D1295488

The Uncollected Writings of Marjorie Kinnan Rawlings

UNIVERSITY PRESS OF FLORIDA

Florida A&M University, Tallahassee
Florida Atlantic University, Boca Raton
Florida Gulf Coast University, Ft. Myers
Florida International University, Miami
Florida State University, Tallahassee
University of Central Florida, Orlando
University of Florida, Gainesville
University of North Florida, Jacksonville
University of South Florida, Tampa
University of West Florida, Pensacola

The Uncollected Writings of Marjorie Kinnan Rawlings

·ı|ı·

Edited by Rodger L. Tarr and Brent E. Kinser

University Press of Florida

Gainesville * Tallahassee * Tampa * Boca Raton
Pensacola * Orlando * Miami * Jacksonville * Ft. Myers

12 11 10 09 08 07   6 5 4 3 2 1

A record of cataloging-in-publication data is available from the
Library of Congress.

ISBN 978-0-8130-3027-2

The University Press of Florida is the scholarly publishing agency
for the State University System of Florida, comprising Florida A&M
University, Florida Atlantic University, Florida Gulf Coast University,
Florida International University, Florida State University, University
of Central Florida, University of Florida, University of North Florida,
University of South Florida, and University of West Florida.

University Press of Florida
15 Northwest 15th Street
Gainesville, FL 32611-2079
http://www.upf.com

To our beloved parents,
whom we sing back home in memory and time,
we dedicate this book

Sara Louise Gaugh Tarr
LeRoy Emerson Tarr
Betty Jeanne Kinser
Ronald Ashley Kinser

Contents

Illustrations

Acknowledgments

We wish to thank all the too-often unsung editors at the University Press of Florida for their continued, seemingly boundless support. It goes without saying that without Meredith Morris-Babb, the insightful and indulgent director, this project would not have been possible. We are also grateful to Gillian Hillis, managing editor, for patiently guiding our way through the labyrinth of manuscript preparation, and acknowledge the stellar work of our copy-editor, Susan Brady, our project editor, Susan Albury, and our volume designer, Larry Leshan.

A long-term project like this involves scores of individuals, past and present. The assistance of the following dedicated librarians and archivists enriched our work markedly: Antol R. Steck and Judy Capurso of the Charles Sumner School Museum and Archives; Jill Rosensihield, Bernard Schemetzler, and David Null of the University of Wisconsin; Linda Henzl and Joanne Hohler of the State Historical Society of Wisconsin; Elizabeth Norris of the YWCA; Dorothy C. Rush of the Filson Club; Sherrill Redmon of the University of Louisville; Leland Hawes of the *Tampa Tribune*; Robin Anne O'Sullivan of the University of Chicago; Chauncey B. Jessup of the National Archives; Jerrold B. Speers of the Department of the Treasury; Patrick F. Gilbo of the American Red Cross; Margaret E. Jaffie of Voice of America; Jean Katona and Betty F. Pilsbury of the Girl Scouts; Linda D. Surles of Phi Beta Kappa; Deborah W. Walk of Rollins College; Heather Moore and Gregory A. Johnson of the University of Virginia; Nanci A. Young of Smith College; Mary Edith Arnold of the Kappa Alpha Theta; and Carl Van Ness of the University of Florida.

Frank Orser, the former curator of the Rawlings Collection at the University of Florida, is everywhere in this book, as is David Nolan, whose rich knowledge of Florida remains a treasure, and with pleasure we welcome the contributions of the newest curator, Flo Turcotte.

Very special acknowledgment goes to Richard Young, the son of the renowned Owen D. Young, whom Rawlings cherished as a close friend, for his kind support and permission to use Rawlings's contributions to the Young family publication, *The Dumpling*.

Rodger Tarr wishes to acknowledge the poet/novelist James Still, since departed in body but not in spirit from his beloved Kentucky, for sharing his memories of Rawlings with me. To Deidre Bryan, my beloved editor at the University Press of Florida for so long, I wish you a wealth of happiness in retirement. And, of course, I am most grateful for the support of the authorities, great and small, at Illinois State University. Carol Anita Tarr and Clayton Carlyle Tarr provide, as always, reason for being.

Brent Kinser wishes to acknowledge Elizabeth Addison, chair of the Department of English, and Robert Kehrberg, interim dean of the College of Arts and Sciences, Western Carolina University, for their continuing support and encouragement. In addition, to his colleagues and friends in and out of the English Department at Western Carolina, and especially to Brian Gastle, Catherine Carter, Mary Adams, Mimi Fenton, Veronica and Karl Nicholas, Leah Hampton, Elizabeth and Sandy Frazier, Lori Seischaba, Chris Coburn, and Chesney Reich, profound thanks for making Cullowhee feel like home. Further, to John McGowan, Beverly Taylor, Joseph Viscomi, Philip Gura, and Robert Cantwell at the University of North Carolina, Chapel Hill; to David Southern and Steve Cohn at Duke University Press; to David Sorensen at St. Joseph's University; to Anita Tarr at Illinois State University; and to D. Paul McCaskill, attorney at literature, thank you all for both your inestimable friendship and your untiring service in the interest of this professional and scholarly journey.

To the two press readers—anonymous, alas—we want to thank you for both for your fine suggestions and enthusiastic support.

Finally, we must thank our valued friends Phil and Gloria May, Bob and Edwina Davis, and Bob and Barb Middendorf, who somehow manage to deal with our enthusiasm gracefully and to share our Rawlings sojourn joyfully.

Editorial Note

The purpose of *The Uncollected Writings* is to reproduce the publications of Marjorie Kinnan Rawlings that have hitherto been lost to the literary scholar and general reader. Beginning with her first publication as Marjorie Kinnan in the *Washington Post* in 1910 and ending with her last in 1953, the year of her death, these publications range from poems, to essays, to letters, to short stories, to newspaper articles, to reviews, to introductions, to blurbs. *The Uncollected Writings* includes all the published material we could find, including a few new items not listed in *Marjorie Kinnan Rawlings: A Descriptive Bibliography*. We have tried to be inclusive. However, we have not reproduced excerpts and serializations of her novels. Neither have we reproduced the material found in *When the Whippoorwill*—and *Short Stories*, nor the poems found in *Poems of Marjorie Kinnan Rawlings: Songs of a Housewife*. The only other material excluded, because of space, are the occasional letters she wrote to the *Washington Post*.

Nearly all of the material in this volume is reproduced for the first time since its original publication, hence the title *The Uncollected Writings*. There are a few exceptions, and these are identified in the appropriate bibliographic notes. None of the material in this volume appears in print for the first time.

We have chosen to present the material in chronological order to preserve Rawlings's daily, yearly literary activities. We have begun with what we have titled "Juvenilia: 1910–1914," and followed that with "University of Wisconsin: 1914–1918" and "The Newspaper Years: 1919–1928," ending with "Florida: 1928–1953." This decision results in an eclectic text—that is, the material is not presented by individual genre but in chronological order. To assist anyone who wants to consult only a single genre, we have listed in the Index of Titles the genres represented, and the reader need only consult the specific genre to find page references to all the poems, to all the short stories, to all the essays, to all the letters, and so on. In addition, we have provided an index of titles.

No substantive editorial alterations have been made to the texts. Rawlings's idiosyncrasies have been preserved, namely her proclivity for coining words and inventing spellings, not to mention her erratic punctuation, especially the seemingly perverse habit of separating subjects and verbs with commas. What was the rule of composition for Rawlings is not the rule in the postmodern academy. Where a coinage or a spelling is especially outrageous, we have used the editorial [*sic*]. However, where the mistakes in the text are obviously typos, such as "hte" for "the," we have corrected them silently. We have not excised any material. We call attention to [MKR's ellipses], even though the ellipses in question might in fact be those introduced by a compositor and/or an editor. We have translated foreign-language expressions in brackets.

Brief biographical summaries to each section are provided to establish the context. Explanatory notes are provided to identify allusions and references and to enhance context and meaning, if necessary. A cross-referenced index is also provided.

Chronology

MKR's major publications are included below. For a complete catalogue of her writings, see Rodger L. Tarr, *Marjorie Kinnan Rawlings: A Descriptive Bibliography* (1996).

1896   Born 8 August, Washington, D.C., to Arthur Frank Kinnan and Ida May Traphagen Kinnan. Father was an examiner for the U.S. Patent Office; mother taught school before MKR's birth. The Kinnans also owned a dairy farm in Maryland.

1900   Arthur Houston Kinnan, MKR's brother, was born.

1910–12   Publishes a number of letters and award-winning stories in the *Washington Post*; "The Reincarnation of Miss Hetty" in *McCall's Magazine* (1912); and several stories in her high school magazine, *Western*.

1913   Father dies.

1914   Graduates from Western High School. The family moves to Madison, where MKR enters the University of Wisconsin and majors in English, with serious interests in journalism and theater.

1915   Begins to publish articles of current university interest in the *Wisconsin Literary Magazine*. Acts in various plays.

1916   Achieves sophomore honors and is elected to Mortar Board. Is on the staff of the school yearbook, *The Badger*. Initiated into the sorority Kappa Alpha Theta.

1917   Elected to Phi Beta Kappa and vice president of Red Domino, the women's drama club, and has the leading part in the junior play, *Green Stockings*.

1918   Announces engagement to Charles Rawlings. Writes a senior English thesis and graduates from the University of Wisconsin with honors.

1919   Works at various editing jobs and for the YWCA in New York City, while trying to sell, unsuccessfully, her stories. Marries Charles Rawlings, and they remove to his hometown of Rochester, New York.

1920   Moves to Louisville, Kentucky, and becomes a feature reporter for the *Louisville Courier-Journal*. Writes a column called "Live Women in Live Louisville."

1921   Returns to Rochester, where she writes feature articles, mostly on social issues, for the *Rochester Evening Journal.*

1922   Continues to write for the *Evening Journal* but has no success in selling her own work.

1923   Mother dies.

1924   Lands a job as the society editor for the popular magazine *Five O'Clock,* writing under the nom de plume "Lady Alicia Thwaite."

1926   Begins, in May, for the *Rochester Times-Union,* a syndicated series of poems generally titled "Songs of a Housewife" that appears almost daily until February 1928. There are 495 of these domestic poems, which run the gamut from advice, to recipes, to gardens, to anecdote on the "Romance of the Housewife." See *Poems by Marjorie Kinnan Rawlings: Songs of a Housewife* (1997).

1928   Completes her autobiographical novel, *Blood of My Blood,* published posthumously in 2002, largely about her conflicted relationship with her mother. Buys a 72-acre orange grove near Cross Creek in remote North Central Florida and moves there with Charles in November.

1930   Sells "Cracker Chidlings" to *Scribner's Magazine,* followed by the novella "Jacob's Ladder," which brings her to the attention of the famed editor Maxwell E. Perkins.

1931   Publishes "Cracker Chidlings," about her impressions of her new neighbors; "Jacob's Ladder," about a young Cracker bride who must learn to survive in a male's world; and "A Plumb Clare Conscience," about a moonshiner whose Cracker ingenuity prevails over civil authority. Writes "Lord Bill of the Suwannee River," about a railroad foreman whose exploits rival those of Paul Bunyan, published posthumously in 1963. Lives with the Fiddia family in the Big Scrub to gather material for a novel.

1932   Publishes "Dutch Oven Cookery," which features her talents as a cook; "A Crop of Beans," about how a man, suffering from avarice and pride, is saved by his wife; and the expressly feminist "Gal Young 'Un," about a woman who empowers herself after suffering humiliation at the hands of her abusive husband. The last was awarded the O. Henry Memorial Prize for the best short story of 1932. Works on the manuscript of her novel about the Big Scrub.

1933   Publishes *South Moon Under* and enjoys immediate critical acclaim. Perkins compares the novel favorably to *Huckleberry Finn.* Lives with the Cal Long family and learns more Cracker lore, part of which later finds its way into *The Yearling.* Goes to England to gather material for a novel Perkins does not want her to write. He encourages her to write a "boy's book" instead. Publishes "Hyacinth Drift," an account of the boat trip she and Dessie Smith took up the St. Johns River; "Alligators," a chronicle of her alligator hunts with Fred Tompkins; and "Benny and the Bird Dogs," a satire about a man who sells his dogs knowing that they are trained to come home. In the last story, she introduces Quincey Dover, a recurring female foil based loosely on MKR herself. Divorces Charles Rawlings in November.

1934   Publishes "The Pardon," about a misfit who is unexpectedly pardoned from prison for a crime he did not commit, and who returns home to find his wife living with another man. Completes draft of *Golden Apples*.

1935   Publishes *Golden Apples*, a psychological novel about an Englishman who finds himself unsuited to life in Florida. It was not a critical success, but Perkins thought it had great technical merit. Abbreviated version appears in *Cosmopolitan*.

1936   Publishes "Varmints," about two slippery friends who own a mule, but who avoid responsibility for its burial when it dies; and "A Mother in Mannville," about an orphan boy who invents a mother to hide his shame. One of MKR's most celebrated stories, it was later adapted for the so-called Lassie story, "Mountain Prelude." Fishes with Ernest Hemingway in Bimini; hunts with Barney Dillard in the Big Scrub; and meets F. Scott Fitzgerald in Asheville, North Carolina.

1937   Works on the manuscript of *The Yearling*, the "boy's book" Perkins had wanted her to write. Meets Thomas Wolfe in New York City at the urging of Perkins, who hopes she can convince Wolfe to shorten his manuscripts.

1938   Publishes *The Yearling*, which becomes an international best seller, and sells the film right to MGM for $30,000. The novel is serialized in the *New York Post*. Becomes a celebrity and goes on the lecture circuit, which impacts her health.

1939   Publishes "Cocks Must Crow," where Quincey Dover learns the lesson that "Man-nature is man-nature, and a woman's a fool to interfere." Elected to the National Institute of Arts and Letters. Receives the Pulitzer Prize for fiction. Buys the cottage at Crescent Beach.

1940   Publishes "The Pelican's Shadow," in part a retrospective on MKR's marriage to Charles Rawlings, about a woman who purchases a life of ease at the expense of her dignity; "The Enemy," about frontier justice set in the cattle country of Central Florida; and "In the Heart," about racism with the twist that she treats black prejudice toward other blacks. Also publishes a nonfictional essay, "Regional Literature of the South," in which she disavows the term *regional*. Publishes a collection of previously published stories, *When the Whippoorwill—*. Completes "Fish Fry and Fireworks," about Quincey Dover introducing a rattlesnake to a political rally with near tragic consequences, which was published posthumously in 1967. Begins work on the manuscript of *Cross Creek*.

1941   Publishes "Jessamine Springs," about an itinerant preacher whose meaningless commitment leads him to loneliness and despair; and "The Provider," about a railroad fireman who gives coal to a destitute family, only to be fired for his charitable spirit. MGM begins production of *The Yearling*, starring Spencer Tracy, only to scrub it later because of costs and actor disenchantment. Marries Norton Sanford Baskin.

1942   Publishes *Cross Creek*, a collection of vignettes about her life at Cross Creek, which becomes a best seller; *Cross Creek Cookery*, a collection of recipes with anecdotal interlinear commentary; and the nonfictional "Trees for Tomorrow," about the need to preserve the forests. Awarded Doctor of Humane Letters by the University of Florida.

1943   Begins work on the manuscript of *The Sojourner*, the writing of which plagues her for nearly a decade. Zelma Cason files the lawsuit accusing MKR of libel for the characterization of her in *Cross Creek*. Norton enlists in the American Field Service and is assigned to the India/Burma campaign.

1944   Publishes the nonfictional "Florida: A Land of Contrasts," another ecological appeal; and "The Shell," about a retarded young woman who, when rudely turned away by the Red Cross, walks into the ocean to join her soldier husband who is at war. MKR is coming under increasing pressures caused by the lawsuit, by Norton's absence, and by her determination to answer literally hundreds of letters from servicepeople.

1945   Publishes the nonfictional "Florida: An Affectionate Tribute," yet another ecological appeal, which is entered into the *Congressional Record*; "Black Secret," about a boy who learns accidentally that his favorite uncle fathered a child by a black woman; and "Miriam's Houses," about a girl who is envious of her friend who seemed to have everything, only to learn later that the friend's mother was a prostitute.

1946   Publishes "Miss Moffatt Steps Out," about a teacher who mistakenly abandons the ideal of books for life in the raw. MKR is found innocent of "invasion of privacy" in the *Cross Creek* trial. Zelma Cason appeals the decision to the State Supreme Court.

1947   "Mountain Prelude," the so-called Lassie story, is serialized in the *Saturday Evening Post*. Publishes "The Use of the Sitz-Bath," one of many contributions to the *Dumpling Magazine*, an annual publication by the family of Owen D. Young. The Florida Supreme Court reverses the *Cross Creek* trial decision and orders MKR to pay a one-dollar fine and court costs. MKR rents and then buys the farmhouse in Van Hornesville, New York. Maxwell Perkins suddenly dies, "an unspeakable grief" from which MKR never recovers.

1948   Continues work on the manuscript of *The Sojourner*, now made more difficult because of the death of Perkins.

1949   Publishes "The Friendship," about a boy who learns the value of friendship after lying to his policeman friend. Continues to be frustrated by her inability to finish *The Sojourner*.

1950   Publishes "Portrait of a Magnificent Editor," about the importance of Maxwell Perkins as an editor.

1951   Begins revision of the first draft of *The Sojourner*.

1952   Suffers a coronary spasm. Convalesces at Crescent Beach. Robert Frost visits her. Completes the revision of *The Sojourner*. Begins preliminary work on her biography of Ellen Glasgow. Takes a trip to England and Ireland with Norton.

1953   Publishes *The Sojourner*, a novel that explores in transcendent terms the subjects of betrayal, redemption, and brotherhood. It is received with mixed reviews. Removes to Richmond, Virginia, to continue research on the Glasgow biography. Five-part autobiographical sketch appears in the *Los Angeles Times*. Suffers a ruptured aneurysm on 13 December, and dies the next day at Flagler Hospital, St. Augustine, at the age of fifty-seven. Buried at Antioch Cemetery, near Island Grove.

Introduction

·||·

Marjorie Kinnan Rawlings is now most often remembered for her Pulitzer Prize–winning novel *The Yearling* (1938) and her autobiographical vignette *Cross Creek* (1942). However, during her tenure with Charles Scribner's and Sons, she was one of their most celebrated and best-selling writers. Thus postmodern scholars of American literature are running out of excuses to continue to exclude her from the highest rank of twentieth-century authors. The number of texts now available for the study of Rawlings confirms this truth. In addition to *The Yearling* and *Cross Creek*, *Cross Creek Cookery* (1942) also remains in print. Further, the recent publication of her novel *Blood of My Blood* (2002) adds yet another work to her canon. The University Press of Florida continues to publish scholarly volumes of primary material that enhance our understanding of this remarkable artist and personality. *Selected Letters of Marjorie Kinnan Rawlings* (1983), *Short Stories by Marjorie Kinnan Rawlings* (1994), *Poems by Marjorie Kinnan Rawlings: Songs of a Housewife* (1997), *Max and Marjorie: The Correspondence between Maxwell E. Perkins and Marjorie Kinnan Rawlings* (1999), and *The Private Marjorie: The Love Letters of Marjorie Kinnan Rawlings to Norton S. Baskin* (2004) demonstrate Rawlings's relevance to the literature and the literary community of an American period that might someday be matched in greatness but never transcended. Now, with the publication of *The Uncollected Writings*, the historical and cultural significance of Rawlings's place in American letters is confirmed. The material presented in this volume, much of it once lost or difficult to obtain, provides even more detail to our understanding of her life and work.

Publishing previously uncollected materials always carries with it a certain amount of risk. Often there are reasons why material has not found its way into anthologized versions of artists' works. In addition, Rawlings might well be angry if she knew that some of the material in this volume, especially that of her early years, was again seeing the light of day. But the material's literary, cultural, and historical worth to scholars would perhaps assuage even her famous temper.

It may be that the greatest value of these texts rests in what they reveal about the development of Rawlings as a writer. To postmodernists, and rightly so, the process of writing has become an immensely important focal point for the study of literature, and critics relish the opportunity to witness writers' development over time as they hone their skills and relate the experiences of their lives. Tracing the progress of a writer from youth to fully formed artistic consciousness holds an essential place at the intellectual table, especially now that the very process of writing is acknowledged not only as a window into the creative mind but as an essential aspect of the creative endeavor we call literature. To have access to the texts of artists and thus to be able to view them refining their skills and discovering their voices is invaluable to both the professional and the general reader.

With these developmental considerations in mind, we have divided the works in this volume into the four major periods of Rawlings's literary life: her juvenilia, her University of Wisconsin publications, her years as a journalist in Louisville and Rochester, and the previously uncollected writings that were written in Florida during the height of her writing career. In doing so, we can view more clearly Rawlings as a writer, one who knew very well that writing was no inspirational accident. Although a self-confirmed Romantic, and in many ways a Transcendentalist in the tradition of Thoreau, her vision of the writing process was anything but naïve. Nor did she claim to be the transcriber of fully formed ideas of divine literary inspiration. For her, writing was a matter of experiment, of experience, and, most of all, simply hard work. Her writing process thus unfolds on the pages of this volume as she proceeds from youth to adulthood, from aspiring author to international celebrity.

Rawlings (née Kinnan) began to publish at the surprisingly young age of thirteen. At the time, she lived with her parents in Washington, D.C., but the source of her inspiration was the dairy farm of her father, Arthur Kinnan, a place that helped to shape her love of nature and her wish to describe life itself through the written word. The proximity to Washington made publishing in the *Washington Post* an obvious choice, especially when the newspaper's children's editor began to encourage young people in the area to contribute to the paper. The young Rawlings's first story, "The Best Spell," reflects all of the innocence one might expect from a person newly arrived in her teen years. Here, love and romance conquer all. She finishes the story with an allusion to a favorite of yesteryear, "Love's Old Sweet Song," the use of which identifies Rawlings's position as a young writer in the transitory period between Victorian and Modern: "So to the end, when life's dim shadows fall, / Love will be found the sweetest dream of all." Her use of this song also creates a great literary coincidence, for when James

Joyce later wrote *Ulysses* (1922), the book that would establish him as an icon of modern literature, he used this very song as one of Molly Bloom's concert pieces. Although absolutely nothing more than a coincidence, Rawlings's use of the song does demonstrate a trait observable from her earliest published writings, her literary instinct. This instinct for what is valuable in a literary sense pervades her juvenilia, and it would never desert her.

Although there are high moments of literary clarity in the juvenilia, the materials also display the unevenness and obsessions of youth. Still, even in her most juvenile moments, there are points of interest and significance. In "The Traveler," she reveals an immense curiosity and wanderlust in terms of language and image as she describes the flowery kingdom of Japan and other places she dreams of visiting. In "Carmenite," a youthful fascination with fairy tales complements her natural propensity for storytelling, yet another attribute that became a hallmark of Rawlings's later writing. In addition to a compelling interest in fairy tales, her juvenile stories also exhibit a rather romantic teen obsession with death. In "Old Friends Are Best," Rawlings reveals her lifelong love affair with animals at the same time that she shows her youthful sense of the sentimental as the rejected mongrel "Doggie Brown" dies saving his master while the pampered purebred looks on with indifference. The "Sad Story of Little Pip" is even more morbid, replete with a suicidal duck intended to establish an emotional bond with the audience, a skill she was later to master in *The Yearling*. But there are also moments when Rawlings uses death and sentiment to great effect. In one of the most successful stories of her early years, "The Reincarnation of Miss Hetty," Rawlings's protagonist loses her connection to life after the golden-haired baby brother she has raised as a son drowns, only to rediscover it when she comes upon and accepts an orphaned child as her own. Rawlings also wrote a fair amount of poetry as a young person, and nowhere in the juvenilia are her emotions at a greater height than in her encomium "To James Whitcomb Riley": "His dear words—I love them—I love them—rest always / As cool hands upon my oft feverish brow. / And I am quieted, e'en as a restless babe, by his singing." Overall, as sentimental as many of these stories and poems may be, they provide a clear indication of Rawlings's innate sense of narrative timing and emotional drama, two skills that would later help to make the Pulitzer Prize–winning *The Yearling* a timeless classic. She often dismissed her early work as overwritten or too intellectual, but this perhaps overly modest assessment does not alter the value of these works as important moments in her creative development.

There are other moments of literary foreshadowing in the juvenilia. For instance, as the fearless Captain Brullen and his "negro" cook, Jim, make their escape in "A Battle for Life," they are faced with a choice of direction: "Being in doubt as to which stream to follow, the men took the one which seemed to have the most northerly direction." Anyone familiar with Rawlings and her writings will remember the problem that she and Dessie Vinson faced in finding the channel in "Hyacinth Drift," a journey not unlike that found in *Huckleberry Finn*. Throughout *The Uncollected Writings*, there are moments of association with Rawlings's more familiar works, some coincidental, some not, all significant in delineating the growth of her literary mind.

Emotion and sentiment are not the only apparent features of Rawlings's writing in the juvenilia. Many of her stories reveal a keen and playful intellect. "The Reforming of a Mala Puella" pokes fun at her own lack of serious focus in her Latin classroom at the same time that it reflects the ease with which she learned languages. The play on gerundial and gerundive constructions can be made only by one who understands the language better than she allows. In addition to foreign languages, the musical qualities of the English language, especially when uttered by rural people, were especially fascinating to her. In "Alonzo Perceval Van Clyne," a story of a young, Huck Finn–like boy's inability to be contained in the classroom, Rawlings describes his classmates' unwillingness to reveal where he has gone into hiding from the authority of his concerned teacher:

> Don'cher 'spose they knew that the only place where you could find those graceful, speckled trout was off over Squire Simm's place, through the forest, beyond the distant hills, and in some mysterious region close beyond, in a clear purling stream that laughed and sobbed and sang, until you thought it must be the river of Heaven, and—but they weren't going to tell on him.

Later, Rawlings often wrote about her struggle to lose her youthful habit of overwriting and overintellectualizing. But, if this passage is somewhat overwrought, it is also in fact very beautiful, especially when one considers that it is written by a fifteen-year-old. In it, one finds significant themes that captivated Rawlings throughout her working life, in particular nature and humanity's relationship with nature. Further, there is the implied desire to understand the way people really speak and to recapture the flavor of that language in written form. Rawlings understands the musicality of language at a very early age, and she would continue to be captivated by it. More important, there is something beyond youthful wonder in the manner she describes the world and the characters of her stories in the juvenilia. The ability, nascent though it may be, to see deeply into the world as an observer of nature and the human condition is clearly percolating.

If some of the characteristics of Rawlings's early writing stem from her identity as a typical, albeit very sensitive, adolescent who is exploring her abilities as an artist, her feminist sensibility is even more remarkable. In "The Love of Adventure," for example, two young girls camp out in a barn that becomes the context for a spooky tale of female community, including the requisite anxieties, sexual and otherwise, of food, father, and stranger. When the father finds the two girls "snuggling up together," unaware that men have been roaming the area—a danger that adds greatly to their sense of fright and to the sexual anxiety underlying the story—Rawlings reveals a notable sense of metaphor and symbol, as well as an astute psychosexual awareness. She confirms her attraction to this literary approach later in her poem "Company, Halt!" (1912). Here, her childhood fascination with death takes on a prescient quality as she anticipates the sexual politics of war: "Their arms for our defense, / And *ours* their recompense—/ Fall, in!" Two years prior to the guns of August, Rawlings has constructed a metaphor that perhaps might even have been appreciated by the World War I poet Siegfried Sassoon (1886–1967), who in his bitingly sarcastic "Glory of Women" (1918) complains about the women who enliven the chivalric hero-worship of the fighting men for whom they manufacture shells. Like Sassoon, Rawlings understands the troubling relationship between sex and war.

Rawlings was, of course, not an entirely morbid youth, and she yields often to her innate comedic sense of playfulness, as in "Once upon a Time a Black Demon Invented Powder, and——." Here, the practical frustrations of becoming a woman:

Oh Powder, boon of maidens fair,
Oh Powder, brunette, pink, and white,
To you I dedicate my song,
To you attribute I my plight!

Rawlings's humorous take on the challenges of makeup does not belie her clear perception of the inner workings of sexual politics. That she would always rather enjoy writing about and participating in the struggle between male and female is not a rejection of her identity as a female but a revelation of it. She wanted to be one of the boys not because she did not wish to be a woman—she wanted to be one of the boys because she wished to do what she wanted when she wanted. Thus in the silly story of the heroic lover Pierre De Salle O'Hooligan, "A Romance," Rawlings adapts Longfellow's "The Psalm of Life," wherein he claims that "things are not what they seem," and she alters it to reflect her own understanding of her feminine self:

I tell you now, in solemn numbers.

Love is but an empty dream,
For the man is dippy who lovest—
    Women are not what they seem.

Pierre goes on to kiss his true love, who happens to have yellow lips and blue
cheeks. Beneath the inherent, youthful silliness, however, is an important point
that is essential to understanding Rawlings both as a youth and as an adult, for
this passage is not an expression of latent misogyny. Rawlings is more compli-
cated than that; she does not hate being a woman; she revels in it.

At the same time that she grapples with sentiment, death, and the challenges
of being an Edwardian female, Rawlings always seems to return to what is clearly
her first love—language. This is not to say, of course, that her investigations of
language caused her to put aside either life questions or nature, both of which
were ever more serious concerns for her. Also in "A Romance," accidentally or
not, Rawlings experiments with nonsensical paradox in a way that suggests she
had been reading Lewis Carroll. Still, the playful way that she constructs para-
dox in this story stands firmly within the context of the problems of being fe-
male. Thus she declares of the absurd Pierre, "He was a typical type of American
womanhood," and "[H]e made a womanly picture indeed, as he coyly toyed
with his bonnet strings." Convention, in both literary terms and those of the
psychological aspects of gender roles, is thrown out of the window as a young
writer tries figuratively to lift herself up and to walk on wobbly legs. To extend
the metaphor, even her first uncertain steps predict a literary future in which she
was able to race with other, more privileged writers.

When Rawlings matriculated to the University of Wisconsin, she seemed
to move into the literary community of fellow undergraduates with ease. She
made close, lifelong friends, met her first husband, acted—even starred—in
plays, wrote articles and plays and stories, interviewed poets, and won academic
honors. Overall, university life gave Rawlings the chance to be and to act like a
literary artist. She took great advantage of her opportunity. While many of the
underlying concerns that had appeared in her earlier writings remained of great
interest to Rawlings and provided themes and images for her writings at Wis-
consin, her interest in sexual politics and its effects on characters became more
mature and stronger as she grew into her college persona. "The Brute," a tale
of the struggle to reconcile animal force and justice, expresses her continuing
desire to understand the inherent struggle in the interactions between male and
female. As Rawlings grew toward maturation, her feminist sensibility became
stronger. For instance, in "Curls and Curlers," a woman who is convinced her
husband will desert her if he finds that she has to wear curlers to make her hair

curly, comes to realize that he is not as shallow in his attraction to her as she thought, although her own shallowness is manifest. The underlying implication that women are made to feel this way in their relations with men makes the story a multileveled discourse on the problems associated with gender roles.

Another theme important to Rawlings throughout her mature years as a writer was food, and it is during her time at Wisconsin that this theme begins to rise to the surface of her writing. In the two-part story "The Captivating Odors of the Kitchen," food and authorial playfulness come together in an extended metaphor:

> I shall talk about things to eat, good things and unpalatable things. I show no preference. Is it not dreadful? If you are one of the disgustingly healthy type of person, robust, ruddy, and complacent, who can devour soft-shelled crabs, warm milk, tomatoes, apple dumplings and ice cream, all within the period of one meal, and live to tell it; if you are the boarding-house sort of person who longs for just one chance at a palatable, well-cooked meal; in either case it will be safe for you to read this story.

During the first part of the story, Rawlings's hero, Jedediah Hoskins, comes to know the joys of food when he is invited to dinner at another household. His attraction to food drives him away from his mother's ruinous kitchen, in which he has never had a decent meal, in search of true love, which he has of course conflated with the joys of eating good food. In the second half of the story, Jedediah's search for utopia becomes disastrously dystopic as he mistakenly concludes that his neighbor is the author of the smells from her kitchen. After they are married, Jedediah finds that he has in fact married the culinary parallel of his mother. Jedediah's eroticization of food becomes an allegory of sexual anxiety. Issues of domesticity, images of forbidden fruit, and an overall Naturalistic sense of doom, makes "Captivating Odors" one of the young Rawlings's most successful stories, and it is certain that after graduation from Wisconsin she would have carried it in her briefcase as she pounded the streets of New York in search of work as a professional writer.

It is also during her Wisconsin years that Rawlings began to become self-reflexive about her writing. After she met Witter Bynner and Vachel Lindsay and reviewed their works, her tone exudes a palpable sense that she is addressing fellow authors, and her "When the Muse Knocks" reveals a writer growing into her own voice. Her command of metaphor and allusion is now an established and important aspect of her growing maturity, and her authorial voice begins to sound more like Rawlings as we know her—ironic, funny, and forceful: "My muse has no sense of the fitness of things. She knocks at the door, boisterously, regardless of whether I am ready to receive her, or am in my kimono and curl-papers—intellectually speaking." That the feminist sensibility of her youth appears here as a characteristic of Rawlings's self-identification as an artist is no accident, for by the end of her school days she had come to the realization that things had changed for the future of women. She expresses this fact with great acumen in "[The Old Order Hath Changed]," an editorial for the *Wisconsin Literary Magazine*:

> Of course, there will always be a large percentage who honestly prefer "home-making" as a profession. That is all right, too. But to the keen, ambitious type who wants something else, this hint: get a professional or commercial training—and your own mentality, your own ambition, alone limit the peaks that you may reach.

This passage reflects Rawlings's inclusive vision of women as the arbiters of their own futures. For her, the power to choose a career path, domestic or professional, was the key to full and true equality for women.

Although her student days ended soon after this editorial was written, she continued to negotiate the domestic and the professional possibilities of her own future, but she would do so in another place and sphere. She went to New York, where she found entry into the world of professional writing. She also succumbed to her college romance with Charles Rawlings and began a domestic venture that seemed doomed from the beginning. But for Rawlings there was to be "something else," and her years as a newspaper writer served as an important step along the way toward her own artistic life, in which she would eventually make peace between the domestic and the professional, the classic dilemma for the female artist who incorporates domesticity into her writings as she questions societal expectations.

Rawlings's initial experience in New York was nothing short of Naturalistic. She arrived in the Big Apple with a valise full of her literary accomplishments as a successful collegiate writer and member of Phi Beta Kappa. New York, to say the least, was unimpressed. Although she did publish at least one story, "His Little Cabbage Head," which was yet another foray into the challenges of male-female relationships, she did not publish enough to live as she wished, as a writer. But Rawlings did not give up, and when all seemed lost she found work with the YWCA that allowed her to practice the feminism that she had developed in high school and college. In "To the Women of France," written in the aftermath of World War I, Rawlings's vision of sisterhood took on global proportions:

> All women, whatever their race or creed, are sisters—daughters of the

modern order—servers of humanity. In this era of rebuilding, French and American women are joining hands with one purpose—to be constructionists; to make industries, mining, manufacturing, canning and the rest, work of any sort, a means, like the Foyer, to an end; to build so well that *liberté, égalité, fraternité*, become incorporated into the social, economic and spiritual fabric, not only of France and America, but of all the world.

The vision of female ascendancy that was expressed in her school days as a kind of personal awareness is transformed in this passage into a pluralistic worldview that seems well ahead of its time. World War I had helped to open the doors of opportunity for women, and in her work for the YWCA, Rawlings participated in the process of trying to force them open further toward full societal inclusion for women.

There was perhaps no better place to take part in such a mission than at the YWCA in postwar New York. Much of Rawlings's writing for the "Y" had to do with enabling young women. In "Here Is Fun for Girls," an article meant to encourage these women to take an active part in their world, Rawlings expands on her developing pluralistic vision of female inclusion:

> Girls in their teens who have taken a keen interest in helping the government in war time, through canteen service, patriotic leagues under the Young Women's Christian Association, Red Cross work, war gardens, and help in the Liberty Loan campaigns, now want to go on and use their new-found power and knowledge to make democracy come true, and to do their share toward the new social order.

This passage does not merely state the official policy of the YWCA; rather, it clearly emanates from Rawlings's own beliefs about what such an organization could and should be. True, the idealism of her vision for the future fits well within the goals of the YWCA, but her own personal feelings are also surely finding expression. Rawlings's ability to be faithful to the true elements of her subject made her an effective spokesperson for the YWCA, and this same faithfulness to the truth would later torture her as she strived to hold herself to the same standards in her writing of fiction.

Not long after her marriage to Charles Rawlings in 1919, Rawlings found herself in Louisville working as a journalist. A remarkable aspect of her work during this time is that she was able to continue to find an outlet for her interest in the issues related to female inclusion. She did so in a series of articles entitled "Live Women in Live Louisville." In this series, she investigated several local women of distinction: Lillian South, the only female bacteriologist in Kentucky; Nora

Dean, a roentgenological nurse of great ability; Emma Hegan, an effective chief probation officer for Jefferson County; Blanche De Rose, an essential financial officer for a large Louisville company; Theresa Moellman, a successful fire insurance underwriter; and Nora Kirch, an influential banker. For Rawlings, these women were more than heroic females who had transcended the societal restrictions on women to achieve in a male-dominated world. As she constructed them, they were in fact female parallels of Emerson's "Representative Men," types from which a new kind of woman could draw inspiration and direction. Thus, Rawlings uses the stories of these women from a wide range of professions to demonstrate the breadth of possibilities on the not yet wide enough horizon of female opportunity.

Soon after the completion of the "Live Women" series, the Rawlingses made their way to Rochester, New York, where she continued her work as a journalist. Themes of food and feminism remain dominant, but Rawlings's writing begins to show a sarcastic edge that the journalistic imperative to "stick to the facts" simply could not suppress. Her description of the new Mechanics Institute in Rochester, "Wives' School First Aid for Peeved Hubbies," for example, drips with sarcasm at the condition of females:

> There isn't much wifely lore left out of the curriculum of the "school for wives." In fact, if you will furnish a nice, roomy, empty cave, the 100 per cent Mechanics girl can provide everything else—and I mean it literally!

Of course, Rawlings does not "mean it literally," and although funny, the article cannot conceal her frustration at the constrictive attitudes that formulated such "female" activities: "Innumerable branches of home-making are taught, all of them calculated to develop an all-round, old-fashioned, cave-woman wife." As her earlier pieces on "Live Women in Live Louisville" had clearly indicated, Rawlings's vision of female opportunity went well beyond the domestic sphere, even though she too found comfort and reveled in the accomplishments of that realm. The essential aspect of her satisfaction in the domestic, however, is that she was able to choose to pursue the activities of kitchen and home, largely because of her later success as a professional writer. Thus it is curious that Rawlings has suffered from the charge that she was overly domestic in her worldview. If she often sounds old-fashioned in these articles, her sarcastic wit is also undeniably present, which may very well have been the product of the growing bitterness she felt toward her own domestic situation in Rochester. In any case, if there is one revelation in Rawlings's *The Uncollected Writings*, it is her concern for the challenges of being a woman in the first half of the twentieth century.

In addition to her resistance to the idea that only certain careers were fit for women, Rawlings also has much to say about the post-Victorian strictures on women's behavior. In "No Place on Campus for Knickers or Cigarettes, Say Graduates," for example, she defends young women of Mt. Holyoke and Wellesley who have chosen to exhibit their own independence and quit because they have been prohibited from smoking and from wearing knickers:

> Does it make any difference that the college girl's manners are ladylike? Does it interfere with her education if she adopts the most startling modes? Do these things have any bearing on the value of her diploma?

The answer to all of these questions, of course, is no. Rawlings felt that women should have both the unlimited opportunities for advancement and the same expectations of behavior that were accorded to men, who of course were able to smoke and to dress casually.

Near the end of her career as a journalist, Rawlings moved back toward the fictive mode. Under the pen name of "Lady Alicia Thwaite," she published a series of comical articles that poked fun at Rochester social life. The playfulness that had informed much of her earlier writing reasserted itself as she was given the opportunity to transcend the factual limitations of journalism. In the guise of an absurd, aristocratic British socialite, Rawlings mocks local theater, athletic clubs, professional wrestling, all in the spirit of good fun, although with a cutting social commentary running just beneath the surface. As her career in journalism came to an end, the lessons she had learned about the importance of description, faithfulness to the truth as she saw it, and objectivity of vision had been ingrained in Rawlings as a writer, which prepared her for Florida, where she would bring her artistic voice to full maturity in *The Yearling* and *Cross Creek*, works that by themselves secure her literary immortality.

The writings included in this volume from Rawlings's Florida years are unique because they in a sense run parallel to the works that have been previously collected. It is not surprising, therefore, that much of this work exudes a self-reflexive quality. People had begun to ask Rawlings about the secrets of her achievement, and she had begun to accept offers to write reviews of and blurbs for other authors. Although there are a few previously uncollected poems—of particular note is "Having Left Cities behind Me," one of Rawlings's favorites— the vast majority of this material is the product of a successful author's reminiscences on her pathway to artistic accomplishment. She defends her portrayal of Florida Crackers in a letter to the *Ocala Evening Star*. She devotes an article to "Dutch Oven Cookery" and reveals ways in which her early fascination with food and cooking had become fully integrated within her artistic vision of the world. Similarly, in "Abe Traphagen's Farm," she recalls her experiences on her grandparents' farm and connects them to her philosophical outlook: "I am not a social philosopher nor a political economist, only a lover of peace and order and social cooperation and individual self-sufficiency." Rawlings was a fully established and widely acclaimed literary artist, one who suffered both the travails and the benefits of celebrity. Many of the texts in the Florida section of this volume contain important biographical information that has often been briefly cited in Rawlings criticism, although the narratives themselves have not been collected since their original publication. Thus, in "I Sing While I Cook," the reader will find the original source for the well-known story of her blackbird pie, which she made for the actor Sam Byrd (who thought it delicious), although she did not know at the time that red-winged blackbirds were a federally protected species.

Of particular importance in the Florida section are Rawlings's discussions of regionalism. In "Regional Literature of the South," she draws an important distinction between regional writing and literature. Here her good friend Ellen Glasgow plays a prominent role:

> To my mind, Ellen Glasgow stands alone in our generation as the creator
> of the only unmistakable regional literature of the South. Pulitzer Prizes
> for "distinguished" novels are amazing anomalies when they ignore work
> of her literary distinction.

Unlike Rawlings, Glasgow never received a Pulitzer Prize, but that had little effect on the friendship between the two authors, and it had even less effect on Rawlings's estimation of Glasgow's work. Rawlings's rejection of regionalism, from which her own reputation and those of other female writers have suffered greatly, is an important moment of self-defense. Her cogent argument that the terms *regional* and *literature* cannot exist in the same phrase serves to place her writings—as they and those of other writers who suffer from the demon appellation "regional" should be placed—in the halls not of regional writing but of literature. For Rawlings, the deep, abiding love she had for Florida and its people, which defined much of her life and work, and which is pervasive in the writings of this section, spoke not to one region but to the universal condition of being human.

In addition to reflections on her own writing, there are significant moments of analysis of other writers. An introduction to Katherine Mansfield's short stories; reviews of works by Maxwell E. Perkins, A. J. Cronin, and James Still; and blurbs for F. Scott Fitzgerald, Marjory Stoneman Douglas, and others speak to Rawlings's status as one of the stars of the house of Scribner. Throughout the section, one recognizes the confident voice of Rawlings that we have known in her other collected works, especially in her always fabulous descriptions of Florida and Floridians. As we have seen into the victories and struggles of her life, the Florida section serves as a culmination of four periods represented in this volume. Gone is the sense of apprenticeship that informs her younger writings; present is the skill with which she had learned to capture the world in language and in print. Rawlings thus offers her experience up to young writers in articles such as "If You Want to Be a Writer," in which she divulges her struggle to master her profession. Thus it is fitting that the book ends with a blurb for a young writer named Doris Betts, for it represents an attribute of Rawlings's writing life that is often overlooked, her desire to be of service as an established author in the encouragement and development of younger writers.

For admirers of Rawlings, justification of such a volume as this is unnecessary. They are happy to know the smallest detail of her extraordinary life, and they never tire of reading the products of her celebration of nature and humanity. On the other hand, some in academe remain skeptical of Rawlings's worth, both as a writer and as an influence. She is not the first woman to fall from favor, and, sadly, she will not be the last. Still, the stories, poems, articles, essays, reminiscences, and ruminations in this volume delineate the intellectual journey of an enduring literary mind. Wordsworth, after all, was correct when he called to Coleridge toward the end of his *Prelude* (1805): "It will be known—by thee at least, my friend, / Felt—that the history of a poet's mind / Is labour not unworthy of regard" (13: 407–10). Those who dismiss Rawlings on the grounds that her approach to race is too stereotypical, that her feminist sensibility is too old-fashioned, that her body of work is too insufficient, that her reputation is too minor should find this volume illuminating because it provides insight into the growth of her poetic mind as it brings complexity to her vision of the world. This Wordsworthian approach to reading Rawlings's *The Uncollected Writings* participates in the needful critical project of demonstrating that Rawlings's struggle with race was heartfelt and honest, that her domestic sensibilities were grounded in her adamantine sense of independence, that her body of work was carefully constructed and immensely respected. Most important, we are able to see Rawlings's work through her dream of being a writer, which she achieved by practicing and experimenting continually. In many ways, *The Uncollected Writings* resembles a *Künstlerroman*, a fictionalized account of an artist's maturation, a record of a remarkable intellectual journey.

One word more. We have here and elsewhere made the case, repeatedly, for the inclusion of Rawlings in current critical and theoretical discourse. Yet there are books published and articles written on the topic of American writers of the twentieth century, not to mention southern writers, where she is barely, if at all, mentioned. This neglect by those purporting to advance the cause of women writers is a disgrace, a blot upon American literary scholarship. Let us be more frank: critics and/or theorists interested in women's writing and its role in the formation of American multiculturalism, identity politics, conceptions of race, narrative theory, community, ecocriticism, cultural history, cultural anthropology, language preservation, gender roles, literature of place, historiography, sexuality, domesticity—*especially* in terms of southern literature—who do not take Rawlings fully into account compromise the integrity of their work. Rawlings is no less an American treasure than Kate Chopin, Zora Neale Hurston, Ellen Glasgow, and Eudora Welty—to name but a few. Her home at Cross Creek itself is now recognized as a *National* Historic Landmark. How can we say it more bluntly? Rawlings's work demands inclusion, significant inclusion, in any discussion of twentieth-century American literature. She was a bright star among the shining stars—in the words of Wallace Stevens, a "very remarkable woman" (308).

Juvenilia

֊ı|ı֊

1910–1914

From her junior high through high school years, MKR published a number of stories, poems, and letters to the editor in the *Washington Post*. The children's editor of the newspaper, Cecelia Reynolds Robertson, whose pen name was "Aunt Anna," encouraged young people in the Washington, D.C., area to submit stories and poems on specific topics. Before long, the Children's Page of the Sunday supplement of the *Post* became immensely popular. MKR submitted her first story at the age of thirteen in 1910, and before she matriculated at the University of Wisconsin in 1914, she had published thirteen stories and poems, many of them winning first or second prize in various contests sponsored by the *Post*. In addition, MKR wrote a number of letters (not reproduced here) to the newspaper, principally relating to the Cousins' Club, formed by the *Post* to honor the young people who were its contributors. Each child adopted a nom de plume; MKR's was "Fidelity." MKR is prominent in the literary discussions that were the focus of the Cousins' Club letters, and on two occasions pictures of her appear on the children's page. When MKR entered Western High School, later the Duke Ellington School for the Performing Arts, in 1911, her work began immediately to appear in the pages of *The Western*, the school's literary magazine, of which she was associate editor from 1911 to 1912 and literary editor from 1913 to 1914. Perhaps MKR's crowning achievement during her high school years was winning a second prize of $75, awarded by *McCall's Magazine* in 1912 for her story "The Reincarnation of Miss Hetty."

The Best Spell

It was New Year's eve outside; the snow was falling in huge flakes, covering the bare branches of the old oak trees down the lane. Inside, the children gathered around the open fire and begged grandpa for a story.

"Once upon a time," he began, "there lived an enchanter in a castle. It was only a castle of dreams, but it meant a great deal to him, and all day he sat in his castle writing spells to enchant people, but he did not always succeed. He had two little nieces to provide for, and sometimes it was hard to make ends meet, for he had ogres to fight, called editors, (although all editors are not ogres.)

"And one day the enchanter met a beautiful lady, who had a great deal of gold, and who loved him. So she said to him, 'I can give the best spell in the world to you, the spell of gold. Gold will buy anything, and mine is yours if you will marry me.' The enchanter was tempted, but he shook his head and went away, saying, 'No. it is not the spell I want.'

"Now when he got home the nieces came running to him, and said, 'Look this is our new music teacher!' And there was the prettiest lady he had ever seen, and so sweet that he told her of the golden spell, and asked if that was the best spell in the world, but she shook her head. 'Love's dream,' she said 'is the best.' So the enchanter took her hands in his, and looking straight into her eyes, said, 'Yes, dear, love is the best spell after all. May I cast it over you?' And when she said 'Yes' he married her, and the spell of both love and gold has been working ever since, for I was the enchanter, and grandma was, the one who showed me real love, as it should be."

The fire had died down and the children were asleep on the hearth when the door opened and a beautiful old lady came in, straight up to the enchanter, and looked right into his eyes with her own blue ones, in which the love light beamed like sunshine, and as she stood there the church bells began to chime out their silvery peals, ringing out the old year and welcoming in the new, and they seemed to be singing to the old couple that beautiful song:

"So to the end, when life's dim shadows fall,
Love will be found the sweetest dream of all."[1]

"FIDELITY."

---

[1]   MKR closes the story with the last two lines of the second verse of "Love's Old Sweet Song" (1884); music by J. L. Molloy and words by G. Clifton Bingham. James Joyce (1882–1941) later used this song in *Ulysses* (1922) as one of Molly Bloom's concert pieces.

"The Best Spell," *Washington Post*, Sunday magazine section, 2 January 1910, 5. MKR was awarded "Second Prize" for this story. Afterward, she wrote to "Aunt Anna" about the award: "This is the first money I have ever earned. So this morning I went downtown with father and started a bank account. I will get 2 per cent on my money. . . . Also, compound interest is allowed. I was very happy when I made my first bank deposit" (30 January 1910, 5). At this time, MKR was in her last year of junior high school at Brookland School (northeast of Washington, D.C.).

*　*　*　*　*　*　*　*　*

The Traveler

I guess I have the wanderlust.
　　For I am always on the go;
Behind the plow's too tame for me,
　　As also is the hoe.
I really don't see what's the fun
　　In drudging all the day
In just the same old poky town,
　　In the same old poky way.
Some fellows are content to live
　　Their lives out in one place;
"Variety is the spice of life"—
　　A cap can spoil his face
With wrinkles, bald spots, and the like,
　　Unless he starts to roam.
So I guess I've got the wanderlust—
　　I want to leave my home.

And so I wander o'er the world—
　　I know each country well—
The times I've called on Africa
　　I really could not tell.
In Venice and its gondolas
　　I've often loafed around.
From thence I ship to Switzerland,
　　Where you get good, solid ground.
Yes, Scotland is a bonny land,

But it's France I love full well.
I love to go to old Cologne,
   And hear the deep church bell.
O'er the frozen wilds of Russia
   I travel in a sleigh,
While in jinrikishas I ride
   In the Flowery Kingdom gay.[2]
So on and so forth, for I could
   Not really name them all;
And traveling, like other things,
   May soon begin to pall.

I fear you'll think that I am not
   Loyal to my country;
That "anywhere I hang my hat
   Is home, sweet home, to me."
But we'll settle that affair right here,
   In argumentative tones,
For it's the dear old States for me,
   Where I would rest my weary bones.
When I get tired of traveling
   I scamper home with joy;
It does me good to hear my chums
   Say, "Welcome home old boy!"

And when I gaze upon the tall
   Goddess that lights the bay,
And see the huge skyscrapers loom
   Up Wall street and Broadway,
I have a choky feeling in
   My throat, and then—and then—
Pshaw! The simple fact is merely this:
   I'm glad I'm home again!
Now fellows, even if you have
   The wanderlust, and know
That in a short time you have got
   To just clear out and go,

---

2   In Japan, the emperor sits upon the Chrysanthemum Throne.

Remember this: no matter
> How much abroad you roam,
"Be it ever so humble,
> There's no place like home!"[3]

FIDELITY.
(Marjorie Kinnan, age 14,
Western High School,
Garrett Park, Md.).

"The Traveler," *Washington Post*, Sunday magazine section, 11 September 1910, 5. The head-note by the children's editor reads, in part: "I wonder if some of the boys and girls who have written verses for this contest will one day be known to fame. . . . The first prize of $3 was won by Marjorie Kinnan, who is 14 years old and a pupil of Western High School. Marjorie is still at her summer home." See Tarr, "Marjorie Kinnan Rawlings and the *Washington Post*." The "summer home" is the dairy farm owned by MKR's father, Arthur Kinnan, just outside Washington, D.C.

*   *   *   *   *   *   *   *   *

Carmenite

It was a typical spring day in the Italian Alps. The birds were singing as they had never caroled before: the sky had never been so blue or cloudless, and at the foot of the lofty mountain which reared its towering and snow-clad peak toward heaven nestled a rippling lake, which seemed to catch the sunbeams in its dimpling bosom and hold them captive there. Nature was arrayed in her most gorgeous raiment, and the whole world was glad.

With one exception, however, for, far up the mountain, seated on the step of a tiny white vine-covered cottage, was a wistful and sad-faced Italian girl, of about 14 summers. The cause of her unhappiness will soon be seen. The blinds of the cottage were drawn, and in a few minutes the village doctor, known to be a sordid, grasping man, came from the house.

"Carmenite," he said gruffly in Italian, "your mother will die if she does not receive the proper food. The work has been too much for her, and she cannot live long without something besides rye bread."

---

3   John Howard Payne (1791–1852), "Home Sweet Home" (1830), originally written for his comic opera *Clari the Maid of Milan* (1823).

Poor little Carmenite! She had no other relatives save her mother, and perhaps the doctor read the appeal in her lustrous eyes, for he said, "I would give you money if I could, but I have not enough to keep my own children."

"I would not take one lira from you," she answered proudly, drawing herself up to her full height, "for I have two hands, and if I cannot find work here I shall go to the good queen, for I know she will help me."

The doctor had soon hastened down the steep descent and was hardly out of sight when a magnificent equipage came into view around the bend, surrounded by mounted soldiers. What could it mean? The carriage contained a beautiful lady and a stately gentleman, and it drove right up to Carmenite's door. "Can you give us a cup of cold water, my dear?" sweetly asked the lady, and Carmenite hastened with alacrity to bring a pitcher of the delicious spring water. After quenching her thirst, the pretty lady said, "My dear, is there anything I can do for you? I think there is a sad look on your face."

The sympathetic tone encouraged Carmenite, and she frankly told her poor little story, adding, "But I think I shall go to the good queen, for she will surely help us." "Dear child," responded the lady, tears filling her beautiful eyes, "your simple trust is pathetic, and unlike the deceitful flatteries of the world, and I shall do my best for you, for I am the queen herself."

From that moment life was one delightful dream, for the queen was true to her word. With plenty of nourishing food, Carmenite's mother became strong again, while the little Italian maid grew up to be a cheerful, helpful companion for the dear mother.

FIDELITY.

Marjorie Kinnan (age 14.)

"Carmenite," *Washington Post*, Sunday magazine section, 19 March 1911, 7.

*   *   *   *   *   *   *   *   *

Our Cloak-room Looking-glass

We girls are plunged in direst grief—
   Our cloak-room's like a tomb;
Its atmosphere's pervaded by
   A solemn, sombre gloom.

No longer are our happy laughs
    In that sad cloak-room heard—
We walk about with muffled tread,
    And speak aloud no word.

And oh, how sad the bitter cause
    Of all this gloomy woe—
It is our cloak-room looking-glass
    Ah me!—we loved it so!

It had no frame of shining gold,
    It was a mirror plain;
Yet it was dear as life to us,
    That modest mirror plain.

How oft before it we have stood,
    And "fixed" our tumbling hair—
And then the other morn we came—
    To find it wasn't there!

Ah me!—that agonizing search—
    What frenzy seized us all—
And then we found it on the shelf
    Against the cloak-room wall.

We found it, yes, yet what a "find!"
    What superstitious token!
For ah! We found, to our dismay
    Our looking-glass was broken!

                            Marjorie Kinnan, '14[4]

"Our Cloak-Room Looking Glass," *Western* 16, no. 1 (November 1911): 22.

---

4   MKR was in the class of 1914.

A Battle for Life

Ah, gentle reader, 'tis a fearful tale I shall unfold—a story that will make cold shivers run up and down your spine, a narrative calculated to make your nerves tingle, to make you shudder and grip the steady arms of your cozy chair and peer fearfully and apprehensively into the darkness of the hallway—the story of the weighing in the balance of seven human lives in the scales that ever tipped toward death.

When the members of the crew of the Despardiena,[5] consisting of six brawny seamen and a negro cook, found themselves cast upon the mainland of South Africa they reluctantly gave up life. When they were captured by a huge band of African savages they resignedly prepared themselves for residence in a new world. When they found the natives eyeing curiously the flagons of whisky they had rescued from the wreck they clutched at the proverbial straw.

It was the tenacity with which they grasped this straw that gives me my story.

The heathens dared not touch the strange objects while the captives lived, for they feared, being superstitious, the wrath of the white man's gods should they do so; yet they were consumed with an insatiable desire to know the contents of the bottles.

Being rather familiar with the natural curiosity of the Africans, the captives conceived a plan of escape—and herein lay the straw.

The plan, in a nutshell, was for one of their number to offer the chief the liquor, by signs, of necessity, and when the dusky warriors were stretched out intoxicated, if they could be made to drink the liquid about the campfire the prisoners could make good their escape. Where they could flee they knew not—it was a slender straw, indeed.

Their arms were tightly bound behind them, but that night Brullen, the worthy captain, rose and walking toward the chieftain, told him with eloquent gestures, coined by necessity, that sharp-witted mother of invention, that if he were to be unbound he would show the chief the contents of the flagons.

Dubiously, yet longingly, the chief unbound him, and whilst the savages closely guarded Brullen he opened one of the flagons, and filling a huge gourd with the "fire water," touched it to his own lips as a sign of his good faith.

---

5   The ship and place-names in this story are fictional. Captain Brullen's name may be derived from *brüllen*, a German word for "roar."

Cautiously and slowly the chief took a sip of the liquid. A diabolic grin spread over his features, and in a few moments the followers of the chieftain were all rushing about looking for gourds.

Gourd after gourd was filled for the clamoring natives, until the huge flagons were entirely emptied, and the warriors, worn out by much singing and dancing, threw themselves down upon the ground, forgetting all in their drunken slumbers.

With reckless haste, Brullen seized a knife from the snakeskin belt of a savage, and in a few moments the men were free, for the time being.

Making hasty preparation for their journey by seizing a number of the primitive bows and arrows and as large a quantity of provisions and fresh water as they could find, they hurriedly set off for the river, where their good friend, the lifeboat of the Despardiena, lay as they had left it.

One thing only to guide them in their course they knew, and that was the fact that the river on whose banks reposed their means of escape flowed into the Bay of Delhi Kahr; on this bay was the seaport of Hehlin del Fu, where they probably could get passage on a northbound schooner.

It was a distance of some 850 miles, and their chance of escape was small, for when the natives found them gone, they would speedily try to overtake them in their swift-running canoes, many times as quick as the rather clumsy boat of the fugitives.

Hastily pushing off their boat, the refugees took the oars and rowed with all strength through the sluggish waters in the all-enveloping darkness.

Some few miles on the river seemed to be divided by a large island, on either side of which the river flowed, the two streams taking different directions as far as could be seen.

Being in doubt as to which stream to follow, the men took the one which seemed to have the most northerly direction.

The sun arose in all its sultry splendor, and yet they rowed on, stopping neither to eat nor to sleep. Midday found them still toiling, in turns, at the heavy oars. The banks were growing higher and more rocky, the jungles much less dense, and just a little while before sundown they entered through a narrow pass into as eerie a place as they had ever seen.

It was a small body of water, much resembling a lake, some 200 rods across,[6] framed with high, overhanging cliffs of dull-gray limestone. There was no outlet

---

6   Two hundred rods equal approximately .85 miles.

to the lake apparently. Everywhere there were walls, walls, walls, impregnable and ancient—only the tiny pass gave any suggestion of an outside world.

The water was thick, thick as oil, dark and cruel. As the oars dipped into the strange substance no gentle splash followed—only a dull gurgle. The air was calm, so calm that its very stillness was pregnant of forebodings of evil. The skies overhead were dull and leaden. The gentle rose-pink rays of the setting sun seemed to shun the place. Half-terrified, the men pushed the boat against the only semblance to a beach offered, a small terrace at the farther end.

They had all stepped out save Brullen, when out from the slimy waters by the side of the boat appeared a creature they had learned to fear—the octopus, or devil-fish.[7] With its huge form lashing the water furiously into hundreds of thick, shiny bubbles, its two monstrous red eyes glowing like fiery caldrons of boiling blood, its eight prickly tentacles waving like so many snakes, it was, indeed, an object to be feared.

Seizing an oar, Brullen held it aloft to strike the creature upon the head, but in a second the oar was seized by one of the huge arms, while another wound itself about Brullen, with a malicious, ever-tightening grasp.

Those reptile-like arms seemed to be everywhere at once—about the boat, around Brullen, and darting angrily at the horrified men upon the bank, who seemed likely to be deprived of their strong, young captain. What a death it would have been!

Brullen ripped his knife out from his belt and desperately went at the creature.

Jim, the negro, whose devotion to his master was almost dog-like in its servility, made several futile attempts to injure the octopus with his knife. Each time it lashed him back with its tentacles.

The sailors, even yet, cannot think of the battle under the frowning precipice without shuddering.

Brullen, with tight-set lips, from which every vestige of color had fled, slashed at the demon, that, like a veritable fiend of Hades, fought, and fought, by nature the stronger of the two.

At last, with a powerful lurch, it threw itself at Brullen—to meet the cruelly unrelenting steel of his knife in one of its venomous-looking eyes—its only vulnerable spot—and a monster stream of blood dyed the sultry waters as the "seamen's horror," as it is sometimes called, still fighting, sank from view.

---

7   The *Oxford English Dictionary* attributes the first published usage of the term *devil-fish* to describe an octopus to *Catholic News*, 15 June 1889.

Brullen threw himself, white and quivering, upon the bank, deeming his escape from death not only more than miraculous, but providential.

FIDELITY
(Marjorie Kinnan, age 15,
306 Hammond court.
Western High School.)

"A Battle for Life," *Washington Post*, Sunday magazine section, 25 February 1912, 5. The children's editor writes of the story in the headnote: "The first prize of $3 in the story adventure contest was won by Marjorie Kinnan. . . . She has told a thrilling story of the sea."

*   *   *   *   *   *   *   *

The Reforming of a Mala Puella

Being the Confessions of the Reformer

Prologue:

Listen, my dears, and I will tell
A fearful tale to you,
A tale of rules and idioms,
And of case-forms not a few.
Go home and think it o'er,
And, render wise my dire grief,
Be wicked nevermore.

I

Once on a time, long years ago,
In the days when I was young,
When in Latin classes gay
The praises of Cæsar were sung,
A parva puella [little girl] went to school,
And her name was Mar-jor-ie,
And the wicked things she did, my dears,
Would have made you weep to see.

She hated Latinus-a-um,[8]
She never liked to work—
And as for learning grammar rules—
You should have seen her shirk!

II

But, ah, the "worstest" things she did
To plague her teachers all,
Was to talk on entering Latin class,
As she strolled in from the hall.
As she'd come in, she'd talk and talk
And talk, and talk, and talk—
And then, not satisfied with that,
She'd talk, and talk, and talk.
How wearied grew Miss Rupli then,
(That was her teacher's name)
She knew not how to stop it, and
In sooth, it *was* a shame!
Four times this wicked girl had sinned,
'Twas four times she had talked.
Full seriously Miss Rupli said,
In voice of fearful tone:
"You may write me an apology,
Tonight, when you go home!"
That Smarty only tossed her head,
And thought: "Now, just for spite,
I'll do no Latinus *at all*,
When I go home tonight!"

III

So all that evening she played,
And left her work undone,
Nor went to bed 'til 12 o'clock,
The naughty, naughty one!

---

8   The adjectival forms for Latium, the district of Italy in which Rome is found; in other words, Latin.

She scarcely had her eye-lids closed,
When, right beside her bed,
Appeared a Latin bogie-man,
With glaring eyes of red!
The genitive of quality
Described his garment brown,
Which was a third declension word,
An-I-stem—oh, that noun!
His eyes were gerunds, bloody-red,
"Videnti" was their name,[9]
While a forehead high, of finite verbs
Lent him an aspect of fame.
"Magno cum strepitu" [with great uproar] he talked,
In indirect discourse, too,
While substantive clauses of purpose played,
With infinitives, peek-a-boo,
Out of his pockets ablatives peeped
Of quality, time and place,
While the case-forms of separation ran
An idiomatic race.

IV

His hair was a wig of curly-cue rules,
Those elusive creatures bold,
And verbs of "telling," in ribbons bright,
Their subjects accusative "told."
His altitudo erat [height was] high,
Mr. Genitive measurely said,
And, oh, those gerund eyes of his,
As he stood beside her bed!
He snatched that naughty, naughty one,
Right up by her two pig-tails,
And carried her off to Latin-land,
Not heeding her loud wails.
He plunked her down on a seat of stems,
And then, oh horrors great,

---

9   Gerundial derivation of *video* [to see].

He gave her an oral prose exam
From Virgil, Book 28![10]
The thing after that he asked her, though,
Was, "Why don't you like to work?
And why do you plague Miss Rupli so?
And talk and laugh and shirk?"
"Oh, sir, it's the causal particles, sir,
That have caused my sad downfall.
If you'd take them out of our Book of Rules,
I wouldn't mind at all!"

V

Not heeding the piteous answer then,
The Latin bogie-man said:
"Do you know what a gerund is, eh, what?
Have you got that through your head?"
And when she replied: "It's an adjective, sir,"[11]
He would have liked to kill her dead.
Two hours that fearful test did last,
And, then, when he was through,
His captive was so Latin-ized
She didn't know what to do.
Then picking her up by her two pig-tails,
The bogie-man took her home,
And so roughly he pulled her hair that he
Nearly shattered her ivory dome.
"Now, where have I brought you, puella bad?"
With wrath he loudly cried,
"I really think, though, I'm not sure,
In domum," [homeward] she replied.
"Oh, wretched, wretched!" hissed the beast,
In spectre-like position,
"Islands and towns, and domus [home] and rus [the country],
Omit the preposition!"

---

10 "Virgil, Book 28" does not exist.

11 A verbal noun form; cf. MK's use of "Videnti," above. A verbal adjective is called a gerundive.

Then in the air he ghostly rose,
Place from which hurried on,
(With ab or ex, whiche'er you choose)[12]
Full anxious to be gone.

VI

Ah, dears, next morn you should have seen
That chastened girl, ah, me!
She crept with mien so meek
You would have wept to see.
She wrote a sweet apology,
With many sobs and tears,
And from that day on, talked not *once*
In all her High-School years.
She learned her Latinus-a-um,
And fairly loved each rule,
A model girl, and praised by all
In that delightful school.
With manner soft she entered class,
Nor even *wished* to talk,
And in the olden days she loved
To talk, and talk, and talk.
This moral then, I'll leave with you,
Ere on my way I go:
Obey your teachers, love your rules,
And they'll love you, you know.
For, if you don't, well, just watch out,
Some night while in the park,
Or a great big Latin bogie-man
Will grab you in the dark!

M. K., '14

"The Reforming of a Mala Puella [Bad Girl]," *Western* 16, no. 5 (March 1912): 17–20.

---

12 The prepositions *ab* and *ex* both mean "away from."

Old Friends Are Best

"Yes, you must give up Doggie Brown: he's too old to play with any more. I shall tell daddy-man to get you a new doggie," said mother to Curly Boy Brown.

Oh, no, Curly Boy was not his really, truly name. He had a very long and dignified name—Christopher Chauncey de Longueval Brown—but his long, sunny curls had earned for him the appellation of "Curly Boy."

"'Es," he echoed blithely, "nuvver doggie dus as dood—Doggie Brown too old?"

And so wobbly old Doggie Brown was relegated to the regions of the kitchen. His eloquently soft brown eyes spoke volumes against this strange injustice—why should he, the constant comrade and protector of Curly Boy ever since his advent into the Brown family, be left to ponder lonesomely by the fire all day long, while Curly Boy and his new doggie romped in the garden? He could not understand.

The new doggie was not given to play—he was too dignified and well-bred, and, besides, he had a pedigree. He was No. 15823 in the Registrar, and had two blue ribbons and a medal to his credit. He lifted his white paws very daintily in the air as he picked his way, and held his pink nose high. Upon his first visit to the kitchen that same pink nose seemed to inquire of Doggie Brown, with all due hauteur, "Well, pray, who are you?"

And Doggie Brown's patient eyes responded, "I was once the favorite and play-fellow of Curly Boy, but now I only eat and sleep, and sigh, waiting for the end, for I can no longer run and frisk about. My old legs give way beneath me. I am too old. But if needs be, I will do my duty for Curly Boy, even though he has neglected me."

But the new doggie only sniffed; he was not interested a particle.

A few days later, Doggie Brown saw the kitchen door standing open.

It was a crisp October day, and the merry out-of-doors invited him to wander.

The sun shone coldly from the autumn sky, the seared brown leaves scurried about, oh, so gayly, a huge crow high in the cloudless sky cawed joyously in appreciation of the perfect day.

Doggie Brown accepted the call that all nature was giving him in its own language to come out into the great open road.

He stumbled feebly along the garden path. Suddenly he bent his keen nose to the ground, and sniffed eagerly. Curly Boy's trail! What wonderful luck.

Hurriedly he shambled along, following the trail.

It led direct to the pier at the river, so blackly cold, as it glided along between its bare banks.

The poor, old fellow hesitated a moment, as he stepped upon the cold, slippery wood, but catching sight of Curly Boy far at the extreme end, he hastened joyfully on, his bushy tail aloft in mute welcome.

Curly Boy was kneeling at the edge of the pier, gazing into the ever-changing, fascinating depths beneath. The new doggie was sitting on his haunches, in a decidedly bored manner.

As Doggie Brown approached, the child bent still farther over, in his effort to fathom the dark waters below, lost his balance, and a faint scream was the only sound, until, a moment later, the waves parted with a gurgle, and the ripples closed over the head of Curly Boy Brown.

This was a trifle more interesting to the new doggie. He actually deigned to stalk over to the edge of the pier, and look over, then stalked back, and sat down again.

Doggie Brown was stunned for a moment. Then, quick as a flash, he was all action, as he struggled to the edge of the wharf, and plunged in. His trembling legs and weak body were forgotten; his master was in danger. He must do his duty.

A dripping, golden head appeared above the surface of the water, and Doggie Brown was there—ready.

Seizing the child's collar between his teeth, he began the desperate struggle, while the new doggie yawned and blinked sleepily. How he ever reached the shore with his limp burden no one ever knew. It seemed supernatural. Yet it was sheer love, strong and unflinching, that gave him the strength.

He laid the unconscious little form upon the beach, and, completely exhausted, threw himself down upon the sands, panting and shaking. His eyes closed wearily, he was so tired. Everything was misty now. How cold he was. And then he sank into merciful oblivion, whence he was never to return. Doggie Brown had done his duty.

* * *

When the new doggie returned alone at midday for his dainty fare, nurse and mother immediately set out on a search with the gardener. They knew Curly Boy's, alas, too well-loved haunts, and it was not long before they came upon the still little figure, so pathetically appealing and beautiful in its helplessness. The transparent eyelids fluttered as they picked him up gently and fearfully. The blue eyes opened wide, the red lips curved in a faint smile, and the mother clasped him to her with an inarticulate little cry of gladness. And then it was that she espied Doggie Brown, stiff and cold. As she knelt beside him with sadly grateful eyes, guessing the whole story of his sacrifice, and thought of the new doggie at home, lapping daintily his saucer of cream, she murmured to his unhearing ears, "After all, dear Doggie Brown, old friends are best."

FIDELITY.
(Marjorie Kinnan, age 15,
Western High School.)

"Old Friends Are Best," *Washington Post*, Sunday magazine section, 3 March 1912, 6.

*   *   *   *   *   *   *   *   *

Sad Story of Little Pip

"Good day, Mrs. Duck. I'm very glad to see you. How is Pip? Oh, my dear, haven't you heard? Dear me, how dreadful! I really must tell you all about it. Yes, it is very sad, my dear, very sad; and, aside from that, it is very disgraceful, very. Nothing of this kind has ever happened before in the family coop. Poor Pip!

"The whole trouble began when that girl, Marjorie Kinnan, came out here to camp out for the summer. My poor Pip was just a wee, fluffy little baby chicken then, chirping just as cheerfully as if he had two eyes and two good legs, instead of only one eye and one lame leg, as you know. My Pip and this girl took to each other immediately. I remember so well when they first espied each other. I was down in the pasture with my babies, hunting for grasshoppers, when she came along with a pail of blackberries. My Pip stood and looked at her, and she stopped and looked at him. Then she held out a blackberry. 'Here, chickie!' she called. And what did he do but run right up to her. 'You look just like a little yellow pippin—you're so round and golden. I'll call you Pip! Here, Pip!'

"'Pip!' Just imagine!" What a name for a chicken! I had originally named him 'Beelzebub,' but from hearing him called Pip all the time, I fell into the bad habit of doing so myself.

"Then, to my amazement, Mrs. Duck, I saw all the results of my two weeks of training fly to the winds, as he, my only son, a chicken surely destined to become the most powerful rooster of the barnyard, ate the blackberry from her fingers.

"After that, Pip would run to her whenever he saw her, and, to my disgust, for I am a respectable, sensible hen, would hop into her lap, and cuddle down as comfortably as if it were my own warm back, where he once warmed his feet.

"Pip was a sly little rascal, wideawake, even with only one eye and a lame leg. He had his eye always open for something to eat, and when he one day saw this girl sitting down, eating a piece of cake, he slipped very quietly up behind her, suddenly jumped up on her shoulder, and made a wild dive for the cake, which was on its way to her mouth. This unexpected action knocked the cake into her lap, where Pip immediately followed, as a matter of course, and made haste to devour as much as possible.

"Marjorie taught him to chirp three times whenever he was hungry, and as a result, whenever he caught sight of her, morning, noon, or night, he would at once utter a series of very loud shrieks, three at a time.

"Pip was of a very jealous disposition, I am sorry to say. Marjorie had several other pets that summer, in particular a cat, and two pigeons that she had raised from featherless babies, and that would fly to her at her call.

"To these pets Pip would never allow her to pay any attention when he could help it.

"He eyed the pigeons with distrust. If Marjorie stooped to pet the cat when he was around, he would peck her legs to attract her attention, and then would look at her in a self-satisfied air, with his head cocked on one side.

"We made our home under the tents when Marjorie camped out, for Pip tagged after her half the time, and I felt that I could not have him out of my sight so much. For my part, I thought the beams under the tents were delightful roosts, but Pip did not seem to think so. He much preferred Marjorie's bed, and it was no unusual thing for her to go into the sleeping tent at any time and find him roosting peacefully on the coverlet. To this she, and particularly her mother, objected strenuously, but, no matter how often Marjorie remonstrated with him, he would seize every opportunity for taking a comfortable nap inside the tent.

"Then, my dear Mrs. Duck, came the day from which I date my son's downfall.

"It was early in September, one of those ideal Indian summer days when nature seems to have reached the highest culmination of her glory.

"My Pip was laying fast asleep under the shade of a locust tree.

"Along came Marjorie. She could not resist the temptation; she crept up behind him, then suddenly pounced upon him and seized him.

"With a huge shriek the poor dear jumped up and flew down the hill in a perfect frenzy of fear and trembling.

"After that, his ideals of perfect happiness shattered, he never dared come within three or four yards of her.

"He was miserably unhappy. He pined and pined, grew thinner and thinner. He had never grown to be more than half the size of his sisters, and, by the time he lost a pound or so of flesh, my dear, you can imagine how he looked.

"Then, Mrs. Duck, came the heart-rending climax.

"We found him, my handsome and only son, in the shade of the same locust tree where his best friend had betrayed him—dead! Yes, my dear, dead!

"He had died from fly poison!

"Those dreadful people had had a plate of fly poison out of doors, and although they all attributed my Pip's death to the fact that he thought the fly poison to be water, I know better—he committed suicide!

"Yes, Mrs. Duck, I believe from the depths of my heart that my poor boy knew that harmless-looking dish to contain poison, and deliberately drank it. I am absolutely certain of that fact, Mrs. Duck.

"Yes, it is very sad, but still it is very, very fashionable to commit suicide, you know; so I really wouldn't mind if you told the news, for our family, Mrs. Duck, has always set the fashion.

"Of course I will miss Pip very much, but yet—oh, well——

"Good-day, Mrs. Duck. So glad you called."

FIDELITY.
Marjorie Kinnan (age 15).
Western High School

"Sad Story of Little Pip," *Washington Post*, Sunday magazine section, 16 June 1912, 6. MKR was awarded second prize, $2, for this autobiographical story. The mother is Ida Traphagen Kinnan, and the farm is the dairy farm of MKR's father, Arthur Kinnan, whose agricultural experiments brought him recognition in Washington. As alluded to in the story, during the warm Maryland summers, the Kinnans would set up tents in a locust grove on the farm and live there (see Silverthorne, 13–14).

*   *   *   *   *   *   *   *   *

The Last Day of School

A ripple through the room, a vague, soft stir—
And then the bell, in accents harsh and loud,
That signals the release of all within—
And out we rush, a free and hurrying crowd.

Yet few the signs of gladness in our feet,
That lag reluctantly down the stair—
The closing day of school has come at last—

The gloom of parting lingers on the air.
'Twas but a day ago we, weary, sighed,
And fretted for the day that now is here.
Yet tears drop mocking from half-laughing eyes
That strive to smile, to buoy gloom with cheer.

We known not why thus strangely sad
We children are, and in our hearts we find
Small recognition of the fact that now
Another milestone soon is left behind—

We sigh, and sighing, sudden laugh,
And mock the glist'ning tear that mutely falls,
The servant of this cloak of sorrow drear
That on the lightness of our laughter palls.

The partings are so hard—so hard to those
Who launch upon the sea of life today;
Who nevermore, perhaps, shall taste the joys
Of youth, who in her holiday array,
Has led them with her through the flowers of May.

A newer day has dawned, the milestone passed,
That promises new hope, new faith, new joys,
Rich in the vestments of a sunrise gold—
The dawning of the future for these girls and boys.

FIDELITY (age 16).[13]
Marjorie Kinnan, Western High School

"The Last Day of School," *Washington Post*, Sunday magazine section, 14 July 1912, 4.

---

13   MKR was not quite sixteen; her birthday was 8 August 1896.

The Love of Adventure

"Oh, Miriam," I groaned, "isn't it dreadful, though, the lack of adventure? Nothing exciting ever, ever happens—we've just simply got to do something."

"Yes," my chum sighed back, "it's perfectly fierce. All our plots for running away or taking a voyage down the creek are thwarted. Let's think hard. You think, and I'll think, and we'll both think, and maybe we can manage to think up something."

Through the big haymow of the barn floated the soft, sweet odor of clover, mingled with straw. Great round, "slidy" mounds of hay offered delightful prospects of hiding and "jumping-off" places. The huge rafters overhead sighed with the burden of many secrets told beneath their shadow, and now and then creaked laboriously, knowing creaking to be the solemn duty of all well-behaved, old-fashioned rafters.

Indeed, the whole atmosphere was old-fashioned, although the barn itself was very new, for where, I ask, where in all this world, could one find an alluringly sweet-scented haymow that did not call up poignant memories of "grandma's," and many joyous revels in the country hay of the old barn!

It was of that same barn at grandma's that I was thinking as I sat by the window with my chin in my hand, gazing at the landscape.

How long I had been musing I know not, when a big, black, crawly spider squirmed down my neck, and brought me back to earth.

"Goodness!" I exclaimed as I revengefully "squashed" him. "I don't know what's the matter with me—almost went to sleep—in broad daylight in a haymow, too!"

And then I looked at Miriam, and Miriam looked at me. Mutely we gazed for a moment, then fell into each other's arms with sobs of joy.

Call it mental telepathy, hypnotic suggestion, anything you want to—for the heavenly inspiration for an adventure had certainly entered both of our minds at the same time.

"We will sleep in the haymow," I gasped, as I recovered my hairpins and my equilibrium. "We will sleep in the haymow!"

"Yes," solemnly replied Miriam, "you have said it. We will sleep in the haymow tonight."

Then, bless my buttons, the hurrying and scurrying that we did do! From the barn to the camp, from the camp to the barn, with surreptitious loads of comforters and "eats." One would have thought, to see us, that we were going to take a voyage of at least a month.

A comforter apiece, a dozen apples, three boxes of cakes, a box of crackers, a box of candy, and over half of a fried chicken, while our paper dolls and two cards games, stuffed in a couple of pillows, completed the array.

Mother caught us on the second trip.

"What on earth are you girls doing with all that stuff?"

"You'll have to tell her," I moaned in Miriam's ear. "She'll find out sooner or later."

"Tell her yourself," retorted my generous friend; "you've lived with her longer than I have—she's your mother!"

Seeing the truth of which statement, I made my plea, the outcome of which was that mother laughed, and said that she had done the same thing herself in her girlhood days.

Oh, merciful Providence, that placeth such humanity in otherwise stern mothers.

*   *   *

Off through the friendly darkness raced two figures. Slinking around the corner of the barn, evading, like two little thieves fearing detection, the moonlight, that lent a ghastly hue to the suddenly unfamiliar haymow, the apparent fugitives finally reached their destination.

Yes; it was "us."

How dusty the haymow was—the straw tickled our noses, making us cough and sneeze. A huge black giant leaped across the windowsill, but finally resolved itself into a 3-inch mouse.

"Say, Miriam," I whispered, as I picked a Junebug out of my hair, "I've heard of snakes in haymows, haven't you?"

"Yes," came back a shaky voice, "and I just know I'm covered with spiders— ugh!"

"Never mind," I reassured her, helping myself in the darkness to some chicken, "this is a real, sure-enough adventure—one that we can tell our grandchildren some day."

"Y-y-yes, but maybe we won't live to tell the story. They'll just find our poor little bodies in the morning, with snakes and things all around them."

But our eatables soon made us forget our troubles, and in a short time we were cuddling up together, whispering and laughing.

The novelty of the situation got the better of us, and all suggestion of fear had vanished, when, suddenly, a dark form hurtled through the window, and with a peculiar, ghostly flapping of the wings, circled about our terrified heads, then dropped into a distant corner, only to start up every now and then, weirdly suggestive of some fairy tale demon in the wan moonlight that filtered through the big window at the south.

Thoroughly frightened, no thought of bats ever entered our heads, and during the remainder of the sojourn in the barn our primitive couch could hardly have been termed a "bed of ease."[14]

Miriam finally dropped off to sleep, but I stayed awake, trembling at every rustling in the straw, and imagining all kinds of impossible things, including burglars, fire, snakes, and dragons.

I was almost suffocated, for little air circulated through the haymow. All longing for strange adventure had left me, and the one desire of my life was my own cool, clean bed over at the camp.

Suddenly a light appeared at the top of the ladder by the door.

"Our time has come," I thought, mentally eliminating burglars and snakes from my list of impossibilities, and then a well-known voice, that of my father, broke the silence with—

"Are you girls there? Come down this very second! I don't believe you have the sense of a last year's bird nest. Don't you know that tramps are more than liable to go into barns at night to sleep?"

(Ah, mother, where is that humanity now? You have disclosed our secret!)

Inwardly sheepish, but with heads held proudly high, we stalked back to camp, our comforters dragging behind us like the blankets of an Indian brave.

And, as we stretched our tired, hot limbs under the cool sheets, and sighed luxuriously, I whispered to my chum, "Oh, Miriam, isn't this glorious?" and Miriam whispered back, "It's perfectly heavenly!"

*   *   *

Were you to ask us now about our experience, we would say enthusiastically, "It was perfectly great!"

But, alas, we are far from being George Washingtons, and when we speak to each other of the affair we solemnly vow that we will nevermore be led astray by the love of adventure.

FIDELITY.
(Marjorie Kinnan, age 15.
Garrett Park, Md.)

---

14 In this passage, one biblical allusion, "sojourn" (cf. Abraham, Genesis 12:10) emphasizes the next, "bed of ease" (cf. Job 7:13–16).

"The Love of Adventure," *Washington Post*, Sunday magazine section, 28 July 1912, 4. This story was awarded first prize, $3. The character of Miriam, here a childhood friend, appears again in MKR's "Miriam's Houses," *New Yorker* 21 (24 November 1945): 29–31 (*Short Stories*, 352–58), a story in which the narrator—MKR writing about her youth in Washington—is shocked to learn that Miriam's mother is a prostitute.

* * * * * * * * *

The Reincarnation of Miss Hetty

Miss Hetty Simpkins sat alone on the side veranda, knitting. Her flying needles defied the heat of the June day, although the rest of the Burnesville ladies had given up all attempt at labor, and now sat upon the adjacent porches or under the shade of the door-yard trees, gossiping and fanning themselves. Miss Hetty did not approve of sitting on the front porch. It subjected them unnecessarily to the gaze of passers by. And as for gossiping Miss Hetty would no sooner have thought of gossiping as of killing something or missing church service. In respect to that destroyer of reputation she would have quoted tersely, "'Let your conversation be yea, yea and nay, nay, for whatsoever is more than this cometh of evil.'"[15]

Neither did she care to fan herself. As for that, "Humph!" she would have said. "If a lady hasn't any more to do than to sit and twiddle a fan, I haven't much use for that lady!" Wherefore she was sitting, alone, on the side veranda, knitting.

The stillness hung sultrily; not a breath of air stirred. Off in the fields, and in Miss Hetty's prim, old-fashioned garden, with its wealth of sweetness, the bees droned busily, the steady hum and buzz the only sound that broke the quiet, save when now and then a wood-thrush called to his mate from the lilac bush.

As she worked at her knitting, Miss Hetty allowed her mind to roam back over the past; a dreary past, that had made her crabbed, as the villagers said. Her parents had died when she was little more than a child, and with no relatives or friends to assist her, she had assumed all the responsibilities of a woman and mother in bringing up her baby brother, a golden-haired child in whom her whole soul had been centered. Her one delight was to satisfy his whims, and love and cuddle him.

---

15   From the Sermon on the Mount, Matthew 5:37: "But let your conversation be, Yea, yea; Nay, nay: for whatsoever is more than these cometh of evil."

By twenty she was a fully matured woman; And then one day they brought him home to her from the river, drowned, the golden curls dripping, the fair face blue and ghastly. Forty-two years had passed since that day, and at sixty-two, Miss Hetty was as bitter as the wormwood in the medicine chest. She remained as bustling, as neat and as precise as ever, (and incidentally as unapproachable), through all the years. The Burnesville ladies had long since ceased to be friendly, and now scarcely bothered to chatter about her behind her back; the village boys never molested her apple tree; no stray cats or dogs ever visited her back yard—for boys, cats and dogs alike were wise, and from experience.

Suddenly Miss Hetty gathered up her knitting, thrust it into her workbag, and hurried into the house, to emerge in a few moments with her best bonnet tied carefully upon her white hair, and her black lace mitts upon her hands. With a great deal of bustle and excitement she locked the door, and slipping the key under the door mat, settled her silver-rimmed spectacles more firmly upon her nose, then started briskly toward "town." She had almost forgotten that she was entirely out of calico, and it was time to make some new aprons.

*   *   *

Miss Hetty was tired.

"Please, lady——"

She started. The voice, tiny, high-pitched and quavering, seemed to come from nowhere at all.

"Please, lady——"

Miss Hetty looked down—and located the voice. It came from a wee mite of a child, with two white streaks running down its face, marking the passage of tears; his yellow hair was tangled; his elbows protruded from the ragged shirt; his legs were bare, his face, naturally chubby, was pinched—but he was a dimpled, lovable child—in spite of the dirt and the ragged clothes.

Miss Hetty edged away. "What is it, child?" she said harshly.

The red lips quivered, although the blue eyes raised to hers were hopeful.

"Please, lady, don'—don' cher wanter buy a dorg?"

She raised her hands, deprecatingly. Involuntarily she closed her eyes and shuddered. "Gracious child, no!" she gasped. "I detest dogs!"

The child fought back the tears disappointedly. "It—it's a very nice dorg," he said. "Look, lady! He likes yer—he's a-waggin' of his tail!"

Miss Hetty glared down at the dog. It was just an ordinary little pup, with a stumpy tail and foolish watery eyes, but the child hugged it affectionately. One glance was enough for her, and picking up her skirts, she started down the road once more. "Don't ever say 'dog' to Hetty Simpkins," she announced decisively.

The wee boy buried his face in the puppy's fur; stifled sobs came to the ears of Miss Hetty. But she seemed quite deaf to them. All during her shopping trip, and all the way home, a vague sense of uneasiness pervaded her. Poignant memories of a golden-haired child in a little white basket assailed her. Something pricked her conscience—the remembrance of two blue eyes raised confidingly and hopefully to her face, the remembrance of the baby's lips quivering at her harsh, unkind words. She thought of her own lonely, useless life, and again the image of the white casket rose before her.

Miss Hetty was not one to hesitate long. She stopped directly in the road. "Bless my stars!" she announced. "I'll wager anything that that child is starving, and was selling that horrid dog to keep himself alive! There's something queer about it, at any rate. Hetty Simpkins, it's your bounden duty to go back and find him! Here you are, a lone woman, with never a chick nor a child to take some of the sourness out of life, when you might be helping some poor orphan, and yourself at the same time!"

Her mind made up, she retraced her steps. The sun was sinking, and one star in the east announced the coming of night. She was almost back to Burnesville, and nearly despairing of finding the child, when a low whine called to her notice the "dorg."

The child must be somewhere near, she reflected. Yes, there was a flutter of something white in the bushes. She hurried towards it. There he was, fast asleep, a sturdy specimen of childhood, despite the wan shadows beneath the big blue eyes. An awful doubt assailed he—perhaps the child was not an orphan, after all—perhaps she had no right to him.

"Dearie," she said, very softly indeed for her, "where are your folks?"

The child shook his head sleepily. "Hain't got any folkses. Me lives at orphan asylum. No folkses 'tall."

And Miss Hetty's heart was at rest.

The summer moonlight streamed in through the open window of the upper bedroom of the trim little cottage. The gnarled old apple tree swayed dreamily in the soft breeze, and peeped quietly in the window. What it saw made it wave a green bough softly and whisper, "Hush! Hush!"

In a little white bed by the window lay the child asleep. One dimpled arm lay outside the coverlet, and his golden curls were spread out on the pillow. Miss Hetty watched by his side. Then she did an unheard of thing. She leaned over and kissed him gently—oh, so gently, on his rosy lips. She knelt down softly—so softly by the bed and buried her face. The child opened his eyes and laid one chubby hand caressingly against her wrinkled face. The old apple tree drew away, scarce rustling a leaf.

"Sh-h!" it murmured. "Sh-h-h-h!"

"The Reincarnation of Miss Hetty," *McCall's Magazine* 39, no. 2 (August 1912): 27, 72. Another version of this story was previously published in the *Washington Post*, 12 February 1911, 5.

*   *   *   *   *   *   *   *   *

The Freshman's Side of It

[*The Western*] Editor's Note—This is to be taken seriously only by the Freshmen.

Once more the sound of baby feet,
    Shy pattering o'er the floor;
Once more the go-cart hinges creak;
    The Freshies come once more.

Soft childish lisps sound through the halls,
    Great screams of fright, as some
Tall Senior takes an infant's doll,
    Its bottle, or a drum.

The nurse maids quite distracted are,
    Their charges don't behave,
This High School life's too much for them—
    All that they see they crave.

They want the Senior's beaver hat,
    The Junior's walking cane,
They want to play the graphophone—[16]
    O'er all they want to reign.
If they're not humored, they begin
    To cry, to scream, to squall;

---

16 Developed in the laboratory of Alexander Graham Bell (1847–1922) in the early 1880s, the graphophone was the first practical sound-recording device.

The more they're spanked, the harder they
    Emit their dreadful bawl.

One little auburn-lock'd chap
    Sits in his classroom, where
He frowns and glowers, in manner fierce,
    And tears his curly hair.

Great round glasses to him lend
    An air almost studious;
Compassion moves your mighty soul—
    "Wha's matter, son, tell us?"

He shakes his bright-hued pate, and says,
    "It wouldn't do me no dood
To tell oo, oo'ld dus laugh at me."
    "Not so, my boy, it would."

"Well, den, I'll tell oo, but I fink
    Oo'll only pull my hair.
De twuble is, we fellows fink
    Dat oo don't tweat us fair.

"We Fweshmen do to all de games,
    An' join de 'ssociation,
An' pay our dues, join de debate
    An' den our consolation.

"Is habbin' Seniors take our hats,
    An' spank us, take our lunch,
An' chase up de twees, an' all,
    An' say, I dot a hunch

"De Seniors aren't no dood at all,
    Nor needer are de Juniors,
'Cause de ones dat support de High School are
    De Fweshies an' de Sophomores.
"De Big-Bugs talk so fwesh, an' say
    We chillens are so bad,

But when it turns to do weel stuff—
    Oo fellowsh makesh me shad!

"We's nebber late to school, an' we
    Don't work de car-line dope.
We do's to classes, an' don't hab
    To be dwagged dere wif a rope.

"We studies lots and lots, an' den
    We always knows our leshons,
An' when we're wicked, wun an' make
    To de office our turfeshons.

"Oo big guys don't do zis at all,
    Oo don't pwetend to work,
Skip clashes, flirt wif girls, an' all—
    Don't do a fing but shirk!

"But, shay, dere's one fing I can tell,
    I'm goin' to do it, too;
Shum day, yuh big stiff ober dere,
    Me'll be as big as oo!!

"Shum day me'll be a Taptain in
    De company, an' den
Perhaps me'll be de President—
    Oo bet I'll lick oo den!

"Oo ain't so monshtrous, anyway,
    Oo ain't so werry tall—
Onsh on a time, oo know, my fwend,
    Oo weally were twight shmall.

"Oo weren't a Senior all oor life,
    (I s'pose oo finks oo were)
Oo ownce was teensy dus like me,
    Yuh big stiff, dere. Yes, shir!

"Me no will shay no more, me do
    To play de gwaphophone;

But after dis, I hope dat oo
    Will leab me wight alone!"

The baby toddles off, and you
    Near burst your sides with laughter,
As he goes strutting off so proud,
    His puppy tagging after.

You clap your comrade on the back,
    And double up—but say,
Old chappy, did you ever think
    The kid's right, in his way?

He told the truth, so what d' you think
    Of taking his advice?
Let's treat 'em square, so they'll all say
    The Seniors are "twight nice."

Let's leave their bloomin' toys alone,
    And don't let's swipe their eats,
And don't let's hook their dollies when
    We meet 'em on the streets.

And don't let's pull their wooly locks,
    And don't let's spank 'em, or
Don't let us chase 'em up the trees,
    Or paddle 'til they're sore.

Let's pat 'em on their curly pates,
    Let's mollify their squealin's,
And let's be dignified, so we
    Won't hurt their little feelin's.

Some day, you know, the dippies *might*
    Be Presidents, and we
The Mighties, might be gone dead broke,
    Without a cent to see.

And then how great 'twould be, old boy,
    To have 'em say to us,

"Please be my Sec. Of State, my friend—
    When I, a little cuss

Was in my Freshman year at school,
    You Seniors sure were great—
I ne'er forgot it, so I beg,
    You to be Sec. Of State!"

M. K., '14

"The Freshman's Side of It," *Western* 17, no. 1 (October 1912): 24–26.

*   *   *   *   *   *   *   *   *

To James Whitcomb Riley

I'm awfully lonesome; seems to me
There's no one else in all the world
About, it is so still.
The night clouds in their nest are curled
And the heavens shiver, their night jewels sparkling.

I'm awfully lonesome; through the bars
Of every window appears the moon,
Harsh, smiling, cold, and far away,
Mocking the bareness of the room.
The asylum wall looms cold and drear.

I'm awfully lonesome; all the rest
Are sleeping in their orphans' beds;
I watch the graveyard, watch the low,
Small mounds, with tombstones at the heads.
The graveyard must be lonesome, too,
    clasping dead orphans to its breast.

The trees are watchman-like and bare
As steel swords from their scabbards drawn.
Sharp-cut, loud swishing in the wind
That moans all weary 'till the dawn.

They watch, the trees, but not o'er me;
　　they have no hearts, no pity.

Dark shadows slip across the snow,
Revengeful of the moon's bright gleams;
They fall from tree, from wall, and glide
Down to the tarn where the waters freeze.
And the shadows speak to the nighttime,
　　and they scoff at the day and the light.

I'm awfully lonesome; no one cares
About me, or my loneliness.
I am but one of many here,
One grain of sand in the wilderness.
But my heart cries out in its grief for love.

I'm always lonesome; my brown-striped frock
Of gingham, my neatly platted hair,
Put me apart from the rest of the world;
"An orphan child," and so I bear
The stamp of my isolation in my garb.

I pass down the street, and I see at their play
The children in well-fed, dear-loved homes,
Of fathers who cherish, and mothers who love.
And a heartsick feeling over me comes.

Here in the home, as the townspeople call it,
The others regard me suspiciously, say
I am different, since I am quiet, a dreamer.
They, all-content, living from day unto day,
Yet fate mocks me, and scoffs at me,
　　tearing my heart strings.

　　　　*　　*　　*

Six months have passed since I stood at my window
By night, and resentfully called out to fate.
Six months have passed—I have found my consolation;

Found it, discovered it, ah, not too late!
And the springtime sings in my heart, for
 the time of the violets and robins is here.

There, on the red wall, the ivy grows greener,
There, on the bough, sings the bluebird his song;
Far in the meadows the flowers bloom sweeter,
"Spring" sing the streamlets the joyous day long.
I am glad, I am glad, and I chant in the
 morn to the meadow lark's music.

Into my life there has crept a new meaning,
Existence means more than the presence of life;
Freed is my heart from its sad contemplations,
Freed is my soul from its conflict, its strife.
And one person, only one, has given me this;
This wonderful joy of living.

He always is with me, though I never have seen him,
His presence, his spirit, encompasses me now;
His dear words—I love them—I love them—rest always
As cool hands upon my oft feverish brow.
And I am quieted, e'en as a restless babe, by his singing.

Six months ago—what an age—what an eon!
Then did I find by the roadside a book
Filled with the most loving phrases of solace,
Of beauty, of joy, that into a nook
Of my heart, tenderly crept as a spirit of love.

Verses that sang of the sheer joy of living,
Verses of people as sad as myself;
Verses of poverty, verses of riches,
Riches of happiness, yea—not of pelf.
And I pondered and took to my heart the
 deep lessons he taught, oh, so sweetly.

There were songs of the glories of God, there were songs
Of the works of His hand, of the birds, of the trees,
Of the deep-laid divinity shown in all nature,
Her rivers, her children, her flowers, and her bees.
And I gazed at the Earth, with her garment
   of snow, and the mother-love deep hidden in
   her breast spoke to me.

There were words of a wonderful love and compassion,
That told me, a stranger, they understood all,
The first one to know, and the first one to pity,
The only one loving or caring at all.
He was there, and the dawn broke with splendor,
   and the sun of my comprehension appeared
   above the golden horizon.

The only one knowing how much I had suffered,
That sympathized; ah, how I loved him along
With his verses, his sonnets, his words that so moved me,
That made my starved heart turn to ecstatic song!
And he understood me, the poor little orphan.

Now I am learning to live, and 'tis through him
Who knew of the grief of a tired, lonesome child,
Longing for sympathy, longing for pity,
   longing for all that he gives in his mild
All-enveloping manner, the Poet Compassionate.

Ah, I should love but to see him—I know that
His face is as kind as his comforting words.
Yet all I can do is to wish that his lifetime
Be happy and free as the songs of the birds.

My Wish.

And one thing I wish him, upon his birthday–[17]
I should like, oh, so much, that my prayer he should see.

---

17 Riley's birthday is 7 October.

May all of his life, lasting long, be as happy
As his cheerful poems have often made me.

FIDELITY. (Marjorie Kinnan, 306 Hammond court,
Western High School

"To James Whitcomb Riley," *Washington Post*, Sunday magazine section, 27 October 1912, 6. MKR was awarded first prize, $3, for this elegy to James Whitcomb Riley (1849–1916), the Hoosier poet, who was especially known for the blending of sentiment and pathos into uplifting moral meaning.

*   *   *   *   *   *   *   *

Company, Halt!

The little tin soldiers have come to town,
Their heads held high, their muskets down,
Scaring the cop from off the street,
As he strolls up Reservoir[18] on his beat.
    Forward, guide right, march!

The little tin soldiers have come to stay,
You can hear them drilling 'most any day;
Their guns are clean, their caps on straight,
For drill days they can scarcely wait.
    Inspection, arms!

The awkward squad inspireth fear—
(Like the poor, my friends, it's always here)—[19]
It almost tears the drill-hall down,
As it rolls and stumbles o'er the ground.
    Present, arms!

The new-made officers, darling things,
Go strutting around on angels' wings,
Beaming and smiling on all the world,

---

18 Reservoir Road, in northwest Washington, D.C.

19 As in Matthew 26:11, Mark 14:7, and John 12:8.

Especially on the little girls.
    Left front into line, march!

They don't have to do much grinning, though—
You can leave that to us girls, you know,
Who want to go to the company dance,
And with the "gold-braids" gaily prance.
    Right dress, front!

But don't despise the ladies' charms,
That lend new courage to your arms,
For they get up the company "feeds,"
To tend to your tender tummies' needs.
    Squads right, march!

They hie them to the Competitive Drill,
To see that Western gets her fill
Of cheers, applause and pennants gay,
To liven the ever-toilsome day.
    Column left, march!

Oh, the soldiers of tin are jolly boys,
And even if they're only toys
To amuse the babies and smile at the girls,
And arrange their hair in cunning curls,
Their arms are strong, and their hearts are true,
And they stand for the honor of me, of you,
And gladden old Western's Assembly Hall
With their sweet little faces, their uniforms all
Rebraided, and some of them even brand-new,
To uphold the honor of me, of you.
    Port, arms!

Then here's to the boys of H and L,
Their arms for our defense,
And *ours* their recompense—
    Fall, in!

M. K. '14.

"Company, Halt!" *Western* 17, no. 2 (November 1912): 18–19.

Our Triumph

Every one knew, or thought that he knew, that Western could do absolutely nothing against Technical. The papers were full of talk about Western's "crippled team" and Tech's mighty one.

And here I had best say that Western and Tech have long been rivals in the athletic world, although friendly in other respects. Twice in the last two years has Tech snatched the baseball championship from our hands; both times in the last game of the season.

Western is doomed, it seems, to always go down before the Maroon and Gray battering ram, although our teams have sometimes humbled their rival.

And Western did have a crippled team. "Serious injuries," "parental objections," said the papers.

Western had a lightweight team, the guards averaging much less than 150 pounds. Tech's men were giants, as usual.

The day of the game came, with Technical absolutely calm and sure, expecting a walkaway.

The Maroon and Gray team strutted on to the field, and their rooters scarcely bothered to cheer. They needed no encouragement.

The Red and White boys trotted out, and from Western's stand went up a mighty cheer; a cheer that made the oncoming team lift its head in pride and determination; a cheer that came from the hearts, and said, as plainly as if spoken: "We're with you, boys. Don't give up. Old Western's spirit is in you, and you can't lose. Stick to it, lads. Win or lose, we're with you."

And the Tech rooters sat up very straight on their board seats and took notice. Western was mighty cheerful for a team going to its own funeral.

And the game began.

Back and forth, to and fro, over the long gridiron surged the two teams, fighting, falling, and pulling.

Back and forth, and the stronger team was slowly advancing toward the Western goal posts, yet checked, checked by something; some vague, intangible something, that they could not locate. It was the school spirit. Western was outplayed by Tech. She was outweighed. She was lacking in technique, in experience, in cunning.

Yet it was only with a most terrible effort that a huge figure in Tech colors pushed the pigskin over the line.

Again the Maroon and Gray boys crept up to the goal, like a slowly coiling serpent ready to strike, and again a tall figure darted between the posts, and thrust the ball over for a second touchdown.

The referee blew the whistle; the first half was ended.

Across the field floated the strains of "Hop along, dear old Western, hop along," sweet and clear. The boys' caps were off, the whole school was on its feet, girls and boys alike.

In every one's throat there was a hard, dry lump, and in many eyes were tears. Never in all my life have I heard so sad a thing as "Hop along, dear old Western," when we were losing.

There is a peculiar tone about the song that makes it plaintive, almost despairing, in defeat. Yet it is "Hop Along" that has often turned the tide of battle and swept the Western teams to victory.

The second half began. Technical's third touchdown was scored.

"Hold 'em, Western. Hold 'em, Western! Hold 'em, Western," came the cry.

With renewed vigor, enthusiasm, and strength Western went at her enemy.

Like a mad bull she tore through her opponent's ranks. Like a bulldog she gripped the ball and held it. Cunningly she broke through her rival's ruses, feints, tricks. Calmly, quietly, but with the light of a conqueror in her eyes, she stole up to the goal posts. With almost a superhuman strength the Maroon and Gray tackled in one mass.

A short, stocky figure, in a torn sweater, red and white stockings, and with a bleeding face, gently, easily, laid the pigskin on the opposite side of Technical's goal, and when the conglomeration of humanity arose, disentangled itself, one from the other, Western's captain lay senseless upon the ground, and was delirious for nearly 24 hours.

The referee blew the whistle once more.

The game was over.

"Western defeated by Technical," said the papers.

But as the battered Red and White team limped from the field, a mighty cheer went up from all throats, Technical and Western together, a cheer for Western and her captain, a cheer for the indomitable will and courage of an inferior team, realizing its failings, but laboring on and on, saving itself from "whit[e]washings" by the sheer pluck and the knowledge of loyal hearts behind.

"Western defeated by Technical." But as our boys went off, their heads held high in grim determination to be "game," there was not a person present but what felt in his heart of hearts that Western had triumphed, despite the score, simply because there was a spirit in the school that would not give up in the face of terrible odds, but kept on nobly, doing the best work possible. And it is the spirit that counts in school life. It is the spirit that makes men and women, and puts character into their makeup.

And it is this spirit that proves "the stuff of boys from across the creek are made of."[20]

FIDELITY.
MARJORIE KINNAN (age 16.)
Western High School

"Our Triumph," *Washington Post*, Sunday magazine section, 17 November 1912, 6. This story was awarded first prize, $3.

*　　*　　*　　*　　*　　*　　*　　*　　*

H'it's a Bear, H'it's a Bear, H'it's a Bear, There!

H'I h'am a bally Hinglishman,
　An h'I love my cup of tea,
H'I like my roast-beef very rare,
　A joke h'I cannot see.

H'I do my best to be a duke,
　A bloomin' one h'at that,
H'I wear a h'eye-glass h'in me h'eye,
　H'I 'ave a stove-pipe 'at.

H'I h'am quite 'ansome, so they say,
　And whondrous h'is my chawm,
My mutton-chops, my cane, my 'air,
　Fill many with h'alarm.

Sir Persë Peachë h'is my name—
　Mah word, h'I love h'it so!
H'it sounds just like h'I look, bah Jove,
　H'it's deucedly swell, you know,

In shawt, h'I'm h'awfully, h'awfully "cute,"
　H'as people h'often say,

---

20 Cf. Shakespeare's *The Tempest*: "We are such stuff / As dreams are made on" (4.1.156–57).

A bally Britisher h'I was,
　　H'I thought, 'til yestuhday.

But now, deah me, h'I'm quite confused,
　　H'I don't know what to think,
My wits are, h'as the d'U. S. says,
　　H' extemely "h'on the blink."

H'I'm visiting New Yawk, you know,
　　And fwends, when yestuhday,
H'I took a walk h'in Central Pahk,
　　H'I 'eard somebody say.

Most beastly rude and loud, you know,
　　"Say, fellows, 'e's a bear,
A Hinglish bear—some bear, eh, wot?
　　A bear! A Hinglish bear!"

Ill-mannahed brutes! What beastly taste,
　　To say a thing like that!
(H'I smoothed my frock-coat down h'in front,
　　And straightened my cravat).

Deah fwends, h'I was so worried, h'I
　　Quite ran to my 'otel,
To get a looking-glass, to 'ave
　　H'it quick the dire treuth tell.

But nay, not so, no vision fierce
　　Of grizzly met my h'eye
My monocle, my 'at were there,
　　My pink and purple tie.

My face was bally round and fair,
　　My h'eye was calm and blue;
The rowdies lied; no bear was h'I—
　　H'I knew h'it was not true.

But yet, to be quite sure, you know,
    H'I h'asked my small bell 'op—
H'I saw 'im running past my door—
    "H'I say, h'old chappy, stop!"

"H'I want that you should h'answer me
    Quite honest and quite square;
Look jolly well h'at me—reply—
    H'am h'I—ha'm I—a bear?"

The bell 'op grinned, 'e rolled 'is h'eyes,
    And started down the stair,
"Ah guess you am, suh; guess you am
    A bear, suh; yas, some bear!"

H'imagine, fwends, my feelings then,
    What trouble stirred my 'eart,
My Hinglish, London, roast-beef soul,
    'Ow keen, 'ow strange the smart.

"A bear, some bear, a Hinglish bear—"
    H'oh, puzzling h'U. S. h'A.—
But now h'I've found the trouble, fwends;
    You know, h'its just this way:

These bloomin' people over here
    Don't know a bear, h'I say;
They don't know what a bear h'is, fwends—
    H'oh, puzzling h'U. S. h'A.!

                                        —M. K., '14

"H'it's a Bear, H'it's a Bear, H'it's a Bear, There!" *Western* 17, no. 3 (December 1912):
10–11.

"Once upon a Time a Black Demon
Invented Powder, and——"

Oh Powder, boon of maidens fair,
Oh Powder, brunette, pink, and white,
To you I dedicate my song,
To you attribute I my plight!

When I rush forth, at 9 o'clock,
From home to school, half frantic, wild,
For fear that I'll be late—Ma-ma
Doth nab me at the door—"My child,
Just wipe that powder off your nose!"

When I arrive at school, and find
My clock was fast, and I'm on time,
Near fainting from the shock, I'm grabbed
By Mr. Young—"Oh, Youth's Decline!
Child, wipe that powder off your nose!"

When I am sallying down the hall,
Important with my weight of years,
I meet my Senior crush, who cries,
Almost upon the verge of tears,
"Oh, wipe that powder off your nose!"

Oft, weighted with the burden great
Of tests, am I, the coming hour;
My own chum brings me back to earth,
With bitter words, full curt and sour:
"Child, wipe that powder off your nose!"

All ready, oft, I am, to go
Into Miss Westcott's office—Jean
Doth halt me with a worried look,
"My dear, don't think I'm awfully mean,
But—wipe that powder off your nose!"

My best beloved called last night;
He took my trembling hand, he sighed—
I thought, "He will, he must propose!"
The picture of despair, he cried,
"Dear, wipe that powder off your nose!"

—M. K., '14.

"Once upon a Time a Black Demon Invented Powder, and——." *Western* 17, no. 4 (January 1913): 27.

* * * * * * * * *

Perse and the Baseball Game

I.

Oh, Perse was a British lod,
  A British lod was he—
Carnation in his buttonhole,
  An eeglasss at his ee.
"Bah Jove!" his fav'rite by-word was,
  "Mah Word!" he'd often say;
A' those wha ever heard him would
  Frae lauching faint away.[21]
He dearly, dearly loved himsel'—
  A joke he couldna' see—
That he was the biggest joke of a'
  Ne'er wot that proud Perse.

II.

Now Perse to the U. S. cam',
  As bauld as bauld could be,
Carnation in his buttonhole,
  His eeglass at his ee.
'Twas the springtime that he cam',
  When baseball held full sway—
He ne'er had seen a baseball game,

---

21 *Lauch* is the Scots word for laugh.

And sae ane bonny day
He hied himself to the Baseball Park,
    To see the "Giants" play.

III.

Sair swagger in a long-tailed coat
    Upon a bench he sat;
Sair swagger, when wi' bat in hand
    A man stepped to the bat.
The pitcher sent a lovely curve
    Right past the batter's head—
The batter swung his bat, and then
    "Str-r-r-ike one!" the Umpire said.

IV.

Dear Perse quite excited was,
    Up frae his seat sprente he.
"Bah Jove! Mah Word!" he shouted forth,
    "Me thinks that looks easy!"
The people on the grandstand lauched
    "An' wha are ye?" they cried.
"I'm Perse Lenfall," answered he,
    "I crossed the ocean wide
To see a U. S. baseball game—
    I wot 'twas something fine—
An' now I find, mair wae to ye,
    'Tis but a pantomine!"
"Oh, merce, Perse," then they howled,
    "Wha tied your tie?" they yelled—
But Perse anely swately smiled—
    Wi' pride his bosom swelled.
He dinna' ken they lauched at him—
    A joke he couldna' see—
He merely smiled, an' put once mair
    His eeglass to his ee.

V.

"Can you do bether, Perse dere?"
    "Can Perse bat a ba'?"

"Why don't ye fa' your luck, my dere?
    Because ye can't—that's a.'"

VI.

But Perse turned, wi' hauteur in
    His every move, and said,
"I'll do it! I con bot a ba—!"
    And soon his coat is shed.
He sprint onto the diamond,
    And piked up a stick,
"Bah Jove! Come on! Send out your Ba's!
    Come on—an' send 'em quick!"

VII.

The pitcher lauched, the batter lauched,
    And every rooter squealed.
"Aw, let 'im plat!" each cried in glee—
    The players in the field
All cried aloud, "Yes, let 'im play,
    Let Perse take the bat!"
Sae Perse, wi' out mair ado,
    Discarded his plug hat.

VIII.

Wi' shirt sleeves up, wi' frown on brow,
    He waited for the ba—
The pitcher sterte, lauchingly,
    A slaw one at his braw.
Dear Perse squealed—"Hell-up!" he called—
    The Ba' 'gan to come on—
"You'll kill me! Take the Ba' away—
    Ye fause, ye wicked mon!"

IX.

"Why don't ye hit it, Perse dere?"
    Each rooter yelled aloud.
Sae Perse swung his bat sair hard,

And then—a dusty cloud
Shawed whaur the catcher bit the dust,
　　As grass to the earth is mowed.

X.

The Ba.' had not reached Perse yet—
　　The sweat upon his brow
Did trickle down his British cheeks—
　　The Ba' is there!—and now—
It strikes dere Perse on the nut—
　　It passes thro' his head—
(His brain is empty) sae ye see
　　It kills poor Perse dead!

XI.

Alas! Alas! He's dead! He's dead!
　　He lies upon the ground!
An' a' those cruel rooters do
　　Run 'round him, 'round and 'round!

XII.

They carried him hame to England—in
Westminster Abbey buried him;
And there his grave it lies to-day—
The grave of Perse Lenfall gay.
This is the epitauph on his tomb—
'Twill last until the day of doom:
　　"Here lies dere Perse Lenf',
　　Was hit in the head by a baseba'
　　He couldna' stay, he had to go—
　　Praise God frae whom a' blessings flow."[22]

　　　　　　　　　　　　　　　　—M. K., '14.

"Perse and the Baseball Game," *Western* 17, no. 5 (February 1913): 25–28.

22　From the Christian hymn known as the "Doxology"; words by Thomas Ken (1637–1711),
Anglican bishop, and music by Louis Bourgeois (ca. 1510–61), French follower of Calvin.

A Romance

This, my friends, is a tale of the Northland; of the wild and frozen North, where balmy southern breezes stir faintly the broad leaves of the palmetto and snow lies five feet deep upon the grassy flower-covered plain. The North wind howls softly through the bare, verdant trees; no sound is heard, while the songs of birds float through the still, noisy atmosphere. Silence reigns over tumult.

The sands of the desert shift beneath the icy sun; and the bleak pines wave their branches dolefully and gladly in the North wind, warmed by no sun, for here is eternal night, and the sun shines always.

This was the land to which our hero, Pierre De Salle O'Hooligan, had come.

Stage coaches were the only vehicles in use at this time, and as Pierre stepped from his Pullman car,[23] this was the scene that greeted his ears.

He was a typical type of American womanhood. His appearance was that of an Italian Frenchman, and one could easily discriminate by glancing away from him, that he was the daughter of the English Kaiser. His complexion was as dark as the ace of spades; he had black, curly hair, a black eye, and a rosy olive-green skin, while straight golden hair was combed crooked back in a Teddy Lion, over a brow, low and high, of ivory-white redness. Blue eyes gleamed from an exquisite mouth, while pearly teeth were set on either side of a straight, Jewish nose. He was of medium height, measuring 8 feet 11 inches in his stocking-hands.

Gazing over the desolate, busy scene, he stepped into an exquisite Paris waiting-room, a low, one-room shack, covered with rose vines of honeysuckle, blooming gaily, void of leaves or blossoms.

Our hero was attired in strictly up-to-date costume, having purchased all the garments in Plunkville, Ohio. Natty white duck trousers of blue serge clothed his pretty pink legs, while Scotch kilts exposed to view three dimpled knees. An Indian blanket was wrapped about his maternal bosom, and a Wellesley sweater clothed his upper half. Gilt sandals of purple suede enhanced the beauty of his tootsie-wootsies, while tennis-slippers of green and pink covered modestly his feet. A plug hat sat off his brown locks, while a poke-bonnet framed his sweetly shy countenance. Immaculate white silk gloves of yellow kid clothed his soft, white ears, and he wore no gloves. A scepter in one foot, an umbrella in the other, he made a womanly picture indeed, as he coyly toyed with his bonnet strings.

---

23 The railway sleeper car invented in 1857 by George Pullman (1831–97).

No house was in sight; on the hill a huge mansion was gaily lighted, and people passed to and fro before the shutters.

Just then a murderous appearing individual of the Louis XIV style came up, attired in a Roman toga and bedroom slippers. Gathering more closely about his loins a bathrobe, he stepped up to our hero on tiptoe.

"What would ye?" he asked.

Pierre laid a finger upon the intruder's tulips.

"A place to work I desire, for I—but no, I cannot speak—I must not—but, ah, what a weight upon my poor feet!"

The station-master, for such it was looked about to see that the cat was asleep, then said in a low, mysterious voice: "Hist ye! Go ye to old man Jones' house, beyond the cross-roads. And mind ye that he does not murder ye in your very bed! Go!"

Our friend shuddered boldly. He was to go to a murderer's dwelling! But he would be brave! Perhaps he could kill him! He must go!

Gathering up his baggage on his shoulders, he started off for the river, where lived old man Jones.

His luggage was a very light affair, consisting only of twelve trunks, thirty suit-cases, and three hundred hat-boxes. Thus you may see that Pierre cared nothing at all for his clothes.

Reaching the pier, he set off up the mountain, and finally came to the cross-roads. Which road should he take? He closed one eye, the blinded one, turned a flip-flop, and found himself facing the South-Northern road, down which he went.

What luck! There was the house! It was an exquisite Newport barn of logs, with glazed paper for windows and a stove-pipe (hat) for a chimney. How exquisite! Pierre caught his breath as he gazed at the magnificence, knocking timidly, he prepared himself boldly for the murderer.

The door swung open—Pierre almost swooned from terror, for there was the murderer himself! Pierre could see immediately that he was as desperate a villain as ever lived.

He wore spectacles, from over which he beamed benevolently. A Van Dyke beard adorned his jaw. His face was kind and insane-looking. His head was almost bald, and a black skull-cap was perched upon it. He had a habit of rubbing his hands together.

"Pardon me," he began softly, "can I be of any assistance to you? What say?"

Pierre was ready to die from fright. So this was old man Jones! He could well see why the station-master had cautioned him against him.

Quaking boldly in his boots, he said shyly, his eyes dropped coquettishly to the ground, "Please, dear Jonsey, I desire work."

Old man Jones smiled fiercely. "You shall have it!" he thundered in a low, soft voice. "I shall employ you in carrying the shredded wheat biscuit to and from the lunch-room."

Pierre sighed—how could he perform such a murderous task? "How much do I get?" he asked.

"You shall get but a penny a-day, because you can't work any faster," he roared benignly.

Pierre was ready to weep on his neck. Murderer or not this terror was generous. A penny a day! What could he get with all that untold wealth! Already he saw in his mind's ear the chewing-gum and the hokey-pokies that he would buy![24]

But just then the violent-looking old man Jones led our sweetly sour hero into the kitchen, where he saw a sight that made the blood rush violently to his feet. It was Sally Jane Jones, the murderer's daughter!

She was as fair as coal, and as dusky in hue as a fleecy cloud. She was slender, yea, unto the verge of skinnyness, and was so plump, yea, unto the verge of fatness, that she resembled nothing more than a barrel of flour tied about the middle. Her golden locks of raven hue stuck out all around her shiny countenance in myriads of kinky pig-tails, and Pierre was like to faint from love of her. She was richly attired in a Paquin gown of green calico,[25] trimmed with Valentine lace, and she wore dainty No. 9 shoes. She was monstrous tall, about 4 inches high, and measured 8 yards about her slender waist. She was like unto an American beauty butter-cup blooming shyly by the road-side in a greenhouse in the wilds of Siberian steppes.

She was perched lightly on the window-sill, partaking of black-berry jam and cream tarts, and the rich mixtures were strewn up and down the length of her dainty gown. She turned and saw Pierre.

Her hair turned gray at sight of him, and her pink, elephantine ears waved back and forth in a mute welcome. Her tiny mouth, just twelve inches across, flopped open—a bold fly ventured in, trickled down her red lane—and still her mouth flopped open. Another fly—then suddenly she swooned into his waiting arms.

---

24 According to the OED, the term *hokey-pokey* appeared in the early 1880s and described an inexpensive ice cream sold by street vendors.

25 The House of Paquin, Paris, cofounded (1891) by the first major couturiere, Jeanne Paquin (1869–1936), winner of the French Legion of Honor (1913) and known for her elegant yet practical designs.

Old man Jones hastened for milk to throw upon her to restore her consciousness. While he was gone, Pierre kissed her back to life.

"My rescuer," she cried, as she opened her eyes and her mouth, "I knew you would come. I have waited long years for you. You are the ideal of my dreams! Let me follow you to eternity and the altar!"

He kissed her cow-slip lips,[26] and her sky-blue cheeks.

"Marry me, oh angel!" he cried in grievous distress, "I love thee!"

She smiled coquettishly. "I reciprocate," she blushed boldly, "I will marry you!"

"Let us elope, sweet, honey-bunch, angel, doodles, ducky, lovey, tootsie-wootsies darling," he cried, "thy father is not nigh. Thou needst no trousseau. Come!"

She pressed a kiss upon his forehead with motherly solicitude, and just then old man Jones entered the room.

"I overheard thy loving talk," he said in a fierce, mild tone, "look not at me with that tone of voice. I am not so harsh as I seem. I will let you elope. But first, let me give you my blessing."

"I tell you now, in solemn numbers.
  Love is but an empty dream,
For the man is dippy who lovest—
  Women are not what they seem."[27]

Then the loving elopers slipped out of the house, out into the cold world, out in the snow. But, out, they slipped, until they came to a frozen lake, slipped upon its glassy surface, and were precipitated to union forever, over the cliff. They plunged over the mountainside, were carried away by the rushing torrents, and were seen no more, save in a warmer place than they had ever visited before.

This, my friends, is a tale of the Northland, of the wild and frozen north, where smudge-fires are always used to keep away the mosquitoes, and lovers live and die.

Found in the Annals of a Dippy Freshman, who expired from Teacheritis. Discovered by

M. K., '14.

"A Romance," *Western* 17, no. 5 (May 1913): 21–24.

---

26 Both the American cowslip (*Caltha palustris*), also known as the marsh marigold, and the English cowslip (*Primula veris*), or primrose, have yellow flowers.

27 Cf. Henry Wordsworth Longfellow (1807–1882), "The Psalm of Life" (1838): "Tell me not, in mournful numbers, / 'Life is but an empty dream!' / For the soul is dead that slumbers / And things are not what they seem" (1–4).

A Surprise

Mandy was coming over to Betty's house for Sunday night supper, and there were to be there also as guests Jeanette and an old friend of Uncle Bob Covington, Judge Anderson.

Jeanette and Betty were conversing earnestly in the latter's pretty room, the girlish faces puckered into most distressing frowns and worried wrinkles.

"You know, Betty," Jeanette was saying, "I do feel sorry for Mandy. The other girls have treated her terribly this last week—and so have we, for that matter. Of course, she is a perfectly dear, whole-souled little thing, once you penetrate her reserve and awkwardness, but you know as well as I, dear, that you couldn't expect the girls to take her up. She is funny and queer and countrified, and she shouldn't count on being received into the most exclusive circles. I do wish, though, that we could help her out a little. You know, I've found her crying twice in her room, although in the school she always has a pleasant smile."

"Yes," frowned Betty; "we want to help her along, but aren't willing to sacrifice ourselves for it. We're afraid that the other girls will laugh at us for being nice to her. We're afraid they'll think there is something queer about us for taking her up. Now isn't that so? Aren't we just afraid to do the square thing because of what other snobbish girls will think?"

"I expect that's so," sighed Betty's pretty cousin, "but, oh, dear, Mandy is so awkward in some ways, and—and—sort of funny looking."

"Yes," agreed Betty again: "and then there's another thing. She's beginning to go with that Blanche Kline and Mildred Brown. I'm going to speak to Mandy about it."

And so the conversation continued, until Mandy appeared, smiling radiantly, her soft eyes sparkling with unalloyed delight. Betty and Jeanette were kindness itself to the rather pathetic little figure in the dress that was too short and made in an astonishing fashion. Finally Betty said to the girl:

"Mandy, I'm awfully sorry that you are going with Mildred and Blanche. They are not refined. Please don't do it anymore, dear."

And the speaker was dumbfounded to see the Western lassie stiffen in an astonishing manner, her eyes kindling.

"Betty," she said in a tense voice, "I don't reckon you ought to talk about the girls I go with. Mebbe they ain't what you all call ladies, but I think they've got a good bit more manners and refinement than some of those you think are the finest in the school. You and the girls in your set let me alone, 'cause I'm queer and awkward, and ain't dressed up stylish-like, but they are mighty nice to me in spite of all that. They don't keer 'bout what I've got on, it's the heart that's under my old-fashion dress. Even if they don't talk as pretty as you an' your crowd, and even if they get in bad with the teachers, I 'spect they're nearer ladies."

Betty and Jeanette gasped. The blow had struck them harder than the free-spoken Mandy had intended. It was all true, what she had said, but they resented it after a fashion. They looked at each other in dumb amazement.

Suddenly the electricity in the stormy atmosphere vanished away as if by magic, pierced by the warm sunshine of the little Westerner's dazzling smile.

"Come on," she said, "let's don't talk 'bout that any more. 'Taint very fun. I didn't mean to hurt you all's feelin's. I just kind of exploded. My, you've got a nice room, Betty. 'Taint much like mine back home, all dark and queer up next the roof, with only one little window, an' the ceilin' so low you bump your head on it all the time if you ain't keerful. There's the supper bell, least that's what we call it. Guess I heard you call it a gong. I'm real hungry, I do declare. Somehow I haven't been so hungry since I left home. Bein' out in the open air helps your appetite lots."

And the two city cousins led the way for the Western one with a relieved, though puzzled and yet almost conscience-stricken, manner.

At the table, Mandy was placed beside Judge Anderson, the white-haired, kindly-eyed, Southern lawyer, who came "of family."

The old gentleman was a splendid talker, and Mandy, fascinated by his tales and remarks, was not even noticed by him, until he came to speak of the immense irrigation schemes of the Southwest.

"I know practically nothing about those wonderful plants, but I would like to know about their workings."

"Oh," cried Mandy, "I know about them, sir, 'deed I do. We use artificial irrigation on our place altogether." And she proceeded to give the astonished judge so detailed and comprehensive an account of the great Western plants that the judge afterward said to Mr. Covington: "That little Western girl has as keen a mind, suh, as clear an intellect, as I have ever been lucky enough to meet with. You mark my words, she'll make something of herself."

By Marjorie Kinnan, age 16,
Western High School,
306 Hammond Court, northwest

"A Surprise," *Washington Post*, Sunday magazine section, 8 June 1913, 4. MKR was awarded first prize, $3, for this story, which is chapter 8 of a longer story, "Jeanette at Boarding School," cowritten with other members of the Cousins' Club.

Class Song

To the tune of "Believe me, if all those enduring young charms."[28]

> There's a song on our lips, but our hearts hold a sigh,
>   As we leave Western's portals so dear;
> For the time has come when we're saying goodbye,
>   And we shed at the parting a tear.
> We will go forth with mirth,
> We will part with a smile,
>   We will laugh o'er the tear and the sigh,
> Yet not once will our class of Fourteen e'er forget,
>   What it owes to dear Western High.
>
> From our memories' past, comes a clear and sweet call,
>   Alma Mater's dear voice sounds afar,
> 'Tis the call to class spirit, to loyalty, love,
>   For the school that is our guiding star.
> From the blackened remains
> Come the words to us here,
>   As we part with a smile and a sigh,
> "Class of Fourteen, remember, 'midst all you hold dear,
>   There's a place for our old Western High."

Marjorie Kinnan

"Class Song," *Western* 18, no. 8 (June 1914): 19.

*   *   *   *   *   *   *   *   *

Alonzo Perceval Van Clyne

With a name like that, he ought to have been good, but he wasn't; he should have worn a black velvet suit with a real lace collar, but he didn't; he should have

---

28 "Believe Me, If All Those Enduring Young Charms" is set to a traditional Irish tune, composer unknown. The lyrics were written by the poet Thomas Moore (1779–1852) and published in volume 2 of his ten-volume *Irish Melodies* (1808–34). The school song of Harvard University, "Fair Harvard," is also sung to this tune.

been possessed of soulful blue eyes, long golden curls, and a slender, sensitive nose adorning a lily-white countenance that bore every mark of aristocracy, but he wasn't.

Alonzo Perceval Van Clyne's spring and summer raiment consisted chiefly, and one might almost say solely, of a pair of faded blue overalls that struck him midway between ankle and knee, patched with threadbare brown squares where he wore out the overalls by too much sitting down, and a gray cotton shirt, turned in at his thin, brown neck, with the sleeves cut off above the elbows for greater convenience in digging frogs' eggs and tadpoles from the mud ponds.

His hair was an unruly mass of reddish brown, and freckles of a harmonious shade were literally bestrewed across his tanned face, and most generously upon the uplifted nose that had earned him the appellation of "Snubby," and bespoke his plebeian birth.

Small brown eyes looked earnestly and clearly, if sometimes shyly, upon the world, while a tender, wistful droop to the broad mouth bespoke love, imagination, and an innate craving for sympathy. But bad?

"My goodness!" often exclaimed Miss Seaton, "if that young one isn't headed straight for the county reform school, just as tight as those skinny legs of his'll carry him, then Jenny Seaton doesn't know what she's a-talking about!"

Alonzo Perceval Van Clyne played hookey [*sic*]! Not at rare and stated intervals, but constantly he would wiggle from his hard, wooden seat in the little white school house, and squirm unobserved in the crawling manner of a young snake, across the splintery floor, and out the open door.

At times he reappeared within a day or two; again, ten days would pass before his towsled [*sic*] head would be seen bent over the spelling book.

The grown-ups of the village and countryside never ceased to bewail the misfortune of his existence. More than one worthy mother would have turned pale could she have seen her sons clustered about the awful one in respectful admiration.

He was a hero, a demigod, filled with inexplicable courage. Would one of his satellites have dared to do what he had done? Uh-uh! No sir-ee-ee! Who but he would risk parental ire and see the dusky woodshed, the teacher's rod, and horrors of horrors, the truant officer, with bony hands eternally restless, and bead-like eyes that glittered behind the black-rimmed spectacles? Who save Alonzo Perceval Van Clyne would tell ghost stories of stellar magnitude, and dreamy tales of far-off hills and streams, where millions of guileless fish were simply waiting to snap the shining hook?

No one could produce from his pockets such treasures as were continually found in Alonzo's scanty overalls, such an ever-changing array of shells, frogs, birds' eggs, marsh grass twine, and—but they weren't going to tell all they knew, no sir-ee-ee-e!

Don'cher 'spose they knew all the wonderful things that Snubby brought back from his rambles? 'Course they did, sure! Don'cher 'spose they knew that the only place where you could find those graceful, speckled trout was off over Squire Simm's place, through the forest, beyond the distant hills, and in some mysterious region close beyond, in a clear purling stream that laughed and sobbed and sang, until you thought it must be the river of Heaven, and—but they weren't going to tell on him.

Let the truant officer search as far as he liked, they alone had any idea of the haunts of the bold one, and they weren't going to tell.

Miss Casterlin's big heart was full of sympathy for the little lad.

A frail, pretty, little creature, with quiet gray eyes, her sympathy and under-standing were unusual. From the day when she first came to the tiny schoolhouse and had taken Snubby into her arms and given him his first kiss, he had wor-shiped at her feet.

The tragedy in her eyes tore at his heartstrings, he loved her, but—he con-tinued to absent himself at regular intervals from her adored presence. For as a country school teacher, something went wrong somewhere, and she was not a success.

To her side one day she summoned Snubby, as all the other boys and girls trooped from out the schoolhouse. Putting her arm about him, drawing him close, she began to talk to him, calmly at first, then with rising agitation, until, at mention of her father, one tear after another welled up in her eyes, and trickled down her cheeks.

"Snubby," she said, "you're simply breaking my heart." Miserable silence from Snubby.

"The superintendent came to see me yesterday, dear, and said that he was afraid I would have to give up the school. I am not succeeding very well at teach-ing."

"No," cried Snubby.

She nodded her head.

"He said that he would let me stay on one condition—that I keep you from running away from school."

An alarmed cry rose to the boy's lips.

"He knew that you and I were such good chums"—Snubby cuddled closer—"and thought that perhaps you would promise never to do it any more, for my sake."

Dry sobs were choking the boy now.

Suddenly the little teacher held him tight.

"Dearie," she cried, "what makes you do it? Why must you run away?"

The dreamy look crept into his eyes. He smiled, a far-away, loving smile, that told of great joys, great cares, great services, great need. His voice was low, sweet, thrilled as he spoke.

"Somethin' pulls me, an' I—I jes' go. It's mostly him, I guess. I can always feel when he is lonesome, or sick, or tired. It's 'cause he loves me so. I 'spose, an' I love him, 'cause I always know when he wants me, or has somethin' in the woods to show me, or a new story. When I'm a-sittin' in the room, an' I look out the door, an' see the trees a-swaying, an' the clover growin' green an' smellin' sweet, an' hear the birds a-singin' like to burst their throats"—he drew a deep breath—"somethin' says, jes' as clear as day, 'Lonso, come on out. He's a-waitin' fer you, off over them fields an' hills, an' through them woods there; he wants you. He'll take you down the stream an' tell you—things—an' love you, an' show you where to find all sorts of things, like nobody else in the world can find. Come on'—an' then—I—I—jes' go!"

Miss Casterlin sighed. This little gypsy wanderer was difficult. It must be the call of the wild, but this mysterious "him."

Then, earnestly, "Well, dear, I've got to ask you not to go any more. If I lose this school, I'll—I'll just starve, that is all."

"Haven't you got any folks to take care of you?" he asked.

She shook her head.

"No father?" with increasing fascination.

The tears came fast now. "No, dear. In a dreadful shipwreck I lost my father. He loved the woods and the fields, too. My mother died when I was small."

Snubby was tense with excitement.

"What did your father look like?"

From her watch Miss Casterlin produced a picture.

The boy scanned it long, smiled. "That is your father?"

Puzzled, Miss Casterlin assented.

"Well, I won't run away any more," he said, and hurried from the school-room.

*   *   *

It was warm and sunny that next day in May. The children stirred restlessly, and as they conned alone their lessons, the room was filled with a buzzing as of many bees.

Out of the open door gazed Snubby. Then he shifted his gaze to Miss Casterlin's pretty head, bent over her desk. Slyly, smoothly, he wriggled from his seat and squirmed across the splintery floor and out the open door.

Miss Casterlin raised her head in time to see him speeding across the open fields toward the nearest woodland.

*   *   *

The sun was at its hottest in the late afternoon, as a small, ragged urchin led an eager, white-haired man across the meadow. They were dusty, perspiring, fatigued. In the man's eyes was the same dreamy look as the boy's, the same wistful droop to the mouth. They came hand in hand.

Miss Casterlin started as if at a ghost, as the odd couple entered the schoolhouse. There was one awful moment of doubt, as father and daughter surveyed each other, and then with joyous cries, the two had met, and laughter, tears, and questions followed.

That evening Snubby marched proudly down the village street, surrounded by a crowd of excited youngsters.

"Yep," he was saying proudly, "I always did know I'd o' made a good detective. You see, when she began to tell me 'bout losin' her father in a shipwreck, it jes' came to me right off, quicker'n scot, how much she looked like Daddy Joe, an' I jes' 'membered how he cried an' told me that he wasn't ever a-goin' to leave the woods again, 'cause there wasn't anything in the world for him.

Marjorie Kinnan, age 17,

Western High School.

"Alonzo Perceval Van Clyne," *Washington Post*, Sunday magazine section, 10 May 1914, 7. This story was awarded first prize, $3.

1. Rawlings as one of the "Representative Women" at the University of Wisconsin. Courtesy of the Department of Special and Area Studies Collections, George A. Smathers Libraries, University of Florida.

2. Rawlings in her early twenties, circa 1918. Courtesy of the Department of Special and Area Studies Collections, George A. Smathers Libraries, University of Florida.

3. Rawlings, circa 1918. Courtesy of the Department of Special and Area Studies Collections, George A. Smathers Libraries, University of Florida.

4. Rawlings as Celia Faraday in the 1917 junior class production of A.E.W. Mason's *Green Stockings*. Courtesy of the Department of Special and Area Studies Collections, George A. Smathers Libraries, University of Florida.

| Durrie | | Adler | Fehrenbach | Simpson | Meyer | | Forbes | |
| Clarke | | Pruett | Knowlton | Linen | Kinnan | Evans | | Ochsner |

5. Editorial board of the *Wisconsin Literary Magazine*; Rawlings appears in the first row, third from right. Courtesy of the University of Wisconsin Libraries.

MARJORIE KINNAN . . . . . . *Madison*

LETTERS AND SCIENCE

Kappa Alpha Theta; Phi Beta Kappa; Mortar Board; Associate Editor Awk 3; Associate Editor Wisconsin Literary Magazine 3, 4; Badger Satire Board 2; Woman's Editor 1918 Badger; Badger Special Feature Editor 4; Red Domino, Vice-President 4; Junior Play 3; Union Vodvil 2, 3; German Play 2; Red Domino-Edwin Booth Productions 2, 3, 4; Junior Play Committee 3; Shakespeare Masque 2; Senior Play Committee 4; Assistant Chairman Prom Refreshment Committee 3; Sophomore Ways and Means Committee 2; Noon Convocations Committee 4. Thesis—Paganism in Modern English Poetry.

6. Rawlings in *The Badger*, the University of Wisconsin yearbook. Courtesy of the University of Wisconsin Libraries.

7. House at Cross Creek, 1939. Courtesy of the Department of Special and Area Studies Collections, George A. Smathers Libraries, University of Florida.

8. Rawlings in the flower garden at Cross Creek. Courtesy of the Department of Special and Area Studies Collections, George A. Smathers Libraries, University of Florida.

9. Rawlings with Pat at Cross Creek, circa 1939. Charles Scribner's Sons. Courtesy of the Department of Special and Area Studies Collections, George A. Smathers Libraries, University of Florida.

10. Publicity photo of Rawlings at Cross Creek house. Courtesy of the Department of Special and Area Studies Collections, George A. Smathers Libraries, University of Florida.

11. Rawlings and Moe at Crescent Beach cottage, early 1940s. Jacob Lofman, photographer. Courtesy of the Department of Special and Area Studies Collections, George A. Smathers Libraries, University of Florida.

12. Rawlings on the dunes at Crescent Beach, early 1940s. Jacob Lofman, photographer. Courtesy of the Department of Special and Area Studies Collections, George A. Smathers Libraries, University of Florida.

13. Rawlings in the mid-1940s. Courtesy of the Department of Special and Area Studies Collections, George A. Smathers Libraries, University of Florida.

14. Rawlings at Van Hornesville house before its restoration, 1947. Courtesy of the Department of Special and Area Studies Collections, George A. Smathers Libraries, University of Florida.

15. Rawlings with Siamese cats at Van Hornesville house after its restoration. Courtesy of the Department of Special and Area Studies Collections, George A. Smathers Libraries, University of Florida.

16. Portrait of Rawlings by Carl Van Vechten, 18 January 1953. Courtesy of the Department of Special and Area Studies Collections, George A. Smathers Libraries, University of Florida.

University of Wisconsin

◂‖▸

1914–1918

MKR entered the University of Wisconsin in the fall of 1914 and became active immediately in campus literary and social life. Known especially for her wit and confidence, she joined the Red Domino and Edwin Booth Dramatic Society and, together with her lifelong friend Beatrice Humiston, later "Bee" McNeill, became well known also for her acting and dramatic skills. Her work was reviewed regularly in the *Daily Cardinal*, the campus newspaper. In 1916, she played the kitchen maid "Tweeny" in *The Admirable Crichton* (1902) by J. M. Barrie (1860–1937). She also wrote *Into the Nowhere*, an original pantomime, which took first prize for best play in the annual contest held by Union Vodvil, a group that produced shows in order to raise money for the university's student union building, and that would later feature MKR's friend Fredric March (1897–1975) after his return from service in World War I. In 1917, she played the lead role in *Green Stockings*, the junior play. "Miss Kinnan's ability as an actress," according to the *Daily Cardinal*, "needs no comment. She has taken part in nearly all university theatricals during the past two years" (6 March 1917, 7). In her senior year, 1918, she starred in the comedy sketch *Lima Beans* with Humiston, which led the *Daily Cardinal* to acknowledge that both "had drawn freely upon their imaginations" was "evidence enough of their ability, versatility, mobility of expression and real enjoyment ipso facto" (29 January 1918, 3). As a senior, she also wrote a "snappy farce" entitled *Born to Blush*. Drama, of course, was not MKR's only literary endeavor. She was named associate editor of the *Wisconsin Literary Magazine* in her junior year and became an editor in her senior year. She was active on the staff of *The Badger*, the yearbook, and served as the woman's editor her senior year. MKR was also recognized for her accomplishments as an English major. She was elected to the Mortar Board for outstanding academic achievement. In her senior year, she won first prize in the Vilas contest (1918) for her essay on Emile Derbaere, and was elected to Theta Sigma Phi, the honorary journalistic society. Her senior thesis was entitled "Paganism in Modern English Poetry." She was elected to Phi Beta Kappa her junior year. Her active and prominent life on campus, however, did not escape controversy. She was fiercely independent, and during her senior year, as a member of Kappa Alpha Theta, she had second thoughts about the exclusivity of sororities. She subsequently joined a movement to ban sororities because she felt them to be "unwholesome, pernicious, and undemocratic," concluding that they "perpetuate a caste system that is unfair to other university alumnae who are not from sororities" (*Daily Cardinal*, 29 May 1918, 1, 4). This spirit of independence followed MKR throughout her life, not always to her benefit. In the spring of 1918, with World War I approaching an end and with the feminist movement gaining momentum, MKR was graduated with honors in English from the University of Wisconsin.

*   *   *   *   *   *   *   *   *

Who Will Take This Money

Is the average Wisconsin student so well off that he doesn't care to compete for the numerous prizes offered in the university for special work? It seems so, when the fact is stated that there are hundreds of dollars available in special prizes which have not been competed for in years. The little blue handbook edited by S. K. Hornbeck and S. H. Goodnight, and obtainable at the registrar's office, contains a wealth of suggestions as to special honors and prizes.

Wisconsin students have assumed that scholarships and fellowships are practically the only forms of merit awards bestowed by the institution. Although The Wisconsin Magazine has always faithfully made announcements of prize offers, it seems that this condition of general student apathy is due in part to lack of popular appeal in arranging prize contests. It is wrong to imagine that every announcement is meant only for the further benefit of a few who have already won recognition along some lines of work.

Wisconsin men and women should consider that every prize offer is made for them, individually. They should use determination, perseverance and ability in competing for honors. Every effort may not win a prize or honor; again, it may. The chances are even; but whether or not successful in winning tangible recognition of merit, the one who makes the effort will have gained an invaluable knowledge of some particular subject, a realization of the essential of all competition.

The Lewis essay prize of twenty-five dollars has not been awarded since 1907. No one seemed to be interested in it and it was ignored. A cash prize of fifteen dollars is given annually by the junior class for an original Prom waltz. The Wisconsin Alumni Association of Chicago announces a song contest with a first prize of fifty and a second prize of twenty-five dollars. Haresfott [*sic*][1] lyrics, book, and musical score, and orchestration of the score, are paid for in terms of from $100 to $200.

Oratory and debate are rich with prizes. Honors are awarded in the sophomore year for good work in two or more departments. Half a dozen essay contests exist which are more than worth while. The chief of these is the William F. Vilas essay contest with two prizes, of fifty and twenty-five dollars each. For the last few years this contest has been extremely popular in the university as a short-story contest, but this year it will take the nature of an essay contest.

University students are urgently advised to keep their eyes and ears open for material which will aid them in competing in different departments for special prizes. There are engineering and political science prizes and any number of others, as the little blue book will reveal. This article gives merely a meager idea of the possibilities lying dormant in the university. The Wisconsin Magazine will contain special announcements from time to time.

—M. K. and D. B.[2]

"Who Will Take This Money," *Wisconsin Magazine* 13, no. 1 (October 1915): 24.

*   *   *   *   *   *   *   *   *

The Brute

Brute Friedsen was standing before his wedding-altar, amid the odor of lilies and the rustling of gowns; it was Easter morning. The chimes pealed from the

---

1   Haresfoot is a musical club named for the rabbit's foot used to apply stage makeup.

2   "D. B." is Dorothy Bell, who would publish "Vilas Prize Particulars" in the next issue of the *Wisconsin Magazine* (13, no. 2 [November 1915]: 19-20). In it, she clarifies the rules for the Vilas Prize and refers to "Who Will Take This Money."

belfry as he paced down the aisle, towering above the girl upon his arm who was become his wife. The sunlight greeted them as they reached the door, dazzled them. To Brute it was the welcome of Life, Life as he had never known it before, never dared to know it, and he fondled the hand in his as a child caresses a gift that has been for a long time in the realm of dreams. A bundle of rosiness and laces was cooing honey and nothings towards his bride, who answered with further nothings. Brute reached out his hand, slipped it along the plumpness of the baby's neck, murmured a word or two. The child turned at the touch, gurgled, then, as it saw the giant's face, startled, shrank, hid its eyes on the mother's shoulder and began to cry.

Through the man's brute-form, through every inch of six feet eight of virility, passed a shudder. A cloud skipped across the sky, and for an instant the sun darkened and disappeared. The man lifted his wife into a cab, giving no heed to the crowd that tittered and stared and gossiped. A quantity of rice showered through the air; the carriage clattered away over the asphalt.

Inside, Brute covered his face with his hands, the face that had the scar across the left half, that had the jaw and mouth that carried one back for thousands of years, to an age when giants won food and dwelling and wife alike, by the club of stone. His body was shaking.

"I hate it—I loathe it!" he panted. "This body—this face—they're afraid of them! I love them—the children—all the little things, the tender things—but they don't trust me—they cry when I look at them—the dogs—even the dogs, the puppies in the streets, snarl when I try to be kind to them! The men—my friends, fawn on me if they've made a mistake. They don't dare prove the Brute. I've always been called so, the Brute! I hate it!"

The girl slipped her arms about his neck. He made no motion to take her to him.

"You—you aren't afraid—anymore?" It was a plea.

"No—I'm not afraid, I—" but she gasped a little, shivered, as she had never ceased to do when she saw the ugliness of that animal-face above her, and felt the power of that body close to hers. The man saw, winced.

"I will not be afraid!" she said. "My dear, I love you so, I will not. I know, oh thank God, I know, the goodness and the tenderness of you. Your heart, I think, must be that of a woman."

The Brute took her in his arms, not with passion, but with the adoration, the worship, of a child. His kisses [text is missing].

"Perhaps it is so," he said, "my heart must be that of a woman."

"Do you remember? Five years ago today we were married."

"What a memory you have, my dear! So few men remember the little things."
The wife smiled across the breakfast-table.

"The little things! It's the biggest thing in my life—my marriage—you—what
you have meant to me."

"Yes?" encouraged the woman.

"Don't I tire you, telling you about it? But your sympathy hides even that.
You have always understood. You let me bubble over as much as I choose—"

The words tumbled out with the enthusiasm of a child's, and the woman
laughed, so that the man's heart, and the room, were warmed with the sound.

"You must relax somewhere, mustn't you?" She leaned across the table and
patted his hand. "Your heart is one of love, love that cannot restrain itself, that
craves a return, in sympathy, and more love. I give you that return, I let you pour
out all the love within your soul—here. Out there," and she waved her hand
towards the window, through which could be seen the tramcars, the taxis, the
swarm of life, hurrying along in the rain, "out there, they are brutes. Of you,
of you especially, such as you seem, they expect brutality, that shall outreach
theirs."

She rose.

"You must go. And wear your greatcoat this morning. You dread the rain, and
you must not take cold."

"No. It—it chills me, out there." But he was not thinking of the rain.

Pushing his way through the crowds, he repeated to himself, "Such as I am,
they expect it of me—brutality." His face had taken on a gloom and a coldness.

And the people turned, and stared. "What a brute!" they said. And the
women would add, "Can he have a wife? Poor thing! I pity her!"

He walked into his office. The French windows, three stories above the street,
had been opened, and framed in one stood a clerk, glaring upon an urchin of
the gutter, who sobbed and pled beside the clerk's bundle of laundry that he had
dropped in the mud and wet. The angered clerk, in the midst of maledictions,
clenched one fist, and with the other seized the gamin by the throat.

It was the sympathetic woman-heart of the Brute that gave the cry of horror,
but it was the man-strength behind the arm of iron that caught the clerk be-
tween the eyes. Under the force of that blow he wilted like a child, plunged, face
down, onto the floor, and lay without a sound or motion. Brute passed a hand
across his forehead. The stillness of the room surprised him. And then he looked
at the figure there lying on the floor. For the first time in his life he had struck a
man. Flecks of gold danced before him. The figure on the floor became that of
his wife, and she was saying, "You have killed a man. And now, more than ever,

they will expect brutality of you." The flecks of gold whipped into his face. He drooped, and lunged backward, through the French window that opened into the grey and drizzle of the rain, and on down to the pavement, where the crowds were swarming to and fro.

III[3]

Brute was readjusting his mind to the world that had evolutionized within a month. At present, that world was bounded by four walls, in one of which was a vista that gave a peep into fairyland. There were parks there, and fountains and trees and birds and children, all the paraphernalia of fairyland, and out beyond all that, a bit of the harbor, blackened by ships and smoke, had been placed, lest the fairyland work enchantment. The characters within the world were a nurse and many doctors, one of whom was just coming into the world of four walls and a vista. He walked across to the bed.

"Today," said the Brute, "today you will tell me—many things. You will answer the questions I have asked you, even in my delirium."

"The clerk," began the doctor, "is dead."

"Yes, I knew." "How, may I ask?"

"I knew, as I saw him lying there, without a motion. I know my strength. Go on."

"The coroner has dismissed the case. The boy, you remember, was a witness of the incident. But you—you will never use that strength again."

"Why not?"

"Your limbs were paralyzed by the fall. It would have been the neck if it had not been that."

"Go on."

"You will be able to keep up your office from a wheelchair, if all goes as it should from now on."

"Yes?"

"Your wife—"

"Yes, go on! Tell me, man, has—"

"A few days after your accident, a son was born to her. She will be here—"

"Yes?" "Tomorrow."

The four walls of the world seemed to stretch out and away, so that an eternity was enclosed therein.

"The son has the beauty of his mother. And now we can take you down into the park, in the wheel chair [*sic*]."

---

3   Apparently, the editor here again has dropped a portion of MKR's text; note that section III is not preceded by either a section I or II.

Some minutes later, the doctor left him beside a fountain, in his chair.

"I'm afraid he'll be a madman when I get back. Think of caging that body and that strength! The brute of him will rage against his weakness. A brute in chains! Poor devil!"

Across the fountain, a mite of some five years was studying the face in the chair. All of its ugliness had been softened by pain, and the network of lines, under the hair streaked with the white of suffering, seemed the map of a heart, all gentleness, kindliness and love. The child edged up to the chair, rested one hand on that of the Brute.

"Nice man?" she queried.

The Brute scarce breathed, fearing to frighten the vision away.

"Nice man!" she answered for herself.

He slipped an arm about her, tingled at the warmth and closeness of her. She rested her head on his shoulder.

"Nice man!" she sighed.

"It seems as if I had waited all my life for just today," he breathed. And the child unburdened her soul to him as to a mother.

"They will never expect it of me again—brutality," he said to himself, "they will not fear me anymore, And I have a son! A son—who will love me, and will not be afraid of me."

The doctor had come back. He patted the man's shoulder.

"Much of a fight, eh? You've got my sympathy, friend."

The Brute smiled.

"I don't need it, sir; don't need it."

But the doctor shook his head.

"Poor devil! Poor devil!"

Marjorie Kinnan

"The Brute," *Wisconsin Literary Magazine* 13, no. 4 (January 1916): 7–9.

*   *   *   *   *   *   *   *   *

Curls and Curlers

It was a long time before the family really found out that Betty was engaged to George. From Christmas until May they had had an uncomfortable feeling that something was wrong, but they had blamed it on everything but an engagement. Mother was sure that a gas-jet was leaking in some undiscoverable place. Sister

Mildred flounced her short skirts, tossed her stiff little pigtail over one shoulder, and sniffed, "Mother, I shouldn't be one bit surprised William had snakes in the house!" William himself probably came closest to guessing the truth. He had a surprising habit of tumbling into a room unexpectedly, and his long thin legs, that usually knocked into every noise-producing object in sight, could slide over the floor without a sound, provided only you were saying something you didn't want him to hear, and thought him safely canoeing on the lake.

"Mebbe there're going'—on's a-tween Betty 'n George," he would say tantalizingly. Then he would grin to himself, as he recalled the afternoon in the dusky front hall when George was just leaving, and the evening he had burst into the parlor to see Betty quickly separate herself from the previous oneness on the davenport, and hear her say to George, in an all-of-a-sudden clear and distinct voice, "I think it's so funny you don't like her. She's really very nice." William was nobody's fool.

Betty herself was elusive, vague, when questioned. Boredom shadowed her eyes as she answered that George was a very decent sort, she supposed, and was there any more red silk in the house?

But when Mother came into the hall, a certain evening in May at parting time, exactly one minute too soon, the whole affair just naturally had to come out, because—oh, well, you know yourself that some people will insist on explanations when things like that happen. Mother was surprised; in fact, very much more so than William, for instance, and the Jacksons, who lived directly across the street, (you know how sometimes you forget to pull down the shades), but at any rate she cried much less than would have been expected.

"I suppose it's all right," she said to Betty last night, as they sat on the bed in their kimonas [*sic*], "George is very nice, and can take care of you, only—," she stopped and surveyed critically her eldest-born, "somehow, I can't think of a girl that looks as funny as you do when you are ready for bed, getting married, or going on a honeymoon. But that's no real reason for keeping you an old maid. Go ahead and marry him, child," and she took a dry handkerchief from the bureau drawer.

Betty looked into the mirror opposite.

"It's—it's the curlers, isn't it?" she asked despairingly, then began to cry softly.

"I may have to be an old maid yet," came from between sobs, "George—George—yes, I know it's the curlers!"

Now, Betty, when clothed for the day's sojourn in the public eye, and under George's cool appraisal, was a most attractive woman, with a tendency toward side-tilted large hats, and sketch effects in black and white, with a dash of red or orange at the girdle—you know the kind. She was more sensible and capable than she looked, an artist with the needle and the oven. Men liked her cautiously, her clear blue eyes, half-way pug nose, child mouth and fluffy hair; and here, ladies and gentlemen, you see before you the sword of Damocles, hanging most appropriately in this case by a hair.[4] Betty's hair was *not* fluffy, except when daytime saw it released from its steel bonds of the night, and coaxed into a curliness that deceived all except the family. It was as straight as a poker by nature, and Betty crowned with straight hair, hopelessly sparse and stringy at that, was far from the alluring being she became under the circumstances previously mentioned. As for the periods of preparation for beauty, when dusky night mantles the procedure, and Betty took her six-for-a-quarter curlers from their box, and used them according to the scheme of curlers! The devil himself wasn't in it when it came to the two long, stiff, upright horns that menaced one from Betty's forehead. A similar one over each ear, and an extra-perky one at the back of her head, completed a halo scarcely angelical in effect. Under this crown, of glory or otherwise, that defied the kindly boudoir cap, Betty's features took on sharp angles, her eyebrows tilted alarmingly as they followed the tightly drawn hair in the curlers, and the expression of her whole face was the completely surprised one seen on some good-natured puppy that has just been slapped across the nozzle.

"Do you think George will still want to marry me after I've told him?" she queried between tears.

"Told him what?"

"Why, that my hair isn't curly, and that I have to put it up at night on curlers?"

"Betty, child, what nonsense you're talking. You don't need even to mention the subject to him. He's probably never given it a thought. He'll get used to the curlers. Don't say anything about them. Act as if they were a matter of course, and he will too."

"But Mother, you don't understand at all. It would be all right with most men, but George—George—," more sobs interrupted the protest.

"Well," came Mother's tart voice, "George isn't any better than any other man. I guess his nature isn't so sensitive but what he can stand seeing your hair in curlers at night. Only—you do look awfully funny."

"Mother," desperately, "don't you see? George—George thinks my hair is naturally curly—"

---

4   In classical myth, the tyrant Dionysius had a sword hung by a hair over the head of his courtier Damocles in order to teach him the precarious nature of rank and power. The phrase "sword of Damocles" thus alludes to the perpetual possibility of impending doom.

"Well, he can change his mind, can't he?"

"—and he said—he said—one day—that he was so thankful I had curly hair, because—because—he never in all the world, could never marry a girl who put her hair up on curlers, and looked like a fright when she went to bed at night, and got up again in the morning!"

"That was your chance to break it gently. What did you say?"

"Oh, Mother, that's just it! I simply didn't have the nerve to tell him I was one of those frights, so I—I—I said I was thankful too!"

"Well," said Mother, "you *have* done it now!"

*   *   *

II.

Some weeks later, Betty stepped up to the altar, and her face was calm, nay, triumphant. She could look marriage with George unflinchingly in the face.

"Betty," Mother said one day, "I have it. You can put your hair up during the daytime, while George is at the office. Three or four hours a day, on those electric curlers, would make it just right."

And Betty, glorious under orange blossoms and a halo of fluffy hair, with a wayward curl or so, became a smiling bride.

*   *   *

III.

The newly-wed apprenticeship was over. Clerks no longer smiled when Betty had patent egg-beaters and new fangled dishpans sent to Mrs. George, with the accent on the Mrs. George. [George] had stopped addressing Betty as Tweetie. They had become enrolled under the great genus of sober American married folks. It was the second anniversary of their wedding.

George kissed Betty affectionately as he left the breakfast table. She watched him with loving eyes as he took his hat from the hall rack, and went out the door and down the street. Leaving the table, she went up stairs, took a small box from the left hand bureau drawer, drew out five of the half-dozen curlers therein, and proceeded to use them according to the scheme of curlers—two in front, one over each ear, and the extra-perky one at the back. Then, with her temporarily ruined beauty she went about her household tasks.

She had given orders for the day to Susan, planned her dinner menu, and gossiped over the 'phone with two of her friends, and was now dusting the library, on the first floor. She heard a step outside, and then, suddenly, the quick opening and shutting of the front door. A man was coming through the hall. The library door opened; and George walked in. Betty gave a little shriek of relief, and started toward him with outstretched hands.

"I thought it was a burglar. Has anything happened?" she said in a voice that sounded like a long-distance from New York to San Francisco.

And then—she remembered the curlers.

She put her hands up to them to make sure that it was not a nightmare; and they were there, hornlike and uncompromising. It was too late to run. Betty buried her face, slapped-puppy expression and all, in her hands. After two years of cautious deception, she had been caught in her own net. The sword of Damocles had fallen, and in her very heart she felt the cruel point. George, trusting her and her curls implicitly, had been betrayed. For the first time he saw her as she was, one of the frights he had refused to marry under any circumstances. The storm of rage would break in a moment. She could feel his eyes, wounded, outraged, upon her in reproach. She lifted her head to meet his gaze—and he was not looking at her at all. He was fumbling anxiously in his desk.

"You let me forget that Harrison letter after all," he was saying, "where the deuce is it?"

Mechanically she found it and handed it to him. In an instant he was gone again, with the merest nod of thanks, and not a glance for the deceiving curlers.

"He was too angry to even look at them again," she sobbed, and dropped into the Morris chair,[5] on top of the plaster of Paris Romeo and Juliet she had set there for advantageous dusting.

As she picked up the fragments, she debated as to her mode of conduct for the evening, when he returned, *if* he returned, she added to herself, and became horrified at possibilities. Perhaps it would be wise to leave the curlers on. And have the whole thing out at once. She finally decided to dress her prettiest, look duly penitent, and let George broach the ghastly subject.

George returned for dinner, smiling, a huge box of roses under his arm.

"You know that I haven't forgotten that my Betty and I were married just two short years ago to-day," he announced as he gave her the roses, and Betty was sure that the tenderness in his voice was condescension. He had such a big heart she thought, as a stray tear fell among the flowers, and all evening she waited for him to speak on the one and only subject. He was voluble in his good-nature,

---

5 First manufactured by the British designer, artist, writer, and socialist William Morris (1834–96) and used mainly for reading, Morris chairs feature a wooden frame, an upholstered seat and back, and a reclining mechanism.

and chattered on of acquaintance, business affairs, and so forth. Only once could Betty feel battle nigh. He was telling her of a new stenographer. She had curly hair, he said, and looked at Betty's wavy locks. She shut her eyes, gripped the arms of the chair, and waited. But his cheerful voice went on, and he was speaking next of the Harrison deal.

"Apropros [*sic*] of that," he remarked, "I'm awfully sorry I scared you this morning when I breezed into get that letter. Next time I come home unexpectedly I'll ring the bell."

Betty went to her rest that night a little calmer in spirit, but wondering at the ways of men.

Her wonder diminished, but did not cease, during the several months that followed. And then, one glorious day, George went up-stair[s] on tiptoe to make his acquaintance with the latest representation of the Eternal Miracle. It lay, very small and very pink, on Betty's arm, and though bearing what George at once insisted a striking resemblance to its father, gave little promise of the greatness that would undoubtedly come some day. George looked at it with the reverence that is always new.

"By Jove, Betty!" he exclaimed after a cautious scrutiny, "he's got curly hair! Look!"

Betty looked at the sparsely covered little head close beside her, and saw that what there was of hair, was without a doubt arranged in genuine ringlets.

"Just like his mother," added George whimsically.

Betty looked her husband squarely in the eye. Maternity had given her a sudden courage.

"George!"

"Yes, dear?"

"I cannot bring up this child under deception. George—I thought you must have realized it that morning when you came home suddenly, but now I know that you were in such a hurry that you didn't notice the curlers. George—my hair is not curly. I put it up while you were away at the office."

George was distinctly puzzled.

"Why, yes, of course," he said, "I knew that."

"What?"

I knew that. I noticed the curlers that morning, but I knew you used them. I thought that was an understood matter."

"You thought—"

"Why, sure!"

"Then you—oh, George, you don't really mind? Even when I look such a fright in them?"

"Why, of course not. A woman with straight hair has to use them to look flossy. I've been brought up on curlers. Mother and the girls always used them."

"But George, what you said when we were first engaged, that you would never marry a girl who made herself a fright by using hair curlers—"

George chuckled.

"Your small brother William," he answered, "was a most astute youth. He informed me of the true state of your hair, let me in on the family secret as it were, and said you could be most beautifully teased along those lines. I tried to tease—and when you agreed with me as to its natural curliness,—why I thought it was all part of the family joke!"

He looked at her curiously.

"And you thought I never knew. I hope it hasn't worried you any?"

"Oh, no," replied Betty weakly, "O—oh no-o!"

"I was so used to the idea of curlers" George went on, "that I never thought to mention your using them. Here—" he took from a notebook in his vest pocket a square piece of paper, "look at this. William told me how you and your mother had planned to spare me the agony of actually beholding the curlers on you, so he took this for me, for fear I'd miss something."

Betty took the paper in her very shaky fingers. It was a snap-shot, showing her seated at her dressing-table in the period of preparation for beauty. The horns, the crown of glory, the tilted eyebrows, the slapped-puppy expression, were all there. Because of the mirror opposite her, both front and back views of her face were plainly visible. On the back of the picture was scribbled, "I took this from the fire iskape [*sic*]."

George grinned in recollection.

"Every time I feel blue, I take that out and have a good laugh. It's so fierce I never dared show it to you. I knew something would happen to William if I did."

"God bless that little demon William," sighed Betty, "Hadn't we better name our youngster after him?"

"Nope," returned the proud father, "this is George Junior."

He surveyed his offspring critically.

"Wonder where the little cuss *did* get the curls?"

By Marjorie Kinnan, '18

"Curls and Curlers," *Wisconsin Magazine* 13, no. 6 (March 1916): 3–5, 31–33. According to the cover, this is a special "Mortar Board Number" of *WLM*; it is described on the table of contents page as a "Women's Number"; and the frontispiece is a chronology, "Women at Wisconsin."

The Barrier

Beyond the tottering wall, rose-fondled, sob
The dancers' violins, that half regret
Their singing to the drowsy, drunken mob—
Sing on, sweet voices, that I may forget
This sorrow in my breast, that, like yon wall,
Keeps me from the dancers, and from folk, apart!
Over the murm'ring, night-kissed waters fall
Echoes of mirth, not, not on thee, my heart.
It is so dark, the way that I must go,
I stifle in the solitude, the shades;
Dearest, if to-night I did not know
That Dawn and Thou were waiting past the glades,
To let the sun into my dusty soul,
Into the void I'd pass; nor try the goal.

M. K.

"The Barrier," *Wisconsin Magazine* [16], no. 1 (October 1916): 4.

*   *   *   *   *   *   *   *   *

The Captivating Odors of the Kitchen
[Part I]

Friend, if you read this story, there is a strong possibility that you will regret having done so. In that respect my tale will not differ from many others, but that is not the point. I believe in a square deal for everyone; something in me rebels at taking advantage of a fellow-mortal; and I wish to give fair warning to all those who indulge more or less indiscriminately in light literature. I refuse absolutely to take any blame or responsibility for this story; if you read it, it is your fault, and you will do so with your eyes open. I speak both literally and figuratively. My title—I feel it is my duty to tell you—I fear that my title is misleading. Reading it, you have expected a feast for the intellect, a philosophical appeal to what we imperfectly call the soul. You have believed, trustingly, that I was catering to your aesthetic sense. You were flattered. I took it for granted that you had an aesthetic sense. Is it not so? Friend, something prompts me to a disclosure of the truth. I am appealing, not to the artistic sense, nor to the intellectual sense, no! but to the gastronomic sense! I am going to talk—how can I confess it—about things to eat. Yes, I agree with you, things to eat are both pleasant and necessary. But they are among the things not mentioned at length or in detail in really good literature, along with nightgowns and corsets and the retention of the Philippines.[6] Nevertheless, I deliberately intend to fly, on the wings of my Muse, in the very face of prejudice. I shall talk about things to eat, good things and unpalatable things. I show no preference. Is it not dreadful? If you are one of the disgustingly healthy type of person, robust, ruddy, and complacent, who can devour soft-shelled crabs, warm milk, tomatoes, apple dumplings and ice cream, all within the period of one meal, and live to tell it; if you are the boarding-house sort of person who longs for just one chance at a palatable, well-cooked meal; in either case it will be safe for you to read this story. In the first instance, you would be able to stand anything. In the second, you would be just the person to sympathize with Jedediah Hoskins. But, and I cannot emphasize this too strongly, if you have lived all your life on buttermilk and toast, with stewed prunes and beef extract as your wildest diversions, or if you have just completed a meal so satisfying as to make the merest mention of food repulsive, then, I prithee, turn to some other tale.

Just to make the thing artistic, we will begin by talking about Jedediah Hoskins' mother, as if we were nosing out his shabby little biography from the records of fame, rather than from the limitless, colorless ones of mediocrity. And having mentioned his mother, that is about all there is to say about her. The senior Mr. Hoskins himself could scarcely have described her. She was heartrendingly unobtrusive, a washed-out, undersized nonen[t]ity. She gave the impression of nothingness; not the intangibility of a fairy, filmy being, but that which some of us are accustomed to connect with the idea of original Chaos—a dimly gray, shapeless, dismal mass of neither meaning nor purpose; coming from Nothing; passing to Nothing. And her cooking was worse than nothingness. It would have shamed a cannibal. It rebelled [sic] even the multitudinous Hoskinses, brought up on it, before eating, choked them on the way down, and left unpleasant when not painful mementoes when it had passed to despa[i]ringly would-be digestive regions. Caviar, lobster á la, all things we see on hotel menus and can't order because of flabby pocketbooks, would have been totally unrecognizable to the connoisseur after they had passed a period in the sticky general stewing pot through

---

6   The Philippine Autonomy Act (29 August 1916), also known as the Jones Law, committed the United States to a policy of eventual independence for the Philippines.

which voyaged all Hoskins viands. That pot was to Hoskins food what the grave is to mortal man; the place where everything has to go some time.

The day came when Jedediah was celebrating his thirtieth birthday. The packing house where he did specialized sorting work decided that he had become invaluable to the firm. They raised his salary from fifty-five to sixty dollars a month. The head of the dried apricots department invited him to his own house for dinner that evening. Jedediah sauntered home to his noonday meal feeling like the original millionaire, with none of that gentleman's worries. He realized that his mother had prepared a sumptuous meal in his honor. He counted the scorched potatoes, and there were thirteen instead of twelve. He was to have two, it being a great day. He looked at a flat, black, mysterious mass on his platter, mildly curious.

"Liver?" he queried pleasantly.

"No," replied Mrs. Hoskins with pride. "Om'let."

He looked forward to the dinner that evening with the casual interest shown by all of Mrs. Hoskins' offspring in a meal. It was a game with them, which Jedediah had not truly outgrown, to guess what different edibles on the table really were; the individual nearest right winning a bite from every other of the ten plates. Mrs. Hoskins' table gave excellent practice in this. Seldom, if ever, could anyone guess correctly. Jedediah, on his way to the home, wife and dinner of the head of the dried apricots department, took it for granted that all cookery was like unto that of the parental board; never having dined away before in his life.

"I hope your appetite isn't spoiled, waiting so long," said his hostess.

"Well, no. Can't say it is."

"And I do hope you won't dislike what I have for dinner."

"Well, no," said Jedediah, wondering why he should dislike it. "Well, no. I'm—I'm not particular. I wasn't—wasn't brought up that way."

He blew his nose, not that it needed blowing, but it gave him something to do, sparing the necessity for speech. Knowing something by hearsay of dining room etiquette, he jogged his brain for subjects of conversation whilst he should be choking away through dinner. All that came to his mind were dried apricots and liver. He dismissed these as unworthy. Would they have either of the two on the table? If so, would he recognize them? And then he forgot his dining room etiquette-by-hearsay, and expressed himself in one long-drawn "A-a-ah!" of delighted wonder. He was seated at the table, his back close to the kitchen door, whence came odors such as might be wafting directly from Paradise. And before him in a graceful dish, wide and flat, was a lake of soup, definitely, deliciously tomato. It was roseate in hue, smooth as butter, and flecked with tantalizing islands of whipped cream. The German army en masse could not have convinced

Jedediah that this dazzling concoction was even second cousin to the Hoskins puddles of mud that bore the same name. Before he was aware of it, the beautiful lake was gone, and he was staring at a spray of pink pansies on the bottom of the plate. There had not been a single choke, and he was conscious of a warm, grateful sensation in gastronomic regions. He riveted his eyes in awe on a comfortably round and snug fowl, exuding spicy vapors from a crinkly, seal-brown surface, and completely surrounded, like a mother hen with her chicks, by potatoes, glossy, even, and steaming. He became absorbed in the little waterfalls of shiny juice that sprang from under every movement of the carving knife, then came to his senses with a jerk. In a moment, he argued to himself, he would wake up with a stomach ache. He smiled nervously toward his hostess, and passed his hand across his forehead.

"I suppose—suppose—you get special rates on—on—dried apricots?"

The lady questioned leaned towards him with a mysterious air of confidence, shaking her finger under his nose. It had jelly on the tip of it, did the finger, and it smelled of crabapple, with an insinuation of mint leaves.

"Now, Mr. Hoskins, do you know, there's just the trouble." Her eye lit on the jelly. Her speech was halted until the finger could pop into her mouth and emerge pink, moist, and comparatively clean. "You know," Mr. Hoskins, "we get such special rates on dried apricots, we could almost live on 'em, for next to nothing, you understand, but—" her voice was as low, as far away, as a dying wind over the prairie, her wagging finger almost in contact with Jedediah's nose, that followed it hypnotically in its gyrations, "Mr. Hoskins—we don't like 'em! Don't like 'em."

She hung breathless, attendant, on his sympathetic response. Jedediah's face was blank. He sensed that something definite was expected of him, what, he could not tell. He did not like beef stew and cabbage, but he ate it twice a week like a hero, saying nothing, almost thinking nothing, about it; he did not like his mother's sticky, leaden puddings, but—etc. What he liked or disliked had nothing to do with the business of self-nourishment. He studied the primrose plant in the center of the table, brows knit. His hostess was trembling with eagerness.

"Is that—so?" he ventured. "I always sort of—sort of—fancied—dried apricots myself. Stewed—real thick and soft," he finished hopefully.

She settled back in her chair mournfully. He could see that she was vastly disappointed; he was sorry to have failed her.

"It's just our luck, I tell my husband," she began determinedly again, as if Jedediah had satisfactorily soared to heights of agonized pity, "not liking 'em. We've tried, and just can't, that's all. But, I tell him—"

But Jedediah's mind was elsewhere. It was floating on the billows of the little boat of rich gravy directly in front of him.

"Help yourself to the gravy, Mr. Hoskins, and pass the rolls."

The rolls! Were those golden morsels, folded over on themselves, with satiny buttered lining, mere rolls? Rolls in the Hoskins household were weapons with which to repel invading dogs and cats, the sound alone of the black objects crashing against the wall sufficing to terrify away the intruders. No one ever dared surmise what would happen if one struck anything alive. A large-sized one, coming in contact with a man's head with any amount of force would have meant certain death. Taken internally by anyone not brought up on them, they would probably have meant the same thing. Fortunately, no guest ever dined at the Hoskins' frugal table. And Jedediah, speechless, well-nigh senseless, before the new world that had opened up before him, was eating and eating and eating.

"You must save room for a couple of slices of my apple pie," his hostess said; and then—It was brought on.

It seemed to Jedediah Hoskins as if that apple pie represented the culmination of life's ideals and ambitions satisfied. His soul went out to meet it. It linked him forever to a hitherto undreamed-of perfection, made him part of it. Every finger-print about the edge of the crust was an impression on his inner being. As the last mouthful of the third slice sped on its way to oblivion, he realized for the first time in his life that there was something in him far removed from other Hoskinses, and mountain-high superior to the general stewing pot from which he had been nourished for thirty years. Jedediah was a changed man.

It was late when he wandered home in the starlight, with the curious restlessness of Spring, that had just a touch of languor behind it, tugging at his newfound being. He thought with revolt of the parental abode, dark and odorous. He thought he must stifle if he went inside; so, when he reached the house, he sat down on the doorstep, and looked at the watery moon (a thing he had never before deliberately done), and thought. He realized that a great intellectual shifting was going on within him. His apathetic attitude towards existence in general was being relegated to his mental attic. Fiery ambition to lead a new life, untouched by the products of the general stewing pot, enthused him. It was impossible for him ever to partake of another meal at the Hoskins board. One evening had revealed to him a world into which he felt impelled to enter, and he resolved, passionately, to take his meals around at restaurants until he found the place, The Ideal Place, where he might embrace Edible Perfection forever. And then—then—another idea insinuated itself into his surprised mind. He found himself thinking of a wife in connection with his new culinary ideal. Upon this,

his overtaxed brain registered a distinct shock, and Jedediah crept away to bed, horrified. It was twelve o'clock.

Morning yawned dully over the Hoskins abode. It was time for a listless descent to the breakfast table, though why that should be differentiated from any other kind of table, dinner, supper, or mahogany, no one knew. The same streaked, gray tablecloth was there, the same disarray of eating utensils, and the same pervasive odor of something with a fire under it and boiling water over it. Jedediah's head was heavy from his late hours of the night before, and he had lost two collar buttons and found them again before he came to an acute awareness of a strange heart palpitation hitherto unknown to a Hoskins. It was the day of the great rebellion! To-day, purposely, cruelly, he was to sever the bonds that had linked him to many Hoskinses, dead and alive. He was to throw a crashing, screaming thing into the smelly darkness, stillness of the dining room. His hands trembled; in halting to quiet them he noticed that he was putting on a collar intended for wash. This condition he remedied; and then he felt better. He was glad to have discovered his mistake in time. Somewhere in his make-up was a genuine germ of elemental neatness. He brushed his shiny new blue serge coat, slid into it, and creaked down the stairs. He creaked down for two reasons: the stairs had been built that way, and his shoes were new. In the hall he stopped to put his hands in his pockets and to moisten his lips. His mother! He could see the wavery [*sic*] lines of distress that would amble nervously across her vacant face when he told her what he had to tell. He had read somewhere of filial in-gratitude. Was he ungrateful to the hand and breast that had nourished him? Was he overturning household gods in repudiating the general stewing pot? A spasmodic flicker of anxiety passed through him. He was taken unawares, and the ground beneath him swayed back and forth. The green animals in the carpet were chasing one another around the border in a dizzy fashion. Jedediah caught hold of the newel post and choked on nothingness that was filling his throat. He was honestly alarmed. He gasped, closed his eyes. And before him there passed, in regular file, like an army going forth to glorious battle, a line of grace-ful dishes, one wide and flat with a pink lake in it, one large and square with a crinkly brown fowl sleeping on it, one crystalline with a castle of quivering jelly built in its bosom, and so on to the end, where three triangles of appled perfec-tion danced in the rear.

Jedediah opened his eyes, lingeringly. Hopefully, he peered to the left, to the right. The little army had surely gone away, but behind it was left, in his heart, the lust of conquest, the glorious loyalty to a principle, that marks the fighter. He realized he had a sacred duty to fulfill, to himself and to his stomach. He had built for himself a goal, an ideal, and to that everything else must give way.

He would be a coward if he allowed this to go the misty way of all his former uncertain ambitions and longings.

He marched into the dining room with his long, thin head held high, and his pale eyes glittering like dirty water in the sun. He greeted his family silently, and was surprised to find himself shaking out his red and white fringed napkin and spreading it over as much of his knees as it would cover. Hurriedly he re-folded it and put it back on the table; then satisfied himself that no one had noticed his unwonted procedure. Mrs. Hoskins had dished out a nondescript porridge of soap-suds hue and odor, and now held it out to her son. The moment had come. He faced it with perfect equanimity. He lifted his right hand with the majestic, awesome gesture of a traffic policeman, and checked the progress of the porridge. Mrs. Hoskins' hand and the dish wavered unsteadily in mid-air; then fluttered down to the table again. Jedediah's gesture had been unquestionabl[y] magnificent. Mrs. Hoskins stared first at the porridge, then at Jedediah. He met her anxious gaze squarely.

"You don't want it?"

He shook his head gravely. She edged her chair closer to the table and leaned over it, her hands hovering over and among the various dishes, under the immediate necessity of handing him something, anything. Omitting the porridge upset the usual order of things, and she sank back into her chair, helpless.

"What—what can I give you?" she queried pleadingly.

Jedediah's tones were portentous.

"Nothing, mother, nothing."

She was baffled. She stirred her coffee rapidly, her frightened eyes on him. Then she breathed deeply, and stroked back her hair as bright relief came over her. Her voice was maternal.

"Now, that's a shame, Jed. You're bilious, I just know it, bilious. After I get through eatin' I'm a-goin' to give you a good big dose o' colomel [*sic*]."

·In the old days she could have offered him calomel at any time, yes, fed it to him, and it would all have been in the day's work. But now! The insult of tendering him this, the new Jedediah with new dreams! His eyes flashed. His electrified manner made the younger Hoskinses, who had been contentedly smacking and slobbering over their plates, pause and watch him. He held the wondering attention of the whole table.

"I'm no more sick 'n you!"

He waited for this to dig its impression.

"I'm not going to eat to home anymore!"

Jedediah was not going to eat at home anymore. The little Hoskinses went on with their interrupted business. But Mrs. Hoskins still gazed at the outraged male, her offspring, and her lips quivered.

"But, Jed, why? Ain't you satisfied with what I give you? Lord knows I do the best I can, with them kids always empty, and nothin' must [more] to do on. Ain't I always fed you enough?"

She looked so pitifully weak when she asked questions, and her eyes looked hurt like that, and her voice wobbled! Jedediah felt the bite of remorse. She had worked hard for him, and she had fed him enough, good heavens, yes; he had always had *enough*! He was on the point of taking up his napkin and asking for a cup of coffee.

"Oh, say, Jed, are you—are you—goin' to get married? Maybe?"

And again the tremor that had come upon him the night before assailed him. He shut his eyes and swallowed, hard. The physical exertion of the swallowing increased his self-respect, and he was offended again, mildly insulted.

"No," he said with dignity, "I'm not—not—a-goin' to get married." The word seemed to stick in his throat like a crooked fishbone. Why should he stumble over the word—"married"—? Who, indeed, would he—marry? He mopped his face, in his horror, with the red and white fringed napkin. When he looked at his mother he experienced the same guilt, and the same terror, that he had felt when she had caught him in his first theft, that of a dirty cur from a neighbor's yard. He gulped. "No," he repeated, "it's just that—"

If only she wouldn't look at him so steadily. He shivered. He would not hurt her feelings with the truth. He would lie nobly, although it was disappointing to lose the effect of the bomb he had planned to throw.

"I thought as how—as how—maybe a change would do me good. Perk me up a mite. Maybe," he added reflectively. "And seein' as I got a raise, I could spare to eat—to eat—around—places. I was readin' the other day where a doctor said as—"

He coughed, and spent much time in getting out his handkerchief. It came harder than he thought.

"—as a man was apt to get all kinds of d'seases by never gettin' a change, and always etin' in one pl[a]ce."

Mrs. Hoskins pursed her lips and studied her son. She nodded her head slowly.

"Mebbe that's so. You can try it, at all rates. Though old Ma Hoskins et here forty years before she died, and it didn't never 'pear to hurt her much. But you've been lookin' kind o' peaked o' late, Jed, seems to me. You try eatin' around a while." She cocked her head on one side to get a better view of his face. "I'm real glad you read what the doctor said." Economic conditions came before her. "Now I can make two pounds o' rump so, 'stead o' two 'n a quarter. It always made it come out half a cent uneven, an' they charged me the whole cent. I can save money on my meat good, an' cents by the day make dollars by the year," she said with real pleasure, both in her housewifely thrift and the cleverness of saving.

It had not come out at all as Jedediah had planned it, and he was conscious, strangely, of being very hungry. Such a thing had not happened in years.

"Hadn't you best have some bread an' coffee anyhow? You won't have time to get nothin' downtown this mornin.' 'Fore you start eatin' around?"

"Well, yes, I guess maybe," said Jedediah. "Well, yes. Not a full cup, an' lots o' milk in it."

—Marjorie Kinnan.

"The Captivating Odors of the Kitchen," *Wisconsin Literary Magazine* [16], no. 2 (November 1916): 41–42, 56, 58, 60.

*   *   *   *   *   *   *   *   *

The Captivating Odors of the Kitchen
(Part II)

For twelve months Jedediah had been eating around. He had had soup and coffee spilled on him in hustling cafeterias, had ordered shredded wheat and rice pudding in clattering restaurants with whirring electric fans that only added to the general din, had tried city boarding houses where gaunt, weary individuals turned suspicious eyes on one who asked for a second helping. He had searched so long and so diversely without success, that the inspiration within him had shriveled like a withered pomegranate that was once plump and glowing and rich. But although his failure to reach the goal had dulled him, so that he was almost the old Jedediah again, and his watery eyes had lost the spark of his first enthusiasm, he had no desire to return to the Hoskins dining room. That was a nightmare that had made him shudder at the recollection. He now stayed at the plant until he was sure the supper dishes were washed, and the thick odors had partly vanished from the house. In the morning he left just before it was time for the sickish coffee scents to come wafting up over the banister to his room at the head of the stairs.

This particular noon-time he sat in a little Quick Lunch restaurant with blue-tiled shiny walls and clean table-cloths. It was soothing to him. The snub-nosed waitress shoved a card under his hand. At the bottom of it was printed:

"COFFEE JUST LIKE MOTHER USED TO MAKE IT."

Jedediah pointed to the statement.
"Is it really just like Mother used to make it?" he asked.
The homely one nodded. Jedediah looked at her pityingly.
"Bring me tea," he said.
He ate plaintively. He was not hungry. He was not anything. Except pensive, perhaps, or tired. He pushed away his custard unfinished, and ambled out into the chill April sunlight, vaguely cross. He began to think and to recollect. He went back over the failures of the year until he reached the night when he had made his vow to arrive, some day, at a world of culinary idealism. He remembered the moon, and the lateness of the hour when he had retired, and the damp, restless air. He went back further still into memory, and saw again the three flaky triangles that had opened portals to him. And it had all gone the way of the other things of his life, the way of meaningless oblivion. For the first time he saw himself a colorless mediocrity, one of the many who are nothing, one who is marked forever as a nonen[t]ity, because he sought and did not find.[7] Was his life always to be so? Was he never to attain, to exult in mastery? Was he always to acknowledge himself baffled and beaten? He had had one aspiration gleam out like a solitary star in his life. Was that never to be fulfilled?

He walked into the employees' entrance with bowed shoulders, and hung up his hat and coat on one of the long line of pegs behind the door. An office boy, strolling down the corridor, whistling, lifted a finger to catch his attention.

"Been lookin' for you, Jed. Old man Whittaker wants you at the office."

Jedediah drew his left hand slowly across his mouth, as if to loosen the sudden constriction of the muscles. His face twitched, and his heart was beating a boisterous reveille. The official summons seemed to come as a climax to his despair, and shocked him into acute dread. Trembling he crept to the door of the head of the firm, and scraped his knuckles over the painted, "PRIVATE." At a brisk "Come!" he pushed open the door and slid through. He wondered if Mr. Whittaker could see his knees knocking together, and he thought [to] himself that if he were a woman, it would not show through the skirts. Wearing trousers, however———. He wanted to make a careless remark about the weather, or packing and sorting conditions, or Mr. Whittaker, but nothing would come. It was Mr.

---

7   Cf. Matthew 7:7, Luke 11:9, and the final line of "Ulysses" (1842), by Alfred Tennyson (1809–92): "To strive, to seek, to find, and not to yield."

Whittaker's place to speak first, after all. That gentleman, white-haired, wrinkled, round-faced, kindly, tipped back in his swivel chair and peered over horn-rimmed glasses at Jedediah. He studied him so for some minutes, then nodded to himself as if satisfied with a judgment. When he finally spoke, it seemed to Jedediah that life and the universe had completed a vast cycle of time.

"Well, Mr. Hoskins, have you been contented with your position with us?"

"Yes—yes, sir. I like—like—my work. Pretty fair."

"Haven't thought of branching out into more clerical work? Office work? Instead of special sorting?"

"No—no, sir. I never thought—thought—I could do it."

"That so? We rather think you can. You know your end of the business from the ground up, and we want a man to go to Clarkston, Ohio,[8] and take charge of the new buying and selecting office there. A hundred a month. Want to try it?"

Jedediah gulped. He had passed through too many phases of emotion in an hour for the good of his coherence. His tongue was lost somewhere in his throat. He recovered it and stammered an acceptance.

"You can be ready to leave in a week, I presume. Come to me tomorrow at nine to talk it over. I have plenty of pointers for you. Thank you, Mr. Hoskins."

And Jedediah, sputtering joyously, backed out of the presence, and finding the door-knob somewhere in the region behind him, got out. The rest of the afternoon was an unreal thing. He put half a barrel of worm-eaten peaches in with a carload of "Royal Crown Specials," and spent from four until six-thirty sorting them out again. To have charge of a buying and selecting office! At the salary of a prince! He could go to this, a new town and a new position, with actual prestige, and with authority. At supper he ordered kidney stew, which he detested, and enjoyed it as if it had been ambrosia, until he remembered on his way home that it was kidney stew he had had on his mind to avoid, and not to order.

The week was gone in what seemed a day. Jedediah learned a great deal from Mr. Whittaker, of office management. He soaked up all such information handed him as if he could not get his fill. He found that there was to be a clerk under him, to typewrite orders and attend to all correspondence. This cleared away all clouds, and he sold, at a distinct loss, the already second-hand dictionary he had purchased for his new position. He bought a suit, a beautiful creation with only one button on the front of the coat, and a deliciously narrow purple stripe down the brown background. He was prepared to conquer Clarkston on first appearance, and arrived there one gaudy Spring afternoon, a dazzling creature that failed, some way or other, to make the stir he had expected. He had counted

---

8   Clarkston, Ohio, is a fictional town.

too much on the splendor of the purple stripe. He could not see the thin, pale face above it, nor the too narrow shoulders, nor the wrinkles in the back of the coat. But the new work engrossed him, and he found deep intellectual satisfaction in overcoming the difficulties, and in receiving favorable reports from headquarters. He was very much of a business man, indeed.

Clarkston he found a sleepy little place, with the town population needlessly concentrated into a few acres; shiftless people, for the most part, who had managed to save or make enough ready money to live within a half-mile of the barn-like Town Hall, and who avoided labor as carefully as possible. Outside of the town proper were many prosperous farms, of rich lowland soil, where thrifty, elemental folks raised corn and fruits and vegetables, and stayed uncouth and pious and healthy. The women had large arms and full bosoms, and even the Sunday clothes of the men smelled of horses and cows and barns and clover. Jedediah found them a little strange. He lived on the outskirts of the village with a very old, very ancient couple, and took his meals at the only restaurant, or eating-place, as it was known, in the town, where two dirty men took turns at cooking and waiting on table. Morning and evening he had a brisk little walk to and from his office. On the way he passed a brown, dingy, little house, with a brick walk and scraggly garden, and neglected rose vines sprawling over the sides and roof to hide the scarred, weather beaten ugliness as best they might. A little care, and the place might have been attractive. Being neglected, it was dilapidated and down-at-the-heel and pitiful. Jedediah found it interesting. Its dustiness and dark color reminded him of the parental Hoskins dwelling-place. Once he was almost homesick when he went by. He wondered often what sort of tenants it contained. For two weeks he saw no one about. He had come to the conclusion that it was deserted.

And then, the evening of all evenings. He was going home early, in the mellow glow of the warm, late-setting sun, and someone was preparing supper in the dingy brown cottage. The caressing touch of bowl against bowl, the clink of spoon on tinware, the whirr of the busy egg-beater, sounded merrily from quite far away, and made a pleasant music. It had a cozy, homelike tinkle that all other meal preparations of Jedediah's experience had lacked. Such sounds might have been made by the wife of the head of the dried apricots department. His ear became alert, and he quickened his step. Then he stopped before the gate, assailed by odors such as he had met with once before—only once. They floated out lazily, smugly, yet their very indifference to him held him in an iron grip. He stood entranced. He sniffed. There was frying chicken. He sniffed again. A crisp, baked odor! It must be biscuits, little ones, crumbly, melty ones. And, surer and surer, asserting itself gradually above the others, came the smell of fresh apple pie. It was rich, tart, delicate, at once. There could be no mistake. Jedediah had known it once in its perfection. He could never forget it. His soul answered. And he sniffed and sniffed, running his hands along the fence palings as if in them he might press the secret lock that would open the immediate door of his heart's desire. A snatch of song, in a woman's voice, filtered out to him. He came to himself, then, and fled, rather terrified. It was the realization of the close connection of the feminine with the culinary ideal that frightened him.

The next morning he managed to pass the brown cottage at breakfast time, and was rewarded for his carefully figured mathematics with a glorifying whiff of coffee, aromatic, alluring, almost passionate. He passed the day under the influence of a kind of awe. He had come so close, so close to the shrine! He had been permitted to breathe the incense of the inner temple. He was bewitched, transported with a sort of religious fervor. When he went home once more in the early evening, he did not meet the spicy odors, but in the front yard, trimming the rose bushes, stood a young woman, and he knew her for the priestess of the sanctuary. He looked on her cautiously, worshipfully, and it was not until the next night, when he saw her there again, that he realized how homely she really was. This inflamed his admiration of her abilities, but rather served to dampen his ardor for the priestess herself. In fact, as time went on, and they grew accustomed to the sight of each other across the safe separation of the fence, he became more and more convinced that never, in all his thirty-odd years of existence among unattractive females, had he seen a woman so slighted by the graces. Her tiny black eyes had a tendency to cross at the most alarming moments, her mouth had a listless, pouty droop that betokened a nature of mixed sulks and slatternliness, and her form bore no relation to any previous feminine model. But the odors from the brown cottage kitchen grew more and more delectable, more promising, and varied. Jedediah, in desperation, found out that she attended the Methodist church, went there one Sunday, had the pastor introduce him to her, accompanied her home, smelled the Sunday dinner cooking, and asked to call.

The first visit was painful. He took infinite care with his toilet, and on arrival had it thrust to the attention of his startled eyes that she had done the same, to a degree even more advanced than his. He had been so busy with the external preparation that he had neglected to provide conversational topics for himself, and found himself in a squeaky hammock by her side with absolutely nothing to talk about. She, however, was a cool, candid, self-assured soul, very talkative, for which he was wonderfully thankful. She discussed homely topics at length and in bad grammar, and he found her quite pleasant by moonlight, with a nice voice. If she had been as shy as he, he would have retreated, defeated again, but as it was he felt a strange, warm elation at this intercourse with a young woman, considered the venture quite a success, and called the next night. She received his advances gratefully, for she had been rather neglected by the youth of her native village, and in Jedediah she saw a good proposition, a triumph over former lettings-alone, and the gratification of her natural impulses as a woman.

He outgrew his embarrassment in her presence, and came to feel more at home with her than with anyone he had ever known. He did not realize that this was a part of her encouragement. A simple-minded male seldom does. He acquired the habit of dropping in for a chat at any stray hour of the day. And always, around meal-time, and sometimes in mid-morning, there came to him the sensuous pleasure of sniffing in the sweet breath of cooking viands; foods concocted by a master mind and hand. The intimate, daily nearness of the goal, the consciousness of truly possible attainment, kept him in a perpetual state of inspiration, and made the cross-eyed one a thousand fold more interesting. Ideas once alarming, now commonplace, had long been developing in his mind, and one drizzly night in the early fall, when Jedediah was tramping home cold, cross and hungry, the smell of stewed apricots, heavy with sirup, was wafted out from the friendly house, and stabbed his recollection to the quick. It was too much. He went in, took the woman of his choice into a corner, stammered a great deal, and bolstered by his large purpose overcame himself, and as eagerly as if he were on fire with love for her, begged her to become Mrs. Hoskins. She did not pretend surprise, only puckered her forehead in deliberation.

Jedediah, watching her, thought that never could he endure a lifetime of that face across any but the exact kind of table he knew she would set. Immersed in the glorious things that she would provide, he could be happy with a Medusa;[9] being a man, as we have seen, of simple mind and tastes. To his violent regret he had never, in the several months of his acquaintance with her, sampled her cooking any closer than the steam of it. She had not seemed particularly hospitable when it came to having him dine with her, although he had hinted more than once, and had often stayed long past the hour of dinner in the hopes of being asked to participate. But she had always failed to respond, and being a gentleman, after all, he had not openly asked for an invitation. He thought of all this now, and it keyed up his anxiety and the desire to possess.

"Please! I—I—want you."

Which was the truth.

Having known for a month or so what she would do when he said this, she

9   In Greek mythology, Medusa was a once beautiful woman whose pride, her hair, was turned into serpents by Athena, who was jealous of her beauty. Any human who looked directly at Medusa would be turned into stone.

smirked a bit and lifted her face to his. He understood, and as his lips met hers, it was not the nectar of a woman's kiss that he tasted, but dumplings and roast fowl and gravy.

She consented to an immediate marriage, having quietly prepared the elements of a trousseau in the last few weeks, and Jedediah spent a sleepless night, tossed about on a very stormy sea of conflicting feelings, and repeating over and over to himself, "Tomorrow, I will be a married man. And when we first eat together, I shall have fulfilled my destiny and gained my Utopia."[10] Of course, he did not say it precisely like that.

She had insisted on a week's honeymoon, and they had gone to Dayton, Ohio, and stayed at a hotel on the American plan, where they had horrible food. They had gone to the vaudeville every night, and she had reveled in the worldliness of it. But Jedediah had pled business, and they had come home to begin matrimony in a more sober fashion.

Tonight was the night, and his feet fairly danced down the street. She would have a god-like feast for him. He had asked expressly for fried chicken and apple pie, and she had frowned and acquiesced. He ran up the porch steps and into the house. In the hall something stopped him. It made him sniff, and sniff again, then gasp in horror. It smacked of the Hoskins general stewing pot, and it was burnt. He crept out to the dining room. Dinner was on the table, and Mrs. Hoskins was waiting for him. He looked at a black, sticky mass on a platter. He could not recognize it.

"Is—is that—the chicken?" he asked

"Well, I should say," replied Mrs. Hoskins, "did you think it was liver?"

"It—it—looked—like it," Jedediah whispered.

She sat down and began to serve.

"I ain't cooked for about five years now," she announced with pride, "this is my first meal since then. Pretty nice lookin', ain't it?"

She rose, and took a plate from the sideboard. On the plate was a triangle. It was flat, caved-in, black at the wide end, with a top and bottom layer of what looked the consistency of shoe leather. In between, a wizened piece of apple wandered here and there.

"I thought I'd put the pie on the table, where you could enjoy lookin' at it."

Jedediah's hands were clutching the table cloth frantically.

"Why—you—why—what about all the things I used to—used to—smell cookin'—here? The fritters, and—and—the pies, and—and—the biscuits?"

---

10 "Utopia," an ideal society envisioned in literature by the Catholic martyr Sir Thomas More (1478–1535) in his *Utopia* (1516). Male-centric visions of Utopia, along with male visions of the ideal feminine, here, as in her earlier allusion to Medusa, inform MKR's feminist sensibility.

Mrs. Hoskins laughed scornfully, and buttered a large slice of bread.

"Oh, you know that Mis' Wells that used to have the upstairs of my house when you was a-courtin' me? I think I made you acquainted one evenin' when she come downstairs to borrow some thread. She was a quiet sort of a little thing, never no more noise 'n a mouse. She had the use 'o my kitchen. She was eternally putterin' around and makin' little tasty things fer that invalid husband o' her's. Greatest woman to cater to his fancy. I used to eat with 'em, seein' as I never cooked none myself."

Jedediah was staring straight ahead of him, his face contorted into a queer thing, as if he would cry, but could not. Mrs. Hoskins took another piece of meat and chattered on amiably.

"Funny you thought it was me that did the cookin.'"

She leaned over and tapped her husband on the arm.

"I might as well tell you, Jed, I'm a-goin' to keep a girl. You can afford it all right, and we can economize on the table." Her eyes crossed horribly, and she took a large mouthful before she continued.

"I don't believe in wastin' a lot o' time on fancy dishes for a man."

Marjorie Kinnan

"The Captivating Odors of the Kitchen (Part II)." *Wisconsin Literary Magazine* [16], no. 3 (December 1916): 87–88, 100, 102. MKR is listed as one of eleven editors in this issue of *WLM*.

*   *   *   *   *   *   *   *   *

The Mouse Speaks

I scarce can see your eyes beneath your lashes—
    You drop them, coy, and shy, and most demure;
I only get a bit of blue, in flashes—
    You do it all on purpose, I am sure.

I scarce can see your crown of golden tresses,
    You hide them in a Quaker bonnet, gray;
Yet now and then a wayward curl confesses
    That you are not averse to dance, or play.

I know your tempting lips would take to kisses,
    Although you seem to hold them very prim,

For when you smile, or pout, I know that this is
    The trick you use to take "the stern sex" in.

You're like a fluffy kitten, cuddly, purring;
    But you know a thing or two, for all of that;
And I wonder, when I see your claws a-stirring,
    How much is kitten, and how much is—cat.

Marjorie Kinnan

"The Mouse Speaks," *Wisconsin Literary Magazine* 16, no. 4 (January 1917): 117. MKR is listed as one of eleven editors in this issue of the *WLM*. "The Mouse Speaks" is listed as a poem of distinction in *The Poets of the Future: A College Anthology for 1916–1917*, edited by Henry T. Schnittkind (Boston: Stratford, 1917), 319 (Tarr, *Bibliography*, 271).

* * * * * * * * *

[Give Me My Heart, And I Will Go]

Give me my heart, and I will go.
You're tired; I've wearied you too long.
The fire upon your hearth is low.
It did not please you—that last song?

I'll leave you to your pipe, your dreams
Of bigger things than womankind.
Oh—what a Titan thing it seems
To plan so large, to search—to find.[11]

I gave you all I had to give;
I taught you tone and harmony;
I made your rough-hewn fancies live;
I set your mind, your passions, free.

You have no further need of me;
Your world eclipses mine, I know.

---

11 MKR again alludes to Matthew 7:7, Luke 11:9, and the final line of Tennyson's "Ulysses" (1842).

You strive to touch infinity.
Give me my heart; and I will go.

M. K.

"[Give Me My Heart, and I Will Go]," *Wisconsin Literary Magazine* 16, no. 5 (February 1917): 145. MKR is listed as one of eleven editors for this issue of *WLM*.

* * * * * * * * *

Creation of Soul

The cross-roads Calvary shone ruddy gold,
Warmed in the soft glow of the evening sun,
When he, my vagabond, sweet alien,
Came, framed against it, tall, and dark, and bold.

And I was his from Time's first happy day,
And god-like, did he ask, and take, my all;
And god-like, too, gave radiance to the thrall.
And I shall follow where he leads, for aye.

And while they mock me where I, joyous, pass
And for my vagrant soul all-pious pray,
I move within a starlit world always—
Of singing nightingales and dewy grass—

And from the crystal truths he brings to me,
I build a soul, fragrant, and pure, and free.

M. K.

"Creation of Soul," *Wisconsin Literary Magazine* 16, no. 5 (February 1917): 146.

The Real Thing

He took her to Prom. He had been out with her but twice when he asked her to go with him; and insomuch as he was an easy, though not inspired, dancer and conversationalist, she accepted; the gods not having showered eligible Prom partners upon her that year. The night before Prom he proposed, by way of a vervid[12] and carefully penned note, oozy with passionate ejaculations. She was an astute maiden, and, while seeming to take his peroration in all seriousness, she soothed him, sympathized with him—and proceeded to cool him off by assuring him that he was far too young to have found the great passion of his life, and that he had known her neither long nor well enough to love her. She was maternal in attitude; she told him not to let it bother him—that he would get over it in a very little while. He averred, with tense voice, dramatically subdued, that it was "the Real Thing." But she smiled mysteriously—and smiling, put a great barrier between them. She kept the barrier there; she was kindly, but aloof—oh, so aloof!—and forced upon him, gently, the sensation that he was a very little boy, and a silly one. And by the time the Prom was over, the Real Thing was dead of starvation; having had nothing to feed upon. This was alarming to him; but not nearly so alarming as the remembrance of having asked her for every Friday night in the year. She remarked tactfully, however, that she knew he had not meant it seriously. He looked grave and agreed. Then he disappeared from off her horizon. She smiled.

A year later he 'phoned and asked to see her on important business. She lifted her eyebrows, and named the time. He arrived. With eyes straight ahead, he told her he had a confession to make, an explanation of his disappearance from off her social earth. He had been mistaken in his great affection, he said. But he had to come to tell her that it was not that he merely recovered from a chance fancy—oh, no! He had meant every word of it at the moment—it was just that he had found, suddenly, that there was some "personal element," as he put it, that had unfortunately prevented the permanency of his attachment. He had really loved her deeply at the time—but that there had been some quality or other in her nature that made him realize that they were not destined for each other. He had come to tell her this, because for some time he had been disturbed about the matter, fearing that she misunderstood, that she thought he had merely grown

---

12 Although "vervid" may be a typo for "fervid," it is possible that MKR has coined an alternate form of the adjective "verve."

tired of her. He wanted her to realize the true meaning of his conduct in so carefully absenting himself.

Her lips twitched dangerously. She drew them down as primly as possible.

"Just so it hasn't left any bitter memories," she said, "it's all right."

His eyes grew wide. "Bitter? Why, of course not."

"Just so there's no scar left on your heart," she murmured.

"Oh, no," he answered relievedly, "I should say not." Then, "Say, what are you laughing about?"

"Nothing—nothing. That's merely a habit of mine."

Already his eyes had become dreamy. Suddenly he dived into an inner pocket, and pulled out a small photograph. He handed it to her, breathless with excitement.

"What do you think of her? That's the girl I'm having down for Prom this year."

He swelled with pride as she looked at the picture. It was a pretty face, alarmingly vacant, alarmingly insipid. She handed it back to him.

"Have you got a case on her?"

He was cut to the quick. His manly dignity was outraged. He replaced the picture with ferocity, rose.

"Good Heavens, no! This—this is the Real Thing!"

Marjorie Kinnan.

"The Real Thing," *Wisconsin Literary Magazine* 16, no. 5 (February 1917): 149.

*   *   *   *   *   *   *   *   *

The Stuff of Dreams

I dream of a low-roofed, sprawling house,
Little and brown and wrapped in vines,
With a pebbled path, and a garden, filled
With roses and larkspur and columbines.

I dream of the solitude, the hush,
The rustling of leaves on the tall oak trees,
The touch of a summery moonlight, soft
As fairy fingers on distant leas.

I dream of this—and of nights with rain—
Of pine knots crackling—ruddy flames—
Wavering shadows—little forms
Nestling against me, worn with games.

I dream of misty morns in June,
With the smell of jasmine, the glint of dew,
The thrushes stirring under the hedge,
The fresh, damp air—the world brand-new!

Out of the noise, the push, the whirl,
Out of the aches that will not cease,
Out of unsatisfaction, pain—
I dream of this—of this—and peace.

—M. K.

"The Stuff of Dreams," *Wisconsin Literary Magazine* 16, no. 7 (April 1917): 212. MKR is listed as one of nine editors for this issue of *WLM*. The title echoes Shakespeare's *The Tempest*: "We are such stuff / As dreams are made on (4.1.156–57).

*   *   *   *   *   *   *   *   *

The Singing Link

I cannot think, that when my zealous sun
Has spanned a life across the open sky,
And fades into the night, without a sigh,
Leaving a moment's glow to say, "'Tis done,"[13]
I cannot think immortal life's begun.
My Heav'n, my Hell, are finished as I die.[14]
I smile on life and soul of mine that cry
For full expression in their petty run.
But they find answer in a word Thou lent,

---

13   In the dramatic poem *Manfred* (1817), by Lord Byron (1788–1824), the darkly heroic Manfred begins his last lines, "'Tis over" (3.4.167). Cf. also the last words of Christ according to the Gospel of John: "It is finished" (19:30).

14   Cf. John Milton (1608–74), *Paradise Lost* (1667): "The mind is its own place, and in it self / Can make a Heav'n of Hell, a Hell of Heav'n" (1.254–55).

"Progress," eternal, 'til man's mind espy
Perfection's highest towers and turrets nigh.[15]
That can be never. But I am content.
I am one singing link of Progress' chain.
There's immortality! Is Soul in vain?

Marjorie Kinnan

"The Singing Link," *Wisconsin Literary Magazine* 16, no. 7 (April 1917): 212.

*   *   *   *   *   *   *   *   *

When the Muse Knocks

My muse has no sense of the fitness of things. She knocks at the door, bois-terously, regardless of whether I am ready to receive her, or am in my kimono and curl-papers—intellectually speaking. She is like relatives; she knows neither when to come nor when to go; a nuisance all around. On the whole, I prefer poison ivy to the literary itch; the results of scratching are more gratifying; and once one has had it, one avoids it ever after. But the muse returns anon and anon, like the meat bill.

She called on me the other night in a harsh mood. She inflicted me with a yearning to write a poem about digitalis. It was a passionate yearning. Digitalis is a purplish-blue flower, arranged at irregular intervals (like rain), along a slender stalk. It is a quaint, romantic-looking herb, connotative of old-fashioned gardens and soft young things in lavender cretonne. Just the sort of subject that arouses my sentimental spinster nature; and look at the name! Digitalis! It sounds like a Kentuckian asking, "Did you tell us?"

I have thought that perhaps my Muse, contrary to the custom of muses, was on the side of law and order, and was punishing me for a legal offense which I have hidden from the locals. For the digitalis which stands stiffly before me as I write, was pilfered from a "No Trespassing" garden. Agnes led me into it. Agnes is young and beautiful. And when I said to her, "Agnes, this is stealing, and we could be prosecuted," she only laughed and answered, "They'd let us off, we're

---

15   Again, MKR may allude to Milton's *Paradise Lost*. In book 2, Satan calls on his fellow demons to attack "Heaven's High Towrs" (62), and in book 5, the startled Eve speaks her first words, to Adam: "O Sole in whom my thoughts find all repose, / My Glorie, my Perfection, glad I see / Thy face" (28–30).

so attractive." I resented that "we." It was editorial in that it was cutting. And I plucked a great armful of digitalis by the roots, and vowed viciously, then and there, that I would write a very modern poem about the blue spikes, to show Agnes that there is something in the world besides beauty. At that time I was ignorant of the name of my poetical subject; and when I sneaked home without being caught, arranged my plunder in wobbly art-craft baskets, and got out my floral dictionary, I saw that the Muse had distinctly "wished something off on me." Digitalis! I set womanfully to work. There were rhymes enough. Ye Gods! There were *rhymes!* The ballad must be sweet and sentimental. So far, so good. I glued my eyes on the different posies before me, and crashed down on the type-writer keys as if I had studied music abroad.

> "O digitalis,
> Raised by Alice,
> In the garden
> Of her palace,
> Down in death ole
> Texan Dallas,
> I can-*not*
> *Be*-come j'alous
> Of thy bluish
> Purple chalice.
>
> Though my malice
> Is for Alice,
> Who is so in-
> Fernal callous
> That she's willing
> Just to "pal" us.
> Is such conduct
> Not a fallac-
> Y for Alice,
> Digitalis?"

When I come to, long after, a Grecian petticoat fluttered around the corner of the door, and I heard a silvery giggle in the clematis vines outside my window.

Why do I yearn to write poems about unpoetical things? I remember one of the twenty-five questions Robert Frost prepared on himself for a class in Contemporary Poetry. "Are a 'hundred collars' unbeautiful," he asked. "If so, are they fit matter for poetry? Does calling them 'reality' help any?"[16] "Unbeautiful" things are not fit for poetry; but when the Muse knocks, we tie up whatever we are thinking of, into some sort of rhythmic language; and the damage is done.

I realized with a melancholy consolation, as I sat looking at my stolen digitalis, that I was not alone in yearning to sing of unpoetical things. I would become an Imagist.[17] I would chant passionately and freely of digitalis, and Miss Lowell

---

16 That Robert Frost (1874–1963) and MKR became close friends thirty years later is in itself poetic. She alludes to Frost's "Hundred Collars" in *North of Boston* (New York: Holt, 1914). The lecture is untraced.

17 Imagism, a poetic movement led by Ezra Pound (1885–1972) and Amy Lowell (1874-1925), was characterized by emphasis on common speech, precision of language, freedom of subject mat-

would take me by the hand as one too exalted to be confined by the poetical; and Miss Monroe would give me many pages in "Poetry."[18] Perhaps Mr. Masters began his career by obeying a yearning to sing of the unsingable.[19] Oh gloomy prospect! But at any rate, when next the Muse knocks, I intend to——knock back!

Marjorie Kinnan

"When the Muse Knocks," *Wisconsin Literary Magazine* 17, no. 1 (October 1917): 6. MKR is listed as one of four editors for this *issue* of *WLM*.

*　*　*　*　*　*　*　*　*

The Miracle

I lay with half-closed eyes, worn out with pain;[20]
And day was night, and life a fearful thing.
I heard a stirring, as of flowers in rain,
Or little birds that move before they sing.
And by my side I found a fairy form,
"Your own. A sturdy son," the kind nurse smiled.
A bundle of pink rose-leaves, soft and warm—
And unbelievable! A mystic child!
The white-garbed angel placed it close to me,
Showed tiny face and dimpled fingers bared,
And smiled again, and "Hush"-ed mysteriously;
Then tip-toed 'round the room. And still—I stared!

*　*　*　*　*　*　*　*　*

In dashed an interne with a tragic face.
"My God!" he cried. "My God! What have you done!

---

ter, and experiment in rhythm.

18　Harriet Monroe (1860–1936), Chicago poet who founded the influential literary magazine *Poetry* in 1912.

19　Edgar Lee Masters (1868–1950), midwestern poet known especially for his simple lyric conventions in *Spoon River Anthology* (1915).

20　The poem was composed after MKR underwent a tonsillectomy (see Silverthorne, 29–30).

The infant here? This girl's a tonsil case!
It goes to Mrs. B——, in forty-one!"

Marjorie Kinnan.

"The Miracle," *Wisconsin Literary Magazine* 17, no. 1 (October 1917): 7.

* * * * * * * * *

The Singer

I have a lute that sings sad, sighing numbers—
    None loves my songs save my lute and I—
I play on hills when the windy world slumbers,
    Spinning out melody under the sky.

Plaintive old melody, ancient as folly,
    Built from the tinkle of sheep-bells in rain,
Throbbing with musical, lost melancholy
    Finding her old home, her old haunts, again.

Here with my lute and me, dreaming and singing,
    Here may the sorrows of ages find rest,
Rustling across my songs, like thrushes winging
    Their tired, homeward way to the hedge-hidden nest.

Far goes my melody over the rivers,
    Farther than gypsy tents under the sky,
Far as the loneliest last star that shivers—
    And none loves my songs save my lute and I.

Marjorie Kinnan.

"The Singer," *Wisconsin Literary Magazine* 17, no. 1 (October 1917): 7.

Little Grey Town of Tumbledown

O little grey town of Tumbledown,[21]
You lie by a river of great renown—
A river that's ever a-rolling and rumbling,
A river that's ever a-twisting and tumbling,
Rushing away to find the sea,
Running to kiss eternity—
A river that sings of storm in the hills,
Of wind in the pines, and the clatter of mills,
Singing of cities of loud-voiced renown—
Past the little grey village of Tumbledown.

O little grey town of Tumbledown,
Sleeping like poppy-dreams over the down,
Whence came the stillness that broods by your doors,
Whence came the breath of death over the moors,
Whence came the low, grey mist
Sprinkled with amethyst,
Veiling your tired old breast,
Sealing your lips with rest—
Whence did they come?
Did they come when wearied Time settled down
In the little grey village of Tumbledown?

In the sad little town of Tumbledown
Weary Time halted and settled down—
Ivy and mosses grow over grey homes,
And hushed old grey gardens are teeming with gnomes,
And phoebe-birds whimper at dawn in the trees—[22]
And the golden, mad river whips past with the breeze,

---

21 Cf. the Christmas carol, "O Little Town of Bethlehem" (1868); words by Phillips Brooks
(1835–93) and music by Lewis H. Redner (1831–1908). Brooks, inspired during a trip to the Holy
Land in 1865 by the view of Bethlehem from the surrounding hills, wrote the carol three years
later.

22 The Eastern phoebe (*Sayornis phoebe*), a common flycatcher known for being a loner; mated
pairs spend little time together, and even during nesting, the female will often chase away the
male.

Yearning for palaces, jesters and kings,
For glittering, colorful, frolicsome things—
Too hungry for loud life and sunlit renown
To pause by grey, sorrowful, old Tumbledown.

—Marjorie Kinnan

"Little Grey Town of Tumbledown," *Wisconsin Literary Magazine* 17, no. 2 (November 1917): 39. MKR is listed as one of four editors for this issue of *WLM*.

* * * * * * * * *

Ephemera

Sometimes at twilight I hear a little sound—and I know that An Idea is just beyond me. It flutters around, tantalizing me; sometimes whistling in the radiator, sometimes counting time with the old clock on the mantel. Once I almost saw its shape in a sudden burst of flame in the open fire—once it floated off with the steam from a dish of sweet potatoes. I steal sleuth-like all over the house—pursuing it—but when I think I have found it, it runs laughing away, and I am left clutching my brother's new pajamas—baffled. I may never find it. But I shall know that it is always there—a little whimsic, motley creature with a kiss—or perhaps—a shower bath.

Marjorie Kinnan

"Ephemera," *Wisconsin Literary Magazine* 17, no. 2 (November 1917): 42.

* * * * * * * * *

Plays of Gods and Men

In "Plays of Gods and Men," (James W. Luce Co.), we have Dunsany at his height.[23] The only previous piece that compares with the plays of this volume is

---

23 Edward John Moreton Drax Plunkett, Lord Dunsany (1878–1957), Irish poet, writer, and dramatist whose plays deal with the fantastic, the gothic, and the supernatural. The collection *The Plays of Gods and Men* (1917) contains four plays: *The Laughter of the Gods*, *The Queen's Enemies*, *The Tents of the Arabs*, and *A Night at an Inn*.

"The Gods of the Mountain."[24] In the startling dramatist's latest collection we find his sense of the dramatic keenly developed, his rhythms perfected, his symbols powerful, and, best of all, a seemingly better realization of character. Many, especially his severer critics, have felt that his characters were merely types, or, more accurately, puppets run to suit the atmosphere and the plot. Agmar and Ulf stand out somewhat; Jim and Bill are memorable, though rather from the plot-novelty surrounding them than from any idiosyncrasies peculiar even to burglars. But in the "Plays of God and Men" are found several characters that stand alone, vital; and could play no part other than their own.

The Queen of "little fears" and later "one big fear," in "The Laughter of the Gods,"[25] stands out vividly. She is an individual whom one can never forget. Her King, who is imbued with a sense of the mysterious beauty of the orchid-laden jungle-city of Thek, is interesting, although practically the same man as the King in "The Tents of the Arabs."[26] Both yearn to leave cities and tents forever, to "dwell apart in a dear brown tent of our own," or to watch the sun go down over the purple orchids. The serpent-like Queen in "The Queen's Enemies"[27] is another Lady Macbeth, although, to me, infinitely more subtle and distinctive as to method, and filled besides with the curious haunting charm of the woman of the East.

And the Toff! The Toff, who goes unflinchingly through the unspeakable "Night at the Inn"[28]—he is a work of genius, with his keen, cryptic self-sufficiency, and his intuition—which could not foresee "the blooming god's"

---

24 In *The Gods of the Mountain* (1914), which premiered at London's Haymarket Theater in 1911, a group of seven beggars pretend to be mountain gods and are ultimately turned into stone by the real gods.

25 In the three-act play *Laughter of the Gods* (1917), which would not be staged until 1919 (in New York), the Queen expresses a wide variety of fears. Late in the play, she says calmly, "No more little fears. There is one great fear," but she refuses to reveal its identity. The play ends with the destruction of the city and its inhabitants, as the gods laugh.

26 In the two-act play *The Tents of the Arabs* (1917), which premiered in Liverpool, England (1914), the king leaves his walled city and kingly responsibilities to live in the desert, in "the tents of the Arabs," for one year. As he returns to fulfill his obligations, the camel-driver Bel-narb claims to be king. The real king allows him to and thus returns to live in the desert with his beloved gypsy, Eznarza.

27 In *The Queen's Enemies* (1917), first staged in New York (1916), the Queen weeps because her enemies will not eat and drink with her for fear of poisoning. At the end of the play, she uses the Nile to flood the room in which they are locked and drowns them.

28 The one-act play *A Night at an Inn* (1916), which premiered at New York's Neighborhood Playhouse on 13 May 1916, ends with the killing of three priests who have been in pursuit of a ruby stolen from their idol.

coming from India to England to recover his ruby eye. The "Night at an Inn" seems a literary off-shoot from "The Gods of the Mountain," but that does not spoil its effectiveness. It is, if anything, almost more impressive, for the doom stealing down on the rough Englishmen comes closer home than that descending on foreign beggers [*sic*] of a type not so well known to us. Green jade idols wreaking actual vengeance seem part of the atmosphere of the exotic Eastern drama; but to make a walking idol effective and chill-producing in England is consummate art—imagination become an aesthetic reality.

The collection, "Plays of Gods and Men," is worthy of representing Dunsany's power and charm of plot, climax, atmosphere, character and rhythmic style. It is his one volume that seems most sure of a fame outlasting the vogue accorded his works at present.

—M. K.

"Plays of Gods and Men," *Wisconsin Literary Magazine* 17, no. 2 (November 1917): 48, 50.

* * * * * * * * *

PSI—University of Wisconsin

Psi began the year with several additions. There are the new pledges, of course, nine splendid girls: Eleanor Hughes, Madison, a Psi sister; Frances Dwight, and Marjorie Lange, Madison; Leah Sutcliffe, Chicago; Marjorie Strock, Des Moines, Iowa; Lucille Chase, Greeley, Colorado; Isabel Lowe and Harriet Bartlett, St. Louis; and Helen Sackett, Springfield, Ohio. We have also new furnishings for our reception room, new silver and new china. All this magnificence was purchased when each active girl pledged herself to earn five dollars this summer for the fund. The money was raised in a variety of ways, from home house-keeping to selling poetry to *Snappy stories!* And we must mention Miss Macnaughton, a charming Canadian woman who is our new chaperon.

Last spring we lost many well-loved members to graduation: Mary Ashby, Gladys Buchner, Ruth Chase, Lois Clark, Mary Dunton, Georgia Ebbert, Laura Hayward, Betty Macgregor, Genevieve Penhallegon, Ruth Robertson, and Beatrice Taylor. The spring brought compensations, however, for Mary Ashby, Ruth Chase, Dorothy Bell, Helen Buell, Marjorie Kinnan and Mildred Sprague were elected to Phi Beta Kappa; the last four being juniors; and Dorothy Bell, Helen Cumming, and Marjorie Kinnan were elected to Mortar Board, the senior women's honorary society based on scholarship, womanliness, and service to the university.

The annual alumnæ banquet in June brought back many of the older girls, and we made most merry, except that war cast its shadow over our hearts unconsciously. Its influence was seen in rushing this fall, not only in Red Cross luncheons, war dinners, and the omnipresent knitting, but in the simplicity and informality of the parties. Psi has pledged herself to a thoughtful economy in dress, food, and entertainment. The Wisconsin fraternities have abandoned their formals this year. Alpha Omicron Pi, the newly installed fraternity, is located in an attractive home, and we have been assisting them in every way to gain a foothold. On the whole, with the usual enthusiasm of a university new year, and with the broader vision always given by convention, this time through Dorothy Bell and Hester Harper, we are looking forward to a busy season of larger service and deeper purpose. It seems to us a time when Kappa Alpha Theta must justify her existence by freedom from all pettiness, narrowness, and selfishness.

Marjorie Kinnan

"PSI—University of Wisconsin," *Kappa Alpha Theta Magazine*, November 1917, 71. MKR's report is dated 29 September 1917.

*   *   *   *   *   *   *   *   *

[The Case for the American Drama]

The case for the American Drama sways back and forth like a pendulum. Lovers of the art behind the footlights often become so discouraged, that the rare enthusiasms of the critics fail to lure them from the domestic cigar or mending or bridge-playing. But now and then some play or group of players cajoles them out of their resentment, and they begin to see glimmerings of a saffron, majestic dawn over the dark American stage.

It seems as if we get these insinuations of a glowing future, not from the conventional stage, with is rose-festooned interior sets that would make even the esthetics of a butcher feel dubious, but always from some independent theatrical organization, like the Portmanteau Players[29] and the little theaters, which have the courage of their convictions, and dare offer the public something frankly

---

29 The Portmanteau Players was presumably a traveling repertory company, but it is not further identified.

artistic or literary, perhaps both. Such experiments the general public, as distinguished from the appreciative minority, is free to take or leave; and it is a good sign, not so much for the experiments as for the public, that they have been successful. People enjoy Shaw and Dunsany when presented by artists.[30]

One production which may mark an epoch in the drama is the *Medea* of Euripedes as presented by Maurice Browne.[31] It is undoubtedly a stupendous thing. The striking color effects, gained largely through off-stage lighting, make Belasco stage effects comparatively mediocre.[32] The Gordon Craig doctrine has come into its own in the *Medea*.[33] The work of the Chorus is perfect; in rhythm, movement and voice-music it leaves nothing to be desired.

The *Medea* will probably not be popular with the average audience. It is too magnificent and consistently tense for the "pleasure" that the American public as a whole demands in its drama. But those who get anything at all from it,—get everything.

The Wisconsin Forum was responsible for bringing the Little Theater to Madison. Better drama, live, thought-stimulating drama, is one of the ideals of this courageous institution. There seems to be an idea among the suspiciously-minded of the University that any organization which stands quite frankly and sincerely for "that continual and fearless sifting and winnowing, by which alone the truth can be found,"[34] must be anarchistic and unqualifiedly devoted to whatever is extreme. But the Portmanteau and Washington Square Players,[35] and the Little Theater of Chicago, have not only failed to outrage anyone's sensibilities along any line, but have opened the eyes of many of us to what the drama can really do in the hands of idealistic craftsmen. Putting the University students in

---

30 George Bernard Shaw (1856–1950), Irish playwright and polemicist; Lord Dunsany (see the review "Plays of Gods and Men").

31 *Medea* (431 B.C.), a tragedy based upon the myth of Jason and his wife, Medea, was written by the Greek playwright Euripides (480 or 485–406 B.C.). Maurice Browne (1881–1955), producer, who along with his wife, the actress Nelly Van (Ellen Van Volkenberg), founded the Chicago Little Theater (1912), the vanguard for the American Little Theater movement.

32 David Belasco (1853–1931), playwright, director, and producer, was known for his imaginative stage settings and inventive lighting techniques.

33 Edward Gordon Craig (1872–1966), producer, actor, and screen designer, was especially known for poetic scene designs that reflected the spirit of the play.

34 The expression, "continual and fearless . . . truth can be found," a credo for the University of Wisconsin, is credited to the economist Richard T. Ely (1854–1943), who uttered it in defense of his academic freedom.

35 The Washington Square Players, an experimental theater group in New York, was founded in late 1914 and gave their first performance in February 1915.

touch with true drama, true esthetically and artistically, is only one of the aims of the Forum in its program of helping them to think honestly and clearly, without the befuddling of issues through conventionality—which is often another word for cowardice.

—M. K.

"[The Case for the American Drama]," *Wisconsin Literary Magazine* 17, no. 3 (December 1917): 58. MKR is listed as one of four editors in this issue of *WLM*.

*   *   *   *   *   *   *   *   *

Korlah

The eyes of Korlah, like a half-lit stage,
Are filled with dreams and dusk and shadowy things.
Who knows what fragrance of some ancient age
Still underneath those drowsy eyelids clings?

She speaks as would the dusky Sphinx aroused—
Old inenarrable, cryptic melodies—
Songs of an unseen, weary singer housed
In incensed temple by the sleepy seas.

Ah Korlah! Korlah! If the mist should rise,
And I should see beneath the veil—to thee–[36]
Should I still love those twilight-haunted eyes—
Or shrink as from the cobra's mystery?[37]

—Marjorie Kinnan

"Korlah," *Wisconsin Literary Magazine* 17, no. 3 (December 1917): 66. Korlah is unidentified.

36 Cf. the Romantic poet Percy Bysshe Shelley (1792–1822), "Lift Not the Painted Veil" (1824).

37 In ancient Upper Egypt, the cobra was a symbol of pharaoh, new life, and resurrection.

The Lullaby

Death sang a lullaby to me,
A little plaintive crooning as of wind
Tangled like cobwebs in a tree,
With storm-swept hill and wavering stars behind.

O dim, caressing melody,
Have you forgotten how I slipped away,
And laughing, would not list to thee—
Too much in love with life and mirth, to stay?

I left you humming in the night,
And when some other traveler came by,
Him you seduced with veiled twilight.
It must have been some other—'twas not I.

—Marjorie Kinnan

"The Lullaby," *Wisconsin Literary Magazine* 17, no. 3 (December 1917): 66.

*　*　*　*　*　*　*　*　*

Born to Blush Unseen

I have always tried to love Aunt Jenny; just as I try to love castor oil and mastoid operations and flannel nightgowns. They seem inevitable; and because they are necessary, I try to think affectionately of them. The theory seems all right, and I often wonder why it doesn't work. I should have been glad, willing and ecstatic to love Aunt Jenny, if it had ever seemed possible. But her theories on diet, her New Thought[38] and her dog Peter have always been as dynamite to my nerves. It is all most unfortunate.

You see, the very necessity of making myself agreeable to her made it that much harder. In my easy-going existence, I am a human marvel under circumstances when it doesn't make any difference at all. I missed my calling in not be-

---

38 An outgrowth of Transcendentalism, "New Thought," which emphasized the power of the mind, became popular in the 1890s.

ing a desert rose born to blush unseen. Although I am as plain as a clean sheet of paper, I feel that in a desert I would have been some blusher. But when duty calls I am a regular stick or a Missouri mule as regards my response. With Aunt Jenny I am a combination of both. For Aunt Jenny is the only person in the family with a few kopeks salted down, and I was the logical person to get them—if I had behaved myself. Aunt Jenny's kopeks wouldn't have made so much difference if I were the sort of person who could ever earn a living, honest or otherwise. But the very word "earn" makes me camp harder than usual in my rocking-chair. I should much prefer to have the ravens feed me manna. Ichabod—or was it Isaiah—had nothing on me.[39]

Do I sound morbid as I tell of it? I do want to keep my poise, no matter what happens; but I cannot but feel, under the circumstances, that my life and education have been wasted. I had counted so on the kopeks, and now that they have vanished like a sweet dream, I see that if the ravens don't feed me, God knows who will. I say that hopefully—I hope He does.

It all happened last Saturday when I had luncheon at Aunt Jenny's. I was nearly an hour late in arriving, and of course I was cross. I am seldom more than half an hour late. When Aunt Jenny floated across the hall to meet me, with her cold eyes glittering angrily, I threw my muff across the room. That was hardly the thing to do, I thought afterwards.

"Don't say a word!" I cried. "I can't stand another thing!"

Aunt Jenny folded her thin hands (I never *did* like thin people) across her stomach, and pursed her lips smugly.

"If you would only listen to me, and take up New Thought, you wouldn't have any nerves. I never allow myself to show irritation. Come. Luncheon is ready."

As I looked at the table, my head swam. It was the last straw. I clutched at the chair for support. Mixed emotions are as upsetting as mixed drinks. There were boiled fish without sauce, bran muffins and beets. Fish—bran muffins—beets! If you knew how I loathe them! How I loathe each one—how I grow dizzy at the sight of all three together! The deadly combination had never happened to me before. But I might have known I would get it at Aunt Jenny's, along with New Thought, and Peter, who was rubbing his watery nose against my clean hand. Yes, I remembered that those were the pettest of her dietary pets. She was serving

---

39 *Ichabod* in Hebrew means "without glory." He was born at the time the Philistines captured the Ark of the Covenant and was named to commemorate that tragic event. Isaiah is the biblical prophet through whom God revealed the defeat of the Babylonian king Sennacherib, the method for healing the Israelite king Hezekiah, as well as the coming of Jesus Christ and Mohammed. The faithful prophet whom the ravens fed at God's command—not manna but meat and bread—was Elijah (1 Kings 17:6).

a most miraculous nutritious and calming lunch. Fish! Fish to eat; Aunt Jenny's eyes were fish eyes; her mouth was the mouth of a carp. Brought up on bran and beets and New Thought; even Peter smelled of fish they had recently fed him. Fish!

And all the time I kept crooning to myself, "Oh God! I mustn't forget the kopeks! Oh God! I mustn't lose the kopeks!"

I was served. I took a huge mouthful of bran muffin, and swallowed it like a capsule. Then, desperately, I poked in some fish, for Aunt Jenny was watching me suspiciously. It simply would not go down. I felt as if I had been two days out on an ocean liner, with rough weather. I draped my napkin protectively across my face. Then I made a dive for my glass of water, gurgled happily, and was temporarily safe. The fish was down. After that, I felt privileged to dawdle. Aunt Jenny looked at me reprovingly as I played with the food on my plate.

"Are you playing marbles there?" she finally asked.

I begged her pardon and laid down my fork.

"You don't mean to say that your finickiness extends to food, do you?" she demanded. "Are you refusing to eat my carefully prepared, nourishing dishes in my own house? I shall probably not live much longer, and I should appreciate a little courtesy."

Aunt Jenny had been pulling that one-foot-in-the-grave line for some twenty years, so it seems as if it were about time for it to be true. I smiled soothingly.

"Dearest Aunt, how could you think such a thing! I'm enjoying everything immensely. And I'm so glad to be here with you to-day."

I was glad; about as glad as I would be at waking up in a crematory. I temporized by burying myself again in my glass of water. And then—then—the telephone rang, and Aunt Jenny was called upstairs to answer it.

How did I ever think to do it? I do not know. It seemed genius at first, but now I see that it was merely its close relation, madness. I looked at the platter in front of Aunt Jenny's plate, then at my plate. And with one eye on the door, I scooped up the fish on my plate and dumped it on the platter, where I messed it around until it could not be distinguished from its brethren. It was as much fun as making mud pies. When Aunt Jenny returned, I was scraping my plate with relish. She seated herself.

That woman is uncanny. I might have known—I might have known! Do you know, there may be something in New Thought, after all. Her eyes turned instinctively to the platter. And as she froze, I froze too.

"Well!" she said, smooth and icy as lemon sherbet, "did you eat up the parsley, too, while I was gone?"

And there, innocent as a primrose by the river's brim, in the middle of the fish on the platter sat the one spray of parsley which Aunt Jenny had conceded to my artistic temperament, and which she had carefully arranged on my portion as she served me. If ever I wanted anything inside of me, it was that parsley. I might have known—oh!—I might have known!

Still eyeing the parsley, Aunt Jenny said, "The wanderer seems to have returned."

Then, New Thoughtfully calm, "Won't you at least have the decency to leave?"

And I left, with Peter getting in my way as I did so, waggling his scrawny tail against me. The big oak door banging sonorously shut behind me, sounded like the door of a vault closing—a vault in a bank which had many kopeks.

And as I wandered down the street, I wondered if the ravens *would* feed me. It seems to me I'm just as deserving—certainly as trusting—as Ichabod. Or was it Isaiah—[?]

—Marjorie Kinnan

"Born to Blush Unseen," *Wisconsin Literary Magazine* 17, no. 3 (December 1917): 78, 80.

*   *   *   *   *   *   *   *   *

Nance of the Slums and the Smile

Calvary Alley, by Alice Hegan Rice. New York,
Century Co. [1918]: $1.35

Behind the author of *Mrs. Wiggs of the Cabbage Patch* is a background of tremendous humanity, maternal, kindly and understanding.[40] It never fails her; and that is why her latest book, *Calvary Alley*, is rich with truth and sweetness and humor. The characters are pulsingly human and unfailingly vivid. They are of the sort that one takes to one's heart, and makes a part of one's intimate literary acquaintanceship. Nance Molly is not a girl in a book; she is a friend that you would know at once, if you met her on the street. "She's got a personality that climbs right over the footlights."

---

40 Alice Hegan Rice (1870–1942), novelist and short-story writer. Rice's earlier novel, *Mrs. Wiggs of the Cabbage Patch* (New York: Century, 1901), a lighthearted social commentary on the residents of an area just west of Louisville, Kentucky, known as the "Cabbage Patch," was also her most popular.

The theme seems common enough; it is that of a ragmuffin [*sic*] of keen mind, and big, passionate, but untutored instincts, who develops a character as subtle, fresh and fragrant as a red rose, in spite of the unutterable squalor and hideousness of the Alley where she was bred. Nance was never a "good" child. She was too alive, too filled with animal spirits and daring. As Mrs. Snawdor, her stepmother, said of her, "She's got her faults. I ain't claimin' she ain't. But she ain't got a drop o' meanness in her. And that's more than I can say for some grown folks present."

The trouble with Nance was that no one had ever set up any standards for her. "She simply got the signals mixed." But if she "was to once git it into her head that a thing was right, she'd do it if it landed her where it landed her paw, at the foot of a forty-foot embankment with an engine a-top of her." And when, in Juvenile Court, after a battle royal with some "swells," the judge told her and her pal, "I believe you can both make good, but you'll have to fight for it,"——

Nance's irregular features broke into a smile. It was a quick, wide smile and very intimate.

"Fight?" she repeated, with a quizzical look at the judge. "I thought that was what we was pinched fer."

But she did fight for it. And when, on probation, and under the motherly influence of Mrs. Purdy, she began to see possibilities for the future, she asked of her chum, "Say, Dan, if folks are borned pore white trash, they don't have to go on bein' it, do they?"

Nance got her education at a Reform School. The result, while gratifying to her and to those who know "what is what," was disturbing to Calvary Alley. The inhabitants thereof absolutely refused to sleep with the windows open.

"What's the sense workin' yer fingers off to buy coal to heat the house if you go an' let out all the hot air over night? They filled up your head with fool notions, but you ain't goin' to work 'em off on us. You can just tell that old maid Stanley that when she's had three husbands an' five children an' a step, an' managed to live on less than ten dollars a week, it will be time enough for her to be learnin' new tricks!"

"Don't you ever want to clear out and go to the country?" asked Nance.

"Not me! I been fightin' the country all my life. It's bad enough bein' dirt pore, without goin' an' settlin' down among the stumps, where there ain't nothin' to take your mind off it."

So Nance grew up. She escaped Calvary Alley by her brief sojourn on the stage. But after tragedies of pocket-book and of heart, and after a hospital course in nursing, she found that Calvary Alley was where she wanted to be after all. But to tell you how, or why, and about Dan, and "Mac," the handsome, daredevil youth of wealth, would be to spoil the charm and humor, the pathos and drama for you, when you read the book yourself. And you mustn't expect Nance to become a perfect lady by the last page. She still uses slang, and is still full of mischief—but I think you'll like her better that way.

—M. K.

"Nance of the Slums and the Smile," *Wisconsin Literary Magazine*, 17, no. 3 (December 1917): 78, 80.

* * * * * * * * *

[The Old Order Hath Changed]

The old order hath changed so often, that it has become platitudinous even to mention the fact. But now that suffrage has at last become almost a certainty, and now that we have woman conductors and motormen and elevator "boys," isn't it delicious to think of the days of Grandmother, when, to be a perfect lady, one had to be a clinging vine, or at least a modest violet! Did you know that Grandmother had to walk down the street with her hands folded across her waist just so? That it was immodest, not to say immoral, to let one's ears show? It is even claimed that in marriage, husband and wife were really two souls with but a single thought—and that one his; but it hardly seems possible that the female of the species can have changed her mode of behavior so radically, in so short a time!

Yes, the change has come. And let us hope that out of the new relationships which must follow, will come a wonderful camaraderie[,] in the world of affairs a mutual respect, and a united striving for the Utopia which we cannot altogether relinquish. Do women as a whole realize the present opportunity for making good? Our young men have left their professions for the bigger, more immediate duty;[41] more will follow; our older men are consecrating much of their time, hitherto sacred to Mammon, to a finer cause; and there is not only room, but acute need, for women trained in every conceivable business. A college girl who is willing to devote some three months to a stenographic course, can step into splendid secretarial positions, previously filled by men. Big law offices, corpora-

---

41 MKR alludes to service in World War I, which did not end until 11 November 1918.

tions, insurance companies, industrial houses, all these can use her. Positions as managers of departments in large firms should come available for college graduates, if they are ready for hard work. There is almost no limit to the possibilities at this time. Success should be waiting with open arms for the determined young woman who studies law, medicine, agriculture, pharmacology; or who takes a commerce course, with an eye to big things.

Big things! There we have it! There is a growing number of women who are exactly as ambitious as men; who would be no more satisfied with marriage alone than would men. The doctrine which Browning gives us for men, in his *Meeting at Night* and *Parting at Morning*, is becoming the doctrine for many women. In saying farewell, you remember, the lover sees the sun rising over the sea; and says:

"And straight was the path of gold for him,
And the need of a world of men for me."[42]

With higher education and the changing order, women's needs have increased; for many of them a placid domesticity, or teaching in country schools as an alternative, is not enough for their eager minds. They too, want a world of men and affairs. Of course, there will always be a large percentage who honestly prefer "home-making" as a profession. That is all right, too. But to the keen, ambitious type who wants something else, this hint: get a professional or commercial training—and your own mentality, your own ambition, alone limit the peaks that you may reach.

—M. K.

"[The Old Order Hath Changed]," *Wisconsin Literary Magazine* 17, no. 4 (January 1918): 86. MKR is listed as one of six editors in this issue of *WLM*.

*   *   *   *   *   *   *   *   *

The Gypsy

All the word is fire to me,
And white flame is my kin,

---

42 Robert Browning (1812–89), Victorian poet. "Meeting at Night" and "Parting at Morning" both appeared in the collection *Dramatic Romances and Lyrics* (1845). MKR quotes lines 3-4 of the latter poem.

And red flame, loud with ecstasy,
I love to dress me in.

Red flame and white flame,
And blue flame when 'tis eve,
Life, and love—they're all the same,
And there to take or leave.

And oh! Some morning when the sun
Is burning up the sky,
I'll off to Bagdad, with someone
As fiery mad as I!

Marjorie Kinnan.

"The Gypsy," *Wisconsin Literary Magazine*, 17, no. 4 (January 1918): 91.

*   *   *   *   *   *   *   *   *

PSI—University of Wisconsin

The University seemed almost the same as in the old days, when at Home-coming time this fall, hundreds of "dear departeds" walked once more around the campus; many of them in uniform, very self-conscious in their new role, and very stern under the weight of great determination. Have you noticed how they have aged—these youngsters? The boys we have played with have become men over night, and although it hurts to see it, there is consolation in the fact that they seem infinitely finer and deeper than before. And it does seem so much harder, doesn't it, to stay home and just think! Handling a machine gun must be such a satisfactory way of expressing oneself.

Wisconsin has been unusually fortunate in the war speakers that have come to Madison. General Vignol of the French Army, and Lieutenant Montariol of the French aviation corps have given us a stirring realization of the indomitable French spirit when under unspeakable difficulties. When one hears that, at the moment when the order came from Joffre,[43] just before the battle of Marne,[44]

---

43 Joseph-Jacques-Césaire Joffre (1852–1931) was commander in chief of the French army from 1914 to 1916, and was instrumental in the victory at the Battle of Marne.

44 MKR alludes to the first Battle of the Marne in September 1914, the Allied offensive that halted the German advance on Paris.

for the French to halt their long retreat, and "not to yield one inch more of ground, France expects every man to die at his post"—when this came, the top of the Eiffel tower in Paris was visible; and when one sees pictures of the shell-torn fields taken from a French plane flying ten miles behind the German lines; then one gets a hint, in one's comfort and safety, of the realities of the war "over there."

Most of the university entertainments are giving their profits to war funds.

The huge annual Union Vodvil, scheduled for January 19, expects to so this; as do the three dramatic societies which are planning a series of six joint productions, consisting largely of one-acts from the repertoires of little theaters over the country.

In the university scholarship report for last semester, PSI ranked second among women's fraternities, being exceeded by Alpha Xi Delta by a few tenths of one point. Our pledges ranked first among fraternity pledges. I should add that our chapter at the time had fourteen more members than Alpha Xi Delta.

Since the last letter we have pledged Sada Buckmaster and Helen Gill, of Madison, and Ruth Jorndt of St. Louis. Sada Buckmaster was recently elected vice-president of the freshman class.

Marjorie Kinnan

"PSI—University of Wisconsin," *Kappa Alpha Theta Magazine*, January 1918, 176–77.

*   *   *   *   *   *   *   *   *

Fizz

What is Art? I am twenty-one and if I shall ever know, I know now. And I have decided:

Art is not milk; it is beer. It is not so much a food as a stimulant. It is not a necessity to incipient life but to insipid life. It is a taste; sometimes acquired, sometimes native. Some people can hardly swallow it; again, "Babies cry for it." To some natures it is a necessity; life is a vale of tears without it; and roseate and dizzy and double-mooned after a number of steins. To prove that Art is beer rather than milk: if you skim off just the top—don't you get foam instead of cream? You do.

Marjorie Kinnan.

"Fizz," *Wisconsin Literary Magazine* 17, no. 5 (February 1918): 109; reprinted, *Wisconsin Literary Magazine* 18, no. 1 (October 1918): 15. MKR is listed as one of six editors in the February 1918 issue of *WLM*.

*   *   *   *   *   *   *   *   *

Effectiveness

She knew that when she had on her black hat, with the aigrette, she was much more effective when viewed from the right side; for the shiny straw tilted up from her face, and lent a classical purity to her somewhat Celtic profile. On the right side, too, was the extra lock of hair that could be plastered into a slick elegant protrusion across her pink cheek. So, when she came into the library, she thanked Venus for that glimpse which showed her where He sat. I do not refer to the deity, but to the most desirable Sig Alph.[45] She was thus enabled to choose her seat, without apparent malice afore-thought. Easily, swaggering with the peculiar twist of the hips and shoulders that marks the female on parade, she sauntered to a seat at the table, on beyond him, on the other side of the aisle, which permitted her to give him that satisfactory profile of the right. She felt at once that he was looking at her. Complacently she passed her hand over her back-hair [*sic*]; rested her arm, Cleopatra-fashion, across the back of the neighboring chair that the white roundness of the flesh might be evident through the thin chiffon. Soulfully she lifted her eyes to the ceiling; sighed audibly and obviously; smiled, with uplifted chin, like a Saint Cecilia hearing the heavenly choir.[46]

She planned not to look at him for a long time, that he might indulge himself with the sight of that lovely profile; for after she had spoken to him, he would not dare to stare at her; and she, in her turn, could not plot her angle and her sighs and her smiles so freely, since he would know that she felt herself observed. So she posed; and posed again; and again. She allowed her face to take on one

---

45 Venus, "the deity," is the Roman god of love and beauty. The "Sig Alph" is a member of Sigma Alpha Epsilon fraternity.

46 Cleopatra (69–30 B.C.), last of the Ptolemaic rulers of Egypt, who legend says killed herself with an asp after the defeat of her lover, Marc Antony (83–30 B.C.). Saint Cecilia, patron Saint of music and musicians, told her husband, Valerian, on their wedding night that they could not consummate the marriage because she was betrothed to an angel, one who jealously guarded her body. After conversion, the angel revealed himself to Valerian, who then focused his life on good works.

expression after another, as if in the mental throes peculiar to Nazimova.[47] She frowned; she parted her lips; she closed her eyes; she rested her chin on two clasped hands. And for fifteen minutes she kept it up, knowing that each attitude was the height of effectiveness. Then:—

She looked up casually; she would notice him with surprise, and smile. She turned her head. And her eyes met, not his, but the anxious ones of her room-mate, sitting in his sacred place. The room-mate arose and hurried over to her. She was met with an acrid, peremptory:—

"How long have you been sitting there?"

"Why, I came in just a minute or so behind you. The man there went away as I came along, and I've been there ever since." She patted solicitously the hair under the black straw and aigrette, and went on with a worried air.

"Don't you feel well, honey? You've been making the funniest faces, and rolling your eyes so queer, I thought you must be awfully sick. You look all right now, but I must say, you were the weirdest looking thing I ever saw, when I sat over there watching you."

—Marjorie Kinnan.

"Effectiveness," *Wisconsin Literary Magazine* 17, no. 5 (February 1918): 132–33.

*   *   *   *   *   *   *   *   *

[Letter to the President of the Board of Regents]

February 1, 1918

Mr. Theodore M. Hammond, President of the Board of Regents of the University of Wisconsin,

Dear Sir: We, the editors of the Wisconsin Literary Magazine, wish to express our sincere regret that anything which we may have printed has given offense to you or to any other friend of the University.

---

47 Alla Nazimova (1879–1945), renowned theater actor and silent film star. In her first major film role, the 1916 film *War Brides*, she plays a woman who kills herself to avoid being imprisoned for protesting the king's policy of forced childbearing, by which women would provide soldiers to him for future wars.

We have felt so sure of our loyalty both to the University and to the country as to make it hard for us to realize that others could doubt it.

Whatever unwise criticism you find in our editorials was prompted by a feeling of love and loyalty to our University which we thought was unjustly assaulted. We sincerely regret that the stand we took has been the cause of considerable anxiety to you.

We realize that much of this anxiety would have been avoided if we had submitted the editorials to the University censor.

Allow us to express again our regret, and to assure you of our faith in our government and the cause of the war.

Very respectfully yours,
THE WISCONSIN LITERARY MAGAZINE
[signed by "M. Kinnan" and five other editors]

"[Letter to the President of the Board of Regents]," *Wisconsin Literary Magazine* 17, no. 5 (February 1918): 136. In a December 1917 editorial (*WLM* 17, no. 3), "P. A. A." (Philip A. Adler) frames the position of the magazine on the war: "we insist on keeping wide awake to current problems, to fight jingo-patriotism together with rabid radicalism, and refuse to dilute the high ideals set forth in President Wilson's proclamations with the trite and hackneyed honeyed democracy with which certain 'democratic' elements are now saturated." Claiming that he and his associates were "worthy trustees of the Ideals of Democracy," Adler closes, "if our critics consider this to be treason, we feel sorry for their powers of critical judgment" (58).

*   *   *   *   *   *   *   *   *

Laughter

I laugh, because the world I know
Is made of lies and death and pain;
Because such tragic people go
Across my path, and back again.

I laugh, because the end I see
For men is mists and silences;
Because romance must ever be
Mother to tears and penances.

I laugh, because the flame I sought
Has burned my soul like autumn chaff;
But I must live, for I am caught;
And so, to live, I laugh—I laugh.

Marjorie Kinnan.

"Laughter," *Wisconsin Literary Magazine* 17, no. 6 (March 1918): 154. MKR is listed as one of nine editors in this issue of *WLM*. Charles Rawlings, later MKR's first husband, is now also listed as an editor.

*　*　*　*　*　*　*　*　*

[On Poetry and Vachel Lindsay]

Let us assume that we all have souls. That will flatter some of you; some it will insult. But whether one wants it or not, there is something idealistic enough in one who pursues an education, or allows it to pursue him, to be called a soul-nucleus. Of course, some are more highly developed than others; there are some students who actually possess souls recognizable as such; and I do not refer to Phi Betes.[48] In fact, soul may be the cause of man's flunking out of the University; he may have a truly spiritual longing for the ideal, which leads him along the Middleton road[49] or to a sorority house, to the detriment of his standing with the faculty. That is not wild oats; he is not wholly to be condemned; that is spiritual restlessness, or soul—misdirected. That student has merely to discover that the ideal of soul-satisfaction is never to be found in wine or women; after enough headaches and heartaches he will turn elsewhere; and his pitiful, starved spirit will find real food; and may, some day, put forth a blossom and fruit. I believe that every one of us here has undreamt-of spiritual possibilities; put the baby on the right diet, and he'll grow.

Where is food for the soul to be found? How can one raise a whole soul from a half-soul; a half-soul from a soul-germ? Not, certainly, by starving it; not even by Hooverizing.[50] One must set a lavish table for the spirit; its appetite once

---

48 "Phi Betes" is the honorary academic society Phi Beta Kappa, to which MKR was elected in April 1917.

49 "Middleton road"—that is, the road to Middleton, Wisconsin, now a northwest suburb of Madison.

50 William Henry Hoover (1849–1932) began manufacturing electric vacuum cleaners in 1908. "Hooverizing" is thus to be cleaned by using a Hoover vacuum.

aroused, it is omnivorous. There are many diets recommended, many tonics and many stimulants. But whatever else may be good, one food is guaranteed to bring results. And that? Is poetry. Now, don't stop reading in disgust. Don't you know that poetry may be appetizing as well as nourishing? That, like dentistry, it may be painless, according to the man doing the work? If one dentist hurts unnecessarily, don't you try another? Of course. Why not do the same thing with your poets? Don't condemn them all because the first one makes you sick at your stomach. Poetry can, and should, appeal to "the public." All you need do is start easily, and stick to it.

I have often wondered if it would not be helpful to know one's first poetry through contemporary poets. Poetry from a modern, even a poetically and temporarily conventional, point of view is bound to be closer to one's own line of thought, than poetry, no matter how magnificent and immortal, of a generation or many generations ago. As long as there are any who think of poetry as a different language and a thing apart, would not contemporary poetry along contemporary lines of interest, best break the ice? Poetry dealing with things of our immediate knowledge, voiced in images comprehensible to the modern mind, ought logically be a substantial preparation for poetry in general.

I have in mind Vachel Lindsay.[51] I think perhaps I had him in mind all along. It seems to me that any young college man or woman would care more for all poetry, after Vachel Lindsay as an introduction. To begin with, he is understandable. He is essentially and vigorously American. *The Sante Fé Trail*, *The Calliope*, and *The Building of Springfield* are triumphs of a keen and loving Americanism.[52] That gives one something tangibly appealing to start with. One is fascinated with what he has to say about the things of one's own knowledge. Then gradually his vision, his stupendous and beauty-filled insight into great forces, grips one; one becomes intoxicated with his rhythms; and behold, one has an appreciation of poetry that may be used on Browning or Landor or Shelley or Homer![53] Of course, it must be admitted that Lindsay would serve better for

---

51   Nicholas Vachel Lindsay (1879–1931) was especially known for his powerful rhythms and vivid imagery, realized in his dramatic readings.

52   "The Sante-Fé Trail" (1914) compares the cacophony of automobile horns to the "sweet" song of a representative bird, "Rachel-Jane," along a Kansas highway. "The Calliope [The Kallyope Yell]" (1913) voices the sounds and relationships of the circus calliope to that of the kallyope, or the poet himself. "On the Building of Springfield [Illinois]" (1913) creates a utopian vision of a city transformed from conflict to beauty. "The Chinese Nightingale" (1915), carrying on the long tradition of that immortal bird in poetry, is a poem of lost realizations found.

53   Robert Browning; Walter Savage Landor (1775–1864), Victorian essayist; Percy Bysshe Shelley; Homer, Greek epic poet.

this purpose than most contemporary versifiers, for, whatever his limitations, he has an undoubted genius and power; he is a real poet. *The Chinese Nightingale* stands alone in modern poetry for sheer beauty and music.

Try reading Lindsay, you who "don't care much for poetry." Try other moderns. *Read them aloud.* Read them in different moods. Fit them to your moods. And see if it doesn't satisfy something that beer or canoeing won't touch. Expand your poetry—reading as widely and as fast as you can. See if your soul doesn't grow. Just see!

—M. K.

"[On Poetry and Vachel Lindsay]," *Wisconsin Literary Magazine* 17, no. 7 (April 1918): 169–70. MKR is listed, along with Charles Rawlings, as one of ten editors for this issue of *WLM*.

*   *   *   *   *   *   *   *   *

Witter Binner [*sic*] and Vachel Lindsay

Two well-known American poets, Vachel Lindsay and Witter Bynner, have paid the *Wisconsin Literary Magazine* the very high compliment of allowing poems of theirs to be printed here for the first time.[54] Both these men have shown a friendly interest in Wisconsin students and their literary aspirations; we are deeply grateful for it. Witter Bynner shows his sympathy with the young aspirer in a poem from *The Little Book of Modern Verse*,[55] entitled *The New Life*.

> Perhaps they laughed at Dante in his youth,
> Told him that truth
> Had unappealably been said
> In the great masterpieces of the dead:—

---

54 Lindsay was especially known for his powerful rhythms and vivid imagery, realized in his dramatic readings. Harold Witter Bynner (1881–1968), Harvard-educated poet whose role in the *Spectra* (1917) hoax had recently been uncovered. The new Bynner poems that appear in this issue of *WLM* are "A Hymn against Jehovah," a bitter call to reject Jehovah because he is the god of war, and "Republic to Republic. 1776–1917," a song of the intimate relationship between France and the United States (both appear on page 174). The new Lindsay poems are "The Turtle," described by MKR at the close of her introduction, and "To Rachel M.," a whimsical Valentine poem (both appear on page 175).

55 *The Little Book of Modern Verse*, edited by Jessie B. Rittenhouse (1869–1948) (Boston: Houghton Mifflin, 1917).

Perhaps he listened and bowed but his head
In acquiescent honor, while his heart
Held natal tidings,—that a new life is the part
Of every man that's born,
A new life never lived before,
And a new expectant art;
It is the variations of the morn
That are forever, more and more,
The single dawning of the single truth.
So answers Dante to the heart of youth!

Curiously enough, not one of the Lindsay or Bynner poems printed in this issue is in the poet's most typical vein. Bynner is unquestionably most at home in charming, whimsical lyrics of a peculiarly haunting grace. Take the following, for instance:

To No One in Particular[56]
Locate your love, you lose your love,
Find her, you look away;
Now mine I never quite discern,
But trace her every day.
She has a thousand presences,
As surely seen and heard
As birds that hide behind a leaf
Or leaves that hide a bird.

Single your love, you lose your love,
You cloak her face with clay;
Now mine I never quite discern—
And never look away.

Vachel Lindsay is in a playful mood in the two bits he gave us. *The Turtle* was written for his two little nieces, aged 2 and 4, I believe. Half the joy in it is in hearing Mr. Lindsay recite it. In fact, his reading of his poems always adds joy to the things themselves.

M.K.

"Witter Binner [*sic*] and Vachel Lindsay," *Wisconsin Literary Magazine* 17, no. 7 (April 1918): 174. Bynner's name is misspelled in the title.

---

56 "To No One in Particular," *Poetry Magazine* 8 (1916): 300.

Babylon Undying

I build me dreams, when day is done,
When twilight lulls the drowsy sun,
And soothes the fevered sky;
And all my visions, one by one,
Trooping back to Babylon,
Like horsemen, whistle by.

They gallop here, they gallop there,
They find me temples everywhere—
In many-storied Babylon;
And gardens hanging in the air
Burst into orchid blooms that wear
The purple of the Tyrian.[57]

O city proud in flame and gold,
Whom priests of Bel and Istar told,[58]
'Thou shalt be ever Babylon,'
The sullen fates could not unfold—
A doom to strike thy spirit cold—
Thou wert not for oblivion!

Live on, O city of delight!
Leap into memory from the night!
Build palaces in dreams!
Thine ancient kings may yet invite
Man's beauty-loving inner sight
To share thy fabled gleams.

O! in my heart I'll rear a shrine,
Burn sandalwood and pour out wine,

---

57 MKR alludes to the city of Babylon's legendary hanging gardens and to the Phoenician city of Tyre, the mercantile economy of which was based upon its production of "Tyrian purple," a dye derived from two species of sea snails, *Murex brandaris* and *Murex trunculus*.

58 Bel (also Ba'al) is the Babylonian god of the earth (as opposed to Anu, the god of the heavens). Istar is the Babylonian goddess of love and war.

To unforgotten Babylon!
Thy courts, thy walls, thy gods, are mine—
My worship and my songs are thine—
Thou reignest still, O Babylon!

Marjorie Kinnan

"Babylon Undying," *Wisconsin Literary Magazine* 17, no. 7 (April 1918): 183.

*　*　*　*　*　*　*　*　*

The Monastery

Over the wall is—home. The window of my cell
Stares at my truancy as if to ask,
'Why should a mission to the town mean this—
A day-long absence in the woods and hills?'
It seems so strange, the monastery there,
So questioning, so alien; but I see
The duties filling up the sunset hour,
Picture the others passing to and fro.
There are long balconies above the court,
With lattice-work that checkers out the sun;
And dark-cowled forms behind stalk up and down,
Telling their *Pater Nosters* on the beads.
The court, a still oasis buried deep
Within the monastery's breast, is green
With slender blades of grass and myrtle leaves,
Where spring has wantoned in, and left a kiss.
Shadows are gathering about the shrines,
The tapers down the halls will soon be lit,
When Father André makes his shuffling round,
Dressing the saints and altars for the night.
I know that silence fills the corridors,
Save when a windy sigh goes rustling through,
A door swings wide, and in the distance hums
A resonant chant—then the door's shut again,
Leaving an echo and a memory.

Here in the grove outside the wall I lie,
Where the last ribbon'd sunlight filters in
Between the saplings; shadows here are bold
And purple, warm as the damp earth under me.
Silence is here, as there; but breathing deep,
Pregnant, alive—not ominous and chill.
I had not meant to loiter here so long—
This means a penance and a fast for me,
Who should be now before the crucifix.
Something like hands has kept me here tonight,
Something in tree and bird and wind and sky,
That would not let me go away again.
I must go back—must throw aside this flower
Tight-crushed within my fingers; when it's gone
I'll be myself again; and can go back.

Arbutus[59]—it was waiting here for me—
It was not odor—it was suffering
Borne on the breath of April to my soul,
Out of a past long-buried and forgot.
The earthly incense, passion-sweet, rose up,
And passion-painful curled about my heart,
Bringing remembrance of warm years of Spring,
Filled with arbutus, filled with wind—with life.
And then I digged it, under the mould
Laid bare the fragrance of its small pink face,
And held it to me, drinking in the pain.
I could not get enough, it seemed; must strain
To breathe the utmost of the agony in—
Such, I remember now, were love—and death—
And all the aching mortal things I knew
So long ago.

    Ah, it was sweet to taste
That mad and stabbing passion once again,
That wrestling of the flesh and soul to touch

---

59 "Arbutus" (*Epigaea repens*) is a creeping evergreen plant with fragrant pink and white flowers;
it blooms in spring and is also known as the mayflower or ground laurel.

The infinity of beauty crowned with stars!
To find eternity through hungry sense,
That needed God to be quite satisfied!
I felt it all again; the throbbing surge
That used to stir me like an organ-peal
Thrilling into the cloister; life aflame,
Calling me, world to man, and God to man—
Daring to fight, despite the suffering!
Arbutus—poignant—crushed between my palms—
Burning my heart out with the love of life—
I must go back—the vesper bell has rung—
Twilight is filling up the grove; the stars
Are showing past the monastery dome
Like an old painting. Father André there,
Holding the lamp above the gate. I'll go,
And take my chastisement as is my due—
I'll leave the arbutus here—I have been mad—

                                        Marjorie Kinnan

"The Monastery," *Wisconsin Literary Magazine* 17, no. 8 (May 1918): 205–6. MKR is listed, along with Charles Rawlings, as one of twelve editors in this issue of *WLM*. It is the last issue in which they are listed as editors.

*   *   *   *   *   *   *   *   *

Mother's Misplaced Confidence

"Ed Franklin leaves for Urbana tonight," I announced to the family. "He stopped me on State street today to kiss me good-bye;"[60] and I winked at mother.

Artie boy looked at me earnestly.[61]

"Did you really kiss him good-bye?" he asked seriously.

"Why, sure. Don't you think that's the least a girl can do for the fellows de-

---

60 Urbana, Illinois, location of the University of Illinois, is approximately 250 miles from Madison, Wisconsin. State Street, the main thoroughfare of Madison, runs due west from the State Capitol building (completed July 1917).

61 "Artie boy" is MKR's brother, Arthur Kinnan Jr., and the "mother" is Ida May Traphagen Kinnan.

fending her? I told him to kiss me as often as he wanted to, just so I got home by five o'clock."

Artie boy studied me.

"Ask mother," I said, "if I'm not the kind of girl that would let them do it."

He leaned towards me. "Mother would say you aren't"—he watched me suspiciously for either a blush or a grin—"but," he announced decisively, "darned if I'm so sure."

Marjorie Kinnan

"Mother's Misplaced Confidence," *Wisconsin Literary Magazine* 18, no. 1 (October 1918): 11.

*   *   *   *   *   *   *   *   *

Beginning Early

The Little Lady deposited her last three peppermints on the mantel, and smoothed the ruffles of her short, saucy skirt.

"Why, aren't you going to eat them?"

"No, I'm saving them for Daddy. I'll give them to him when he comes home."

"That's splendid, Goldie," said Mother.

"Yes. And then he'll say to me, 'No, dearie, YOU eat them.'"

She folded her pink small hands together, and smiled with all the triumph of smug virtue.

"And then I'll eat them!"

—Marjorie Kinnan

"Beginning Early," *Wisconsin Literary Magazine* 18, no. 1 (October 1918): 11. Considering the autobiographical element in the previous companion poem, it seems likely that the "Little Lady" is MKR, and the "Daddy" is Arthur Kinnan Sr.

The Newspaper Years

᎐ᎥᎢᎥᐧ

1919–1928

Perhaps the most difficult time in MKR's life began after her graduation from the University of Wisconsin. She was an idealist, full of hope for the future, particularly her future. After a stormy courtship, she finally was married to her Wisconsin beau Charles A. Rawlings Jr., who joined her in New York City after a stint in the army. MKR's Homeric dreams, those experienced by many aspiring creative writers, were almost immediately dashed upon the rocks of reality. New York seemed oblivious of her presence. Her stories and poems were rejected, most often without comment. Nearly broke, and not wanting to retreat back to her mother's arms in Madison, she found a job with the YWCA and began to write promotional ads and features. It was good work for her because it taught her how to cut through to the essence of a story. Gone were the romantic trappings she took on during her student days. Her job at the YWCA soon came to an end, as did Charles's at an export company. The couple was confronted with the practical necessity of moving on with their lives. In 1919, they moved to Louisville, Kentucky, where they took positions on the *Courier-Journal*. MKR thrived as a feature writer. She enjoyed the "hunt" associated with reporting and soon was honing her penchant for description that was to become a hallmark of her later writing. Charles, however, was restless. In 1921, they moved to Rochester, New York, the home of Charles's parents. He was soon on the road as a traveling salesman, and his Willy Loman–like visions of grandeur were out of concert with his abilities. Once again, fortune stepped in. Bored with the duties of home life and suffocated by the proximity of her in-laws, MKR sought work again as a newspaper writer. It was not lucrative, but it kept the bills paid and allowed her to continue to develop her craft. Her stories, including an autobiographical novel, *Blood of My Blood*, continued to be summarily rejected. Charles's failures as a salesman did not help. In 1928, frustrated with the publishing and corporate worlds of the North, they moved to the South, where they bought an orange grove in the remote North Central Florida hamlet of Cross Creek. It would prove to be the most important decision of MKR's personal life and literary career.

*   *   *   *   *   *   *   *   *

The Blue Triangle Follows the Switchboard

For the first time in history a great war has been carried to a successful conclusion with women recognized officially as part of the army. The women telephone operators of the Signal Corps have played an enviable part, not even surpassed by the work of the nurses, for in many instances their units were located only twelve miles behind the firing line, and were subjected to all the dangers of those within range of the sweeping Teuton guns. These girls were under the same military rule as the Sammies in the trenches.[1] They had to have passes galore, had to report to their superior officer, the chief operator. Discipline regulated their comings-in and their goings-out and in reward for their service they wore the symbols of the trust of a nation on their collars,—the letters "U.S."

It is interesting to know that the work of housing these units was also entrusted officially to women. The Government asked the Young Women's Christian Association, prepared for such service by its equipment, personnel, and fifty-two years of experience in housing women, to look after the physical welfare of every unit which arrived in France. This was successfully achieved in every instance, though the difficulties of obtaining lodgings, servants, and rations in headquarters towns were almost insurmountable, and the fearful cost of bare necessities made it a real problem to keep expenses down within the reach of the women, who shared all costs of the housing on a coöperative basis. The fifteen dollars per week which it usually averaged to live was considered an achievement of genius by the interested army men, who had had to pay as much as seven dollars for a single dinner in Paris.

The houses were almost always attractive old French establishments, sometimes with the quaintest of gardens and the most ravishing of shrubbery. Even the officers flocked to the side of the grate-fire and absorbed the undeniable air

---

1   "Sammies"—that is, those fighting for Uncle Sam.

than enough work for all. It has been estimated that six million days of toil are necessary to rebuild the despoiled cities and villages. The women must carry a large share of the burden of peace.

The French women, thrust headlong into industry by the fearful exigencies of the war, which, says M. Clemenceau,[7] "could not have gone on twenty minutes without them," were totally unprepared for their share in the economic life of the nation. Their indomitable will and energy made them equal to the task; but in the intense drive of the days ahead, which must rebuild a material and spiritual foundation for the generations to come, these women need a special knowledge. They must see clearly their own relation to the new social order. Nothing must be haphazard. They must know what they are doing, where and why they are going.

French women of political and social prominence are now devoting themselves to the problem. A commission was recently appointed by the National Council of French Women to study the conditions of women's life in France, and the various organizations for women's welfare. This commission consists of the Comtesse du Portales, Mme. Lucie Jules Siegfried, President of the National Council, and Mme. Max Lazard. Mme. Avril de Saint Croix, acting as a representative of the French government, has also given long study to the woman. They have come to a striking conclusion. Through their study of the Foyers conducted by the Y.W.C.A. in France during the war,[8] they have come to feel that the secret of the Association's success lies in a *co-operation, a directness and a "team-work,"* that are truly American. Get women to work together, whole-souled, with far-seeing understanding—women for women and for society—and intricate problems of the woman in industry, of social morality, of democracy, begin to straighten out. The result is, that French *intellectuelles* are uniting with the French government and with the industrial women who benefit by the Foyers, to ask the American Y.W.C.A. to stay in France and continue its work until French leaders can be trained to learn the underlying principles and to assume the responsibility for women's needs.

During the war there were fifteen *Foyers des Alliées* conducted by the Y.W.C.A., located at the great munition factories, such as those in Tours, Lyon, St. Eti-

---

7   Georges Clemenceau (1841–1929), the premier of France who led the French delegation at the Paris Peace Conference and who lost the election of January 1920 because he had been unable to secure harsher war penalties against the Central Powers.

8   As the Hostess Houses were established for Americans serving in France, the "Foyers" [homes or hostels] served a similar function for the French. They were also called *Foyers du Soldat*. More than 1,500 such homes existed by the end of the war and were intended as places of refuge for battle-weary nurses, workers, and soldiers.

enne, Montlucon, Is-sur-Fille, Bourges, Roanne and Romarantin. Sometimes the Foyer was only a shack; again it was more pretentious, as at Lyon, where twelve thousand girls came daily. But in any case it was a friendly, intimate refuge from the monotony and strain of war and of hard labor; a welcoming place that belonged exclusively to the girls and women of the factory; a place where they might come at noon for rest, recreation and wholesome food from the cafeteria; where at night they might gather to sing, dance, talk and forget their fatigue and their individual sorrows for a time; where they might meet their friends, men or women. At the larger foyers they might even attend classes in English, stenography, gymnastics and domestic science. The Foyer is a means to an end. The sequence might run something like this:

The woman that works must be kept healthy and happy through the proper recreation, exercise, food and mode of thought. When she is happy and healthy she is a better worker, a better woman, and a better citizen to her country. A democratic, constructive co-operation among women is the keynote of the Foyer in attaining its end.

The following letter, directed to Miss Mary L. Dingman, *Directrice de l'Ouvrage Industriel de l'Y.W.C.A.*, who established the Foyers, expresses the attitude of the French government on the meaning of the work.

"Paris, France.

Mademoiselle:

"I must express to you the greatest satisfaction and most sincere thanks of the French government for the services rendered the women working in the government factories, through the establishment of the Foyers.

"These Foyers have been excellent means of bettering the physical conditions and morale of our workers. They have been used constantly by the women workers, who have found in them new elements of dignity and social education.

"I must thank you here for the part you personally have taken in bringing about the result, and I hope that your work will not disappear with the war, but will continue to be carried on for the development, ever more extended, of the principles of social solidarity which inspires it.

"Pray accept, mademoiselle, this further expression of my gratitude and respects."

Ministre de l'Armament et des Fabrications du Guerre,

(Signed) Loucheur.[9]

---

9   Louis Loucheur (1872–1931), French industrialist, would be the chief economic negotiator at the Paris Peace Conference.

Mrs. William Adams Brown, vice-president of the War Work Council of the Y.W.C.A., who returned in December from France, brought with her statements from the most varied sources, conveying the wishes of the French people in regard to American Y.W.C.A. aid to reconstruction in France. As a result of those statements and of Mrs. Brown's survey of Association work in France, the Foyers for women and girls in industry are to be continued; American women are to stand by them until French women and organizations working for women can prepare their policies and their leaders. The Foyers formerly located near munition factories now closed are being moved to the cities which are the industrial centers of their regions.

"Do not leave us," say the girls who must continue to work. They have begged the secretaries in charge of the Foyers not to go away now that peace has come. And the promise has been made.

"As long as you need us we will stay," is the reply of the Y.W.C.A.

A new line of inspiration and enjoyment is now being inaugurated in the form of education exhibits, to be made largely through the Foyers, and consisting of charts, moving pictures, posters and photographs, planned to give an idea of American life, particularly among women and girls. There is a "Better Babies" film showing the most modern methods of infant care. A series of National Child Welfare charts dealing with the following subjects is included in the exhibit:

Prevention of tuberculosis in childhood; healthy babies and children; prenatal care for saving mothers' and babies' lives; early habit-forming; growth through play; growth through study and growth through work.

Showing the work that women are now doing successfully, are pictures of women engaged in various sorts of factories other than war emergency ones, and in work from clerking to farming.

With the increased social responsibility of women the world is holding them accountable, demanding their utmost effort. All women, whatever their race or creed, are sisters—daughters of the modern order—servers of humanity. In this era of rebuilding, French and American women are joining hands with one purpose—to be constructionists; to make industries, mining, manufacturing, canning and the rest, work of any sort, a means, like the Foyer, to an end; to build so well that *liberté, égalité, fraternité*, become incorporated into the social, economic and spiritual fabric, not only of France and America, but of all the world.

Marjorie Kinnan

"Women As Constructionists," *New France* (1919): 434–35.

Through Three Revolutions

A Woman's Experience in Modern Russia

It happened in Russia—the northern Russia of famine, biting cold, revolution and blood. They say that she was the only American woman in Russia through it all. She was in Moscow and Petrograd long after she had been warned that she was in fearful peril if she stayed. And so the American troops who have known her and her work, have called her the sister of the boy who stood on the burning deck![10]

She arrived in May, 1917. Revolution number one had removed the czar from power, and Prince Lvoff was at the head of the Provisional Government.[11] In Petrograd, her first home, she found the streets crowded. The air was tense and filled with a seething unrest. Crowds of workmen everywhere had left their occupations, and stood on the corners indulging the great Russian national pastime—talk. A vague terror looked from the eyes of strangers on the streets. The fear of anarchism hung over the whole city.

Here in Petrograd Miss Boies[12] established a recreation center for girls—girls over whom dark clouds were constantly hovering. And the actual running of the center, similar to those kept up by the Y.W.C.A. in the United States, was not as simple as it sounds.

Russian Reasonableness

Elements other than revolution were in the way. The girls came directly from the factories, and had to be fed a little something in order to have their strength and energy for their classes. Miss Boies was told that it was physically impossible to obtain provisions. The ministries were constantly changing, and any one versed in politics knows that one is never "in with" more than one faction. There being twenty-one political groups at the time, it was inconceivable that a mere

---

10 An allusion to Felicia Hemans (1793–1835), "Casabianca" (1826), a popular poem about a French boy who perished on ship standing resolutely by his father at the Battle of the Nile (1798).

11 The initial Russian Revolution took place in February 1917. Czar Nicholas II abdicated in March and was executed along with his family in July. The provisional government (23 March until 21 July), led by the Russian statesman Prince Georgy Lvov (1861–1925), was unable to maintain civic authority.

12 Elizabeth Boies, a graduate of Smith College, was one of many women sent into foreign service by the YWCA.

woman should procure concessions for some two hundred girls. Miss Boies explains how she procured food from every ministry in turn.

"The Russian has an innate reasonableness. All that is necessary is to insist on discussing the question, and discussing it as often as is needed to come to an understanding. I simply explained what we were trying to do, and invariably found only interest and sympathy."

"Won't You Walk into My Parlor?"

"Did you know that Prince Lvoff was ordered to be executed three different times—and each time persuaded his captors, by amiably chatting with them, not to commit such an unpleasant act? Time and time again guards came to our house in Moscow to requisition our supplies. But each time I drew them into my parlors"—here Miss Boies chuckled, thinking, I would swear, of the well-known spider[13]—"and had a talk with them about—oh, just everything—and they always went away with the friendliest feeling—and without the flour and sugar they had come for."

Six months later, after her cable to "Send them over like cannon-balls" had brought four more Y.W.C.A. secretaries to Petrograd, Elizabeth Boies put her toothbrush in her pocket and went to Moscow.

In the meantime another revolution had shaken Russia. Kerensky had risen against Lvoff, and finally on July twenty-third, had been given unlimited power by the Workmen's and Soldiers' Council. Classes in Petrograd had to stop when the confusion was at its height and the streets were dangerous. Then came the Korniloff fiasco, when the troublesome commander of the Russian armies captured Halicy, and was later repressed in his attempt at a counter-revolution.[14] The Czar was deported to Siberia. In Moscow, on September second, Kerensky "cleaned out" a group of anarchists who were plotting to have the black flag flown triumphant over the city. Kerensky pronounced Russia a republic. And at

13   MKR refers to a poem by Mary Howitt (1799–1888), "The Spider and the Fly," which begins "'Will you walk into my parlor?' said the Spider to the Fly." At the end of the poem, the spider forces the fly into the parlor, and "she ne'er came out again!" (line 40).

14   What MKR describes as the second revolution features the removal of Lvov as prime minister and the succession of Aleksandr Kerensky (1881–1970), who ruled the provisional government from 21 July until 8 November 1917. After Kerensky took power, he named General Lavr Kornilov (1870–1918) as his commander in chief, in part because he had routed the Austrians at the Galician (now Ukrainian) city of Halicz ("Halicy") on 8 July. A month later, Kornilov attempted a military coup against Kerensky in Petrograd. Kerensky had him relieved of command on 9 September and placed him under house arrest. Kornilov called on his Cossacks to rescue him. Unsure of his own generals, Kerensky was forced to call on the assistance of others to put down the rebellion, including the Bolsheviks, who gained substantial power from the "fiasco."

the same time that Miss Boies went into Moscow, the government was moved there from Petrograd.

Here Mme. Morozoff,[15] the owner of a large linen factory, offered to put a beautiful hall and art gallery, which adjoined her residence, at the disposal of Miss Boies in order to begin work among the women and girls of the city. Mme. Morozoff also provided a sun parlor, classroom, corridor, two small rooms and a kitchenette, in which classes were established in Russian, English, French, stenography and gymnasium work. Because of the shooting in the streets after dark, classes were held from four until eight.

When the girls arrived, they were served black-bread sandwiches and tea, with a quarter of a lump of sugar for each cup. To the astonishment of the Russian women, class distinctions dropped away in the gym classes and the informal parties like dead leaves. Day after day slim princesses worked side by side with peasant girls and with wives of Russian officials of all factions, cutting dresses or trimming hats at long tables.

Dealings with the Bolsheviki

In November, bedlam once again broke loose when Kerensky tottered and fell. The Bolsheviki, under Lenine [*sic*] and Trotzky, took over the reins of government[16]—and Elizabeth Boies took up her dealings with them.

"We would have dealt with the czar if he had been returned to power," said Miss Boies. "Our concern was not with politics."

Politics played their part, however. An attempt to capture the post-office stirred Moscow. Plots, counter-plots and insurrections rumbled under the life of the city, orderly on the surface, like hot lava smoldering in a volcano. Over this bed of coals Miss Boies continued quietly, as did the majority of people—so accustomed to the revolutionary atmosphere that they could live normal lives within it. In her home on one of Moscow's two great boulevards, Miss Boies continued to plan and organize.

---

15 Perhaps Daria Morozoff, the wife of Feodor Morozoff; they were forced to flee Russia during the revolution and ended up in Kobe, Japan, where he became a chocolatier.

16 In the third revolution of MKR's account, Kerensky and the provisional government were overthrown by the Bolsheviks, led by Vladimir Lenin (1870–1924), who took power in early November 1917. The Communist Party thus was born, with Lenin as its leader. His comrade Leon Trotsky (1879–1940) was made the first people's commissar of foreign affairs, with the main task of negotiating a peace with Germany, which he bungled by withdrawing from peace talks (10 February 1918). After Lenin's death, Trotsky would lose the ensuing power struggle to another of their comrades, Joseph Stalin (1879–1953).

It all sounds like the Brothers Grimm,[17] doesn't it? No one would be surprised to have Elizabeth Boies discover dragons with horny tails in Russia—and then proceed to "persuade" them to cooperate! Instead of discovering medieval dragons, however, she has discovered something of far greater interest to American women—the medieval Russian woman—who isn't so medieval after all.

Praise for Russian Women

"It is the Russian women who have kept their country from going further astray," says Miss Boies. "While the men were asking for freedom, the women kept things going. They laid railroad tracks, and sidings. The shoveled dirt; did trucking and repairing; they were found at work all about the stations. The Battalion of Death?[18] It was the most natural thing in the world for them!"

"Neechevo!"

"The Russian woman has powers of self-sacrifice, of which we rather selfish American women can never dream. Her creed is an Eastern one—Western women must realize that first of all—a creed of the abasement of the individual. Before eternity, the individual life or death has no value."

"That is why there have been so many suicides. Life is so confused these days, over there, so seemingly hopeless, that when it gets to be too much to manage it seems logical to them to do away with it. Don't you see how to such women, the Battalion of Death was a wonderful medium for sacrificing themselves to an ideal?"

At this point Elizabeth Boies has a message for American women. They must first of all understand these Easterners; they must sympathize, for the Russian knows a friend intuitively. And they must cooperate with Russian women, to help bring about the law and order and the realization of practical ideals for which women the world over have always longed. *Their contribution to Russia is the American ability to play a losing game; to fight to the last ditch, and then fight again, and again.*

The Russians suffer, suffer, suffer. They try one remedy—it does not succeed; they throw up the whole thing. "*Neechvo!*" they say—"what's the use!"

What has stimulated Russian women more than anything else, is the sight

---

17 The "Brothers Grimm," Jakob (1785–1863) and Wilhelm (1786–1859), published their collections of fairy tales in 1812 and 1814. Originally the tales were intended for adults more than children, which enhances MKR's use of "Grimm" here as a pun for "grim."

18 Russian women recruited in Petrograd (May 1917) to fight beside and to encourage valor from, and if need be humiliate, the men. Organized and led by Maria Bochkareva (1889–1920), they served and fought on the front lines and were known as the Battalion of Death.

of these American women, who could be living comfortably at home, fighting against terrible conditions and even greater obstacles, and accomplishing the impossible, such as procuring provisions, through sheer tenacity. It is an eye-opener to the Russian to find that the mere keeping after a purpose brings results.

A Russian Woman's Day

In seeing a woman like Miss Boies achieve things by outlining a definite, however small, object, they begin to realize that they fail because they make their first plans too big and too theoretical. Of course their tenacity of purpose dwindles under the natural obstacles. They are often not ambitious, because they have had little experience with the rewards of labor. And their feeling of transiency also hinders them.

"But on!" exclaims Miss Boies, "it is so easy to talk. And it is so hard to find fault with the peasant woman, for instance, when you know what she has to contend with. Let me give you an idea of her day's work, and you won't be so ready to condemn her for slovenliness."

"She gets up early in the morning—and early morning in fall and winter in Northern Russia is very dark and very cold—she milks the cow and feeds the pigs and chickens; comes back, starts the samovar and puts on the small stove-pipe to make a draft; serves tea and black bread, perhaps, for breakfast. If the house is to be straightened out she must do it now before going to the fields to work, from one to five miles away. She is there all day. If mother or grandmother lives with her, the children can stay at home; otherwise she must take them to the fields with her. She does the sowing, the cultivating, the harvesting and reaping with hand implements. At night she plods home in the gray chill, the children clinging to her full skirt, whimpering.

"Now she must milk the cow again and prepare the evening meal. Butter and cheeses must be made, baking and sewing done. This is her day. Once a week she goes a long distance to the bazaar in the largest town of the district with butter and eggs. There she exchanges ideas and buys cloth and household utensils. One has deep respect for such a woman, especially when one finds that she has an artistic appreciation of all beautiful things."

No Vegetable-Gardens

But much can be done to remedy conditions, particularly the fearful dirt and consequent disease. A large number of diseases peculiar to the race can be corrected through proper food. The Russian diet consists almost altogether of black bread, tea, meat and soup. Fruits and vegetables are an unknown quantity.

The Russian not only insists that he does not like vegetables, but he has not begun to have gardens. This is partly because the peasants own so little garden land, due to the custom of redividing the fertile bits of land every year or so. When Miss Boies returns to Russia—oh, yes, she is going back!—she will take with her an exhibit to include, among the other things, wax models of all the vegetables, with instructions for their growing and cooking.

Yes, they are conservative, those dark-eyed Slav women. But they have also a peculiar quality and chance for leadership. There is practically no prejudice against their sharing in the political and economic life of the nation. There are merely inhibitions in themselves. Where those are removed, they become as Catherine Breshkovsky, Babushka the Beloved,[19] who says at seventy-five, "I feel that I have the whole of Russia on my back."

"You Get Used to the Bullets"

Miss Boies tells of one woman leader who stood for law and order in the midst of chaos.

"It was in Moscow under Lenine [*sic*]. Two friends of the Y.W.C.A. had brought us a sack of flour in an automobile. As they were leaving they were stopped by two big bear-like guards, who put them under arrest without any charge other than their possession of an automobile. Two men, whom I have every reason to believe were disguised German officers, finding the prisoners to be American—'Worse than the English,' they said in German—demanded their immediate execution. Then the secretary who was over the guards appeared. And it was a wiry, skinny little woman not much over twenty!"

A Woman Wins the Day

"'We are not going to do things this way,' she blazed at the four huge men."

"After questioning the captives she had them released at once."

"In another town the Commissar of Finance was a capable, pretty little school-teacher. So you see, that once she is started the Russian woman is a recognized figure. If she has the energy to do things, there is no one to say her nay [*sic*]."

Miss Boies is delightfully cool about this business of immediate executions and revolutions.

"Bullets? Oh yes. Especially at night. But you get used to them. They do come

19 Catherine Breshkovsky (1844–1934), "Babushka" [grandmother], was a social reformer from a noble family who was exiled twice to Siberia (1878–96 and 1905–17). Released by Kerensky in 1917, she fell out of favor with the subsequent Bolshevik regime and was forced into exile again, this time to what was then known as Czechoslovakia.

around corners rather unexpectedly—you stumble on fights when you venture out late—but there isn't any danger if you go about your own business and don't get too curious."

A Close Call

"Under fire?" repeated Miss Boies in answer to a question as to her closest call. "I suppose it was one Sunday morning at the Sucharev market in Moscow. There were thousands of people there, as usual, buying and selling boots, iron, cloth, and valuable loot from the great estates. There were small sheds of dried fish and barrels of milk curds."

"I was looking at linens, when, without warning, concentrated firing began around us. The fish-wives, quiet but tense, closed shop hurriedly. The people tried to get out, but there were too many of them and no place to go. Down one street came a motor-lorry filled with guards. Down another street came an auto with a machine gun in the back. I was about to climb into a big empty barrel when the proprietress of the shop shooed me away. There was nothing to do but make a break for home."

"And then——?"

"Well," smiled Miss Boies, "here I am!"

As if she were not contented with her efforts, Miss Boies has recently established a Y.W.C.A. Hostess House in Archangel for the Allied troops, homesick and comfortless, passing through that bleak neighborhood.

Cocoa $1.50 Per Cup

"When we found that a cup of cocoa cost a dollar and a half at a second-rate restaurant, we decided the need was great."

"There were only log cabins available in Archangel, but a can of blue paint from the Michigan Engineers, and a bolt of gauze from a British surgeon provided stenciled curtains, and the rest of the furnishings were acquired in quite as original a way. From five to eight hundred American soldiers go there daily. Russian women resent interference but they appreciate friendliness. They admire America, because she has attained freedom and they long for her organizing ability and her ambition."

By Marjorie Kinnan

"Through Three Revolutions," *Designer* 50, no 3 (July 1919): 1, 26, 29.

Eight-Week Clubs; Community Service

A most peculiar thing has happened to the boys and girls of the United States. A few generations ago, Grandfather and Grandmother would have said it is impossible.

"Young folks are thoughtless and careless," they used to say. "It is all we old people can do to train them into considerate ways."

But now, behold! All over our great, beautiful country, which danger has taught us to love so deeply, boys and girls in their teens are voluntarily taking the responsibility for community welfare work. The nation is looking at them in astonishment and joy. Of course, the war has done the most to awaken us to our duties. We have bought thrift stamps, Liberty bonds, and made Red Cross dressings, and in doing all of this we have caught a glimpse of how much difference the service of each small, youngish individual makes in the life of a community or a country. If each Mary Jenkins had not knitted a pair of socks and made some bandages each week, what would the Sammies have worn on their long American feet, and with what would the hospitals have bound up their wounds? *E Pluribus Unum* means something more than it did in the care-free days before the war. And we like to think, too, that years and years of fine American training have bred a sense of social responsibility in our youth.

For the last six years American girls have been doing a fascinating sort of work, which is now becoming so popular and wide-spread as to be a movement. "We are busy with our studies and helping Mother during the school year," they said, "but what about our summer vacations? We can help around the house, and yet have plenty of time for other things. What shall we do with those empty eight weeks?"

As it happened, the Young Women's Christian Association had the answer. After fifty-two years of club work with girls, it knew that some sort of organized club was the best means of getting girls together to accomplish anything, from hemming towels to hoeing corn. So the Eight Week Clubs came into existence for the purpose of utilizing the summer months for something worth while to the community. The Y.W.C.A. even set up courses of training for leaders for these clubs. In student Y.W.C.A.'s all over the country, there are Eight-Week-Clubs training-courses for college girls who are anxious to pay back some small interest on the debt they owe their communities. These girls are taught the principles of club organization, types of service that interest girls, characteristic activities for different ages, and various forms of wholesome recreation to increase good health and develop an interest in exercise and outdoor life. Have you someone in your community who has taken this course, but has never been given a chance to use it in action—never been asked to lead a group of girls?

Already the Eight Week Clubs have made themselves felt. The ideal is always community service of some type, and the results have been obtained. Exhibits have been made at county fairs that have "done the community proud"; in one small town girls wrote patriotic items for the local newspapers; in many rural communities the girls did "potato-bugging," hoeing, and haying; in one district in North Dakota they helped in the grain fields at a time when the nation was clamoring for the crop, and help was scarce. Eight Week Clubs have got the community together in countless places—a service invaluable to coöperation. They have bought chairs for a community hall, so that everyone could meet and talk over problems, facing them as a group; they have held "fly-swatting" and anti-mosquito campaigns; have held general cleaning days; circulated petitions for electric lighting and other civic improvements; distributed pamphlets on canning; bought apparatuses for the children's playground; and cut down all the weeds which were making Main Street a disgrace.

Perhaps the most valuable bit of work done by these groups has been the attempt to get a feeling of unity and coöperativeness in communities where there had been friction. One club devoted a summer to getting a better spirit between the high-school girls and the grade-school girls, after there had been petty jealousies and rivalries for several years. Another club united warring factions of the church.

These are all things that any Eight Week Club can accomplish. And even if there is no trained leader available, it is a simple matter to organize with or without the help of suggestions from the national headquarters of the Y.W.C.A.

The principle is to utilize that long summer vacation for community service, for doing for your community whatever it needs the most, whether that be a circulating library, a recreation club, a clean-up campaign, or just good times to get every one, from Grandfather to the baby and from all the families in the community, together—a real American unit.

Marjorie Kinnan

"Eight-Week Clubs; Community Service," *St. Nicholas Magazine* 46, no. 7 (May 1919): 619–21.

His Little Cabbage Head

"I like you," said my friend Stanley, "because you are French. I also like you because you have tawny bobbed hair and green cat's eyes and an ugly mouth. But most especially I like you because you are the only safe Frenchwoman in a naughty world."

I did not become angry at this, which should have been an insult; but then, I am not a Parisian, and I rather enjoy having an ugly mouth. Instead of railing at my friend, I railed at the *garçon*; the stupid beast had bought me a Bacardi without grenadine. I assure you, I told him things to set the pigs uprooting the lilies on his grandmother's grave.

"Stanley," I said, "we will leave my mouth out of the question. It was not meant for kissing; embraces bore me more than American congressmen do. Therefore, my mouth concerns only myself, and I think of it, I will confide to you, merely as a wide doorway for your excellent food. Listen; I have lived in New York for—many years, only because of the food, and the romance of pursuing it in the great illusion of one day adding to its joys a cup of respectable coffee—*café au lait*—to the tongue as Italian silk underwear to the body. It is a constant adventure, and failure only intrigues me. Some day I shall find it; some day——"

"Ah!" breathed Stanley. "You should have been in my shoes those long years ago! Here, in America's most terrible city, you would have found the perfect coffee, with whipped cream upon it like lace upon a creole's pale brown breast. And if it had been served by Nanon——"

"Nanon? I smell a mouse! You like me because I am French? *Diable*, I think I see!" And I banged my fist upon the little table so that its teeth shook.

My friend Stanley laughed. He fitted a cigarette in his silly amber holder— do you not love the bite of saucy wisps of tobacco against your tongue?—and leaned back, luxurious even on a restaurant chair.

"Because of Nanon I like French women," he affirmed. "Because of Nanon I also like you—for exactly what you are. Ah, little frightened Nanon——"

I wanted to say Pouf!—for frightened women are an abomination, and get themselves loved by men more than is necessary. But my friend is so seldom sentimental that I had a great desire to hear him indulge.

"Little Nanon?" I murmured. "She was very lovely?"

My friend shook his head.

"Not at all; and so, in my perversity, I loved her. I liked the idea of sheltering and adoring an unwanted little simple thing, who would develop charm just for me. I called her *mon petit chou*. '*Chou-chou*,' I would say, 'my little cabbage-head, you are stupid; I shall teach you!' But I did not count on——"

"—on her remaining stupid and without charm," I finished for him. "Tell me all of it."

"I hoped you would ask me," said Stanley. "Now listen; I may ask you what you think, so pay attention."

"*Je suis à toi* [I am with you]," I said.

So my friend told me of Nanon, his little cabbage-head whom he had loved.

It was years ago, when I was more of a fool—and so more interested in people. And my ideals—Take my word for it, friend Margot, I was chaste. I looked on women as delicate flowers; each one I classed botanically. You, for instance, would have been an orange-brown zinnia, with your green eyes and orange-brown hair, and your unyielding and amazing sexlessness. One would never cuddle a zinnia, but they are nice flowers for friends. Most women, however, were roses or orchids, with here and there a spray of mignonette.[20] You understand now what I was. It is pathetic, and rather charming, is it not? Yes.

Well, friend Margot, I lived in a very old house just off Washington Square, where I paid a small sum each week for a large brown room and three old-fashioned meals a day. I reported for the *Chronicle* for nothing a week, wrote very absurd poetry furtively, and lived on an allowance from my mother. It was in the days when the Square and the Village were passing through the intermediate stage between the later Victorian era and bohemianism. Respectability clung about the neighborhood like a ghost but recently dead; artists were there, but had not yet begun the semi-annual flight from street to street to escape Missourian tourists and up-towners. There were no red-and-white apartment houses.[21] Most important of all, there were no "March Hare," no "Purple Saucepan," restaurants and tearooms,[22] where one paid twenty cents for coffee, at the rate of five for the beverage, five for the cream, and ten for the idea.

Instead—ah, Margot, instead, there was a little French place, the *Maison*

---

20 Zinnias (*Zinnia elegans*) are easily grown garden flowers that require little water or attention, as opposed to roses, orchids, and mignonettes (*Reseda odorata*), all of which require substantial gardening expertise. Mignonettes, for example, often used in the perfume industry, must be carefully selected in order to maintain their fragrance through generations.

21 Possibly an allusion to the colors of the Russian Revolution, red and white; Washington Square, in the heart of the Greenwich Village area of New York, was a focal point for heightened concerns about communism, known as the "Red Scare" (1919–20).

22 "March Hare" alludes to Lewis Carroll (1832-98), *Alice's Adventures in Wonderland* (1865), but it and the "Purple Saucepan" are unidentified as restaurants.

Richel, where one could go, all night long, for *café au lait* and cinnamon buns and *pâtisserie*. The old papa Richel was fat and gentlemanly, with a tremendous wife—*un bateau*—who quarreled with him, sometimes called him *cochon*, and wore diamonds. The shop was immaculate and quiet, and in the morning the sun came in through the white curtains. I wish that I might be called to my seat by the throne from my corner seat in the *Maison* Richel, with a cinnamon bun and a cup of *café au lait* half-way to my lips. The angels would find me in a most agreeable mood.

In among the suave, dress-suited waiters, who gave an air of Parisian elegance to the little shop, fluttered a girl. She was distantly related to Mama Richel, lived on her bounty, and served all night long and part of the day. They made a dog of her!

Margot, you know me as a cynic, as egoist, as a dilettante extremely selfish; but believe me when I tell you that this child found in me a generous, unselfish friend, and a reverent, tender lover. Believe me also, that she was completely without charm, save in the pathos of her, and the wistfulness of her great brown eyes. I saw her first as she stood taking a rebuke from a patron—a handsome, insolent woman. She stood with her small head drooped on her thin breast, one strand of her black, lifeless hair between her downcast eyes. Her hands were folded together in front like a girl just home from the convent. When she turned to go, she lifted her eyes—wide, bewildered, unhappy, without a trace of tears—and met mine. Then she fluttered away to the kitchen for the woman's order, her shoulders hunched together, placing her feet timidly, cautiously, like a cat walking over an iron grill. In a few minutes she came back to her patron, and the pain in her eyes was a wild agony, the mental crucifixion a child undergoes when it expects a nameless punishment because of some petty misdemeanor.

"Madame," she breathed, "I—after all—I have forgotten what you have ordered!"

And that was Nanon. She was always wrong. She could remember nothing from one table to the next. She would suffer anguish when she was rebuked (and it happened often, from Mama Richel if from no one else) and five minutes later she would commit a worse *bêtise* [blunder]. Oh, Margot, she was so little, so pale, so trembling, so hounded and cuffed—and so unbelievably stupid! All my young chivalry arose in a tidal wave. I wanted to protect her from the world, to fold her thin little body within my arms, and feel her heart beat like a bird's against my own.

"Nanon has never had love," I said to myself. "She has never benefited by the psychology of adoration and praise. She needs a modiste, a hairdresser, and warmth, warmth, warmth. Her heart, her brain, are frozen. I will love her, and she will blossom out and make me proud of her." I wrote to my mother that I was taking a wife. "An old-fashioned, modest creature you would worship," I wrote. My mother doubled my allowance, thinking me safest married.

I went to Papa Richel to secure the consent I knew he would give so gladly. He was talkative that day. I thought I should never get away from him. He insisted on discussing his *ménage*. He forgot his manners and confided to me that his wife was a torment.

He talked drolly of his waiters; of Georges, in particular, who exasperated him beyond all endurance.

"He is slow; *mon Dieu*, one hundred peoples in ze shop, and he move like zees!" and Papa Richel moved his pudgy fingers over the counter at a pace supposed to resemble that of Georges. "He is *artiste*, you know, *oui*! He play ze violin, *oui*! All day he plays, an' when he come here at seex o'clock—*voila*, he is crazy! *Oui*, crazy—an' slow—an' stupid! Almost as stupid as Nanon!"

This was my chance. To the astonishment of Papa Richel I made my proposal for the hand of Nanon and received his vociferous blessing. Nanon agreed, wide-eyed.

We were married. I showered her with my attentions. My mother died shortly after, leaving me a fortune. I made over half of it to Nanon. She dressed in chiffons and laces. Her thin body grew plump. Her lifeless black hair took on a satin luster. Her lips grew red, her cheeks like pink anemones. She was a lovely thing; but she retained always her shyness, her stupidity.

. . . [MKR's ellipsis] My friend Stanley sat with dreaming eyes, tapping the ashes from his cigarette. Then he called the waiter, for his bill, and turned to me with a crooked little smile.

"Ah," I cried, "finish it *mon ami*! Where is she now, *la pauvre Nanon*? She is—dead?"

"Oh no," said *mon ami*. "She is here in New York. You have heard of la Comtesse Lizet?"

"She of the old-world salon? The exquisite, silent Comtesse who is so deep, so subtle that she has never been fathomed—but who many insist, despite her beauty and grace, is a *sotte* [fool], *une femme stupide*?"

"Yes."

"The wife of the famous violinist, the composer, the great artiste?"

"It is she—Nanon."

"But *chéri*——"

"She slipped quietly away with Georges, Papa Richel's violin-playing waiter, the one almost as stupid as she, and also with considerably more than half of my fortune I had given her. Do you see? My money gave him his training, gave them fame—the stupid Georges and the more stupid Nanon!"

Impulsively my hand closed over that of my friend.

"My poor one," I said to him, "my poor dear, dearest one!"

He shrugged his shoulders; laughed easily. Then he sat straight.

"Margot, you have sympathized! Your ugly mouth is soft and beautiful! You have lost your sexlessness. You are no longer safe; you are a woman!"

"*Tais-toi* [Shut up]," I said to him, "you are a silly boy. Did you learn nothing, after all, from your little cabbage-head?"

Marjorie Kinnan

"His Little Cabbage Head," *Young's Magazine* 37, no. 5 (May 1919): 252–54.

*   *   *   *   *   *   *   *   *

Good Things for Church Suppers

Best Recipes from Popular Y.W.C.A. Cafeterias

Many a Ladies' Aid Society or Sewing Circle has racked its brains for the church sociable or supper that will be reasonable in price, pleasing to the most "pernickety" of men as well as women, and yet a bit different from the usual thing.

Here are some of the discoveries made by the Y.W.C.A. in its cafeterias.

Have you discovered that delicious Southern combination—hot waffles and fricasseed chicken? Boil the chicken until tender, remove from the liquor, which should be boiled down to desired strength. Season with salt and pepper. Thicken with two heaping tablespoons of flour to a quart of liquor, the flour being first tinned smooth in about half a cup of cold water, and then stirred rapidly into the chicken liquor until it boils. Remove the bones from the chicken, cut into small pieces, including the liver and the skin, if tender, and the gizzard, which should be boiled separately until tender. Stir into the gravy, and serve hot over, or on the same plate with, hot waffles. The chicken can be prepared beforehand, and reheated to serve. One four to five pound chicken, prepared in this way, should serve a dozen people plentifully.

Waffles

4 pints flour
3 level tablespoons baking-powder

2 teaspoons salt
8 eggs
5 cups of milk
4 tablespoons of melted butter

Mix in the order given; add the beaten yolks of the eggs to the milk, then the melted butter, and the whites well-beaten, last. This should serve fifty people, if "seconds" are not given.

Stuffed peppers is one of the most popular dishes at the Y.W.C.A. cafeterias. The peppers may be stuffed with chopped meat mixed with bread or cracker crums, in the proportion of one-half cup of crums to one cup of meat, one small onion to two tablespoons of chopped parsley, one tablespoons of melted butter, used in a few tablespoons of hot water for basting. Half meat and half rice, or mashed potatoes, flavored with parsley and a dash of onion, makes a good combination.

The peppers should be the large, green, sweet peppers with three or four distinct lobes; should be thoroughly cleaned of inner tissue and seeds, and if not wanted at all strong, may be parboiled before filling and baking. Tomato sauce may be added to the meat-and-rice mixture if desired. Salt but no pepper is needed. Eight pounds of chopped meat (boiled beef, lamb and ham) and eight cups of bread or cracker crums will fill fifty fair-sized peppers.

Twenty minutes should be allowed for baking in a moderate oven. Gem-pans are good, for the individual peppers may be supported in each cup. A little water should be put in the bottom of the pan to prevent sticking, and the peppers should be basted every ten minutes. Serve with cream-cheese-and-nut sandwiches.

Meat loaf is always popular with the men, who like something rather substantial. French roast, as it is called, is delicious filling, and goes a long way. When the meat loaf is thoroughly done, mashed potatoes, beaten light with plenty of milk, are spread on top of the loaf to the thickness of about two inches and browned delicately. Hot rolls or biscuits should be served with this.

Meat Loaf

1 pound fresh pork
1 pound veal
2 pounds beef
1 cup bread-crums
1 cup milk
1 tablespoon salt
1 teaspoon pepper

2 eggs, slightly beaten
1 small minced onion
2 tablespoons lemon-juice

Chop meat finely or force through a meat-chopper, mix and add remaining ingredients in order given. Shape into a loaf, put into pan and lay across the top six thin slices of fat salt pork. Roast in a hot oven for two hours, basting every ten minutes, at first with one-half cup water, and after that is gone, with fat in pan. Three loaves of the size resulting from the recipe should serve forty-five or fifty people.

If made without the mashed-potato topping, this is good served cold, with potato salad or hot potato-balls. For potato-balls, boil and mash potatoes, season with salt, pepper, and butter, chopped parsley and a little minced onion, beat up with enough milk to make the mixture creamy and malleable, shape into balls about two inches in diameter, and when cool and firm, role twice alternately in slightly beaten egg and cracker-crums, then fry in a wire basket in hot deep fat.

Scalloped oysters make a delicious dish for a church supper. Use large baking-dishes; brush with butter, put in a half-inch layer of bread and cracker-crums; then a thin layer of cream sauce: lay the oysters flat, at even intervals, not too close; sprinkle with salt, paprika or black pepper and bits of butter; repeat this alternation of crums, sauce, oysters, salt, pepper and butter until the dish is almost full, covering with a thick layer of crums and bits of butter sprinkled liberally over the top. The cream sauce should be very thin.

Allow four or five oysters for each person to be served. Sweet pickles and rolls or thin bread-and-butter sandwiches should be served with this dish.

Meat croquettes—chopped ham, beef, or chicken—molded into cone-shaped croquettes with the addition of cream sauce and sifted bread or cracker crums, and seasoned with salt, pepper and parsley, are always popular. They may be rolled in egg and sifted bread-crums and fried in deep hot fat or baked in the oven and served with potato-chips or French-fried potatoes or creamed potatoes.

Crisp patty-shells made from ordinary pie crust, and filled with creamed salmon and peas, with creamed shrimps, creamed oysters or creamed chicken with mushrooms or peas, are too good to be true, if well seasoned with paprika and served hot with mashed potatoes and hot rolls.

Pastry for Patty Shells

2 level cups pastry flour
½ teaspoon baking-powder
½ teaspoon salt

⅔ cup butter and lard mix

½ cup ice water

Mix the baking-powder and salt with the flour, and rub in the lard. Mix quite stiff with ice-cold water. Roll out, put the butter on the paste in little pieces, and sprinkle with flour. Fold over and roll out. Roll up like a jelly-roll. Roll out again, and with the top of a large glass or small bowl cut out round pieces to fit into gem-tins, lining the bottom and sides of the little cups. Bake half an hour or until golden brown. The above recipe will make about a dozen patties. It is best not to make the pastry in too large amounts, but to make several batches with smaller quantities.

Thick Cream Sauce for Croquettes and Patties

1 pint hot milk (or cream if possible)

2 tablespoons butter

4 level tablespoons flour

1 half teaspoon salt

1 half teaspoon celery salt

A few grains of Cayenne

Scald the milk or cream. Melt the butter in a granite saucepan. When bubbling, add the flour and stir until well-mixed. Add one-third of the milk, and stir as it boils or thickens. Add more milk and boil again. When perfectly smooth, add the remainder of the milk. The sauce should be almost as thick as a drop-batter. Add the seasoning, and mix it while hot with the meat, fish or whatever the material.

Egg croquettes melt in the mouth and are surprisingly cheap when made in quantities. Chop eight hard-boiled eggs quite fine in a wooden chopping-bowl, season with salt and pepper according to the amount used in the sauce; add several tablespoons of minced parsley and one small onion. Stir into the thick cream sauce listed above, and let it cool for several hours, or until rather firmly set.

Mold into croquettes about three inches long and an inch and a half across, by shaping the right amount of the mixture into a ball between the palms of the hands, then giving the ball a gentle rolling pressure till slightly cylindrical; then roll it lightly in fine bread or cracker crums, clasp it gently, and flatten one end on the board. Turn the hand over and flatten the other end.

Place the croquette on a broad knife, and roll it in beaten egg. With a spoon dip the egg over the croquette, drain on the knife and roll again in crums. Fry in a wire basket in deep hot fat. Drain on paper.

Keep the croquettes as soft as possible, but if too soft to be at all manageable, stir in enough fine cracker-dust to make it hold together, but never add any uncooked material, like flour, nor the dried bread-crums, as these will make the croquettes too stiff.

Serve with currant or grape jelly and either hot rolls or lettuce-and-mayonnaise sandwiches. The recipe quoted makes a dozen or more good-sized croquettes at will. Two dozen and a half eggs make over fifty croquettes.

For a supper given in warm weather, nothing is more appetizing than jellied chicken. Boil a four-pound chicken until tender; remove from the pot and boil the liquor down to two quarts. Season with salt and pepper. Pick all the meat from the fowl, discarding the skin, and cut it into uniform small pieces.

Soak one-half cup gelatin into cold water for a couple of hours, and when quite well dissolved, stir into the chicken liquor. Add the meat and pour the whole into a tin such as is used for individual loaves of bread, which has had the sides lined with slices of hard-boiled eggs and narrow strips of canned sweet red peppers.

Let stand until firm, then when ready to serve, dip the tin quickly in a pan of hot water; turn the jellied loaf, which should hold together firmly, out on a large platter which has been lined with lettuce leaves; cut in inch-thick slices, and serve on lettuce, with olives and parsley garniture.

The following are also good for any church supper:

Potato salad or creamed potatoes with cold sliced ham or tongue, and sandwiches—ham, cream-cheese-and-nut, peanut-butter, lettuce-and-mayonnaise, date-and-nut, roast-beef, olive-nut, or chopped egg with cream.

Cream hard-boiled eggs on toast, with sweet pickles.

Macaroni or potatoes au gratin.

Boiled "wieners" with potato chips or creamed potatoes or sauerkraut.

Lamb stew, with potatoes, carrots, onions and peas.

Oyster stew.

Clam chowder, made with thickened milk and potatoes.

Coffee, tea or cocoa should be served, and a desert, for which the Y.W.C.A. suggests: Fruit jelly, chocolate pudding, blanc-mange, cottage pudding, brown betty, charlotte russe.

Cake: Yellow, with chocolate frosting, sponge, coconut, orange-jelly layer, devil's food, jelly roll, spice, fruit.

Pie: Apple, mince, lemon meringue, peach, custard, coconut, cherry, blueberry, huckleberry.

George Washington pie—two or three layers of light sponge-cake, filled and covered with thick custard, flavored with vanilla, orange or lemon.

For pie-crust, use the patty-shell recipe. For cake, use as a foundation:

1 cup of sugar
2 tablespoons of butter
2 eggs
2 cups of flour
2 teaspoons baking-powder
1 half cup milk

Cream the butter and sugar, add the eggs well beaten, sift the flower and baking-powder into the mixture, alternating with milk until both are stirred in. Bake half an hour in a moderate oven. This recipe may be varied or increased according to need—chocolate or spices added, etc., and the frosting giving the flavor.

Marjorie Kinnan

"Good Things for Church Suppers," *Woman's Magazine* 39, no. 6 (June 1919): 24, 54.

* * * * * * * * *

Here Is Fun for Girls

The Y.W.C.A. Will Plan Just the Club You Want

The war is over. But the world is not settling back into its old habits and ways. American women and girls have realized with a jolt to their pride that they had not been good citizens; the war gave them a civic and national responsibility which put their attainments to the test.

Women had not prepared themselves for their share in the community life. One thing they had not realized was that their health was essential to the life of the nation. But through the long hours and the hard work brought by the war's activities, they found out that they needed stronger bodies to get the most out of their work and out of themselves.

The Young Women's Christian Association, however, realized all this years ago. Girls have always been its one interest, and it has studied their needs from every angle. It knows that the thousands of girls in small towns and cities all over the country must be built up through plenty of outdoor sports and wholesome fun, in order that they may prepare themselves for their life-work, whatever it may be.

Girls in their teens who have taken a keen interest in helping the government in war time, through canteen service, patriotic leagues under the Young Women's Christian Association, Red Cross work, war gardens, and help in the Liberty Loan campaigns, now want to go on and use their new-found power and knowledge to make democracy come true, and to do their share toward the new social order.

They realize that the key-note to service is good health. Physical defects can and must be overcome by wholesome, rollicking recreation. Baseball, played with the indoor baseball, volleyball, tennis, swimming, basket-ball and hockey, camping and "bacon bats"[23]—these give the girl in her teens a physical energy and development that will take her through the difficult years to come. And the glorious part about this build-up process through recreation is that it is literally "all kinds of fun!"

Camping is "a perfect circus." Weekend camps, if summer camping can not be managed, give the "real thing," with the pitching of one's own tent under the trees, building fires in rain or wind, cooking, sleeping, playing out-of-doors. Long tramps bring one back to the camp famished for the crisp bacon and steaming coffee from the fire.

A whole day of fun in the open brings a wonderful peace at night, lying on the grass, studying the stars and reciting their curious legends, singing songs, making up original songs to old tunes, telling stories and exchanging experiences. Bed is the softest, sweetest place in the world, but in the morning with the sun coming up almost a stone's throw from one's face, getting up has none of the horrors that it has at home; one wants most of anything in the world to slip into bloomers and a middy blouse,[24] and have breakfast, then a game of baseball, tennis, or whatever appeals most.

Girls are organizing as never before into clubs.

The Y.W.C.A. is a big sister to these clubs. It can make suggestions for organization into any type of club and for programs of any sort, work or fun.

The Y.W.C.A. will tell them that a certain amount of formal organization is essential, and that recreation, study and service are necessary to make the right balance for a club. A club that does nothing but work is stupid and prosy, and in danger of repeating the things that schools give. A club, on the other hand, de-

---

23 "Bacon bats" were popularized by Smith College students, who to gain relief from the tedium of class would go on hikes (bats) and roast bacon over a fire.

24 Sailor outfits made popular in the 1840s, when Queen Victoria's young sons, Albert (later Edward VII) and Alfred, wore them. Middy blouses eventually became a common form of school dress.

voted to good times alone, soon dies out for lack of purpose to hold it together, and is a waste of time.

After years of experiment the Y.W.C.A. has come to the conclusion which it offers to girls in their teens everywhere, and that is, that the aims of the club should be: Health; second, Knowledge, and third, Spirit. The expression of these aims should come through Service—in the home, at school, in the community, in the nation at large.

If you want to get up a club, the Y.W.C.A. will tell you that three committees make a workable basis: the Service Committee, plans which [sic] for all service activities, both personal and community; the Social Committee, which plans for good times, recreation and entertainments; and the Sentry Committee, which attends to the business affairs and technical matters of the club, secures new members, and so forth. Other schemes are equally good.

Where a club plans to go in for a great deal of study or wide service, it is advisable to have as a leader an older girl or woman, who can make helpful suggestions along these lines. All officers, of course, should be chosen from the girls themselves. Study may range from first aid, through domestic science, canning, interior decorating, to a study of civic and national and even international problems. Service, like charity, should begin at home, and then branch out to the school and to the community.

A club member should be able to make a list of the names and locations of the institutions in her community or the nearest towns to which she would refer a tubercular friend, persons needing food, fuel or clothing; a lost child, a truant-school case, a girl seeking employment, a person taken suddenly ill on the street, a case of fire, or a case for the police; an unsanitary housing condition in her locality.

A completely rounded club will want to follow these lines. If its members wish to organize under the Girls' Reserves, as part of the Y.W.C.A. activities for girls, a complete program may be obtained from Miss Gertrude Gogin,[25] at headquarters, 600 Lexington Avenue, New York City.

Or the Commonweal Club, a working girl program for girls in unorganized districts, may be obtained from Miss Gogin, as a suggestion for organization. In many cases, where the chief interest is in recreation, an Athletic Club, which might include the community at large, is advisable.

Such recreation work among girls can lead to a wider community understanding, as the town takes an interest. Pageantry, as a field of recreation, is opening

---

25 The "Girls' Reserves" of the YWCA was especially popular during the war. They assisted high school girls in everything from the performing arts to practical management. Gertrude Gogin is not further identified.

up more and more as a foundation for community cooperation. Pageantry and the drama are more and more giving Americans an outlet of self-expression, and so taking their place in community programs which have the fourfold aim of Health, Knowledge, Spirit and thence to Service.

Marjorie Kinnan

"Here Is Fun for Girls," *Woman's Magazine* 39, no. 6 (June 1919): 43.

*   *   *   *   *   *   *   *   *

Found: A Practical Artist

Introducing an artist, as "artistic" and ethereal as tradition demands, but one who carries with her a saw, a hammer, bits of wood and a warm, jolly love of "real, every-day, honest-to-God people"—Mrs. Donald Pratt, *née* Margaret Swain, formerly of the Provincetown Players, New York,[26] who says:

"Art for art's sake has no place in this busy world. The Lord would never have tolerated it for one moment."

Mrs. Pratt worked for a year in Kentucky, staging fairy pantomimes with the children of the poor mountain whites, and the transient miners. Then she was dramatic director for the revival of miracle plays, under the Episcopal Church in Ohio, which has since spread all through the West.

She has worked with children, directing two thousand at one time. She has danced—here, there, everywhere—and has acted with many Little Theatre groups.

Now she has turned to the most practical of construction work with the pageantry department of the Young Women's Christian Association, where she sits at her desk, or works at her model theatre, as a boon to the hundreds of communities all over the United States who write in for help in staging pageants and dramas.

Bibliographies of helpful books are sent in answer to countless requests; lists

---

26 Margaret Swain codesigned the play *Fog*, written by Eugene O'Neill (1888–1953) and produced by the Provincetown Players at New York's Playwright Theater, opening 5 January 1917. The Provincetown Players (originally of Provincetown, Massachusetts) had introduced the plays of O'Neill to the American public (28 July 1916), and by 1919, thanks to their success with O'Neill's plays, had adopted their own theater, the Provincetown Playhouse, at 133 Macdougal Street, New York (now classroom space for the New York University Law School).

of plays are given—plays both good and simple; pictures are sent as suggestions for costumes.

Mrs. Pratt has just finished a set of scenery which will be manna from the gods for small communities—a set which is convertible into either a formal drawing-room or a rustic cottage. This cuts the expense exactly in half, and opens up as many possibilities for combination sets.

Perhaps the most practical help to an artistic end is this practical artist's model theatre, where she works out every idea that is to be offered to any one else. Mrs. Pratt expects eventually to make this theatre a "kitbag" theatre, which will fold and unfold, and may be carried everywhere about the country for making demonstrations.

The tiny stage is sixteen inches by five. At the rear is a balcony nine inches high, supported by pillars, with steps of varying heights leading up to it, and suitable for various pageantry groupings. The stage, instead of using the conventional curtain, is approached by long, low steps. The furniture, like the scenery, is made to be as adaptable as possible.

"What I want to do," says Mrs. Pratt, "is to help people to create. The model theatre is like a pen to a poet or a typewriter to a newspaperman. We want to help those who have never expressed themselves before to do so, and to do it well."

"Snobbish artists feel pain when amateurs interpret a great piece of work badly. Yet in the end, the amateur may have something to give the professional. It may take years. But what are years?"

Marjorie Kinnan

"Found: A Practical Artist," *Everybody's Magazine* 41 (October 1919): 124.

*   *   *   *   *   *   *   *   *

A Sanatorium without Mud Baths or Mineral Water

The average sanatorium flourishes if it can boast a few dozen patrons, but Louisville is the proud sponsor of a health center which draws girls and women by the hundreds and thousands. This institution, without mud baths, mineral water or white-garbed attendants, is the Young Women's Christian Association, whose physical department is busily engaged in keeping feminine Louisville healthy and in building up health where none grew before.

A new physical director has recently arrived at the Y.W.C.A., Miss Margaret Leighton, whose vigorous ideas are causing the devotees of the gym and swimming pool to question the necessity of embarking for Battle Creek.[27] With the fall enrollment in physical work passing all records, enthusiasts are prophesying a veritable epidemic of health. It is becoming not only unfashionable but disgraceful to be ill, and Miss Leighton intends to do her share in making it unnecessary. Her theories, which brought results for two years at Asheville, N.C., Normal School,[28] are arousing wide comment among old gym members and newcomers.

"Girls and women," declares Miss Leighton, "need physical exercise exactly as they need food and air and sleep. The more enjoyable way of getting it is in the gymnasium or swimming pool, where the presence of others doing the same thing adds a sociable aspect. It is hard to exercise alone. What most women and girls need is to keep up, rather than to build up. I have never directed athletics with the Y.W.C.A. before, and I find it ideal for my purposes, since the "keeping up" process is made so attractive here. Everyone has so much fun in the gym classes and in the pool, and people get along infinitely faster when they enjoy the work."

In answer to a question Miss Leighton replied that she is finding Louisville girls splendid specimens of health. They have begun to look on the Y.W.C.A. physical department as a general cure-all. The plump girls, who insist on calling themselves fat, come to reduce, the slender girls, who insist on calling themselves thin, come for development. The pale-complexioned ones come to gather roses while they may—but the majority, who are pink-cheeked and generally "just right," come to "keep fit"—and because, truth to tell, they find more fun to the square inch in a gymnasium than in any other plot of ground! It is these latter who scurry to the smooth floor of the gym for a stray dance or two to the new Victrola, made especially for use in gym and dancing classes.

It is they who flock there on Saturday night during the winter for roller skating, hundreds of them. It is they who splash luxuriously in the big pool when the

---

27 After graduating from medical school in 1875, Dr. John Harvey Kellogg (1852–1943) returned to his home in Battle Creek, Michigan, and took charge of what would be called the Battle Creek Sanitarium. The rich and famous were soon flocking to Battle Creek to follow Kellogg's regimen of healthy diet and exercise. The sanitarium was popular well into the twentieth century.

28 The Asheville Normal School, 1887–1944, a teacher's college for women, was later sold to Memorial Mission Hospital.

reducers and developers have lost heart with the first snow fall and retired from the watery field. Although the pool is kept at summer temperatures throughout the year, winter seems to keep away all except those surfeited with animal spirits. As the lady in the play explained, "It isn't the mouse I am afraid of—it's just the idea of it."

Miss Margaret Rawlins, the new swimming instructor, is prevailing on many erstwhile timid ones to continue their aquatic exercise, and is holding out the lure of something new to Louisville swimming classes for women—lifesaving. "Every girl a swimmer and every swimmer a lifesaver," is the slogan of this energetic young lady, who holds numerous medals for rescue work. Miss Rawlins is an accredited examiner in lifesaving and for the American Red Cross. If she and Annette Kellerman could match stories on the beauty-giving value of swimming[,][29] the beauty parlors would be closed and the big indoor pond swamped. As it is, she would doubtless be willing to paraphrase John Keats and remark, "Beauty is health, health beauty"[30]—and so another department is added automatically to the "Y"—a beauty department! All good sanatoriums have them!

For those who need building up there is special corrective work. The physical examinations this year are made partially by a woman physician, who may recommend the seeing of an oculist, a throat surgeon, a dentist, when necessary. Miss Leighton is qualified to make the anatomical examinations, and in these she makes it her business to locate any deviations from the normal, with the view of correcting them later in her classes. Crooked spines, weak ankles, arches and backs, round shoulders, poor posture, all are noted for correction.

"Five minutes a day regularly will take care of most of those troubles," says Miss Leighton. "They are easily corrected if one is only persistent and patient, but they cause untold misery if left alone."

School teachers, who, because of a sedentary life and much desk work, need the stimulus of exercise, come in for special consideration under the new fall schedule. The house from 5 to 6 on Tuesday and Friday is given over to a class for teachers, who may find in the gymnasium the antidote for the confinement of the classroom. Round shoulders cannot last long here, and weak ankles and backs will not be tolerated.

---

29 Annette Kellermann (1886–1975), legendary endurance swimmer and provocative silent film actor from Australia, author of *Physical Beauty and How to Keep It* (New York: Doran, 1918).

30 MKR is alluding to "Ode on a Grecian Urn" (1819) by John Keats (1795–1821): "'Beauty is truth, truth beauty'—that is all / Ye know on earth, and all ye need to know" (lines 49–50).

Every Thursday from 7:30 to 8:30 o'clock there meets the class in interpretive and folk dancing—and here Miss Leighton waxes most enthusiastic. In the first place, she made dancing her specialty, and in the second place, she has the most malleable material to work with, for the Southern girl is known far and wide for her natural grace. Miss Leighton, who in 1917 graduated from Skidmore School of Arts at Saratoga Springs, N.Y., studying also a summer session at Columbia University, has had wide experience with pageantry and the dance, and is ambitious to have her class do a large amount of exhibition work.

"I could never work without pageants and festivals," she declares. "They give point to dancing, just as contests give point to athletics."

Her May Day pageant at Asheville Normal School was the most successful ever given in the locality, and she plans many simple festivals and pageants for her Louisville girls. So firm a believer is she in the value of dancing, that all of her two-period classes are to devote from one-third to one-half of their time to dance work.

Associated with Miss Leighton as Associate Director of Athletics, is Miss Florence Brooks, who has had exactly the same training. She is a remarkable athlete personally, as well as a teacher, and half of the classes are led by her. She has specialized in basket ball and volley ball, and the followers of these sports find it a treat to work with her.

Younger Louisville will be interested in the announcement, just given out, that Miss Mary Neal Barker, who is one of the most popular members of the younger set, has been appointed as a regular assistant to Miss Rawlins at the swimming pool. She has been in attendance all summer, but her formal appointment to a position of responsibility has come as a pleasant surprise to her friends.

All in all, the personnel of the doctor-less sanatorium is proving most delightful, and with the slogan of "Something doing all the time," fun and health loom large for the season. Tonics are discarded, and the negligee is replaced by the middy blouse and the bloomers, which, if it must be known, are even more becoming.

Marjorie Kinnan Rawlings

"A Sanatorium without Mud Baths or Mineral Water," *Louisville (Ky.) Courier-Journal*, Sunday magazine, 24 October 1920, 5. Although MKR and Charles Rawlings were married in May 1919, this is the first article found signed with her married name.

Live Women in Live Louisville

The Only Woman State Bacteriologist in the United States

About the time I was lisping my prayers at my mother's knee, and earnestly invoking heaven to send measles to me in light but school-preventing form, I was taught that for pure, breath-taking speed you couldn't beat the minute man of early Colonial days. But wisdom came to me, perhaps with the measles, and now I know why the minute man is represented by a statue: he was a motionless piece of bric-a-brac compared with the modern phenomenon, the mile-a-minute woman.

I get dizzy when I think of them. They are women on wheels everywhere at once, doing that part of the world's work that seems to be best done by woman's brain. When I shut my eyes, I see them on these little red scooters—the most dignified of them pedaling for mad. Whiz—zip! Around the corner so fast you couldn't recognize her! A cloud of dust—and then "I see by the papers" that the Legislature has at last passed a needed reform bill, or a free clinic of the most vital sort has been opened—and I know she got there! Louisville is full of them, these mile-a-minute women. There are more live women to the square inch than in any other city I know except New York, where it takes a live woman to even hold her seat on the subway. Prosperous shops owned and run by women; a dozen woman doctors; specialists of all kinds; organizers, workers, managers; the city is full of evidence of an enormous feminine activity. And I am so fired by the sight of their energy, that must perforce grasp a nearby megaphone and look for a comfortable house top.[31] If I did my shouting about all of the live women in the town, I should grow hoarse and gray in the work—but until my voice shows sign of hard usage I intend to announce some of my discoveries. Some of them are old familiar friends to Louisville, some are not widely known, of all I remark, "Did you ever realize how live they really are?"

And so, Mr. Chairman, ladies and gentlemen:

"We have with us today"—

The only woman State bacteriologist in the United States—right here in Louisville!—Dr. Lillian South.[32]

---

31 Cf. Whitman, who in "Song of Myself" (1855) sounds his "barbaric yawp over the roofs of the world" (*Leaves of Grass* [1855 edition], line 55), and Henry David Thoreau (1817–62), who in *Walden* (1854) seeks to "brag as lustily as chanticleer in the morning, standing on his roost, if only to wake [his] neighbors up" (Library of America edition [1985], 389).

32 Lillian H. South (1879–1966).

To begin with, there are only as many State bacteriologists as there are States. These jobs are the most coveted of the scientific gentlemen in the medical profession who play fast and loose with antitoxins, vaccines and other weapons used against our enemy, the germ. To be the chief bacteriologist of a State is to have risen to the height [*sic*] of the profession. It is to have responsibility involving thousands of lives. It is to serve all the physicians, and so all the people, in the prevention of rabies, typhoid, diphtheria, pneumonia, whooping cough, influenza and all other communicable diseases. It is to keep constant watch over all municipal water supplies. And out of the small number of directors of such colossal work we find one woman—Dr. Lillian South, "Kentucky born and bred," whose one aim in life is to serve Kentucky and protect her health. Her laboratories in the State Board of Health building at Sixth and Main Streets are open day and night—the only State laboratories to give twenty-four hour service. She has established her residence in the building and the night bell registers at her bedside. A physician out in the country, in any part of the State finding himself suddenly in need of a serum, can telephone in any hour of the night and the precious package will be mailed to him immediately, or given him at once if he can call. So vital a part of the medical profession has the laboratory become that as much is done for Kentucky physicians, on a small appropriation, as is done for the physicians of any other State in the Union, including New York on a large appropriation. There are as many tests made for them, of as many different kinds. Pennsylvania has an appropriation of $2,000,000 for the State Board of health, while that for Kentucky is $175,000. Only a portion of these sums reaches the bacteriological laboratories, $8,000 a year being an average expenditure of the Kentucky establishment, but the ratio is the same. Anybody from Pennsylvania want to fight?

When Dr. Lillian South graduated from the Woman's Medical College in Philadelphia, one of the oldest in the country, she found her home State of Kentucky progressive enough to be interested in her specialty, bacteriology, then a comparatively new study. In 1911, the State bacteriological laboratories were created at Bowling Green, and Dr. South was appointed State bacteriologist. Just there is where the fundamental test came of her ability. Would the physicians of the State trust a woman in such an important position? The answer lies in my remarks above on the enormous amount of work done for the Kentucky medical profession. Her genius is recognized by the entire profession—and specimens for analysis pour into her laboratories at the rate of thirty or more a day.

In the last year, the first year of the laboratories' establishment in Louisville, nearly 12,000 specimens were examined for the discovery of some contagious disease. There were distributed nearly 5,000 free bottles of vaccines, each bottle sufficient to innoculate [*sic*] twenty people. The vaccines are made in the laboratories and sent to the physicians without charge. The resultant saving to Kentucky taxpayers is thus enormous, for the vaccines purchased through commercial channels are expensive.

The laboratories also act as distributing agent for antitoxins. In the last year there have been sent over 6,000 bottles for diphtheria, meningitis, etc., the retail cost of which would be about $30,000. The cost to the users was $12,000. The reduced rates made to the State laboratory make such a saving possible.

Perhaps the department for the prevention of rabies is the most spectacular. Since their founding the laboratories have treated 894 cases for this dread disease. The Federal Government gives the materials, and the treatments, costing $25 each through any other channel, are given absolutely free. And now you must hear about Mary!

Let me tell you first that the heads of dogs suspected of rabies are sent into the laboratories where, after a very careful removal of the brain, analysis can be made. Mary is a colored woman who performs this difficult work—and during her reign she has opened over a thousand canine heads! The work requires the hand of a surgeon, for if the brain is not absolutely intact, the analysis cannot be made. Mary also demonstrates before students and doctors—and the steady hand never falters. She was trained by Dr. South.

Dr. South attributes the confidence of the State and the medical profession to the fact that she has never tried to keep her work to herself. She has taken it directly to the doctors and to the people, showed them what she was doing, and enlisted their co-operation. At the very beginning of her work she made slides of every phase of it, and visited every county Federation of Woman's Clubs in the State, lecturing and showing her lantern slides. The clubs backed her. The medical profession put its official approval on her work by electing her vice president of the American Medical Association in 1913—the first woman ever to hold office in that venerable body.

A year previously, in 1912, she had done the work which brought her nation-wide recognition as a scientist, and which resulted in her appearance in Who's Who; the making of a sanitary survey of Kentucky in regard to the disease known as hookworm. Not only was she personally elevated to fame, but the Rockefeller Foundation appropriated $20,000 to combat the disease in this State—solely as the result of her report.

If I were in Who's Who, and were the only woman something in the country, I should rest on my laurels, go on sending out little bottles of life-saving vaccines with my nose lifted haughtily, and live under the firm impression that I knew it all.

But now that's just the difference between Dr. South and some of the rest of us. Every single year she goes off to some other laboratory to "learn something new," as she puts it, or take a post-graduate course at some learned institution that doesn't even let 'em in until they have written an encyclopedia.

"I want Kentucky to have whatever is up-to-date in public health, whatever curative or life-saving discovery comes out, and you can only keep in touch with the latest medical and scientific developments by going to the great centers of experimentation, to other laboratories, to get your knowledge at the very top."

She has taken a post-graduate degree at Washington, D.C., under Dr. C. W. Stiles,[33] the greatest known expert on hookworm. She has studied at the Virginia State Board of Health; she has studied public health at the great Mayo Clinic. During the war she took the famous war laboratory course at the Rockefeller Institute.

"I went to the Rockefeller Institute the way a dressmaker would go to Paris, and with the same feeling," she said.

She has recently finished a six weeks' course at the Johns Hopkins School of Hygiene, under Sir Arthur Newsholm,[34] famous English scientist. I saw the nicest picture of the graduating class, row on row of lofty-browed gentlemen, and down at the front, next to Sir Arthur himself, was our own private State Bacteriologist, a sure-nuf credit to Kentucky. It's such a satisfaction that she is good looking!

I'd like to tell you, all in a breath, all the clubs and medical associations she finds time to belong to and be enthusiastic over—but my dear, there are eighteen of them that by patient hammering I finally found out about! And I'd like to tell you that she has made her success by drinking some magic bacteriological potion, but alas the truth will be out:

"Hard work and ambition have been my only aids," she said.

Ah—there goes another scooter with another mile-a-minute woman skidding around the corner! Pardon me while I pursue. And when I have her story, I'll pass it on to you. As our mutual friend Petrova would say, "May I?"[35]

Marjorie Kinnan Rawlings

"The Only Woman State Bacteriologist in the United States," *Louisville (Ky.) Courier-Journal*, Sunday magazine, 6 February 1921, 6.

---

33   Charles Wardell Stiles (1876–1941), zoologist with the United States Public Health Service (1902–31).

34   Sir Arthur Newsholme (1857–1943), British public health physician, lectured at Johns Hopkins University from 1920 to 1921.

35   Possibly Olga Petrova (1884–1997), film star, usually cast as a femme fatale.

Live Women in Live Louisville

A Roentgenological Technician

Once upon a time, and this is no fairy story—if anyone had asked me in a low, mysterious voice, "Are you a Roentgenological technician?"[36] I should have held out my paws for the steel-plated handcuffs and said, "I surrender!" knowing I had walked in my sleep and committed some weird, Arthur-B-Reeveian crime.[37] But that was before I knew a Roentgenological technician.

Have you a little Roentgenological technician in your town? Never mind grabbing for the well-thumbed dictionary—unless it is very up to date the term won't be in it. If you live in Louisville you may bow to the applause and admit that we have one. It is young—it is a woman—it has lovely auburn hair—and to put her title in words more familiar to us laymen, she is an X-ray specialist—and her name is Miss Nora D. Dean.

Harrodsburg, Ky., may take a little of the credit, for it produced Miss Dean and turned her loose as a rural school teacher; this in her very, very early youth. Perhaps she questioned the possibility of inculcating knowledge into a mixed school of boys and girls, ranging from age 6 to 20—a condition still existing in many rural sections—for she decided that she had more to give the world in other lines, and in 1912 arrived in Louisville to enter the Norton Infirmary for training as a nurse.

She was graduated in 1915 with honors, and just to prove that youth can't keep a good man down, was appointed superintendent of the St. Rose Hospital at Great Bend, Kansas. Fortunately for her reputation as a mother of great men, Kentucky has a penchant for calling her own back to her. She may let her children roam the world for a time; perhaps even acquire fame in foreign parts; but sooner or later she beckons in the wanderers and gives them work to do at home. The Bluegrass State ran true to form in Miss Dean's case, and arguing that a good Kentucky superintendent of nurses in Kansas was better yet in Kentucky, called her to Louisville as supervisor and instructor of nurses at the Deaconess Hospital. There she held sway, making, among myriad of friends, one enemy—an energetic reporter who, seeing the ambulance chasing down the street, dashed also, arriving far in advance of the dead or dying to elicit information. This ir-

---

36 Wilhelm Conrad Röntgen (1845–1923), German physicist, discovered in 1895 the short-wave ray, or X-ray, for which he received the Nobel Prize in Physics in 1901. A roentgenologist is one who specializes in the taking and interpreting of X-rays.

37 Arthur B. Reeve (1880–1936) was noted for the scientific inventions in his detective stories.

resistible reportorial force met the usual immovable body, Miss Dean, intent on saving the life of the accident case, and with no time to tell the press whether it were murder or suicide. The result of the impact, oft repeated, was the free, gratis, unsolicited name, presented to Miss Dean by the energetic reporter, of "The Wildcat."[38] Which gives you an insight into her character when the performing of her duty is involved. In France this characteristic was turned to account in seeing that her boys had everything that it was within the power of the American Commissary and the French peasantry to procure for them.

France? Well, you might know she'd get there, mightn't you?

In June, 1918, Dr. Irvin Abell of Louisville organized a unit of Kentucky registered nurses,[39] among them Miss Dean, which after preliminary training at Fort Meade, Md., was sent abroad. There the unit was scattered, fifty only going to Base Hospital 59 at Rimaucourt, Haute Marne, France.

Base 59 was in an advance sector, some forty-five miles from the firing lines—which is not so far when you think of the distance that the sound of the big guns carried. Even across the channel, in England, could be heard the deep reverberations. The capacity of the hospital was 1,100 beds at first, but increased, as the need increased to 2,500 by the use of tents. The wounded came by hospital train from St. Mihiel, the Argonne and the Meuse regions, as many coming in one night as 1,100—the hospital's complete capacity. Many of the convoys arrived at night, and the wounded had to be cared for almost in darkness, as orders were strict against the display of lights. An American Red Cross hospital was no safer from Boche [German] planes than an artillery unit. Miss Dean has very little to say about this part of her experiences. Commenting that from twenty to thirty boys died every night, she seemed to hint that that told the story.

Mixed with the tragedy was of course the usual fun, that the American will find anywhere—and even if the occasional dance to which she went was interrupted by a hurry call from her ward to get them cigarettes—necessitating her leaving the festivities for an hour or so—the fun was there. And best of all she made the acquaintance of General Pershing's beautiful horse,[40] almost as widely known as the commander himself. And was allowed to ride him from time to time.

The armistice came, but thousands of wounded were still to be cared for, and

---

38 Dean's nickname is probably derived from the mascot of the University of Kentucky, the wildcat.

39 Irvin Abell (1876–1949), a prominent surgeon in Louisville, was based at St. Joseph's Infirmary, which also had a school of nursing.

40 General John Joseph Pershing (1860–1948) was appointed to command the American Expeditionary Forces (AEF) in France in 1917. His famous horse's name was Kidron.

Base Hospital 59 went on as before. Then in the early spring of 1919 Miss Dean was made chief nurse, a position she held until the hospital unit was demobilized in June. She arrived home on the U. S. S. Imperator and headed direct for little old Louisville. She reached town on July 23—and went to work August 1. I ask you—is that "live" or isn't it?

Since that busy first August she has been engaged with the subtle workings of the X-ray machine, acting as a technician for a local firm of doctors. Her preliminary training was at Camp Meade and the remainder has been acquired in Louisville. The Roentgen ray, as it is now known to the highbrows, is named after Roentgen, the father of the X-ray. Miss Dean, writing in a recent issue of the American Journal of Nursing on "The Roentgenological Field for Nurses," says:

"The study of the Roentgen ray and its usage may be considered new in the nursing world, but it is a lusty infant, and like every other, it required time for development. When the discoveries of Roentgen, Becquerel, and Curie were first put into practical application by the medical profession,[41] they were considered rather dangerous and it was thought that the Roentgenologist would never consent to the assistance of a nurse; instead, there is today a vast field open to nurses who care to devote their time and study to this science."

"The Roentgen ray has been, in the past few years, so studied and simplified by our expert scientists and Roentgenologists, that it proves to have untold value to the medical profession in the diagnosis and treatment of disease."

As Miss Dean indicates, the work is in two sections—diagnosis and treatment, equally valuable. Hidden ills loom obvious in the "shadow photographs."

"The theory of shadow formation," says Miss Dean, "is very important, and as the Roentgenologist depends entirely upon the shadow formation in making a diagnostic reading, a nurse must familiarize herself with the normal shadows and their relation to each other, in their normal position, under normal conditions, or she will not be qualified to make a satisfactory plate."

"There are a few simple laws governing the physics of X-ray that are essential for a nurse to know, such as the laws of governing control, voltage, spark gap, exposure, milliamperes, etc.," she comments.

Miss Dean gives treatments also, using a combination of rubber and lead as a protector for the patient—for there are several kinds of "rays" emanating from an X-ray, some of them undesirable. The rubber insulates against one ray,

---

41 Antoine Henri Becquerel (1852–1908) discovered radioactivity in uranium in 1896, for which he received the Nobel Prize in Physics in 1903. Pierre Curie (1859–1906) and Marie Curie (1867–1934) were known for their work on radioactivity and for isolating uranium and shared the Nobel Prize for Physics with Becquerel.

the lead against another—and the desired rays drift casually through, curing all kinds of diseases, including cancer of certain types. And speaking of danger! The patient is thoroughly insulated, the table on which he lies and the very ground under him being danger-free—but so far there has been found no way of protecting the operator, beyond natural caution. I am told that one day, otherwise sunny and clear, Miss Dean awoke on the couch after a sudden sleep occasioned by something like a live wire, or a spark gap, or something equally strange but deadly. None of which disturbs her enthusiasm. After having been with the A.E.F. as chief nurse of an important base, a mere shock of a few thousand volts of electricity has no permanent effect. She is too accustomed to the unexpected, if I may utter a paradox.

There is one thing alone which causes consternation in the mind of the Roentgenological technician—a nervous woman! The nervous woman is a genus homo all by herself, and black is the day when she comes in for treatment. Everyone flees except the Roentgenological technician, who has to stay to operate the machine. The room is dark, and the only sound is a whirring sputter of the Roentgen ray—and the squeals of the patient, who hears the voice of Gabriel in every sputter. She is perfectly safe; treatments are utterly without sensation; but still she squeals and the technician has to go ahead, manipulating the most delicate machines in the world.

Miss Dean finds the work inspiring, however, because of its incomparable value. With a view to ever increased usefulness, she wishes to become a physician, but meantime, the long hours of study of this remarkable science have been well spent.

Marjorie Kinnan Rawlings

"A Roentgenological Technician," *Louisville (Ky.) Courier-Journal*, Sunday magazine, 13 February 1921, 4.

*   *   *   *   *   *   *   *   *

Live Women in Live Louisville

The Chief Probation Officer for Jefferson County

When the hoofs of my trusty steed the typewriter pound out the words, live woman, I usually try to talk about the woman. But in this case I am going to talk about a live job, and with the remark that it takes a live woman to hold it, let you draw your own conclusions. Along with other women who really accomplished something, Mrs. Emma B. Hegan, Chief Probation Officer for Jefferson County, including Louisville, doesn't enjoy the thought of personal publicity. But her job—that is another matter.

"I want people to know what the Juvenile Court is doing and trying to do," she told me in her office at the Court House.

Mrs. Hegan is, to all practical purposes, the Juvenile Court, and with enchanting graciousness admitted that, to talk of its work, I must perforce talk of her. The job is Mrs. Hegan, and Mrs. Hegan is the job. I couldn't imagine anyone else sitting in her chair any more than I could imagine a statue of George the Third in the place of the statue of Liberty.[42] The success of any Juvenile Court, of any probation office, is dependent upon the personality of the officer in charge and to hear, as I did, the stories told her in such naïve and trusting confidence, would convince you of her influence.

"Just sit in that chair behind mine and listen," she said. "You will learn more about the work than I could tell you."

"But will they talk when someone else is here?" I asked. And she nodded.

"That won't make any difference."

And bless your heart, it didn't! I must be a friend of "Miss Emma," as she is known to many, or I wouldn't be there. And any friend of hers could listen to anything she thought fit for her to hear. So out came the stories regardless of my presence.

As it happened, the visitors during the time I was in the office were parents or relatives of delinquent children. The first was the mother of an 11-year-old boy, who had been in a detention home for nearly a year. Tom acted as a "lookout" in a minor robbery—perpetrated by bandits little older than himself—and while the spirit of the adventure doubtless was as fundamental a motive as the desire to steal, it was thought best for Tom to be withdrawn from society until he could be taught some of the essentials of good citizenship. The mother feels that he has learned a lesson, and came to ask for his withdrawal. Mrs. Hegan is not authorized to order a discharge, and this the mother knew—but she came direct to "Miss Emma" with her plea.

"I think he is broke now, or I wouldn't ask fer him out. I don't want to cause no trouble to nobody."

And then she added, as mothers have added since the beginning of time, "He ain't a bad boy. He just didn't know no better."

---

42 George III (1738–1820), king of Great Britain from 1760 to 1820.

Next came the mother of Jenny L., insisting that "Jenny ain't a bad girl," and asking for her dismissal from a detention home. In this case Mrs. Hegan agreed that Jenny was not bad, but told me afterwards that she was potentially so, and that it was probably vital to her moral well being that she have the supervision and training of an institution until she reached something like maturity—for Jenny is only 15. Mrs. Hegan's job in this instance is to persuade the mother that Jenny is better off where she is. Even the discipline the mother promised to administer at home would doubtless fail of its effect, as her sole idea was to "make Jenny work hard and go to Sunday-school." All of which left out the important factor in Jenny's need for recreation, which she receives in wholesome quantities at her present home.

The next parent was undoubtedly parent to a Booth Tarkington character,[43] Edgar Alfred, age 10, whose "case" will ultimately go to court because of the irate temper of the gentleman who insists that Edgar Alfred is a thief. Edgar Alfred had a job as office boy. Edgar Alfred got another job that paid more money, and he left his first employer flat. His second employer, a gentleman inspiring great devotion from all accounts, remarked soon after Edgar Alfred's arrival, "I do wish I had a dictaphone."

"Why, say," piped up Edgar Alfred, "I know where there is a dictaphone I could get yuh."

"Fine!" said the devotion-inspiring employer, and thought no more about it.

After hours Edgar Alfred beat it to the office of employer number one, and transferred a dusty dictaphone to his new place of business, probably beaming with pride. Unfortunately number one calls the transfer a theft, and will take the affair to court. As a matter of fact, Edgar Alfred did not steal the dictaphone. He simply "knew where there was one"! But even his mother, who visits Mrs. Hegan every day for reassurance that the judge won't lock him up, has to admit that he shouldn't have done it.

Such cases are a minor part of the work, but each one is a matter of delicate adjustment, requiring infinite patience and kindness and understanding of people.

I was not surprised, then, to have Mrs. Hegan say, during our conversation, "No one should go into social service work of any sort without a very deep love of humanity."

---

43 Booth Tarkington (1869–1946), author of romantic novels about growing up in the Midwest.

Interestingly enough, just a few days ago I heard Mrs. Cornelia Parker, author of "An American Idyll,"[44] make almost an identical remark in an address at the University of Wisconsin. I think I may add that the only influential people in the field of social service are those with this love. Mrs. Hegan's success is intimately bound up with it. Certainly, a love of humanity is a primate [prime] requisite to the understanding of humanity. I do not believe that the cynic or the pessimist really understands human nature. Margot Asquith says, "You will seldom find enough pity for the pathos of life,"[45] and I thought of that when Mrs. Hegan said, "My usefulness here would cease the moment I lost my capacity for pity."

Certainly the conditions that bring people to her are the most pitiable possible, for they are the conditions which strike at the welfare of children. And it is the children for whom she is working. One motto is constantly in her mind: "The child first!"

"You cannot change the adult," she says, "but you can change conditions for the child. And the whole world depends on the child, and on the conditions which make him what he is."

Mrs. Hegan's constant efforts are to develop the child, not to incarcerate him. Her work is constructive and positive. "What is best for the child?" is the question she asks herself in every case—and she is deeply wise in her answers.

Anything affecting the welfare of children is her business. Truancy is her concern. Juvenile delinquency, in boys up to 17 years of age, and girls up to 18, is for her. And, what she considers the most important problem, the problem of the dependent child; that is, the child dependent on society through failure of its parents to provide properly for it. That failure may come from any one of a number of causes: actual neglect, illness of either or both parents; poverty due to shiftlessness, lack of ability, illness or economic conditions in the world at large; or either or both of the parents may be dead; or they may be divorced or separated.

One of the, to me, most startling facts relating to the influence of a stable life in juvenile delinquency, and on the problem of the child dependent on society instead of its parents, was the following, made as a positive statement by Mrs. Hegan:

"In practically all of the cases brought before me, the mother is dead or the parents are separated."

---

44 Cornelia Parker (1885–1972), *An American Idyll: The Life of Carleton H. Parker* (Boston: Atlantic Monthly Press, 1919).

45 Margot Asquith (1864–1945), Countess of Oxford and of Asquith, noted for her wit. The quote is from Asquith's *Autobiography* (New York: Doran, 1920), 1: 156.

I prefer to leave this without further comment. Journalism the garrulous is tongued-tied in the presence of such a statement.

The problem of the dependent child, or of parental nonsupport is fundamental. A delinquent child could, if necessary, go unpunished, unstudied, but a hungry child has to be fed, a naked child clothed, and a corner for sleep provided. If there are no parents, or the parents cannot provide for the child, society must take up the burden. In the latter event, the parents must be put on their feet: illness if that is the trouble, cured; a job found, if unemployment is to blame. In many such cases, the children are placed in an institution until home conditions are bettered, the father paying in as much money as possible toward their support—only a dollar or so each week for each child. All this money goes through Mrs. Hegan's office. While I was there, some soiled bills came in from Peter Piper, whose four children are in an institution due to their father's more or less romantic tendency to take to the woods on the slightest excuse.[46] The parents are separated, probably due to the same tendency—but whether he is a-gypsying or a-Maying or what-not, Peter Piper sends money each week toward the support of his quartette. The law says he has to!

What Mrs. Hegan feels is deeply needed is boarding homes for dependent children, to accommodate not more than five or six children at a time. She would encourage working women with homes to open them to these youngsters, as a means of augmenting their incomes, in preference to working in factories. It would be better for the women, and certainly better for the children, who would thus have the advantages of a real home. However fine an institution, it cannot replace a small home, with individual care and attention from a good, responsible woman. Jefferson County detention homes are fearfully overcrowded. The county could not handle satisfactorily its own delinquent children, and there are in addition many children to be cared for of families from other counties who have moved recently into Jefferson County, hoping to find work and better wages in Louisville. A Children's Bureau is needed, to place dependent children in "natural" homes, under the care of capable women. But, in this, as in everything else, the public must realize a need before any legislative action can ameliorate conditions.

"We of the Juvenile Court can do more and more as the public is awakened to the needs of the child of the streets."

It is an encouraging fact to those of us who are the public, that the Juvenile Court, the Schools of Correction, and the board connected with the schools,

---

46 MKR's alias is derived from the tongue twister in the Mother Goose Nursery Rhymes: "Peter Piper picked a peck of pickled peppers."

are nonpartisan, thus auguring well for the passage of goods laws from time to time—and for the continued efficiency of the personnel.

Mrs. Hegan knows the psychology of Louisville. Each section of the city has its own juvenile peculiarities. Born and raised twenty miles from the city, and almost a life-long resident, she knows what she is doing. She broke into the field as a volunteer, doing case and field work for the court. She was later engaged by the Children's Protective Association, and has held her present position—which in a majority of cases is held by a man—for the past three years. She knows when a case rings true; knows from the reports of her worker if the truth has been told them; as she tells them herself, "I walked the beat once myself." Her only fatigue at the end of the day comes when she feels that a problem has gone unsolved.

Her ability to cooperate with other organizations works to the advantage of the children. The Children's Protective Association, the American Red Cross, the Board of Health, the Psychopathic Clinic—which examines children from the Juvenile Court—and Humane Societies all over the country, all work with her.

It is a twenty-four hour job. She is on call at any hour of the day or night, like a physician. She has, literally, no time to think of herself, but only of these children who must have their chance, and back of which are countless evils: bad housing, disease, ignorance, alcoholism and what is temporarily worse, the system of alcoholic substitutes, poverty, feeble-mindedness—and that condition so appalling universal, when a man's income is on the decline, and his family on the increase.

In reality, the Chief Probation Officer of Jefferson County is holding down a job for the whole community. She is looking after the community's interests. That she is live enough to do it successfully, and to hold the confidence of every child and every parent she sees, may well be a matter of pride. In treating more of a world than of an individual, I hope that I have given you a glimpse of a live woman—and, as suggested before, a woman deeply kind and deeply wise. If I also add that a perpetual good humor is necessary to do the job, you will appreciate with me a nature which can be optimistic in the face of daily contact with countless tragedies.

Marjorie Kinnan Rawlings

"The Chief Probation Officer for Jefferson County," *Louisville (Ky.) Courier-Journal*, Sunday magazine, 6 March 1921, 6.

Live Women in Live Louisville

The Cashier for One of the South's Largest Manufacturing Concerns

Most men are willing to spend money on a girl—but not so many are pleased at the prospect of letting her handle it herself. The chap who gives the most liberal box of chocolate marshmallows in his courting days keeps the closest tab on the object of his affections after she has promised to love, honor, and obey—but has carefully refrained from making him any rash promises on the subject of finances.

There seems to be an idea throughout all civilized countries—and I'll wager it holds true in the African jungles—that a woman has no head for figures, and the further you keep her away from your roll, and from your bank the better off you'll be on the first of the month. Probably the dusky Hottentot[47] forbids his spouse to touch his sack of alligator teeth or whatever is the currency of the locality, saying, "You make good soup, but you don't know anything about money."

The feminists would claim that this is part of masculine selfishness. They claim that in the case of ancient Hawaii, where it was once a deadly sin for a woman to eat a banana—not because bananas disagreed with her, but because there weren't enough bananas to go around—and that was the delicate male way of assuring that he would get them. Touch a man's pocketbook and you touch his heart. And whether you want to look on his gold rubles as Hawaiian bananas and call it the instinct for self-preservation that makes him keep up the management of them for himself, or whether you are kind-hearted, you must admit that a man thinks a long, long time before he hands over his hard-earned money to a woman. If banks had women cashiers and women tellers I'd bet—at about 3 to 2—that the instinct would operate to such an extent that the bank's receipts would fall off and the old woollen [*sic*] sock would be brought forth for the hoarding of savings! In making such a statement, I hope I'm not keeping a woman from being appointed to a nice, fat job in a bank! For, by the way, I have so far been unable to find a woman in an executive capacity in any of the Louisville banks.

"Oh, no," officials have exclaimed when questioned. "Oh, mercy, no!"

After reminding you of the usual viewpoint on the relation of a woman to a

---

47 The Khoikoi, or Khoi, people of southwestern Africa were initially dubbed the "Hottentots" by Europeans.

column of figures—particularly when there is a dollar sign at the head—I expect you to be duly impressed when I inform you that one of the most important positions in the world of industrial finance in Louisville is held by a woman— and a very young woman! She is a wizard at figures and is cashier of the B. F. Avery & Sons, an important Southern manufacturing concern. Her name is as far removed from the realms of finance as is possible—Miss Blanche De Rose. I must admit that she looks her name, but far more blooms within her brain than thoughts of summer flowers!

Some few years ago Miss De Rose entered the employ of the Avery Company in a minor capacity as a bookkeeper. Her only previous training had been in the cashier's offices of a Louisville department store. She had been educated at private schools, and had had no commercial schooling—which would seem to show that strong tendencies assert themselves regardless of training and conditions. Step by step she advanced until she had charge of the customers' ledgers of the Avery concern, work which never before had been intrusted to a woman. It was obvious that this quiet young woman brought something to her work that was worth watching.

Then came the war. The cashier of the company was called to Government duty in connection with the income tax commission, where the highest experts were needed. This most responsible position then fell vacant and the surrounding landscape was scoured with microscope, periscope, telescope and stethoscope for signs of a man good enough for the job, and not already engaged in serving Uncle Sam. While the hunt was on, the treasurer of the company bided his time. It was like the old game of hide and seek. Don't you remember how you never thought of looking in the nearest cubby-holes for the person in hiding? And how sometimes he turned up right under your nose—in the clothes hamper, perhaps, where you had passed a dozen times? And so it was in this case. The perfect incumbent for this important position was right there all the time, going on with her regular work, and totally unaware of conditions. It had certainly never occurred to her, of all people, that she was in line for the job.

Then came the day when the treasurer addressed the assembled officials.

"Gentlemen," he said, "gentlemen—I have found our new cashier."

We can safely assume that there was a little rustle as the assembled officials leaned back and took off their nose glasses. If I were a Saturday Evening Post writer, with the courage of my convictions which 5 cents a word brings, I should draw a picture of the gentlemen of business at this moment, impatiently awaiting the denouement. I should describe the president drumming on the desk, and so forth. But I should probably also give quite an erroneous portrait—which would never do in a city where almost everyone knows almost everyone else. But we shall assume, anyway, that someone said:

"And who is he?"

And this paves the way for the treasurer's dramatic utterance:

"It is a woman. It is Miss Blanche De Rose, already connected with our concern.

I have the treasurer's own word for what followed. The officials said, "A woman? Impossible! We have never had a woman in such a responsible position. It is out of the question."

Here was the situation: The firm of B. F. Avery and Sons lacks some four years and some days of being 100 years old. In all that time there had never been a woman in the executive job of cashier of the company. No woman had held a position with the firm even approximating this job in responsibility. That a woman should be capable of handling figures to this extent seemed incredible. But again the treasurer, who had best known the work of Miss De Rose, said:

"I am so convinced that you will find her satisfactory, that I am willing to assume the entire responsibility of her making good."

And that settled it. Miss Blanche De Rose was created cashier. She still holds the position, although the war has come and gone. And this is the consensus of opinion in her firm; never, in a hundred years of existence, has the Avery Company had a better cashier; it has only had one who might possibly be called as good! It was a firm of auditors with an international reputation which dubbed her "the wizard," saying that they had never seen her equal. She seldom needs an adding machine. One slow glance down the column, and the sum total is hers!

"Why," I was told in a hushed voice by one of her admirers, "she picks off figures as if she were picking blackberries!"

Those who have seen bank-tellers throughout the United States say that she handles bills twice as rapidly as the most expert. She is never behind with her work.

"She doesn't have to stay nights and work, as the men did," I was told. "Her work is always done."

If Miss De Rose's admirers were not vociferous, it would be impossible to glean all the remarkableness of her job. She herself thinks there is nothing unusual in a woman's holding such a position. She sees nothing unusual in her ability. She said, however, that it has been her experience that women make better clerks than men, because of greater conscientiousness and attention to detail.

It is on these latter grounds that her own success might be explained.

"I have always taken a personal pride in my work," she said. "There is a superlative joy in doing the immediate task to the best of one's ability. I have always felt that the pleasure of work well done was greater than any monetary gain."

After all, the right sort of business man must feel that way. Isn't it natural to expect a woman to be a success when she puts herself into her work so thoroughly, as wholeheartedly, as a man? She believes in giving oneself completely to the job in hand. If the job happens to be matrimony, or motherhood, she believes that a woman should put her whole brain, as well as her heart, into the work. For there is no successful shirking of the immediate task, in her philosophy.

Miss De Rose believes strongly in a girl's training herself to earn her own living, and feels that there is no job too big for a woman nowadays. She is a recent and enthusiastic member of the Business and Professional Women's Clubs, which she considers a broadening influence for business women.

If Miss De Rose some day becomes a bank president, Louisville will be glad to know that she was "born and raised" in this city, and that all her heart is here. The more I think about it the more I feel that the air of the Ohio Valley must have an especially beneficent effect on women's brains and energies. Something strange in the climate must account for a young woman's being intrusted with columns of figures pertinent to a huge manufactory!

Marjorie Kinnan Rawlings

"The Cashier for One of the South's Largest Manufacturing Concerns," *Louisville (Ky.) Courier-Journal*, Sunday magazine, 13 March 1921, 4.

*   *   *   *   *   *   *   *   *

Live Women in Live Louisville

A Member of the Louisville Board of Fire Underwriters

O for the virile pen of Horatio Alger.[48] What does it matter that the hero is a woman? She has trod the path to success in the very manner which that leader of ambitious youth has sponsored, and I feel the need of his solemn style. I should like to picture my lady hero, surrounded in early youth by a bevy of girls indifferent to their employer's welfare, but with her own eyes fixed firmly on the goal ahead, working whole-heartedly for "the firm." I should like to make you gasp

---

48 Horatio Alger (1834–99), author of idealistic books for boys founded on the theory that if one struggles against poverty and temptation, then one will achieve wealth and fame.

with admiration for her indomitable will?—and make you clutch the arm of your chair for fear the villain was going to keep her for promotion. But there wasn't any villain, and I should only succeed in making my hero sue me for alienation of the public's affections—so I shall forget Horatio Alger with a sigh, and tell the story in my own frivolous way.

My hero is Miss Theresa Moellman, full partner in the firm of Moellman & Hennessey, and a portion of Kentucky's population comes daily to her with requests that she underwrite fire insurance on the family garage, bungalow or chicken coop, whatever happens to be most valuable. She is one of only two women members of the Louisville Board of Fire Underwriters—and if you must know it—I was so busy listening to Miss Moellman's answers to my questions that it never occurred to me to ask the name of the other woman member. I can't listen and think at the same time. But then I have heard of people who couldn't talk and think at the same time, so my case can't be unusual.

If I were Alger, I shouldn't have to tell you until the very end that our hero became a member of a fire insurance firm, with her name in gilt on the glass door. My simpler soul has not the knack of creating suspense. But I had to get that out of my system before I could tell you how she got there.

"How she got there" is the most interesting part of the story. In some cases the job itself is a story. In others, as here, the devious path that led to a job is a movie serial in itself. Ladies, bare your ears:

Miss Theresa Moellman worked her way through business college! Doesn't that alone qualify her as a self-starter for any machine? The school was the Bryan and Stratton Business College of Louisville. When she graduated a job in the County Clerk's office engaged her attention, and there she gained her experience in real estate. She learned to write deeds, to draw up contracts, to close deals. Here an idea entered her clever head, and Part Two shows her working in the office of J. W. Henning & Sons, a firm, now defunct, which was successor to Henning & Speed. If my knowledge does not fail me, Henning and Speed were the original surveyors of Louisville, and Louisville's oldest real estate firm, so our hero's business ancestry is sound.

With J. W. Henning & Sons, Miss Moellman entered on that far-famed pursuit known as "working up," and her success has justified her theories as to the wisdom of staying with one concern and reaching the top. Promotion came steadily. She saved her gold shekels.[49] She invested them, and made six grow where but one had gleamed before. She reached out into real estate transactions.

---

49 MKR is alluding to the parable of the talents, Matthew 25:14-20, where the two resourceful servants invest their money and the slothful third hides his.

She tasted the joys of insuring people, and seeing them alive and their houses unburned—which is good for the people and the insurance companies both. Her ears were gladdened by a rustic gentleman who said:

"Wa'l—it's better to have insurance an' not needin' it, than to need it an' not havin' it."

Five years ago Miss Moellman became a full partner in Moellman & Hennessey, which bought out her old firm of Henning & Sons. Fire insurance is her business, her love and her life. Odds and ends of real estate deals, her early love, come to the firm, which also manages the Todd building. For several years she has acted as a private secretary to Mr. James Ross Todd, whose offices adjoin those of her firm. Her name is on the glass door, in the building directory, in everything. Not enough grass has grown under her feet to make a garden in a bird cage.

I'd like to have every working girl in Louisville know Miss Moellman's philosophy of work. I'd like to have them "get it" with all her sincerity behind it. If they did—well, I'd have enough "live women" to write about to keep me busy until the day I buy me a ghost.

Here is the Mississippi River of her philosophy, into which all of her other theories empty:

"Always do a little more than is expected of you."

The girl who is going to succeed, says Miss Moellman, mustn't be afraid of working overtime. She must never watch the clock. As a matter of fact, there is no such thing as "overtime." There are jobs well done and jobs badly done—and if you would have yours in the former class, you mustn't think that Saturday afternoons and holidays are planned solely for your amusement. They are sometimes mighty convenient for finishing up a job! Miss Moellman found them so—but then:

"I was as interested in my employer's firm as I am now in my own," she told me. Which accounts for many things, including her belief that it is better to stay with one firm and work to the top, than to change from firm to firm, even if the immediate job offered seems better.

"I was offered other jobs with more money, but all the time I felt that if I stayed with 'my' firm and worked up, some day, I would be in the business."

Her confidence expressed itself in her willingness to try anything. She never said she could not do a task asked of her. If other women had done it, she could learn.

Miss Moellman has an interesting theory, with which most thinking people will agree, that one class of girl has held back the advance of women in business—the girl whose whole object in life is to marry. This girl considers her work temporary. No matter how young she is, she feels that the work is of no importance, since she is destined to domesticity. Such an attitude gives an indifference to her employer's interests, and even to her own advancement. She is slipshod and careless, indifferent and bored. These girls, in Miss Moellman's opinion, give women in business a dubious reputation, and are responsible for the fact that many firms still prefer to employ men exclusively. A business house must be able to count on the interest of its employees.

"It would be absurd for a girl to go into business feeling that she will never marry," says Miss Moellman, "but as long as she is in business, she should put thoughts of marriage behind her, and give herself whole-heartedly to her work."

It is obvious that our hero loves to work.

"I love business. I love to write deeds, to draw up contracts. I love to close deals, whether they are ones I am to get a profit on or not. I love the contact with business men, who talk to me as a mental equal. I like to get their ideas."

Miss Moellman chuckled as she told me of one girl whom she informed of her love for work. "Do you know what I think?" whispered the girl to her, "I—I think you're—a—liar!"

But our hero loves business as the girl just mentioned probably loves Mary Garden perfume.[50] Our hero knows the zest of a good scrap against odds, and has tasted the fruits of victory.

Didn't I tell you she needed an Alger to write her history?

Marjorie Kinnan Rawlings

"A Member of the Louisville Board of Fire Underwriters," *Louisville (Ky.) Courier-Journal*, Sunday magazine, 27 March 1921, 4.

* * * * * * * * *

Live Women in Live Louisville

A Pioneer Booster of Women in Business

More than twenty-three years ago the Masonic Home sent a pink-cheeked youngster to the Louisville Trust Company, to be embarked on a business career. At that time the woman in business was as rare as the pterodactyl—and

---

50 Mary Garden (1874–1967), Scottish opera singer who had a perfume named after her by Rigaud in Paris.

you know how few of those we see. In fact, the only man I have heard of who has seen one wasn't [so] sure about it the morning after. Twenty-five years ago a woman must be a teacher, a seamstress, or a wife [who] would pay her way in the world. At that time, then, the little girl who went to the Louisville Trust Company must do one of two things; become submerged, a mere cog in a machine, another example of the theory that a woman was unfit for business—or become considerable of a pioneer in the great world government to increase the value of [man] in the modern scheme of things. Machinery had taken from women many of their earlier functions—the spinning, the weaving, the elaborate sewing, the dyeing—and the turning out came not so much more than a quarter century ago, when the choice must be made between a partial existence of some sort, and a life of real usefulness in the world, working at anything a man might work at.

The girl chose the latter course, chose to exert her influence against the old traditions that were hampering many women in business, chose to work for the welfare of employed women.

Miss Nora Kirch may be presented, then, as a pioneer in Louisville. She is still with the Louisville Trust Company in a position of responsibility. She probably has as wide an acquaintance in Louisville as any business woman. Her work brings her into constant contact with people, as a trained first company woman. Judiciary matters are her concern, and the intricate details of a mortgage are to her as gum-drops to a small boy. Commercial law is a page in a primer to her, and the patrons of her company feel an infinite trust in her ability and judgment.

But it is not her job, nor her vigorous personality, that is intriguing my fancies at the moment, but her ideas on women in business, and particularly on the club movement for business women. Her deepest belief is that the club movement, as embodied in the National Federation of Business and Professional Women's Clubs, is the surest way of "awakening women to greater ambition and higher standards." She is responsible for organizing the Louisville Business and Professional Women's Club, fast becoming an influence in the community. Miss Kirch is a vice president in the national federation. There is one president, and each State has a vice president, the latter making up the national Executive Committee. Miss Kirch represents Kentucky in this important movement, and California never had a better booster than she. She is "bound 'n determined" that Kentucky shall take her place among her Southern neighbors who have already come forward with strong State organizations and with such evidences of power as club houses.

In undertaking the organization of the Louisville Federation, Miss Kirch relied largely on the judgment of Louisville's business men, who have shown a desire to co-operate with the movement. She wrote to more than two hundred business men of her immediate acquaintance, asking for the names of their most aggressive women. And women whose names were sent her in answer formed the nucleus of the federation. The may be considered to represent Louisville business women.

The Altrusa Club was Louisville's first club for business women,[51] and [one] Miss Kirch organized four years ago, acting as its president the first two critical years of growth. This club is small, with a limited membership, and is on the Rotary Club plan. Last week it joined the State Federation of Business and Professional Women's Clubs, organized March 5 by the Paducah Federation; two clubs at Lexington, and the Louisville Federation. Miss Ann Baker, of Paducah, reputed to be Kentucky's highest-paid woman, is president of the State Federation.

The matter of equal pay for equal work is one of the great concerns of the National Federation. "The Independent Woman," the official organ, speaks of the matter thus:

"Is there a need for an organization of business and professional women? Any doubt will be set at rest by an 'ad' which appeared in 'Printers' Ink' under the caption, 'Positions Wanted.'"

"'Because I Am a Woman—You can secure my services for a moderate salary. Few men have had the same training and experience as editor, publicity writer, sales promoter, college professor and business analyst. Ready to work out any difficult problem with busy executive. State nature of the business and problem. Box 769.'"

"The Independent Woman" points out the sermon in the ad, a sermon to make the federation members even more enthusiastic in their work and in upholding the principles of the organization, a sermon for the woman willing to work for less than her services are worth, and a sermon for employers.

The question of eight-hour laws for women will be voted on at the national convention, to be held in Cleveland from July 19 to 22. As the sentiment now stands, the federation has gone on record as standing for a law that applies to human beings, with differentiations made between various professions, not between men and women.

The Chautauqua [New York] authorities have become so impressed with the importance and the momentum of this movement, that they have donated one

---

51 The National Association of Altrusa Clubs, founded in 1917, was the first national organization for professional and business women.

week, gratis, to the national federation. The advent will follow the adjournment of the convention, and will consume from July 25 to 30. When anyone gives something away, you just naturally know they believe in the cause for the gift.

Miss Kirch, if she had her way, would have every business girl or woman in Louisville attend that convention, and a goodly number have readily arranged to go. Their employers are quite naturally interested, because any movement that stirs a girl to greater activity, ambition and energy is to his advantage. The slow girl may not stir up much dust, in an office, but she doesn't mean much extra business to a firm. The interest of several local firms in the movement was evidenced in the courtesies shown to out-of-town guests of the Louisville Federation, recognizing the "arrival" of business and professional women.

What Miss Kirch is working toward at present is a clubhouse that might shelter all of Louisville women's clubs, including the Women's City Club. She has only her hopes to go on, she explains—but what project ever got anywhere without hope for a basis? If the women's clubs could come together in a cooperative spirit to find shelter for their various activities and needs—taking over, for instance, the Elks' Club on Walnut Street if the plans for a new clubhouse on Shirley Place should get through—much might be accomplished. Miss Audrey Cossar, president of the Louisville Federation, is something of a genius in resources, and Louisville had best kept [keep] its ears to the ground for news of some such project.

In all her work for business women, Miss Kirch holds the desire to make things easier for younger women coming along than they have been for the present generation. If they can enter business with more equal opportunities than in the past, the work of the pioneers who always pay the price for advancement will not have been in vain.

The difference between men and women is not that either sex can do what the other cannot, but the difference in [is] personality, is Miss Kirch's opinion. Men have learned to put their personalities across—and a big personality can go further in exactly the same work than a small personality.

Psychologically, women have been, says Miss Kirch, "unconsciously conscious that they could not do what men do." The traditions of the race are to blame, she insists, and no one is responsible. Certainly not the broad minded business man, who has given a helping hand to women in new fields, realizing that her progress is the world's progress as well.

Marjorie Kinnan Rawlings

"A Pioneer Booster of Women in Business," *Louisville (Ky.) Courier-Journal*, Sunday magazine. 10 April 1921, 3.

The Vagrant of Romance Finds Large City Harsh

Young Eloper Anxious to Return to Peace of Small Town She Found Tiresome

Tonawanda isn't very big—as cities go.[52] The woods and meadows are stupidly close to the heart of town, and when night comes down, the street lights don't seem as bright as—well, as bright as Rochester.

Four months ago it seemed to Margaret Bigger, sixteen years old, that she couldn't endure Tonawanda another day. She was pretty, with an elfin charm— and it didn't seem fair that she should have to stay there.

"Nothing ever happened in Tonawanda," she told me. "It was so stupid at home. I wanted to live in a big city. I thought it would be very exciting—so I ran away and came to Rochester."

EXCITEMENT APLENTY.

The little tramp on the trail of romance found her excitement—and found more than she bargained for. The bars of the county jail have shut her off from the big city she found so enticing—and William Holder, twenty-four, of Canada and Buffalo, is being held on a statutory charge and a charge of grand larceny. The pair was arrested in a rooming house at No. 133 Chestnut street, where Holder called them "Mr. and Mrs. Anderson."

"I didn't know that Billy was here when I came to Rochester," she says. "I just met him by accident soon after I arrived. He said that he would take care of me—so I went with him."

In the women's dormitory at the county jail, where I talked with her, she was only concerned with her re-[line missing] refused to remove her, complying with the request of Captain McDonald that she be taken to La Salle to testify against Holder.

"Daddy will take me home when this is all over," she said confidently. "I told him I didn't mean to do anything wrong—and I know he will let me go back."

Margaret doesn't think that she would care to run away again.

"I will be satisfied to stay in Tonawanda now," she declared. "I've seen what

---

52 Tonawanda, town in western New York on the Niagara River between Buffalo and Niagara Falls.

a big city is like—and everything has gone wrong—and I won't want to come back, ever again."

MARRIAGE PROMISED.

Holder, a Canadian war veteran, has a wife in Canada.

"He told me that we would be married when he could get a divorce," the girl explained. "He said that a divorce was very expensive, and he was saving his pension from the Canadian government to get one."

Asked whether she expected to marry him at any time in the future, she answered, very slowly:

"I don't know. I may change my mind. I had expected to—but now I don't know."

During the four months that she was in Rochester, she kept house for Holder, preparing three meals a day.

"He would never let me out alone," she said. "He wouldn't let me meet any boys, or go any place where I might see some. He said that he wanted to protect me."

NOTES TO OTHERS

Questioning revealed the fact that Holder's chivalry was a bit one-sided, as he had social engagement with numerous girls.

"I used to write letters for him to some of them," she told me. "I was never jealous, because Billy said everything was all right."

Throughout the episode of Holder's arrest, Margaret had attempted to shield him. She persistently refused to give the police any information, until Holder himself broke down and made a confession. He is said to have admitted the theft of an automobile.

"I can't believe that he took it," the girl declares. "He doesn't seem like that kind of man. I have trusted him always."

Margaret's father, as well as the police, feel quite different about it. The charges against him will be pressed to the limit. Then, if the girl's belief in her father's forgiveness is not mistaken, she will be taken back to the little town she ran away from.

"I won't leave Tonawanda again," she promises. "I've had enough of the city— I wan't [*sic*] to go home."

Marjorie Kinnan Rawlings

"The Vagrant of Romance Finds Large City Harsh," copy from an unknown newspaper, clipping at Smathers Library, University of Florida.

* * * * * * * * *

"Women Are Spoiled" Protests the Romantic Lou Tellegen

Matinee Idol and Divorced Husband of Geraldine Farrar Lets Cat Out of the Bag

He didn't mean to give anything away, when I talked with him at the Temple Theater yesterday, for I understand he is very touchy on the subject—but as far as I am concerned, Lou has explained the blighting of what seemed the most hopeful romance in many a long, romantic moon.

And as he did this, Geraldine Farrar in New York was announcing that she would sell at auction all the furnishings of the home where she and Tellegen passed so many romantic hours before their separation.[53]

When Geraldine Farrar, operatic, dramatic and personal idol of thousands of fans, forsook her lonely apartment life for housekeeping on a grand and glorious scale, of course—with Tellegen, likewise idol of innumerable sentimental damsels, a fairy tale seemed to have come to life in prosaic little Main Street-y America.[54] The fair princess had married the prince!

ALL SEEMED SO HOPEFUL

Usually, you know, they marry a tobacco merchant, as did Connie Talmadge,[55] or a plumber or janitor, or somebody equally unappealing as a hero. But Lou Tellegen! He was handsome—as any school girl could tell you. He was famous—as all the world knows.

And he had such an undeniable technique at love-making—as evidenced by his dramatic work on the stage and screen—that every one was tickled to pieces to see pictures of the fascinating Geraldine with her hand in his.

It all seemed so very hopeful. Photographs of Geraldine in her elaborate suite,

---

53   Lou Tellegen (1881–1934), a dashing silent film actor, married Geraldine Farrar (1882–1967), the renowned operatic diva and dramatic actor, in 1916. They were divorced in 1923, after considerable public scandal.

54   An allusion to *Main Street* (1920) by Sinclair Lewis (1885–1952), a novel about a woman lost in the narrow-minded atmosphere of a small town in Minnesota.

55   Constance Talmadge (1897–1973), another silent screen actor.

and Lou in his very dressy rooms, all within the Farrar-Tellegen mansion, looked so happily domestic on the grand scale.

And then the photographs of the two together—dearie, dearie me: Lou and Geraldine on the steamship—it was all too good to be true!

BLACK LINING DISPLAYED

The silver cloud turned inside out after a few brief years, showing its black and horrid lining.

And now His Royal Highness of hearts has cast the first bit of illumination on the subject, from the masculine point of view.

"Women are spoiled!"

Seen at the Temple Theater, where he is playing this week in a condensed version of his own play "Blind Youth,"[56] Mr. Tellegen spoke highly of American women—of all women—with the grace of tone and of gesture that have won him his popularity.

But one little phrase slipped out—one little phrase that shows the fairy princess in a new role—that of a captious lady who simply must have everything her own way—or else Biff, Bang, out of the pumpkin coach must fly Romance itself.

Did the magnificent Farrar expect too much of the magnificent Tellegen? Did she fail to make allowances for his regal habit of doing as he pleased, both as regards money and Cinderellas? Or was she, too, so accustomed to having her way that she was, in plain American, downright spoiled?

Remember, Tellegen has been surrounded, as have few men, with feminine admiration. Before the war the stage entrance was always mobbed with "matinee girls" waiting to do him homage. He says:

"The matinee girl has gone, because the war has made the younger generation not only more serious, but more blasé. Young girls do not have the delightful spontaneity of former days. It may come back again—I hope so. I like the inspiration of their youthful enthusiasm."

Did Farrar's enthusiasm likewise die? Did the consequent lack of inspiration turn the perfect lover into a mere every-day husband? Is the key to the ruined fairy story in Tellegen's casual words:

"Women are spoiled?"

Now please he didn't say a word about the lovely Geraldine! He didn't discuss his marital catastrophe at all. And as I told you at the very start, I'm quite sure he didn't mean to give anything away.

---

56 *Blind Youth* (1920), written by Tellegen and Willard Mack (1873–1934), opened on Broadway in December 1917.

But it seems to me that the cat's out of the bag—a spoiled woman can explain so much!

Marjorie Kinnan Rawlings

"'Women Are Spoiled' Protests the Romantic Lou Tellegen," copy from an unknown newspaper, clipping at Smathers Library, University of Florida.

*   *   *   *   *   *   *   *   *

"Flapping Is Merely Joy of Living," Explains High School Flapper

Psychology of the Species Laid Bare by Editor of East High "Clarion"

We all seem to agree that a flapper is any personable female of the younger generation who is obviously enjoying herself. And because she is personable, and because she enjoys herself, she has come in for an enormous amount of fuss and feathers.

But now we are given to understand by a priestess of the cult, that there are two kinds of flappers—brainy flappers and dumb-bells!

The spokesman in behalf of justice is Miss Elizabeth Slayton, daughter of Dr. L. E. Slayton of Spencerport,[57] a senior at East High School. She has just vindicated the younger modern girl by a triumphant issue of "The Clarion," the East High School publication.

As editor-in-chief, she is the third girl in the history of the school to hold such an important position.

It has usually been held that only the brains of an East High boy are equal to the duties of chief editor—but now and then along comes a damsel so obviously equipped for the work that male superiority is temporarily eclipsed, and the damsel is elected to the position.

You will grant, will you not, that a flapper of such caliber is competent to speak on the subject of her kind? Miss Slayton has given real thought to the problem, and knows whereof she speaks.

---

57 Spencerport is ten miles west of Rochester on the Erie Canal.

"There are two kinds of flappers," she protests. The kind that has caused all the trouble really doesn't have 'anything above the ears'[58]

Marjorie K. Rawlings

"'Flapping Is Merely Joy of Living,' Explains High School Flapper," copy from an unknown newspaper, clipping at Smathers Library, University of Florida.

*   *   *   *   *   *   *   *   *

Do American Women Appreciate Good Points of Their Men?

Beautiful Artiste Calls Typical U.S. Husband Jewel Beyond Price

Of course, we like our men—but do we appreciate them? Mlle. Herma Menth, the dazzling Viennese who presided over the piano at the Eastman Theater last week,[59] has put a burden on my overtaxed conscience.

Mlle. Menth has known, and been adored by, men of almost every nationality. She has been fêted in Paris, Vienna and London—and she insists, for all the world to know, that the woman who owns a typical American husband, owns a jewel beyond price! Is this news to you—or was I all alone in the darkness?

"I grant you," says Mlle. Menth, with an enchanting wave of her graceful hand, "that the European makes love more—shall we say—entertainingly? I grant you that he makes those little unnecessary speeches that render him so attractive. He is gallante, he is enormously flattering—but nowhere on earth can he compare to the American man!

"The American man lacks the technique of love—but he has everything else that makes him desirable as a husband."

WE OWN THE EARTH.

In the name of St. Valentine, is this the way the wind blows? Here we are, divorcing our husbands, maligning them, warning our sweethearts that we will

---

58   The rest of the article is missing.

59   Herma Menth, classical pianist. The Eastman Theater, at the University of Rochester, New York, opened in 1922.

stand for no nonsense after marriage, crying out that we are misunderstood and oppressed—and from abroad comes a beautiful woman, a sensitive artist, who plays the piano as if all the music of Heaven had been let loose at once—and she tells us that we own the earth! Surely, a man is without honor in his own country!

Here are the points, that, according to our lovely lady of Vienna, pile up the score in favor of the American man as donor of the wedding ring:

He has a splendid physique, with broad shoulders seldom possessed by the European. In fact, whenever Mlle. Menth saw a pair of broad shoulders on a street in Vienna, she thought, "He must be an American!"

He is sincere. A few words from him mean more than an hour of blandishments from a Parisian.

He allows his wife to be as independent as she wishes.

He loves more steadfastly. This alone would make for greater marital happiness, for it would mean less of a tendency to stray from the fold and tread the primrose path.

And, most important of all, he not only demands little—oh, very little, from a woman, but he places her on a throne.

"You American women are queens!" cried Mlle. Menth. "Your men have given you crowns!"

SCEPTERS ARE READY.

Will you please step forward and receive your scepters, ladies?

Yes, we have certain claims to the throne. According to Mlle. Menth, we are beautiful and graceful. We wear clothes superbly well.

"Europe designs the clothes, but American women wear them."

And there is one black mark against the American husband—he is too deeply absorbed in his business.

Who is the supreme example of this American manhood? The American policeman!

"I adore American policemen," says our oracle. "They are courtesy, bravery, chivalry incarnate. When I came to America eight years ago, speaking no English, American policemen made life possible for me. They saw to it that I reached my destination safely. I almost learned English from them! One policeman at Seventy-second and Broadway, in New York City, to this very day, stops traffic to let me pass!"

From American doctors Mlle. Menth first learned to enjoy an American audience.

DOCTORS APPLAUDED.

"It was in Vienna. A group of American doctors, studying in our hospitals there, lived in a pension across from my father's house on an old, old street. My piano was at the front window on the second floor. I used to go to my piano and play—well-known airs from Cavalliera Rusticana, Mendelssohn's Spring Song[60]—and the lovely doctors across the street would listen, and applaud, crying, 'Bravo! Herma! Encore!' I would go to the window and bow very deeply. Then—my mother would catch me at it, and punish me!"

"So," with a bewildering brilliant smile, "from the very first I have loved your American men!"

Do we appreciate them? Had we all better begin to tell them how much we care for them? Shall we make obeisances to them? Or shall we go on the way we have been going—neglecting them a bit, scolding them more—and loving them the most of all?

Between you and me and the American cupid—and I think Mlle. Menth agrees with me—they would be greatly obliged if we would stay just exactly as we are!

Marjorie Kinnan Rawlings

"Do American Women Appreciate Good Points of Their Men?" *Rochester Evening Journal*, 19 September 1922.

* * * * * * * * *

Wives' School First Aid for Peeved Hubbies

Mechanics Institute Converts Modern Girls
into the Old Fashioned Product

Graduates Home Builders

Man Needs to Furnish Them Only Large Empty Cave
and They Will Do the Rest

Are you satisfied with your wife?

Does she measure up to the cave-woman standard, which says that a woman should be able to attend to all the little details about the home, such as hammer-

---

60 *Cavalliera Rusticana* (1890), an opera by Pietro Mascagni (1863–1945). Felix Mendelssohn (1809–47), "Frühlingslied" [Spring Song], published in 1844 as volume 5 of his *Lieder ohne Worte* [Songs without Words], forty-eight songs for the piano in eight volumes (1829–45).

ing a rocking-chair out of a few logs, and moulding the family tea pot out of a handful of clay?

She doesn't? Say, isn't that too bad!

But cheer up—Rochester has the answer. If you want a little cave-woman in your home, send her to Mechanics Institute![61]

There isn't much wifely lore left out of the curriculum of the "school for wives." In fact, if you will furnish a nice, roomy, empty cave, the 100 per cent Mechanics girl can provide everything else—and I mean it literally!

What about furniture? The School of Applied Arts has a thorough course in wood-working, in which the industrious student can learn to make anything for the home, from a dining-room buffet to a pipe-rack.

Do wife or daughter, as the case may be, nail together a padded foot-stool. Would you like a cedar chest to hold your fishing tackle? Put her to work! Bookcases, tabourets, writing tables, mahogany candlesticks? Take your choice!

RUGS FASCINATE.

What about rugs to cover the dirt floor of the cave—or the hardwood of the modern apartment? One of the most fascinating courses in the whole institute is that in weaving, where the beautiful and substantial rugs of our forefathers come to life on enormous looms. In rich blues and creams, they are lovelier than any department store product.

Fabrics to make bed coverlets are woven there, from pure woolen or linen threads.

Do you need a new shirt? Does the housewife need a new dress? She may weave the loveliest of materials in this remarkable class—and then she may take them across the hall to the School of Home Economics—and make them up into finished garments! Even intricate batik work comes forth there, for pillow covers, scarves and blouses.

When it comes to household crockery, the most expensive art shop can't better the utensils whirled out on the institute's potter's wheel. Mixing bowls are easy; lamp bases are quickly evolved by the skillful; flower bowls; fruit compotes, tiles to keep the coffee pot from burning the table, all emerge from the dull gray clay, are painted, glazed and baked in the big kilns.

COLOR HARMONY TAUGHT.

And dishes for afternoon tea! How would you like to say to your guests, instead of, "My wife made the tea,"—"My wife made the tea-pot?" Not so poor, eh?

---

61 In 1944, The Mechanics Institute became the Rochester Institute of Technology.

When it comes to interior decorating, you need never suffer because a white lamp is placed beside a bright red davenport. The well trained wife doesn't do these things. Even if she starts out with the taste of a sea cook, she can be taught harmony in color schemes, the planning of rooms, the placing of furniture and the graceful arranging of curtains.

And if she has any talent at all, she can be trained to the point where she can execute a few tasteful paintings for your walls! This is the one place in the institute where the perfect wife must have a little ability—for the Futuristic system of art, which paints pictures entirely void of rhyme or reason, has no place in the school's sane, conservative programme.

The subject of interior decoration brings us to what most men would concede the really vital work of the institute—the teaching of cookery.

COOKERY MADE FINE ART.

How far cookery ranks above the other fine arts! How more important a perfect pie than a perfect poem! Poetry must catch one in just the right mood—but what mood is necessary for apple pie?

If you have been sawing away lately at leathery pie-crust, or choking over dry biscuits—enroll your wife, or, if possible, your cook, in the course in cookery. And if you are just contemplating matrimony, in the name of hot waffles, persuade your elected to take up the study of the kitchen stove!

Make her understand that a man can forgive a flirtation—but never poor food! I know a man who threw a dish of macaroni at his wife because it was underdone. She tried to divorce him, but the jury held the husband was justified, and censured the wife severely!

Cookery students at the institute are taught neatness—that staunch ally of the successful wife. They dress in trim white uniforms, with ravishing little white caps that make any man want to kiss the cook. They are taught marketing, and are actually taken out to buy foods. No danger that one of them might buy a pint of spinach because she didn't know it cooked down to about one-tenth of its original amount. A bride that did that fainted when she took the spinach out of the kettle and found a scant tablespoonful.

DIETETICS IMPORTANT.

Students may take up dietetics—that valuable study that prevents one from offering ham and eggs to an invalid, and serving ice cream for dessert after a lobster dinner. Some may say that common sense knows such things—but dietetics are scientific common sense that may well be learned by many cooks.

Menu planning is a factor in the happy home. Household administration, with its budget handling, saves many a matrimonial shipwreck. Innumerable branches of home-making are taught, all of them calculated to develop an all-round, old-fashioned, cave-woman wife.

Mr. Clifford Ulp, director of the School of Applied Arts, and Miss May D. Benedict, director of the School of Home Economics, are busily engaged in insuring the efficiency of the teaching.

TRAINING ENJOYED.

The best of it is, the students thoroughly enjoy the training process. Learning to be a perfect wife is a very satisfying job.

What's that? "Practice alone makes perfect?"

Right-o! At No. 36 South Washington street, the institute maintains a "practice house," where for three weeks each semester, juniors in the four-year training course, and students in the one-year home-making course, try out their theories.

No casualties have yet been reported—which alone explains the enormous prestige of the institute as a wife-trainer.

So realistic is the atmosphere of the home "practice" house, that it is seriously considering the adoption of a baby.

Marjorie Rawlings

"Wives' School First Aid for Peeved Hubbies," *Sunday Rochester (N.Y.) American*, 1 October 1922.

*   *   *   *   *   *   *   *   *

The Rev. Clinton Wunder
Is Pioneer Efficiency Pastor

Builds Remarkable Church Organization by Applying to Religion Principles That Are Successful in Business

Here in Rochester stands one of the most amazing churches in the United States. In the heart of the city, at North and Franklin streets, the Baptist Temple has succeeded in the most spectacular fashion, through its publication of modern principles to its work. It is planning the most startling move that a church can make:

The erection of a million-dollar office building on its present site, with the church built in the very center!

"The failure of the church" is a modern phrase that has swept the country as the church-going population of the United States has become converted to the moving pictures and the Sunday automobile instead of to religion.

The public—potential movie audience or church congregation—has said nothing, but from religious leaders, newspapers and magazines has gone forth a great hue and cry.

"The church has failed! People are refusing to be saved. What is to be done?"

Success Assured

From a portion of press and pulpit has come the answer:

"The church must adjust itself to changing conditions. The religion of our fathers must put on modern guise, or go the way of all outworn institutions."

The recent history of the Baptist Temple is in itself a treatise on success in religion. That success is due to three factors: A thoroughly modern church membership, anxious for progress; an efficient church staff; and one of the most remarkable young ministers in the country.

The Rev. Clinton Wunder, twenty-nine year old pastor of Rochester's downtown church, is a religious pioneer.[62] He came to the church from business and the world. He brings to his work the best business and the best of the world, and is "using his brains to make, not less, but more of a church."

---

62   Clinton Wunder was pastor at the New Baptist Temple from 1921 to 1929; his business instincts are suggested in the following ad campaign for the church:

New Baptist Temple, Rochester, N.Y.

THE NEW BAPTIST TEMPLE and OFFICE BUILDING (Now under Construction)
Clinton Wunder, Minister
'In the Heart of Rochester' (Organized 1834)
THE BAPTIST TEMPLE and TEMPLE BUILDING
The new Temple, now being erected at North and Franklin Streets, inclusive of the site will be valued at $2,750,000. Fourteen stories high, it will contain an office buildiong [*sic*], retail stores, thelatest church equiptment [*sic*] for recreation, religious education, community service and worship. A Hook and Hastings organ, specially designed and the largest most complete church instrument in this section is now under construction. The congregation this year is giving $100,000 to current expenses, benevolences and the building fund.
The Temple is a church of, for and by the People who "heard Jesus gladly." 100,000 people attended services last year.
When in Rochester, worship with us.

"God gave men brains with which they make fortunes in business," he declares. "They should use the same brains in the church."

Mr. Wunder was successful in the world, in newspaper work and in advertising. He was successful in the army, where he combined his duties as chaplain with those of a first lieutenant. He is a success in the church, where business methods have helped make it possible for him to reach the hearts of more men and women than ever before in the history of the Baptist temple.

"Modern conditions have made the church a competitor with numerous pleasurable attractions," says Mr. Wunder. "People used to go to church because it was the thing to do. Now other things compete for their time—and the church must be made appealing through every modern resource."

"This is only legitimate. St. Paul rode about his missionary work on a camel. But if the Twentieth Century Express had been available, St. Paul would have used it—because it would have enabled him to take the Gospel to a greater number of people."

Modern Methods

"In the same way the modern church must use every power at its command to reach people. Just as advertising makes the world try a certain brand of soap, so it can be made to make the world try religion. The Gospel must be given every assistance to make itself heard."

"Every principle that is honest and safe in business is good for the church," sums up Mr. Wunder.

[line or lines missing] may be had from a picture of the modern minister at work in the modern church. First of all, a thorough business organization runs through all church activities.

The minister's study, despite the thirty years of the Temple, is up to date, with complete telephone equipment, a modern filing system and a business-like calendar of appointments for the day.

Instead of attempting to attend to minor details himself, the minister has a secretary, Miss Cora Armstrong.

Miss Margaret Schultz is church secretary, in charge of finances and collections. She acts as a "purchasing agent" for the church.

Mrs. Grace B. Marriott is the minister's assistant, and is in charge of social service work.

The Rev. Robert V. Russell, a 1922 graduate of the Rochester Theological Seminary with Mr. Wunder, is associate minister, in charge of educational activities.

Mr. William Hartman, as chairman of the Building Committee, is an important factor in the development of plans for the new church building.

J. Alfred Spouse, a vocal instructor in the schools of Rochester, as director of music plans the elaborate musical programs that have proved such a drawing card.

Arthur Stewart, as chairman of the Board of Trustees, Arthur Castle as chair of the deacons, and Dr. Henry B. Robbins as chair of the Board of Religious Education, contribute materially to the businesslike distribution of church work.

In the second place the modern minister appeals to the intellects of his congregation. To this end, Mr. Wunder has reviewed many of the "best-sellers" in his Sunday evening meetings. He has held open forums in which the audience participates, expressing their own ideas.

Advertising Is Vital

"Advertising is a vital element in adjusting the church to the times," says the business minister. "People will not go to church unless they want to—and advertising makes people want to do things."

The advertising appropriation of the Baptist Temple has been increased during the year and a half of Mr. Wunder's pastorate to the sum of $2000 a year. This pays for newspaper advertising, electric signs that point out the church to the stranger at night, printed posters and attractive signboards on the building.

The Baptist Temple spends nearly $32,000 a year, a sum raised almost entirely by contributions of members and by collections. Parts of the sum are spent each year for unusual bits of service to the community.

The benches and drinking fountain in the church vestibule were given by the church. They are used every day by tired wayfarers, and at noon by dozens of workmen who spend their lunch hour there, eating, laughing, resting, partaking of the hospitality of bench and fountain.

The plans for a new building are based on the sound economic value of the church property. Located at the very core of the downtown business district, it is believed that an enormous revenue can be obtained by putting the site to work.

Self Supporting

The rentals from an office building as large as planned would pay for the structure in twenty years, it is claimed. After that, the revenue would constitute a permanent endowment fund, which could do incalculable good because of its size.

Church work on so vast a scale is, naturally, an enormous drain on the modern minister. He must act as a preacher—with a large amount of preparation to be spent on his sermons; he must do pastoral work; he must be an executive; he is a promoter; and he is publicity man.

But the modern minister, says Mr. Wunder, finds that it pays. He finds that he can reach more people than the old-fashioned preacher ever dreamed of addressing.

Clinton Wunder speaks to over 700 people at the morning service, and more than 1,300 at night. Business principles as applied to religion have brought new thousands to the Baptist Temple. So eagerly does modern Rochester respond to a live church, that complaint was made of the packed conditions of the aisles and stairways.

Marjorie Kinnan Rawlings

"The Rev. Clinton Wunder Is Pioneer Efficiency Pastor," *Sunday Rochester (N.Y.) American*, 8 October 1922: C3.

*   *   *   *   *   *   *   *   *

Romance of Fifty Years Ago Key to Lonely Life of Spinster Slain in Bethany

Brother of Miss Kimble Tells Story of Her Love for Young Farmer—She Broke Engagement.

On Monday afternoon a lonely old woman of seventy-three was murdered in her isolated home, "The Evergreens."

Fifty years ago, a beautiful young woman in her early twenties, pursued by the youth of the countryside, gave her heart and the promise of her hand to a farmer lad of her own age.

The woman was the same. Lovely Frances Kimball passed through the heartbreak of a shattered romance[63]—and with the passing of time, became the solitary figure of "The Evergreens," whose death has been a tragic ending to an unfulfilled life.

---

63   Frances Kimball (1849–1922). Her murder has never been solved. Linden, the site of the murder, is in southern Genesee County, near the northern border of Wyoming County. The counties are approximately half way between Rochester and Buffalo. The villages mentioned are all in these two counties.

In the old homestead in which the spinster had lived alone, for more than twenty years, Charles Kimball, sixty-eight years of age, her oldest brother, told for the first time in fifty years, the story of a romance which removed his sister from a life of gayety to a life so lonely that her dead body was not found for hours after her mysterious murder.

HOUSE SHOWS HER TOUCH.

The weather-beaten gray house, hemmed in by dark, lowering evergreens, standing far from any other dwelling, was filled with hints of the old woman's presence. In the windows stood pots of begonia, ferns and geraniums. A great bowl of leaves of geranium stood on a shelf above the kitchen sink,[64] where she had placed them shortly before her death. The white curtains at the small windows were immaculate. On a shelf over the table which did dining-room duty in the large, sunny kitchen, stood the ancient clock by which she had timed her methodical life since her girlhood.

"As a girl, Frances was very gay and popular," began Charles. "She had dark brown hair, soft dark eyes, and pretty pink cheeks. She used to go to country dances and husking bees and on buggy rides with young men. When she was living in Dale, N. Y., not far from here, she met the only man she ever cared for—Walter Spaulding of Wyoming village—and became engaged to him."

FEW REMEMBER HIM.

Walter Spaulding has been dead for some ten or fifteen years. Scarcely half a dozen people remember his name—Charles Kimball of Attica; Spaulding's half sisters, Mrs. Will Wilson and Mrs. Delia Eastland of Wyoming, and two old friends of his boyhood, Mr. and Mrs. Ed Dodson. But memory of him so strongly influenced Frances Kimball that after she broke her engagement to him she never married—and became, first, a strangely unsociable village seamstress, and later, a lonely old woman whose solitude gave her murderer the chance to cover his tracks.

"Frances was engaged to Walter Spaulding for several years," said Charles Kimball. "They were very much in love, and went to all kinds of doings together. I was younger than she, but I remember seeing her go out with him, all dressed up in her best bib and tucker.

EACH TOOK LONELY PATH.

"Then—she found that she didn't approve of lots of things he did. Walter was a fine chap, but Frances was very strict. She tried for a long time to make

---

64 Rose geraniums (*Pelargonium graveolens*) are often used in the making of potpourri.

him stop doing the things she disapproved of—but he was obstinate. He had a stubborn streak she couldn't seem to reach—and she decided not to marry him, although I believe she never stopped loving him."

Walter Spaulding never married. Frances Kimball never married. Each took a lonely path. His ended peacefully at his sister's home. But that of pretty Frances Kimball of fifty years ago, led to her death at the hands of an unknown killer. Her life was bleak and bitter. The highlights of adventure touched it only at its beginning—and at its end.

With Batavia, Bethany and county authorities searching, so far vainly, for a clue that will lead to the motive of the murder of an unhappy old woman, the question has been constantly asked:

Why should a woman, once gay, with devoted friends and relatives, live a life so solitary that her murder could pass unnoticed?

Charles Kimball's revealing of her hidden romance of fifty years ago, explains it.

* * * * * * * * *

Clue Seen in Aged Spinster's Diary Details of Her Life Bared

Continued from First Page

[text missing] written in a shaky hand on slips of paper that hang over the old-fashioned kitchen pump.

The old homestead, which she had tended for more than thirty years, will soon be deserted, or perhaps sold into strange hands.

"There is no one to take care of it now," said Charles.

Confidence was still high among authorities as the fourth day of their investigation into the mystery drew to a close that an early solution of the murder mystery would soon reward their efforts.

Clues and theories have been sifted down so that today attention is centered on four men, two of whom are kin of Miss Kimball and all of whom are well acquainted with her methodical habits and the interior of the old farmhouse where she had lived, practically a recluse for the past fifteen years.

Microscopic examination today of a jack knife taken from William Kimball, fifty-eight, bachelor brother of the slain woman, and questioning of Andrew

Michel, forty, farmer living a mile distant from "The Evergreens," may have important bearing on the investigation, authorities said.

William Kimball's knife, on the blade of which a microscope shows an eighth of an inch of black fuzz, is being examined by a chemical expert in Rochester, Sheriff Daniel Elliott stated.

"We are attaching some importance to the findings of the Rochester chemist," he declared.

Cutting the telephone wires at the lower northwest corner of the Kimball home was one of the precautions against discovery taken by the person or persons who committed the crime. From the beginning authorities have looked upon the wire cutting clue as one of the most important they have unearthed.

District Attorney James L. Kelly, Sheriff Elliott, Detective John A. Doyle of Rochester engaged by county authorities to assist in the probing, and troopers under Captain Winfield Robinson attended the funeral this morning.

All residents of Linden and Bethany township are aroused over the brutal slaying, which is the chief topic of talk when farmers or their wives gather.

"If the authorities have as much evidence as they say they have, why is an arrest being delayed?" they are asking.

Before the funeral, authorities visited the home of Andrew Michel, farmer, living with his wife a mile distant from The Evergreens.

Michel, when questioned Wednesday by District Attorney Kelley, explained his whereabouts late Monday afternoon, the time when Miss Kimball was murdered, authorities have determined, by stating he went to his mother's home at 4 o'clock. He brought her to his home, a half mile distant, where she had dinner and spent the evening with him and his wife, Michel declared.

Several weeks ago Michel was arrested for the alleged selling of hard cider to William Kimball. Complaint has been made to authorities by Mrs. Willis Kimball, William's sister-in-law. A grand jury, however, failed to indict Michel. Since then it was learned that relations between Michel and the Kimballs were somewhat strained.

Michel has also been in trouble with the police over his alleged cruel treatment of animals, brutally beating a cow and horse he owns.

A will, left by Miss Kimball, and deposited, after he discovered the paper in her effects Tuesday, by Charles Kimball, brother, in the bank at Perry, will probably be read today by District Attorney Kelley. It is believed the articles of the will may throw valuable light on the case.

State troopers have been busy checking up [on] activities of everyone living within the radius of a mile from the Kimball home Monday and another man, whose name authorities refused to disclose, entered into the investigation to-day.

A "two-man" crime. That is an important theory upon which the police are working.

Harry Volz, Batavia steamfitter, who, authorities learned, quarreled with the aged spinster when the latter befriended and took into her home Mrs. Pearl Kimball Volz, daughter of Charles Kimball, when Mrs. Volz separated from her husband a fortnight ago has not been further quizzed. He accounts for his presence working in Le Roy last Monday, authorities declare.

Volz went to The Evergreens and had a word battle with Miss Kimball over her championship of her niece's side in the marital disagreement two weeks ago, according to information authorities received.

Harry Nelson, nineteen, arrested in Rochester Wednesday night for alleged theft of an automobile in Attica, was absolved last night of suspicion in connection with the Kimball slaying. Nelson was brought to the Batavia court house late yesterday afternoon by Sheriff Nate Conger of Wyoming County, to whom Rochester police turned over the youth.

Marjorie Kinnan Rawlings

"Romance of Fifty Years Ago Key to Lonely Life of Spinster Slain in Bethany," *Rochester (N.Y.) Evening Journal*, 20 October 1922.

* * * * * * * * *

Lonely Spinster Had Premonition of Death

Neighbor Tells of Warning in Dream

Victim Pleaded with Friend to Hunt Down Slayer
If She Ever Was Found Killed

Clue to Lost Brother

Letter Asking Money Came from Ed Kimball
before Tragedy, Mrs. Speed Asserts

Did Miss Frances Kimball, whose slaying near Bethany has furnished a baffling mystery, know that she was to meet her death in a violent fashion? Were strange psychic influences at work that warned her of her end?

Mrs. Charles Speed, who lived nearest her in a little brown house down the lonely road that passes the two homes, has told me a remarkable story of weird premonitions and warnings which came to the lonely spinster. She whispered:

"Miss Kimball dreamed that someone came and killed her!"

The story as she tells it gives hint of psychic forces acting on the old woman several days before her death. It also throws light for the first time on the trail of a vanished brother, Edwin Kimball, who disappeared in the Klondike twenty years ago, and has not been heard from since.

Old Mysteries Cleared

Old, old mysteries have been unearthed and clarified in connection with the woman's life. Only a few days ago, Charles Kimball, the older brother, sixty-eight years old, told for the first time in fifty years the story of his sister's unhappy love for Walter Spaulding, now long since dead.

After breaking her engagement with the farmer lad in Dale, N. Y., because he did not measure up to her Puritan ideals, neither married. Both led solitary lives within a few miles of each other the rest of their days.

Mrs. Speed's story, along with her revealing of Miss Kimball's death warning, also gives a sudden and unexpected clue to the whereabouts of her lost bother, Edwin.

"Good Kind Woman"

Mrs. Speed, rocking back and forth in her antiquated black painted rocking chair, told me:

"Miss Kimball was my friend. Oh, she was a good, kind woman! I loved her. She used to bring me apples. Lots of times we came home together from the village, and sometimes she would light me home with a lantern, and sometimes I would light her home."

"She used to spend a lot of her time making her house look pretty. She had the best luck with plants and ferns. They grew for her when the rest of us couldn't get a sprout. She had about twenty-five geraniums all in bloom at one time—red and pink and white."

"She was a fine housekeeper. Her stove was always polished till you could see your face in it—and tablecloths? Land, she had a clean one every few days! She always did things on time and had two or three clocks all going at once."

"She used to write lots of letters, and she had a little book she wrote in. She kept track of everything she did and everything she spent. She made quite a few dollars here and there selling potatoes and apples and things like that. She was honest as the day is long, and never cheated a man out of a penny. Nobody could ever have complained he didn't get justice from her."

Had No Enemies

"Have you ever heard of anyone who had any complaint against her?"

"I can't see how any man on earth could have brought himself to do it. She never harmed a soul—and she was so old, with not many more years to live. Why couldn't she have died in peace?"

Here Mrs. Speed took me into the best parlor, where a large crayon portrait was prominently displayed. She said with tears in her eyes:

"That is my dear mother. She's long since gone to her rest. Before she went she often said to me, 'Kind o' look after that poor Miss Kimball. She's a good woman, and you mustn't let any harm come to her.'"

"Oh, it's so awful, ain't it? Well, ma'am, just a few days before she was found murdered, Miss Kimball came to me. She had had a dream. She dreamed that someone came and killed her. She said her mother was there when he did it. She was scared, and so was I."

"'Please, Mrs. Speed,' she said to me, 'If I should ever be found killed—try to find the man who did it!'"

"I promised her—and then that night I had the dream, too. I dreamed she was murdered—and when Charles—my husband—found her dead body—I was ready for it. Poor soul, she'll never have to go through it again."

Edwin Asks Money

Mrs. Speed's information on the whereabouts of Edwin Kimball is the first clue to the fact that he may be alive. She said:

"A considerable spell before Miss Kimball was taken she came down to the house one morning with a letter. It was from Edwin Kimball, 'way out in California."

"Now Ed had always been jealous of Miss Kimball. He thought that she had more than the rest of them—the house and farm and furniture and all. He always had acted as if she should help him out. In this letter he asked her for money. He said he was in trouble, and he thought she ought to give it to him. She asked me what I thought—she was real worried about it."

"So she wrote Ed that she couldn't let him have any money—and she never heard another word from him."

Where is Ed Kimball? The family knows nothing of his whereabouts. Said Charles Kimball:

"We have considered him dead for many years."

According to Mrs. Speed, Miss Kimball had more than once told her that she did not believe her brother was dead, and that she was sure he would some day return.

So far as I have been able to determine, none of the family knew of a recent letter from Edwin. Mrs. Speed asked:

"Do you know where Ed is?"

I shook my head. She said plaintively:

"I wish they could find him."

At this point we went outside into the yard, yellow and red with fallen maple leaves. I had seen two handsome black and yellow cats in the house, one of which had jumped up in Mrs. Speed's lap, and had sat gazing into her face.

I suggested that she hold one of them as she had her picture taken. But as I went towards them, they flew wildly away and could not be coaxed back. Mrs. Speed shook her head, and came close to me, as she whispered:

"They won't come. They've been acting up for more than a week. They know she's dead. THEY KNOW!"

Marjorie Kinnan Rawlings

"Lonely Spinster Had Premonition of Her Death," *Sunday Rochester (N.Y.) American*, 22 October 1922.

*   *   *   *   *   *   *   *   *

No Place on Campus for Knickers or Cigarettes, Say Graduates

Rochester Alumnae Back Deans in Conflicts with Students at Wellesley and Mt. Holyoke

Do manners, modes and morals have anything to do with a girl's education? When a girl of eighteen enters college, should the authorities limit their activities to matters concerning the classroom alone?

Two Wellesley freshmen, Billie Burse and Jean Roth, have just withdrawn from college because the authorities found them smoking—and forbade them to do so again. The girls said:

"It was a question of quitting college or cigarettes. The school frowned on our knickers and on our ideas—and now on our cigarettes, so we decided to leave."

KNICKERS INAPPROPRIATE

Now comes Dean Purington of Mt. Holyoke,[65] who has just announced that knickers are henceforth forbidden in the classroom. The Dean says:

"We consider the fashion inappropriate for classroom wear."

Scratch! go the matches in the dormitory rooms.

Puff-puff! go the cigarettes in the co-ed fingers—and nimble acquirers of education go tripping across the floor in knickers!

Does it make any difference that the college girl's manners are ladylike? Does it interfere with her education if she adopts the most startling modes? Do these things have any bearing on the value of her diploma?

Rochester graduates of Wellesley and Mt. Holyoke, commenting on the attitudes of their respective Alma Maters in the recent difficulties, in emphatic chorus answer all three questions:

"Yes! Manners, modes and morals are immediately bound up with a girl's education."

Miss Mae Galliger No. 41 Cornell street, president of the Rochester Mt. Holyoke Club, illumines the subject with an analysis of the girl in college. She says:

"A girl goes to college to get something more than an education. She expects to acquire what I might sum up with the word 'Poise.' She enters the institution as a young, impressionable girl."

"She should avoid whatever may lower her standards—because what she learns in college, she retains the rest of her life."

AVOID LAXNESS

It is important, says Miss Galliger, that the college girl avoid laxness—in her manners, in her clothes and, certainly, in her morals.

"If one is lax," she declares, "it is difficult to return to one's original high standards."

Miss Galliger sympathizes thoroughly with both Wellesley and Mt. Holyoke authorities in their stand. She explains:

"College authorities are naturally anxious that every graduate should represent the best that the school has to give. Every Mt. Holyoke graduate is a symbol

---

65 Florence E. Purington, first dean at Mt. Holyoke College (1907–29).

of the college—and the dean—in ruling against frivolous fashions, is trying to insure the developing of the finest type of young woman."

Mrs. E. B. Nell, No. 195 Vassar street, also a Mt. Holyoke graduate, feels that the college girl cannot be too cautious in her acceptance of bizarre fashions and habits. She says:

"The college girl should be most conservative—in her dress and in her habits—for the reason that she is copied by others. She gets [sets] the styles in many ways. Knickers have no place on campus or in the classroom, because they are not conservative—and in wearing them, the college girl is setting a wrong example."

Mrs. E. L. Sunderlin, No. 1139 Park avenue, Wellesley graduate with the class of 1917, speaks decisively against the use of cigarettes by college girls. She says:

"I believe that cigarette smoking is unwomanly—and that is the one thing the college girl should not be. I fear, however, that girls are not to blame, and that the authorities will have difficulty in controlling the matter—because the mothers themselves set the example."

So wages the warfare!

The college girl herself keeps a smiling silence—except when the kettle bubbles over, and the word reaches the world that two saucy freshmen have left one of the most famous institutions in the country—rather than give up cigarettes and knickers!

Marjorie Kinnan Rawlings

"No Place on Campus for Knickers or Cigarettes, Say Graduates," *Rochester (N.Y.) Evening Journal*, 2 November 1922.

Tragic Drama at the Corinthian
Stirs Rochester's Elite

Editor's Note: Lady Thwaite, who is visiting in Rochester, is not only a third cousin of the Earl of Bentleigh, but one of London's most scintillating *cognoscenti*.[66] Her profound dramatic reviews of the more important English productions have made her a favorite fiction writer of the Prince of Wales.[67]

"The Big Sensation" has paused at the Corinthian Theater for one little week in its meteoric coruscations across the United States—and Rochester the pure, the noble-minded, has given its approval![68]

Here at the Corinthian is a company of artists battling against terrific odds to present the ancient Greek ideal that Form is Everything, or, as the French have it, *La figure, c'est tout*. The brave struggle against poverty is recognized in the painful lack of material for the gowns of the chorus; but Rochester audiences are above such things and the scantier the costume, the louder their cheers. Indeed, when Miss Pauline Russell bites her lips, lifts her chin and steps bravely before the footlights in three pitiful little squares of silk, the pit, galleries and stalls unite in their applause and call her back again and again and again to show their appreciation of a true artist's indomitable pluck.

The drama itself? Ah, it is burlesk as it should be!!![69] "The Big Sensation" whirls through two acts with the swiftness of Destiny. Everything about it is very, very swift indeed. It is a fantasy in the Fourth Dimension, for the char-

---

66 MKR most likely had a hand in the content of this "editor's note," for it contains her flair for comedic irony. There was no "Earl of Bentleigh." The wordplay is on the Bentley Motor Co., which built cars driven by the British nobility, none of whom, as Thwaite (MKR) points out, can be found in the barbarous American city of Rochester. The primary meaning of "cognoscenti" is learned connoisseur, but here it also carries the sense of an ironic double entendre, falsely stupid.

67 Edward, Prince of Wales (1894–1972). The delicious irony here, which MKR could not possibly have anticipated, is that less than a year after his ascension as Edward VIII (20 January 1936), he would abdicate (11 December 1936) to marry the twice-divorced American commoner, Wallis Simpson (1896–1986).

68 *The Big Sensation*, an unidentified and perhaps fictional burlesque. The venerable Corinthian Hall, built in 1849, where luminaries such as Charles Dickens (1812–70), Ralph Waldo Emerson (1803–82), Frederick Douglass (ca. 1818–95), and Susan B. Anthony (1820–1906) had lectured, burned down in 1898 and was reopened in 1904. In its later years, many burlesques were staged at the Corinthian; it was torn down and turned into a parking lot in 1928.

69 Of course, "burlesk" is not "as it should be"; it is misspelled.

acters of one act, without explanation, become quite different persons in the next. All but Bevo, a bum out for a good time, played by Mr. Billy Kelly—he is always—just Bevo!

The play is a tragedy. It is instinct with the irony of Fate, for no one gets anywhere. The characters dance, sing and jest, but in what I am told are the immortal words of your artist, Mr. Ruben Goldberg,[70] "it doesn't mean anything." "Miss Lavender" struggles across the stage in the best the production's wardrobe affords, only to have Slim Jake, portrayed by Mr. Andy Martini, in private life a contortionist, dismiss her with the words:

"If that's a chicken, give me fish."

Slim Jake in turn is baffled by life and cries out in despair when a friend refuses to play a little game with him:

"If you don't say '*Give it to me*,' how'm I going to spit in your face?"

And Bevo, the eternal clown with the breaking heart beneath! He wrings one's soul when he staggers from the stage saying:

"I'm going out to the graveyard to dig up a woman for tonight!"

Fortunately, "The Big Sensation" has its lighter moments. Mr. Lew Harris provides comic relief with his song, "Stay Home, Little Gal, Stay Home." Sung in very serious manner, this is choice comedy, because obviously none of the few little girls in the audience have cared to stay at home; the chorus, certainly shows no signs of regret at having left the parental domicile, so the advice to all little girls to stay at home is rare humor, don't you know!

The chorus, posted on the program as "City Girls with high-powered cars, fast horses and country homes," is made up of representatives of the principle American cities and might also have been chosen by Mr. Valentino in his Beauty Contest.[71] After seeing them dance, really, you know, one could believe anything of them. One member was quaintly decorated with a tattooed ship on her right arm, a custom that I confess is new to me. Might it, possibly, indicate a friend or relative in marine service?

It was most gratifying to see the elite of your city at the opening of "The Big Sensation" and to see that your men are foremost acolytes of the Thespian god-

---

70 Reuben ("Rube") Goldberg (1883–1970), cartoonist, wit, and social critic whose primary tenet was that humankind had the unique capacity to make something easy difficult.

71 Rudolph Valentino (1895–1926), the legendary actor of silent film. In 1923, David O. Selznick (1902–65) produced and distributed a thirteen-minute documentary, *Rudolph Valentino and His 88 American Beauties*, which depicted Valentino judging a beauty contest. (Norma Niblock of Toronto, Canada, was the winner.)

dess. The theatre [*sic*] was wreathed with smoke, evidently incense to the virgins of the temple, a delightful reversion to more reverent days.

Among the holders of stalls on the opening night there was pointed out to me Mr. Kid Taylor, a lightweight prominent in Buffalo social circles. Charming informality prevailed during the intermission, when Eskimo pastries were served and boxes of "Chawklits not kisses, an article of value absolutely free in each and every package,"[72] were dispensed. Amid much merriment, Mr. Taylor drew forth from his prize parcels a spoon and an infant's stocking cap. Remarking that he drank nothing requiring the use of a spoon and that *le bon Dieu* knew he had no need of an infant's cap, Mr. Taylor tossed his prizes to Bevo when the curtain next rose.

On the railing of my stall were the initials "T. R."[73] Could your great President Roosevelt perchance have carved them there? I have been told that it was he, viewing a drama at the Corinthian, who first proposed a law to compel chorus girls to wash below the collar bones.

Lady Alicia Thwaite

"Tragic Drama at the Corinthian Stirs Rochester's Elite," *Five O'Clock* 1 (22 April 1924): 9. Henry Clune, the editor of the short-lived *Five O'Clock*, claimed years later that it was his idea to give MKR the nom de plume Lady Alicia Thwaite; see *Los Angeles Times Book Review*, 11 November 1990, 10.

*   *   *   *   *   *   *   *   *

Our Center of Culture—And Mike Dempsey

Editor's Note: This is the second of a series of articles by Lady Thwaite on interesting institutions—and people—of Rochester. Last week Lady Thwaite discussed the trend of modern drama as seen at the Corinthian Theater.

---

72 MKR is poking fun at the class distinctions between fancy chocolates and the more plebian Hershey's "Kisses" (introduced in 1907), as well as the class associations of "Cracker Jack," the popcorn candy immortalized in the song "Take Me Out to the Ballgame" (1908), which in 1912 began including "A Prize in Every Box."

73 Theodore Roosevelt (1858–1919), twenty-sixth president of the United States. Roosevelt called the newspaper magnate William Randolph Hearst (1863–1951) "sinister" and "evil" for marrying one chorus girl while having affairs with others. In truth, Roosevelt feared the political ambitions of Hearst.

Tucked away over Kenealy's little café, in true French fashion, I have discovered your center of culture—and your mute genius, Mr. Mike Dempsey![74]

"Tell me," I had cried impulsively to a policeman, "where I, a stranger, may find Rochester's seat of culture and of the higher force!"

"Madam," he replied, "there's no higher force than what comes straight from the shoulder, and you must be referrin' to the Genesee Valley Athletic Club, just openin' up this next week. They do say Tommy Bresnahan[75] will have a department for ladies. Tell him O'Grady sent you."

So, calling out, "O'Grady sent me," I found myself in the studio of Mr. Tommy Bresnahan, in private life a match manufacturer, but here at his new Club a patron of the arts. And sitting dumbly like Rodin's "Thinker,"[76] dreaming great dreams, was your great Mike Dempsey.

"Who is Mike Dempsey?" I whispered in my ignorance.

"He is an artist, lady," said Mr. Bresnahan simply.

"I knew it!" I exclaimed. "What kind of artist?"

"He lays 'em out cold," was the reply.

"A sculptor in marble!" I cried.

"Have it your way," shrugged Mr. Bresnahan, sweeping several artists and a pack of cards from a table, "but they don't have to be white. Mike takes on niggers just as quick. Have a seat."

"How democratic!" was my tribute to Mr. Dempsey, who still sat dumbly—thinking.

"Mike's all of that," said Mr. Bresnahan. "He was born in Italy, began life as a barber, has an Irish wife, is a member of the Camorra Black Hand Society and of the Moose,[77] so you couldn't call him a snob."

"What may I call him?" I queried humbly. "And tell me about him."

---

74 There was a middleweight fighter in the nineteenth century named Mike Dempsey, but it is unlikely MKR knew about him. She is almost certainly using the name to toy with the celebrated heavyweight champion Jack Dempsey (1895–1983), known as the "Manassa Mauler."

75 There was a featherweight boxer named Tommy Bresnahan who fought in the New York area at the turn of the twentieth century, although it is unlikely that MKR had him in mind for the character of the promoter.

76 Auguste Rodin (1840–1917), French sculptor known especially for *The Thinker* (1880–81).

77 MKR conflates two notorious Italian secret societies. Camorra was founded in Naples in the 1820s, transplanted to the United States in the early twentieth century, and was known for intimidation, blackmail, and bribery. At the same time, the Black Hand, a Sicilian organization famed for sending blackmail letters marked with a black hand (thus the name), became very active in the United States. The Loyal Order of Moose, on the other hand, founded in 1888 and now titled Moose International, is a social organization known for its good works.

"He's often called the Sheik of Hartford Street," said Mr. Bresnahan, "and has been mistaken for Rudolph Valentino.[78] He fights like a mud turtle, with his chin on his chest. He heard someone say he ought to keep his chin in, and since then he's been doing the oyster act. He's a great artist, all right."

"And of course the whole world will hear of him some day," I encouraged, for the modest Mr. Dempsey was still staring into space. "Is he making progress in his art?"

"He's making progress every way but here," and Mr. Bresnahan tapped his forehead.

And then the great Mr. Dempsey stirred, and a radiant light swept across his features.

"I gotcha!" he cried excitedly. "Use th' noodle!"

"Good boy!" applauded Mr. Bresnahan.

"Ah, you are kind to him, I can see," I said to this promoter of art. "But tell me, what is Mr. Dempsey's relationship to your Genesee Valley Athletic Club?"

"Praise be," said Mr. Bresnahan, "he's no relation. He just costs us money."

There was the truth revealed—this good *pere des artistes*[79] is supplying bread and butter and even—I found later—a six thousand-dollar sport car—to this genius. How childlike is the artist in his finances! And then I asked, for one feels so free with these *enfants de l'art* [children of art]:

"But why is his left ear so—so battered?"

"That's a tin ear, lady," answered Mr. Bresnahan, "and he got it listening to the birdies."

I was overcome. What a super-sensitive soul, to have the physical ear so played upon by what the poet Davies calls "the tumult of a thousand wings"[80] as to make an artificial organ necessary!

"Tumult is right, lady," agreed Mr. Bresnahan, "you must o' been to a fight yourself."

And then I asked simpler questions, that would reveal to me not Dempsey the artist, but the man himself.

"What does he do when he is not at work?"

---

78 Rudolph Valentino (1895–1926), the legendary actor of silent film; he is most often associated with his role in *The Sheik* (1921).

79 The phrase *pere des artistes* [father of artists] is used more often in the sense of influence than it is of patronage.

80 Not the Welsh poet William H. Davies (1871–1940) but the English poet John Drinkwater (1882–1937) and the final line of his "A Town Window," which appeared in *Swords and Plough-shares* (1915).

"Well, I tell you, lady," answered Mr. Bresnahan, "Mike's a great boy for Sea Breeze."

"A nature lover!" I cried in rapture.

"Something o' the sort," he continued. "At any rate, he spent seventeen dollars one evening on the scenic railroad."

"And his reading? Does he read, for instance, 'The Dial'?"[81]

"Well, I wouldn't want to give anybody away that runs a quiet little game, but he's been known to have a go at roulette here and there."

"I don't understand. Does he read, perhaps, Haggard's virile stories of Africa?"[82]

"Lady, the only African books he reads are the dice, and he knows 'em coming and going."

"I don't know 'The Dice,'" I puzzled.

"You wouldn't," replied Mr. Bresnahan, "and I think you're rolling all your balls down the wrong alley. And if you'll excuse me, I gotta go to my grandmother's funeral."

"How cruel of me to detain you," I said. "Only tell me, before I go, what I shall say to Rochester about your center of culture?"

"Center of physical culture," he corrected me. "Tell 'em we'll be open for business next week, and will guarantee to keep in the pink of condition both business men and bootleggers. All kinds of apparatus, showers, and a reducing bath for ladies."

"And may I call your club a studio of all the arts?" I asked from the doorway, toward which Mr. Bresnahan had been gently propelling me.

"My God, lady," he exclaimed chivalrously, "call it anything you want to except a snake-hole. Some folks in town are a little touchy on the subject."

Lady Alicia Thwaite

"Our Center of Culture—and Mike Dempsey," *Five O'Clock* 1 (6 May 1924): 12.

---

81 *Dial Magazine* (1920–29) published the work of the new literati, among them T. S. Eliot (1888–1965), Marianne Moore (1887–1972), and Ezra Pound (1885–1972).

82 Henry Rider Haggard (1856–1925), author of romance novels, most notable among them *King Solomon's Mines* (1886), *Allan Quatermain* (1887), and *She* (1887).

Society Divides between Opera and Wrestling

It seems quite unlikely, really, that society attending the wrestling match at Convention Hall[83] on Monday last was a little gayer than society at the opera the same evening. The elite divided themselves between the two social occasions without bitterness, although husbands who patronized the former expressed themselves as amazed at the venom of their wives who, without escorts, attended the latter. As one prominent banker behind me merrily declared:

"I'll catch Hell when I get home, but the match is worth it."

I, really, had a slight preference for the opera, but since my new gown failed to arrive from New York City, I thought it best to choose for my evening's function a place where slightly more informality prevailed. I was not the only one there for the same reason. I feel sure, for many of the guests in my vicinity seemed to have had to get along without even their fresh linen. Laundries are so uncertain, since the war, are they not! But the audience laughed off any discrepancies in costume, and many, to make their less fortunate friends feel at ease, completely removed their coats and vests. The gentleman at my left arrived without a coat, and I heard him say, in jest:

"Had to hock the old mackinaw to get here. The old girl had a fiver hid in the tea-pot, but she caught me at it and I had to beat it while the running was free."

Such jolly souls, your Rochester society men! Always ready for a bit of mirth!

I was gratified to witness the entertainment of such prominent artists as Mr. Strangler Lewis, of Kentucky, and Mr. Cowboy, or Toots Mondt, of Montana.[84] Although I met only Mr. Lewis, both seemed charming gentlemen, more gentle, perhaps, in private life than professionally. Their delightful display consisted of a series of artistic poses in the old Greek fashion, each one trying to out-do the other in the intricacy of his muscular arrangements. The winner was to be he who twice pinned his rival's shoulders to the floor, to remove competition

---

83 The Convention Hall (1907–49), 75 Woodbury Boulevard, was built in 1868–71 as a state arsenal, became a naval academy in 1949, the GeVa Theater in 1985, and is now owned by the Genesee Valley Arts Foundation, which has used the building for a performing arts center since 2003. The Convention Hall is approximately eight blocks south of the Eastman Theater, which is at 60 Gibbs Street.

84 Ed "Strangler" Lewis (1891–1966), legendary heavyweight wrestler, known especially for his devastating headlock. Joseph "Toots" Mondt (1894–1976) once wrestled against Lewis but later became his partner and promoter.

and leave himself free for a statuesque pose. Several poses in which the two combined, struck me as remarkably effective. The thousands in the Hall roared with pleasure when Mr. Cowboy Mondt placed both limbs about Mr. Strangler Lewis' ribs and linked Mr. Lewis' left arm tightly in his own.

"What is the symbolism of that pose?" I whispered to the gentleman in front of me, who seemed quite a connoisseur. He stared at me for several seconds, stroking his chin, before he answered:

"That," he whispered back in a hushed voice, "that is a representation of an angry boa-constrictor protecting its young."

I understood, then, that I had judged correctly, and that pose was really as rough as it looked. I fear that Mr. Mondt actually hurt Mr. Lewis, quite unintentionally, of course. Mr. Lewis, indeed, seemed a bit put out by it, and almost seemed to attempt a retaliation when he squeezed Mr. Mondt's head between his arms a moment later. I trust he did nothing so un-sporting, but I feel it my duty to mention the incident.

Both entertainers were quite gaily costumed, Mr. Lewis in a purple velvet dressing gown and purple trousers, cut very short; Mr. Mondt in a tan checked gown and red trousers, also cut short. I had hoped to meet Mrs. Lewis, who is a famous beauty, having won a beauty contest in Missouri, but she was in Boston that evening. However, Mr. Billy Sandow,[85] Mr. Lewis' financial adviser, told me the charming story of their romance.

Mr. Lewis was under contract not to wed, on the theory, Mr. Sandow told me in confidence, that any sort of fighter should fight only in public. Disagreeing with him, Mr. Lewis locked Mr. Sandow in his room in the Morrison Hotel, Chicago, plugged the telephone, and rushed to his marriage with Miss Bessie McNair of Kansas City.

Again in confidence, Mr. Sandow told me that while he greatly admires Mrs. Lewis, the marriage precludes another trip of the great champion wrestler to Europe, for the Russian Princess Marie Trawaski[86] is only waiting for him to get within subpoena distance to sue him for breach of promise!

"Very distressing!" admitted Mr. Sandow.

Interestingly enough, at the close of the evening I heard an elderly clergyman use the same phrase.

"Very distressing!" he was murmuring. "I had twenty dollars bet on Toots. Very distressing!"

---

85 Billy Sandow, himself once a wrestler, promoted Lewis. Lewis, Mondt, and Sandow, dubbed the "Gold Dust Trio," formed a partnership and by the 1920s controlled professional wrestling; they are credited with making the sport what it is today.

86 Neither "Bessie McNair" nor "Princess Trawaski" has been identified.

An odd little incident occurred to me at the start of the performance. As I sat down, I heard at least half of the audience crying:

"Take off your hat!"

I thought, of course, the expression was merely another of your spontaneous slang phrases, directed at the performers, and I enjoyed the hearty calls thoroughly. After several minutes, in which the cries had doubled, an usher tapped me on the shoulder and said:

"It's you or your head-piece, Madam. You can't both stay."

And then I realized that there were only three other women present, very simply dressed, and that the democratic audience did not wish me to embarrass them with my rather ostentatious Gage model,[87] which has the new high cascade of flowers, topped by an aigrette. I was pleased at their spirit, and much amused.

The audiences from Convention Hall and Eastman Theatre mingled at the close of the two performances, and while the gentlemen who had attended the wrestling match seemed to have a freshness and gaiety lacking in the opera-goers, opinion seemed evenly divided as to the worth of the two functions.

"I tell you Bill," I heard a gentleman who had come from Eastman remark to a friend who had come from Convention Hall, "it's a toss up which is hardest work, singing or wrestling. But the fellow who has to sit in the seat and cheer the performers, catches the devil for different reasons, no matter which one he goes to.

Lady Alicia Thwaite

"Society Divides between Opera and Wrestling," *Five O'Clock* 1 (13 May 1924): 7.

*   *   *   *   *   *   *   *   *

Paint Jobs That Bloom in the Spring, Tra La!

Editor's Note: This is the last of a series of articles by Lady Thwaite. Her life has been so repeatedly threatened that she has been forced to retire, for the time being, from print.

A fresh coat of paint in the spring does work wonders, really, you know! I

---

87 The Gage Millinery, or Gage Hat Company, of New York and Chicago, makers of fashionable hats.

am referring, of course, to the annual May coming-out party of Rochester wait-resses, which burst into full flower last Friday at the State Street hot-house of choice buds—Cooper's Hall.

All winter the shy little waitresses, poor but honest, hide in their places of ap-pointment from the wolves of society who pursue them. In May, with the bright, beautiful Rochester sun upon them, and the hot May Rochester breezes blowing the scent of coffee from their marcelled hair, they become bolder—only a trifle bolder—and fling caution to the winds at the annual Waitress' Ball. They wash their ears, an annoyingly new necessity, since the shingle bob,[88] re-shine their finger-nails, and with the fresh coat of paint of which I have spoken, are ready for Spring and whatever it may bring!

"Let me loose," cried a little rosebud from the Manhattan Restaurant as she strode from the ladies' dressing room at Cooper's Hall to the strains of the first fox-trot. "I got on half a bottle of Mary Garden perfume that they've been ad-vertisin' as perfume with so seductive a lure that men simply can't resist it. I'm gonna give it a good, fair trial, and if they're lyin' I want my money back."

It was a perfectly topping party, as Waitress' Balls go! Cooper's Hall was fes-tively decorated for the occasion with a "No Smoking" sign, and in a tribute to the coming of Spring, the whole ball-room was scented with the unmistakable odor of spearmint. Charming idea! Since Rochester waitresses, I am told, are singularly bashful, not all the members of the Union have what they call their "sweeties," or suitors for their hand in marriage, and so, many of the girlish blos-soms attended the Ball alone. I feel sure that they were quite safe in doing so, for two policemen are always assigned to cover the Ball, undoubtedly for the little waitresses' protection.

These unattended waitresses seemed to have such sweet, trusting natures, for they danced with every indication of life-long friendship with any man who asked them. I should, really, have warned them of the dangers to unsuspecting girls in cities over three thousand population. Further indications of the trust-ing nature of the waitresses lay in the fact that the elevator carried guests up to the ballroom, but not down; that garments had to be checked in advance at the check room; and that one policeman patrolled the corridor until the last guest left in his limousine.

"We've never had no trouble," said Miss Mamie Kelley, "except last year at the Ball at the Liederkranz[89] when six watches and three hand-bags was miss-

---

88 The shingle, or "boyish" bob, introduced in 1923, a short haircut tapered into a "v" in the back.

89 The Liederkranz Club, a Rochester choral society founded in 1873, had since 1919 been lo-cated at the former Westminster Presbyterian Church.

ing, and the year before when we had the Ball at Munz's Hall on South Avenue, and we had to call extra cops to help throw out two Eye-talians. But we let it be knowed that we run a real refined Ball, you know, and we gen'rally have as nice a crowd as you see here tonight."

I was delighted at this news, as I had just heard that the male guests at this year's Ball were a choice assortment of plumbers, taxi-drivers and newspaper men. I cannot vouch personally for the truth of it, however, as I could not distinguish one from the other.

I was charmed to see my acquaintance of whom I wrote two weeks ago, Mr. Mike Dempsey, a center of attraction with a bright green silk handkerchief in his breast pocket, which he kept pulling further and further into prominence until it slipped to the floor, and a well-known pool player was slapped harshly across the face for putting it in his own breast pocket. A bit of clever repartee ensued.

"Who the ?!***!!? are you?" queried the pool player.

"I'm Mike Dempsey, that's who the ?!***!!? I am!" responded the famous welterweight.

"Keep the handkerchief," replied the pool player.

Standing by my side, a witness to the little encounter, was a sad-faced youth with baggy trousers and large, red hands.

"Gosh!" he ejaculated. "It was Dempsey took a girl away from me a minute ago, and I didn't know he was a fighter, and Gosh! I told him I didn't think he oughta do that way. Gosh! That was a narrer escape."

The sad-faced youth sighed.

"I'd just found out her name was Vi'let. I seen her in one o' them cafeteries today, and she looked so purty with a piece o' apple pie in one hand and a dish o' vanilly ice cream in t'other, waitin' on customers so nice, I made so bold as t'speak with her, and she said I could see her at the Ball t'night. And then that fighter took her off just as we started to dance. I always was partial to the name o' Vi'let."

And, seeing this stalwart rural youth retire to a circle of similar rustics, and being informed that they were known to the waitresses as "moss-backs," I remembered that apropos lyric:

Such a starved bank of moss,
'Til, that May morn,
Blue ran the flash across—
Violets were born![90]

---

90 The prefatory lyric to Browning's *La Saisiaz, and The Two Poets of Croisic* (1878).

Indeed, all these flowers of girls, so many named appropriately, Rose, Violet, Poppy, Lilly, seemed made to delight the heart of simple man—and the simpler the man, the greater his delight! Since it had been announced at the beginning of the evening that "the bunny-hug, toddle and ubjexshunubbel [objectionable] dancing"[91] were strictly prohibited, "but aside from that, the sky's the limit to have a good time," the merry-making waitresses were forced to find their jollity within these harsh regulations. It must be admitted that, considering their limitations, they did very well indeed. A late hour found them tripping, weary but still, oh, so gay! out to their cars parked closely for three blocks.

I presume that, their annual May gayety done with, they will go into retirement for another year—Cinderellas of the Ham and Eggs!

One Cinderella at least found her coach waiting and her Prince faithful, for I heard the sad-faced rustic say, as he drew a Ford crank from his pocket:

"Vi'let, will you be ready to go when I get Henry a-breathin'?"

Lady Alicia Thwaite

"Paint Jobs That Bloom in the Spring, Tra La!" *Five O'Clock* 1 (20 May 1924): 9.

* * * * * * * * *

The Price of Marguerite

Like a Mediaeval Romantic Tragedy This Actual News Story of To-Day, in Which the Beautiful Intriguing Wife, the Unsuspecting Husband, the Cynical Lover and the Infatuated Dupe Enact a Passionate Drama That Heads Two for the Electric Chair

Does the blood of the Borgias still flow in the veins of the beautiful Marguerite Lemardi?[92] Five hundred years ago, corrupt Italian beauties of various social

---

91 The "bunny-hug" was a sensual dance invented in San Francisco circa 1911. It was considered indecent and banned at many dance halls before it was renamed the fox-trot. The "toodle" was a sultry dance inspired by the sound of the jazz legend Edward "Duke" Ellington (1899–1974).

92 The political and sexual scandals associated with this Italian Renaissance family have contributed to them being called the "First Crime Family." The sexual intrigues of Lucrezia Borgia (1480–1519), daughter of Rodrigo Borgia, Pope Alexander VI (1431–1503), with whom she may have had a son, are in themselves the subject of legend. There are certain parallels between her love life and that of Marguerite Lemardi; both committed adultery and both incited murder. Lucrezia Borgia's later life has often been laid bare in literature; see, for example, Victor Hugo (1802–85),

classes frequently had stout or otherwise objectionable husbands, who came to be neatly dispatched at the hands of impetuous lovers. To-day in America, for the most part, objectionable husbands are otherwise disposed of.

In Rochester, N. Y., in 1925, Marguerite Lemardi, twenty-six, had an undesirable husband, James, aged thirty-two; an ardent but cautious lover, Joseph Provenzano, twenty-two, and an eager but gullible dupe, Joseph Friia, aged thirty-one. After elaborate plotting and counterplotting, the dupe, at the instigation of the woman and her lover, murdered the husband as he slept, in a fashion that would have interested Lucrezia Borgia.

To-day, Marguerite Lemardi is free of her husband, as she desired to be. But since, after all, it happened in modern America, Provenzano and Friia have been claimed by the State, and are awaiting execution in the death house at Sing Sing.[93] As for the young and fair modern Borgia, she will spend a few years in Auburn.[94] It has been remarked that young and beautiful women seem seldom to have committed first degree murder.

Here follows the story. Most of it from the lips of Friia, the dupe, who in vindictiveness turned in his fellow conspirators, and whose revenge has been almost complete.

"I killed him, I killed him! For the love of her, I killed him, and I'm ready to die for it!"

Such was his confessional cry; but when he should die, he wished to take the lovers with him.

Five hundred years ago, in their ancestral Italy, James Lemardi and Joseph Friia would doubtless have been leaders of a band employed by mediaeval nobility for nefarious purposes, carrying on aside their own sinister loves. Four years ago, in Pittston, Pa., they were fellow workers for the Black Hand. They were friends.

What lovers the unfaithful Marguerite Lemardi had had, no one, least of all Lemardi, knew. Two weeks after her marriage to Lemardi, at the age of sixteen, she had begun her infidelities by eloping with another man. She returned and was forgiven. Mystery hangs over the intervening six years, until we come to Friia, shopkeeper and Black Hander; tall and stocky, a little slow-witted, perhaps, but capable of passionate devotion to Marguerite. They were lovers.

Treachery to the Black Hand made it necessary for Lemardi to leave Pittston.

Lucrèce Borgia (1833), and Robert Browning, "Andrea del Sarto" (1855).

93 The notorious prison in Ossining, New York.

94 Prison in Auburn, New York, known for its reform-minded theories.

He came to Rochester, and with him his wife, who seems promptly to have dismissed Friia from her mind. At least he suffered eclipse in 1924, when she met Provenzano, young and handsome, a vagabond actor. An Italian amateur dramatic society was producing a movie picture, "The Brigand of Spain."[95] Marguerite had been chosen to play the heroine to Provenzano's hero, and they were madly in love.

At that time Friia came to Rochester and begged Marguerite to elope with him—to Spain, he pleaded, where they would be happy in a sunny clime. In her mind, Marguerite doubtless made the reservation that if she went to Spain with anyone, it would be with her beloved brigand, Provenzano. She was wrapped up in the slim, graceful actor, her new lover—more ardent, more desirable than any other man she had known for her twenty-six years. She repulsed Friia and sent him back to Pittston.

Friia knew nothing of his successor. Back in Pittston, he dreamed and planned, for Marguerite had told him that she dared not leave her husband. Meanwhile, the lovers were making their own schemes. Since they had been chosen to play the leads in "The Brigand of Spain," they would elope to Hollywood, where they would win professional fame. In the days of the Borgias, it would have been from the provinces to Venice, where the drama flourished.

Lemardi, unsuspecting, stood like a stone wall in the way. An enraged husband was no part of their plans, to descend on them with a revengeful stiletto. The minds of the lovers went back hundreds of years to the times when lovers adopted what was, after all, the simplest of expedients for removing husbands. Lemardi was in the way, therefore he must die!

Running true to mediaeval form, Provenzano suggested poison. He gave Marguerite four deadly drugs to put in her husband's food. Everything was planned, everything was ready for the fatal dose. But when the moment came, the woman, like Lady Macbeth, dreaded to do the deed. Lemardi, unwitting of danger, lived on, and Provenzano upbraided his mistress for her cowardice.

In the spring of 1925, Friia sold his shop in Pittston and came to Rochester to press his love. He met Marguerite on the street and urged her, in impassioned plea, to go away with him. In an adjacent doorway, where he had come to meet her, lurked Provenzano. As though it had been arranged by a master playwright, he overheard the discarded lover make his plea. Lest he should forget its phrasing, he jotted down some of the conversation on a sheet of paper, where it was later found in his pocket—a serious piece of evidence against him, corroborating

---

95 *The Brigand of Spain* is not further identified.

the story Friia was to tell the police, and which Provenzano and Marguerite were to deny.

Provenzano heard his sweetheart send the man away. And at once, it seems, he realized that he had found the instrument of his desires: the dupe, the infatuated fool, who would do away with Lemardi at no risk to the lovers. Marguerite fell in with the plan. She approached Friia.

"She said that if I killed her husband, I could come to her house to live." In these words the betrayed Friia told of Marguerite's proposal.

At first he demurred. The idea came as a shock to him. But repeatedly the woman urged him. Once, when he refused, she called him a coward, as murderous-hearted women long before her had done. And always she offered herself as the reward. If Friia would kill her husband, he could come to her house to live with her. The temptation was too strong for the infatuated admirer. He agreed.

On March 29, 1925, at Marguerite's suggestion, Friia turned over $2000 to her, the proceeds of the sale of his shop. He little suspected that she planned to use it for escape with Provenzano. Neither did he know that the handsome actor was a more favored suitor than he.

Marguerite urged him to do the killing at once, to hide in the nearby railroad yards, throw away the revolver, and make his escape on an outbound train. But some sleeping instinct warned the dupe. He had the feeling, he said later, that if he did this, he would never see Marguerite again, and it was for her he was to slay. Again Lemardi was spared a little time.

Provenzano was increasingly impatient at the delays. Twice his plans had been frustrated by the hesitancy of his tools. He wrote a note to Marguerite. This also was found later in his pocket.

"If this will not happen to-night or to-morrow night, I am going to leave town Friday night. If you really love me and want to be with me, do it and we'll be happy."

Desperate, Marguerite met Friia twice on April 4. She pleaded, again offering him the supreme reward. He was to come at midnight the following night, and she would let him in. He agreed.

On the evening of April 25, 1925, James Lemardi was away from home. Marguerite waited nervously—she could be nervous, it seems. The husband returned about 11 o'clock, and the two retired soon there after.

The wife left a light burning low so that the murderer might find his way. In an adjoining bedroom slept the three young Lemardi children, who might have been the children of another woman, as far as Marguerite was concerned. Lemardi fell asleep at once. His wife listened to his heavy breathing; to the ticking of the alarm clock on the dresser; to sounds from the kitchen which would tell that Friia, the assassin, the dupe, was coming in through a space where she had removed a window bodily for his convenience.

Shortly after midnight the murderer arrived. And with him was Provenzano, come, he said, to encourage him. Marguerite had slipped from her husband's side, and led Friia to the bedroom. Once he retreated, and Provenzano sent him back. Marguerite led him to the bedside, where her husband lay peacefully asleep.

"Shoot him in the mouth," she whispered.

She indicated the positions at which Friia was to fire. He fired five times, a heavy .38 calibre revolver. The husband, dying instantaneously in his sleep, neither saw nor knew his betrayers.

A sudden suspicion of treachery swept over Friia. He wheeled on the woman he loved, snarling:

"I've still got one for you, if you tell."

He turned to go.

When he went out, Provenzano was near the door, laughing! Did it occur to Friia, a year later, when his testimony was sending Provenzano to the death cell, that he laughs best who laughs last?

And Marguerite?

Her story at the trial in June, 1926, was that she was sleeping innocently at her husband's side, and that she was awakened by the first shot. She said that, terrified, she turned her face to the wall and lay motionless as the killer fired the other four shots.

But over the bed hung a colored picture of a saint. The police found it spattered with blood. Lemardi's blood was on it, and on the walls, and on the bedclothing. The bedclothing had caught fire immediately, from the nearness of the revolver shots. And the nightgown in which the police found Marguerite that fatal night, was spotlessly white! She could not have been at Lemardi's side when he was shot and have escaped the stain of his life's blood. The bespattered picture bore witness to the truth of Friia's story, when he said that the woman stood beside him and told him where to shoot.

Marguerite waited a few minutes to give Friia a start, then went inside and called her neighbors, already awakened by the shots. Friia fled through a side door and went to his hotel room at "Scully" Marino's. Provenzano was identified at his trial as the man who had been running from the direction of the Lemardi house on the night of the murder. The police arrived shortly after, and began their gruelling [*sic*] of the widow in her spotless nightgown.

At first denying that she knew the identity of her husband's slayer, she at last gave in and named Friia. On her information, the police found him pacing up and down in his room. Her betrayal of the dupe was complete.

And the dupe confessed. "I killed him, I killed him! For love of her I killed him!"

And then came the thing that Marguerite and Provenzano had overlooked. Betrayed, trapped, doomed, the dupe turned on the conspirators. He threw away his own chances of life to convict them both. At his own trial he told the story of the whole plot, his knowledge of the lovers' duplicity filling him with vindictiveness. He was sentenced to die in the electric chair the week of July 19. And in June and July he appeared at the trials of Marguerite Lemardi and Joseph Provenzano, to repeat his tale. The dupe was revenged.

The lovers denied any participation in the murder. But their own lies snared and convicted them—their lies and the bloodstained picture of the saint.

Up to the time of their conviction, Provenzano continued his dreams of love and fame in Hollywood. Surely, life would not be taken from one so favored! He was planning, he said, to weave the story of the murder into a moving picture.

"I not only want to be an author but I plan to act in my own productions," he said.

Provenzano, indeed, played the lead in his own production, but other hands than his will write the denouement and the end. He was sentenced to death for murder, first degree.

Justice for Marguerite Lemardi? The beautiful Marguerite, who said, at first, that she slept through the entire murder and did not hear the shots! Who later admitted hearing the first, and having laid trembling beside her husband as the others were fired—and was refuted by the saint she had prayed to! The woman who was actress enough to kiss her dead husband's lips and call to him; and then, still acting, or, perhaps, overcome by her weight of evil, fainted at his dead feet! Who, calm and lovely, for the most part, in the court room, tangles herself in lie after lie.

She was convicted, not for first degree murder but for second. She was sentenced from twenty years to life at Auburn. By the strange provisions of the law, she will receive commutations, and she can actually be free after serving eight years, eleven months and twenty-two days.

Eight years and eleven months added to her twenty-seven! The Borgias were in their prime at thirty-six! So, Lemardi will be dead, and Friia, and Provenzano; and Marguerite Lemardi will be free. Perhaps—who knows?—still dangerously beautiful.

Marjorie Kinnan Rawlings

"The Price of Marguerite," *World Magazine* (5 September 1926): 12ff. Only a clipping has been seen.

Florida

᷍ᛁᛁᛁᛁ᷍

1928–1953

With the publication by *Scribner's Magazine* of "Cracker Chidlings" (1931), MKR's career finally began to take flight. This period of her life was a time of unparalleled success, and it was a time of immense frustration. Under the mentorship of the eminent Scribner editor Maxwell E. Perkins, MKR blossomed as a writer at the same time she continued to struggle valiantly with the process of writing. The success of her first novel, *South Moon Under* (1933), made her an emerging star in Scribner circles. Her next novel, *Golden Apples* (1935), did not receive the critical acclaim Perkins thought it deserved. *The Yearling* (1938), however, brought her instant fame and wealth. The predictable pain of celebrity was exacerbated by winning the Pulitzer Prize in 1939. Her psychological state was always fragile, and such attention took her too frequently from the roots of her stability. She drank, smoked, and ate too much, and she began to suffer from acute diverticulosis. Yet Perkins continued to encourage her, always in his loving and paternal manner (see *Max and Marjorie*). A collection of her stories, *When the Whippoorwill*—(1940), received critical notice and established her as one of the deans of short fiction. *Cross Creek* (1942), a collection of autobiographical vignettes that centered on her life at the Creek, became, like *The Yearling*, a best seller. She followed it immediately with *Cross Creek Cookery* (1942). Written with the help of her "Perfect Maid" Idella Parker, the collection of recipes interlaced with narrative took advantage of MKR's legendary status as a cook. Yet once again personal tribulation confronted her. Her second husband, Norton S. Baskin, joined the American Field Service at the height of World War II. MKR was proud, but shocked, and more than anything, worried. She soon devoted herself to the war effort, all but putting aside her creative work. For eighteen months, during 1943–44, she wrote a letter a day to Norton, who was an ambulance driver in Burma and India (see *Private Marjorie*). She also took on the arduous task of responding to the letters she received from servicepeople, who were reading her novels in Armed Services Editions. The literally hundreds of letters she wrote to comfort these young Americans preparing to go into or trying to recover from battle might very well have been her own finest hour. Such effort, not made easy by the protracted 1943 lawsuit over her alleged "invasion of privacy" in *Cross Creek*, took its toll. Her frustration at not being able to give sustained effort to the manuscript of her novel *The Sojourner* (1953) made life for her and those around her tense. After the war, she rededicated herself to her craft, but the inspiration of her former days was difficult to recapture. She bought a home near Van Hornesville, New York, where she worked in the summer and often well into the winter. The death of Perkins in 1947 was a blow from which she never fully recovered. In spite of the encouragement she received from her friends, most notable among them Owen D. Young and Robert Frost, the recusant *Sojourner* was more frustrating to her than any of her other novels. Still, she pressed on and finally was able to deliver the manuscript to Scribners near the end of 1952. Remarkably, her vim and vigor seemed to return, and she set out to write a biography of Ellen Glasgow, her treasured friend. For nearly a year she did research, interviewed Glasgow intimates, and gathered notes. However, it was not to be. On 14 December 1953, MKR died suddenly, her celebrated life brought to an end unexpectedly by a massive stroke. The true ownership of Cross Creek had reverted back to time.

Letter to the *Ocala (Fl.) Evening Star*

Author of Cracker "Chidlings" Protests[1]

Cross Creek,
Hawthorne, Route 1, Fla.
Jan. 30, 1931

Editor Star: Your comment on my sketches in the February Scribner's, "Cracker Chidlings," was brought to my attention yesterday as I was leaving the hospital in Jacksonville after a recent operation.[2] The paper had been kept from me until that time. Late as I am in taking up the discussion, journalistic ethics of course require that, having attacked my good faith and sincerity, you give space to my communication, exactly as I submit it.

Allow me to point out that one thing that is simply not done by a trained journalist or by any writer careful of her integrity and reputation, is "palming off material collected in the Cumberlands, where she must have visited, as Florida life." I have not visited the Cumberland mountains or any other remote regions. The Florida frontier—unfortunately fast-vanishing—has been my first experience of the kind, and my cracker friends and acquaintances have come into my life with all the freshness of new material.

Reading your editorial, I thought ruefully, "Ah, I must know more than he does about red bugs and mosquitoes." Or perhaps—come, now, take a firm stand—perhaps you deny the red bug and mosquito! My dear sir, either you simply do not know the back woods and back waters of our state, or you are one of those persons Mencken had in mind when he wrote in the September Forum:

"There are men in the world, and some of them not unintelligent men, who have a natural appetite for the untrue, just as there are others who have a natural

---

1   MKR's collection of vignettes "Cracker Chidlings," *Scribner's Magazine* 89, no. 2 (February 1931): 127-34, was reviewed unfavorably by the *Ocala Evening Star* (30 January 1931), which criticized the story as misrepresenting Cracker dialect and culture. MKR responded in the above letter, which in turn drew an equally spirited counter-response by the *Evening Star*. The controversy made it as far as the *Miami Herald* (9 April 1931), which supported MKR's authorial license, concluding that the sketches reveal the "compassion of a woman's great heart." Maxwell E. Perkins, her editor at Scribners, consoled MKR with the observation that such misunderstanding is "what a writer must expect" (*Max and Marjorie*, 36).

2   MKR had recently had an appendectomy, although it is likely that the problem was related to her recurring diverticulitis.

appetite for the ugly. A bald fact somehow affrights them: they long to swathe it in comforting illusions. Thus one hears from them that it is somehow immoral for an artist to depict human life as it actually is: the spectacle of the real must be ameliorated by an evocation of the ideal, which is to say, of the unreal. So Thomas Hardy becomes a bad artist, and the author of Pollyanna a good one."[3]

My artistry I cannot becomingly defend. Of my accuracy I am so positive that I feel, in good time, as your knowledge increases, you will offer me the courtesy of an apology. My dear sir, my sketches are so true, that I have softened them, not colored them, for fear that if they came to the chance attention of the subjects—all within a forty-mile radius of my home—offense would be taken at my frankness where none was intended.

The dialect which to you "sounds as if it must be spoken somewhere" is made up studiously only of idioms, of phrases, of turns of speech, that I have myself heard here again and again. Perhaps my newness in this country gives a pristine quality to the oddities of speech that come to my ears. Perhaps my interest as a student of etymology has made me alert to the quaintnesses and archaisms deep-rooted in the English tongue. One of my cracker acquaintances in the cattle section of recent turmoil, said to me of 'coon-meat, of which he is exceedingly fond, "It has a kind of foolish taste." Do you know that one must go back far into Anglo-Saxon speech to find the word "foolish" used currently in the sense in which he used it?[4] And have you noticed that the Georgia "hit" for "it," which persists hereabouts, is likely to be used at the beginning of a sentence, but not necessarily afterward?

Of course, it would be preposterous to credit me with implying that all crackers or that all Florida natives use the dialectical turns I have suggested. They exist only in sections uncontaminated by the tourist or the Rotary Club. Just as it would be preposterous to insist that I was describing the average Floridian, and therefore insulting him. Heaven forbid that a storied character out of any one locality be forced, by such logic as yours, to represent his whole community. Sir, you would eliminate individuality. You would annihilate personality.

And how we disagree, you and I, in summarizing my characters. You shock me with your classifications. The lack of sympathy is yours, not mine. These

---

3   H. L. Mencken (1880–1956), American newspaperman, editor, and critic. Thomas Hardy (1840–1928), British novelist, renowned for his stark representations of the trials of the peasant class. "Pollyanna," the so-called glad child of the juvenile novels of Eleanor H. Porter (1868–1920). The source of Mencken's quote is untraced.

4   According to the *Oxford English Dictionary*, in the seventeenth century one meaning of "fool" was a kind of custard, or clotted cream. By the mid-nineteenth century, a "fool" would also be a dish of crushed fruit (often gooseberries) mixed with cream or custard.

people are to me all that is delightful. Yet they offend you. I am so sorry. And I am so sorry that you have hurt the feelings of a very good man in your failure to read carefully "The Preacher Has His Fun."[5] The Rev. Mr. Plummer, well-loved chaplain of Raiford, an inspiration to its inmates, who preached what I thought a locally famous farewell sermon in a certain nearby small town, must be cut to the quick at your labeling of him in the public print—for most of the two counties knows the story of his prank—as "a renegade preacher."

And how astonishing to call a Florida moonshiner a weakling![6] This hardy breed made Florida famous long before the day of hard roads and modern hotels, and will, I do not question, in fame outlive them. No, my dear sir, do not let us hustle and deny out of existence the last of Florida's frontier. The state will soon be like any other. Before they have been quite swallowed up, let us know and enjoy these picturesque people, pioneer remains. They are much more vital than you and I.

Let me quarrel a moment longer, and I am through. How, in your glass house, dare you stone my "unsympathetic manner" after the farce your paper made of journalism and of justice, in its handling of the recent flogging in the cattle country?[7] I have met, and have been entertained at one of the hospitable tables of, most of the cattlemen in the Burbank section. I admire them. They are fine, honest, sturdy pioneers, puzzled at the superimposition of involved modern law on the simple frontier law. You called then "hoodlums." You implied, just short of laying yourself open to libel charges, that the particular men under indictment were without doubt the "hoodlums" you meant. Their acquittal has done little to temper the injustice that has been done them.

May I ask you to reserve your charge of lack of sympathy until you have read my short novel, "Jacob's Ladder," a story of a young cracker man and woman, to be published in Scribner's within a few months? With the encouragement

---

5   In "The Preacher Has His Fun" (*Short Stories*, 37–38), the preacher gently satirizes the congregation for its treatment of a preacher, who one day dramatically departs with Christ's injunction: "I go to prepare a place for you. Where I am, there ye may be also." He was leaving to be the chaplain at the state penitentiary in Raiford.

6   In "A 'Shiner's Wife," (*Short Stories*, 31–33), moonshiner Tim and his female companion, not his wife, stay one night ahead of the law and kill without hesitation. The "wife," a neat and obedient woman who follows Tim into the swamp, where "Nobody but Christ would try to walk," concludes, "I reckon Christ don't pay no attention to us mean rascals." Such sympathetic portrayals drew the ire of the *Evening Star*.

7   There had been an ongoing dispute among the locals about establishing a fence law. Several cattlemen who opposed the law were put on trial for allegedly physically beating two opponents. The *Evening Star* called such people "hoodlums." The cattlemen were later found innocent. MKR used parts of this event in her story "The Enemy" (*Short Stories*, 298–314).

of Scribner's acceptance, I have only begun my re-creation of this section and these people. I am going leisurely, for I wish only to write of what I know. Added to the past days and nights in the scrub, there must be weeks or months; there must be longer and further prowlings through the piney-woods and the shadowy hammocks—where, alas, dear sir, I am never likely to meet you. The remote, lovely core of Florida is as yet unexpressed. Having introduced you to some of her unfamiliar people, I think hopefully: perhaps I can introduce you to some of her unfamiliar beauty.

Sincerely,
Marjorie Kinnan Rawlings

"Author of Cracker 'Chidlings' Protests," *Ocala (Fla.) Evening Star* (2 February 1931).

*   *   *   *   *   *   *   *   *

Dutch Oven Cookery

I should like to meet the ghost of the man who invented the Dutch oven.[8] The gentleman himself must be many decades dead, but if ghosts retain the characteristics of the living, his wraith is a kindly one, filled with love and helpfulness for his fellow man, and I should like to shake his ectoplasmic hand.

A favorite indoor sport of the intelligentsia is choosing the one book you would desire for company, if cast away on a desert island. If I am ever marooned in mid-ocean, give me a Dutch oven, and to hell with the book. I have often thought how mournful the life of an ordinary castaway—like that of an ordinary camper—must be, even if he nurses a Bible or a Shakespeare, because of the monotony of his victuals. All his food must be stuck on a stick and scorched over an open fire. With a Dutch oven, any food may be cooked in any way that is possible with the most up-to-date gas or electric stove.

The Dutch oven was the first stove of most Florida pioneers. There is only one that is genuine. Three feet attached to a cooking utensil do not make a Dutch oven, whatever the clerk may tell you. The real thing is of heavy cast iron with three slim sturdy legs, a long flat handle and a cover that fits as snugly as a quar-

---

8   A year later, when MKR and her dear friend Dessie Smith Vinson, later Prescott (1906–2002), took their famous trip described in "Hyacinth Drift," a Dutch oven, of course, accompanied them; see *Cross Creek* (1942), 351–52 and 355.

ter in a slot-machine. A fire may be built directly underneath, but it is usually desirable to raise the oven further from the ground on three bricks, flat stones, or small sections of pipe. The long handle presumably extends beyond the range of the fire. Since there is no way of keeping cast iron from heating itself to the bitter end, a trusting nature is a misfortune in handling a Dutch oven. Gloves are sometimes used by the effete, but the accredited holder is a large handful of Spanish moss.

The cover must, positively must, have an inverted flange an inch high, making a shallow pan of the lid itself. The border is a sacred thing, like the wall of Troy or the Great Wall of China. It means that on the lid, without danger of their getting into the food or sliding off, you can scatter live coals. This in turn means, *Messieurs et Mesdames*, that you can bake, on a camp, raised rolls, hot biscuits, baked stuffed fish, a baked roast of meat or fowl—any of the baked and browned-on-both-sides delicacies that are quite out of the question with the ordinary camp implements. The heat is controllable, top and bottom, to a fine degree. And in the center of the lid is an oval cast-iron eye, through which the pointed end of a long pole may be inserted for comfortable lifting.

Probably nowhere in the world are camping and camp cooking more delightful than in Florida. The very mention of the state signifies life outdoors. Florida has developed a whole technique of Dutch oven cookery. The utensil is perfect for frying fish. Its depth eliminates spattering. Frog-legs French fried in deep fat are a choice out-door delicacy. Florida has recently awakened to the fact that the "peepers" in her countless lakes and marshes are identical with the cultivated specimens grown on Louisiana frog-farms.

Florida frogs are caught at night. A light is shone in their eyes, and a stick with a nail in the end brings them in as fast as the small boat can be paddled. A camping party near water should be able to add them any time to its *carte du jour*. And when you have taken your fried fish, or frog-legs, or peanut-fattened Florida pork chops, or chicken, or ham, from your smoking fat, drop in stiff corn-pone batter by spoonfuls. Fried quickly in deep fat, and eaten "out of hand," these are tid-bits of a peculiarly delicious, nutty flavor.

Among camp dishes most flavory and most suited to the Dutch oven, I recommend Florida fish chowder. This is quite different from New England chowder, and people have been known to devour it in inordinate quantities, who have insisted that they did not care for chowders. The dish is built up, like a skyscraper or a layer cake, and never mixed or stirred. A layer of bacon, of slices an inch or two long, is first browned. Cover with a layer of individual portions of raw boned fish. Add a layer of thinly sliced potatoes, a scantier layer of sliced onions, salt, pepper, dots of butter and a layer of crackers. Begin all over again from bacon to crackers, making as many layers as your oven will hold or the crowd will eat. Add just enough water from time to time to keep the chowder from sticking and burning. Cover tightly. It should be watched closely, and a pancake turner slipped now and then under the bottom layer. When fish, potatoes and onions are tender—in thirty or forty minutes—add enough milk or cream to make slightly moist.

The pilau (pronounced pur-loo) should by no means be omitted from Florida camp cookery. I shall never forget the glorious days when I was first introduced to the dish. And I shall never forget the lone chicken that fed eight starving campers. The fowl was cut into its smaller component of parts. It was boiled in plenty of water until tender. Then two and a half cups of dry rice was stirred into the kettle, with salt and pepper. After half an hour's further boiling, an immense platter of epicurean nourishment was placed on the table. The fluffy white rice, absorbing all the liquid, was so impregnated with the flavor of chicken that it was impossible to tell where breast ended and neck began. Little puddles of golden fat like sunlight lay there. There was a gorging and a smacking of lips—but there was pilau to spare.

Florida did not originate the pilau. It came, perhaps, from Persia or Turkey, by way of Georgia and Carolina, but Florida adopted the dish for her own. Rice, added to meat boiled tender in water to cover, is always the base. There is chicken pilau, blackbird pilau or rice-bird pilau, quail or dove pilau, pork pilau, and pilau of any meat you fancy, the gamier the better. I have had pilau of coot livers and gizzards.[9] The coots themselves were donated to the next day's outing of the Negro Sanctified Church. I make only one suggestion: if you are ever so fortunate as to partake of squirrel pilau, ask for it without the heads. Squirrel brains and jowls are a great delicacy I can vouch for personally—but the eyes are disconcerting.

I remember a Continental newspaper editor who spent three amazed days with us in our rural Florida life. We took him on an outing by the shore of a lake; spats, moving picture camera, foreign accent and all. We gave him a drink of well-aged Florida 'shine and we fed him on a breast of guinea hen, roasted whole in the Dutch oven, and surrounded by young glazed carrots. It was a dish

9   The American coot (*Fulica Americana*), a bird with a light- to dark-gray body resembling a duck, sometimes called a mud duck or a mud hen.

fit for a king, and he quite frankly said so. Then, suddenly, a wild, yet somehow pleased, look came into his eyes. It was not the 'shine, but only astonishment.

"But in Florida," he exclaimed, "you liff like kings!"

Marjorie Kinnan Rawlings

"Dutch Oven Cookery," *Sunrise: The Florida Magazine* 1, no. 2 (February 1932): 20, 46.

*   *   *   *   *   *   *   *   *

F. Scott Fitzgerald's *Tender Is the Night*

Disturbing, bitter, and beautiful. I am totally unable to analyze the almost over-powering effect that some of his passages create. There is something terrifying about it, and the closest I can come to understanding it is to think that he visualizes people not in their immediate setting, from the human point of view—but in time and space—almost, you might say, with the divine detachment.

Marjorie Kinnan Rawlings

"F. Scott Fitzgerald's *Tender Is the Night*," blurb for F. Scott Fitzgerald, *Tender Is the Night* (New York: Scribners, 1934). This appears on the front flap of a later printing dust jacket (see Tarr, *Bibliography*, 239).

*   *   *   *   *   *   *   *   *

Having Left Cities behind Me

Now, having left cities behind me, turned
Away forever from the strange, gregarious
Huddling of men by stones, I find those various
Great towns I knew fused into one, burned
Together in the fire of my despising.[10]
And I recall of them only those things

---

10   The tenor of MKR's opening suggests that of Wordsworth in the first book of *The Prelude* (1850), where the "gentle breeze" (line 1) enables his escape "From the vast city, where I long had pined / A discontented sojourner" (lines 7–8).

Irrelevant to cities; murmurings
Of rain and wind; moons setting and suns rising.

There was a church spire on a distant hill
Clamorous with birds by day and stars by night,
Devout and singing. I have forgot its site—
Boston, or Rochester, or Louisville—
Of a certain city all I can remember
Is wild ducks flying southward in November.

Marjorie Kinnan Rawlings

"Having Left Cities behind Me." *Scribner's Magazine* 98, no. 4 (October 1935): 246; *Journal of Florida Literature* 13 (2004): 31.

*   *   *   *   *   *   *   *   *

Letter to the *Tampa Morning Tribune*

Still Small Voice of Gleam Arouses Loafer

> *Marjorie Rawlings has been fishing down there too.*
> *When she isn't fishing, she's working on a new novel.*
> —Gleam June 19.

Phil: The enclosed in my TRIBUNE reached me while stretched flat on my back on a couch on my Cross Creek porch, abandoned to utter indolence. It was like the accusing finger of judgment. I dashed immediately in my guilt to the typewriter. Then I gathered myself together defensively and decided to protest.

Don't you know—you must—the ghastly hiatus that lies between fishing and working—on a new novel or, I fancy anything else? Work cannot spoil you for fishing, but how fishing can wreck you for work! There are hours, days, sometimes weeks, that must be endured while one convalesces from the orgy, much as one must recover from the delicious but enervating effects of hashish.[11] The

---

11   The range of possible literary allusions for MKR's reference to "hashish" runs from the opium dream of "Kubla Khan" (circa 1797) by S. T. Coleridge (1772–1834) to the extreme enervation of "The Lotos-Eaters" (1832) by Alfred Lord Tennyson (1809–92) to Fitzgerald's *Tender Is the Night*, in which Rosemary claims that the palace of Cardinal de Reitz is "perverted as a breakfast of oatmeal and hashish" (71).

harsh facts of life must be learned all over again. The soul, raw from exposure to one of the greatest delights on earth, must grow a new protective armor. The skin, raw from the summer sun, must heal. The joys of fishing, the joys of companionship with the kind of people who fish, must be forgotten before the burden may again be assumed.

When your paragraph so rudely disturbed me, I was swimming in the delicious haze of memory; memories of glorious days at Bimini with "Bill" Grinnell, the world's grandest sportswoman; of jolly days at Useppa, marooned, thank Heaven, by "a tropical disturbance of slight intensity," with not only Dave Newell as host, but the completely delightful "Kit" Miller as fellow-guest.[12] I have been only recently introduced to the insidious drug of big-game fishing. It has been all the more difficult to awaken from the dream. You have hastened the process. With fury and frustration I return to my work. For I have it on your respected authority that "when she isn't fishing, she's working on a new novel."

Marjorie Kinnan Rawlings

Hawthorn

"Still Small Voice of Gleam Arouses Loafer," *Tampa (Fl.) Morning Tribune* (25 June 1936). In this letter, MKR is responding to a *Tribune* column, "The Gulf Gleam," written by Philip E. Barney, who on the authority of Dave Newell (see below), reported that "Marj Rawlings" had been fishing for tarpon south of Naples and that "When she isn't fishing, she's working on a new novel" (19 June 1936).

* * * * * * * * *

Letter to the *Tampa Morning Tribune*

You Reckon This Mought Be the Same Man, Elmer?

Mr. Barney, dear Sir: I am a poor widow woman living alone in my orange grove at Cross Creek.[13] Your newspaper, dear Sir, in especial the finely wrote verses, is

---

12   MKR neglects to mention here that during her trip to Bimini, "Bill" (Mrs. Oliver) Grinnell had introduced her to Ernest Hemingway (1898–1961). "Useppa" is an island off the southwest coast of Florida. David McCheyne Newell (1898?–1986), explorer, editor of *Field and Stream*, author of *The Fishing and Hunting Answer Book* (Garden City, N.Y.: Doubleday, 1948), announcer for the television show *The Sportsman's Club* (1950–67). "Kit" Miller is unidentified.

13   A colloquialism for a divorcée was a "grass widow."

a great pleasure to my simple life and every morning I do stand by my gate, wearing my blue sunbonnet against the sun, or my gray shawl against the weather, to wait for its coming.

Now I am troubled, dear Sir, to read in it of a gentleman inquiring for a citizen who is missing, a citizen wearing a brown derby, who was a great rider but over-reached himself and was thrown from a donkey and later from an elephant. An elephant is a big creature, I am told, but do you not agree, Sir, that there is a precious little bigness anywhere? But to come to the matter I am troubled, because I believe that I have seen the missing citizen, and can bear witness to his whereabouts. I would not confuse the search, Sir, and I could in any case be mistook. But I will tell you what I saw, only yesterday, for it is my duty to tell it and it happened in this fashion:

I wandered over the bridge across the Creek, gathering poke leaves in my apron, for the winter has been lean, what with so many gentlemen coming to say I might not sell my oranges, so that in puzzlement I left the fruit for the woodpeckers, gathering poke leaves, I say, to make me a little salad. It was my old patchedy apron, but good enough for such jauntings.

Well, Sir, I did lean over a bank for an especial green tender cluster, and there before me was a cave or grotto which I had not noticed before. And lying in the grass before the cave was a brown derby head-piece.

"There is someone here," I said, "perhaps a fellow mortal in distress, and taking refuge."

So I did clamber down the bank and look into the cavern.

A gentleman sat there in the darkness, Sir, and he was tossing a little table back and forth.

"Good day, Sir," I said. "I thought I might be of service, but I see you playing contentedly with a little table. What kind of table might it be?"

"It's a director's table, Woman," he said gruffly. "I have naught else to play with."

Just then I did notice a most shocking thing. The gentleman's breast was bare, and I could see it, and the flesh was eaten away from over his heart, so that I could see it, too, and it was small and shriveled, and it was all but eaten, too.

"Oh, pray, Sir," I cried, "what has happened to your heart?"

He stared at it in something of surprise, methought.

"It was a brave heart, one time," he said. "I do remember long ago in a far northern place I held high office. And rich men came to me and would take from the state a portion of the land to make them a golf course. And my heart stirred within me, and I felt it swelling, and I did say, 'Begone. Boys in ragged shirts and torn breeches do play their games there, and have no other place to play them. You shall not have their playground."'

"And now, alas," said I, "there is not enough heart remaining to make you any protest, and methinks human injustices would find it unaffected."

In the blackness, Sir, I do swear it, a voice said, "It's time to turn your coat again."

And the gentleman did rise and turn his coat, and indeed, he did seem bruised in parts, as though he had fallen from a donkey or an elephant. And I did see that what had spoken to him was so close entwined with him that my eye could not separate them. And what hugged him close was a green-eyed monster.

"Oh, come away, Sir!" I cried out. "It is the beast that has brought you to this sad state."

"Too late, Woman," he answered me. "I do love him, and we are one. Of my own will and nature, I did choose him to be my boon companion."

And the green-eyed monster did lean close and suck another morsel from his heart, Sir.

And could this be the missing citizen? And had I best advise the proper authorities? But who, indeed, Sir, might be the proper authorities in a case so tragic? Does it not seem to you it has passed beyond the power of man? And might it be best to leave him quietly to perish in darkness, since it is of his choosing?

The Widow Rawlings

P.S. If he should truly perish, would it be unlawful, Sir, for me to fetch the hat? I would put it a-top a mop-handle and use it for a scare-booger in my corn-field.[14]

"You Reckon This Mought Be the Same Man, Elmer?" *Tampa Morning Tribune*, 18 March 1937. Published in the column "The Gulf Gleam."

---

14   MKR's piece is an allegory of Alfred E. Smith (1873–1944), a politician famous for his brown derby. He was a Democrat whose landslide defeat by Herbert Hoover (1874–1964) in the presidential election of 1928 and primary defeat by Franklin D. Roosevelt (1882–1945) in 1932 led to much bitterness, the "little green monster." Smith became a staunch opponent of the New Deal and supported Republican presidential candidates in 1936 and 1940. The complete allegory is cleverly worked out in Leland Hawes, "Just Who Was the Gentlemen Sitting in the Cave?" *Tampa Tribune-Times*, 10 January 1988, and "Riddle's Answer—Man in Derby Was Alfred E. Smith," *Tampa Tribune*, 24 January 1988.

Abe Traphagen's Farm

When I think of my grandfather's farm west of Holly, I think of a way of life that was beautiful, and that is gone. Louis Bromfield wrote of that life in a fine book, "The Farm."[15] I, too, should have written such a book about those Michigan acres I knew, but I understood too late their meaning, and before I could gather from the tall gaunt old man who looked like another Abe, Lincoln, enough of his memories, he was dead and buried, along with the rich, the hard-working, the satisfying life that he had lived and of which he was a symbol.

I think perhaps men and women are no longer willing to work as hard as Abe and Fanny Traphagen. We talk now of hours and wages, and do not give ourselves with quite the uncalculating fervor to living.

In 1840, I believe, my grandfather's grandfather migrated to pioneer Michigan from New York state to take up "free land." Any man was entitled to forty acres, free of federal taxes. His sons took up land in their time, and Abe Traphagen found himself at the age of sixteen with eighty acres of land, most of it in timber.

I can see that great lanky, bony boy, serious as an owl, clearing his land. There were not enough hours in a day, he told me, and moonlit nights seemed to him a dispensation by which he might stretch the time and he used the moonlight as he used the light of the sun, for planting corn and wheat, and felling timber. There was marsh across one section of his land, and the rattlesnakes were so thick in it that he killed as many as twenty in one day. And when his hay crop failed him, he cut the coarse marsh grass and laid it by for feed for his stock.

"Good fodder in bad times," he told me.

He built a house that looked out over his rolling acres, green as only Michigan can be green, with a granite-lined lake, in a hollow, so deep that no one ever found the bottom; so blue that the bright Michigan sky seemed pale above it. When he was nineteen, he brought sixteen-year-old Fanny Osmun there as his bride. We should say today that a boy and a girl tended that house and worked those acres. But it was a man and woman. The acreage grew to some two hundred; the house was burned and was built, and burned and built again; seven children were born. And when I first came to know them, they were not Abe and Fanny, but grandpa and grandma. And no life I have ever told seemed to me to hold such peace and comfort, all the finer for being earned.

The first impression that comes back to mind of the farm, is one of spick

---

15   Louis Bromfield (1896–1956), *The Farm* (New York: Harper, 1933).

and span order; not the tidiness of the WPA,[16] but of a family that is proud of the work of its own hands. The plain, even ugly, farmhouse, sat back of a close-clipped lawn with a look of honest cleanliness, like a country boy had just come from scrubbing his face under the pump. A row of poplars put up a stiff front across the line where the yard joined the road. The barns on the opposite side were clean enough to live in. Even wood shed and attic and store room were orderly with hickory nuts and apples and dried corn and vegetables and stove wood and kindling and furnace wood; all in their proper and immaculate places. Even the ordinary kitchen chaos when a meal was in preparation, resolved itself momentarily into order, for grandma was an old-school believer in "keeping the dishes washed up" as the cooking progressed.

My second impression, and the most profound, is of an abundance now available only to the rich. But it was then a common thing, and a farm that did not provide lavishly was, simply, a poor or shiftless farm. The very fragrance of prosperity met the nose at the door of the farmhouse. It was years before I could sort that fragrance into its various ingredients. Some of it still eludes me, but I have identified such goodnesses as crocks of buckwheat and of clover honey; stone jars of sugar cookies and molasses cookies; strawberry and raspberry tarts kept, for some unfathomable reason, in the china cupboard; and an odor of assorted spices, browning butter and roasting meat in a house where three Gargantuan meals were served daily to a number of people that for most of us would constitute a "party."

Those meals were incredible. They cannot have become enlarged by that peculiar magnifying combination of a child's eyes and an adult's memory, for I can name the assorted dishes that covered the table. Della Lutes knows those Michigan farm meals. I refer you to her "A Country Kitchen" for mouth-watering descriptions,[17] and my only complaint against her grand book is that she has not included everything. The lightest "cold supper" after a vast and late noon dinner, would be pickled pork, fried to golden crispness; new potatoes with milk gravy; poached eggs so fresh they quivered with their newness; all the left-over meats from dinner to justify the name of "cold supper;" chicken, roast lamb, pot roast of beef; baked beans; salt rising bread and perhaps hot biscuits, for fear the meal should seem too casual; pickles, jams, jellies, relishes; and such an assortment of cakes, pound cake, jelly roll, nut cake, chocolate layer cake, that it

---

16   President Roosevelt created the Works Progress Administration (WPA) by executive order on 6 May 1935; its name was changed to Work Projects Administration in 1939. A cornerstone of his New Deal, the WPA employed thousands of workers on a wide range of major and minor projects during the Great Depression.

17   Della Lutes (1872–1942), *The Country Kitchen* (Boston: Little, Brown, 1936).

is small wonder that an attendant memory, as a city child, is of castor oil every other Saturday. It took a sturdy race to sit down to those groaning boards and arise none the worse for wear.

The miracle was, that all the lavishness was produced on those two hundred acres. Coffee, tea, sugar, spices—I can think of little else that had to be purchased. Even the flour must have been milled from their own wheat. The garden was perfection. Root vegetables, potatoes, turnips, carrots, beets, onions, were grown in quantities to last the year. Seasonal vegetables would have stocked a city market; cucumbers, spinach, lettuce, beans, peas, cabbage, squash—including Hubbards and pumpkins for a winter's pies. Bordering the vegetable garden were the fruit trees; sickle pears and Bartletts, peaches, Damson plums, sour cherry and oxheart. And at the far end, beyond the grape arbor, were the raspberries and the gooseberries and the currants, so that no visitor, stranger, neighbor or kin, should ever lack for a variety of jams and jellies and preserves. The watermelon patch lay back of the smoke-house and the bee-hives, and the only rule for a greedy grand-child in that patch, was that he should learn to identify the ripe melons, and not waste the crop by cutting the green ones; and that he should not make himself sick.

The stock was supported entirely by feed grown on the place. There were oats for the plow horses—the trimmest of which was used to draw the rubber-tired buggy to go to Holly on Saturday; corn and fodder for the cows and hogs and chickens; silage for winter use. Wood for fuel came from the timbered forty acres. Abe Traphagen was one of the first farmers in Michigan to raise the now-staple navy beans as a money crop. His cash came from beans, from wheat, and from the most beautiful and satisfying source of income a man can possess, after an orange grove—an apple orchard.

From the time the apple blossoms covered the trees like pale careless bouquets, through the long green summer, up to the cool fall, when the fruit hung like lanterns, shining red of Baldwin and snow-apple, wax-green of Greening, gold of sheep's-nose and of banana apple, burnished gold of the russet, and into the snowy winter when the bare gray trunks and limbs were as lovely as a Japanese drawing, the orchard was a thing of grace and beauty. The village of Flint, they tell me, is now a bustling automobile city. But for me it will always be the destination of a wagon-load of red apples on which I was once allowed to ride with Grandpa. And the road to Flint is a road paved, not with asphalt or gravel, but with tales of old Michigan days that Abe Traphagen told me as we jogged along with a load of apples on a crisp October day.

And one of those tales he told me had to do with Indians who fished the lakes of Holly township and trapped along its streams. They were of the Fisher tribe, he said, and as a boy he spent so much time with them that folk said, "Abe Traphagen is half Indian." The friendship with the tribe went back to the days when the first Traphagen—whose Holland-Dutch name was originally Triph'auven—came to clear his government land, and being a man of wide experience, treated the Indians' ponies for their ailments. And even within the memory of my mother, an old Indian came periodically to visit, and might be found any winter morning asleep by the warm ashes of the kitchen hearth, a gift of fish or fur for the Traphagens beside him. Abe "spoke the lingo" as a boy, but as an old man he could remember only one expression. I cannot vouch for the spelling, but it was this, in sound:

"No ka Kanaka-man." The translation: "We do not like the white man."

Strange, but those savages were conscious of a taint in us. Something is the matter with the white man. I am not a social philosopher nor a political economist, only a lover of peace and order and social cooperation and individual self-sufficiency. But I know that the pioneer days and the pioneer people possessed those things, and they were of irreplaceable value, and they are in danger. And it is a fine thing for a township descended from such people, to be looking back over its history, and taking stock, perhaps, of what is transient there, and what is priceless and eternal.

Marjorie Kinnan Rawlings

"Abe Traphagen's Farm," *Holly (Mich.) Herald*, Centennial Anniversary Edition, 30 June 1938, 35.

* * * * * * * * *

Mountain Rain

Only the rain has made me faithless to the lowlands,
Rain slow as tears,
The arrogant hemlocks lifted gentle, dripping hands,
And the junipers.

Eagles cried over granite. I turned away my face, Adamant.
How could I know that rain would make this high, proud place
A supplicant?

Peaks blue with distance, mocking the straining tendons,
I could resist.
Who shall not yearn to the tear-washed rhododendrons
And the wet-lipped mist?

Marjorie Kinnan Rawlings

"Mountain Rain," *Scribner's Magazine* 104, no. 1 (July 1938): 63; *Journal of Florida Literature* 13 (2004): 32.

*   *   *   *   *   *   *   *   *

I Sing While I Cook

It has been a matter of pure joy to me, a very serious woman, to find that the properly planned and prepared food brings acolytes into my life who are unimpressed by my abilities either as a novelist or as a *femme fatale*. Writing is my profession, my exaltation, and my torture. I write as an introvert, attempting to turn an intangible loveliness into a tangible conception. But I cook as an extrovert, singing at the top of my lungs, in ecstasy and certainty of fulfillment. My black Adrina says, "I sho' loves to see you cut loose in the kitchen."[18]

Suppose we leave out of the picture, for the moment, the pale neurotics who genuflect before dreary diets or the this-that-and t'other caloried or documented eating. Let us consider only the pleasing of normal, lusty folk who, after two or three cocktails, sit down with well-bred greediness to my careless and carefree table on my Florida veranda. For these, I dote on planning a meal that shall first titillate, then satisfy, then ease. I play to the gourmet, never the gourmand.

To my notion, the most pleasant way of playing is to make the most of local materials. I can do wonders with asparagus, but asparagus in Florida comes from California, from Colorado, or New York, and is a withered memory of its own early days. So, instead of asparagus with Hollandaise, I stimulate a menu with fresh okra, direct from the field. I use only the young crisp pods, boil them whole, briskly, for ten minutes by the stop-watch—one minute too long destroys their integrity. Then I arrange the pods on individual, small, hot plates like the spokes of a wheel, their firm green tips pointed in thirstily toward the individual

---

18   Adrenna Mickens Samson, the daughter of the old servants Will and Martha Mickens; she is described in *Cross Creek* as a "femme fatale" who could "seduce any man she wanted" (22–23).

tiny bowls of Hollandaise. We dip the still firm okra into the sauce, holding it by the uncut stem end, as unhulled strawberries are dipped in powdered sugar.

Perhaps the loveliest of my local dishes is my crab Newburgh. I can not possibly give proportions, for I never have, twice, the same amount of fresh crabmeat. Robert Frost says in one of his orchard poems, "Something has to be left to God."[19] And in cooking, something has to be left to the instinct, or experience, of the cook, who goes at such dishes not by measure, but by the look and the holy feel of the mixture. In describing my Newburgh at its best, I must stand humbly and acknowledge two miracles that go into its composition. One is Dora, my Jersey cow, who has the rottenest disposition and gives the richest cream in the world. The other miracle is the nature of the crabmeat.

In the middle of a desolate nowhere in Florida, whose location I refuse to reveal lest tourists make a path to its shore, we have the phenomenon of a spring bubbling suddenly from subterranean depths to form a stream that runs into a river, and thence to the sea.[20] In that spring and that stream are found the largest, the sweetest blue crabs I have ever encountered. The cooked meat from them is as white as the breast of a virgin, and as tender. The large flakes fall as exquisitely from the shell as the white garments fall from the bride.

I take whatsoever measure I may have, then, of these unviolated morsels, and toss them into an iron skillet, half-inch deep in Dora's butter. I turn them gently. They must not brown, they must not change the colour of their innocence, but they must absorb the butter as a flower absorbs the sun. Then I add lemon-juice, approximately one tablespoon to a heaping cupful of crabmeat. I toy again. I add salt, a dash of clove, a fainter dash of nutmeg, and a wisp of a dash of red pepper. I pour on, slowly, devilish-Dora's cream, thick and golden. I let simmer. I call for a ritual cocktail. The rest of the meal is ready. The guests are warned to powder their noses, to take their last drink, and to assemble.

I beat eggs. How can I say how many? Probably three eggs to a pint of cream. I fold in the eggs. I uncork the sherry, which should be as dry as possible. I pour slowly, stirring meanwhile as feverishly as though the Prince of Wales were waiting. How much sherry? How should I know? Just enough to thin the thickened blend to something a shade beyond the original thickness of the cream.

Adrina cries out, "Supper comin' up!"

The guests seat themselves. I add two or three tablespoons of cognac brandy, I turn the Newburgh into a red-hot, deep serving-dish, I rush it to the table.

---

19   MKR quotes the last line (29) of Frost's poem "Good-bye, and Keep Cold" (1923).

20   MKR's favorite crabbing spots were Salt Springs and Silver Glen Springs, both of which empty into Lake George, then into the St. Johns River, and finally into the Atlantic Ocean.

Toast points are ready, and parsley for garnishing. I serve. I pray. The Newburgh is tasted—a sip of Chablis behind it. Strong men who have admitted they have not read my writings, who have indicated all too plainly that there are sirens in their lives past my power to dethrone, grope for my hand to kiss its blistered finger-tips. Women who would knife me in the back, if I turned it, murmur, "Darling—." This, then, is a Newburgh.

My blackbird pie, however, came close to costing me a friend. I carried my use of local ingredients, to say nothing of childish innocence, almost too far. I sat Sam Byrd, the actor, of *Tobacco Road* and *Of Mice and Men* fame,[21] down to a pie of blackbirds. I think it really held twenty-four, for there were four of us at table, and I always allow six of the tiny things per person.

Sam said, "You don't mean—blackbirds?"

"Why, yes. It does seem evil to shoot them, doesn't it? Their chirping is so gay in the rushes."

"Not blackbirds?"

"The little red-winged blackbirds.[22] The females are drab and sometimes mistaken for rice-birds. I suppose I should really explain why I began shooting them for pie. I am a rotten shot, and one cold, foggy morning in a duck-blind on Orange Lake back of my place, I had simply missed too many ducks. I was in a fury of frustration. And all around me in the marsh-grass the red-winged blackbirds were cheeping and chirring by the hundreds. I slipped No. 10 shot into my double-barreled twenty-gage, and two shots dropped a dozen birds. Pie for two."

"And what possessed you—pardon me—how did it occur to you that they might be edible?"

I stared at him.

"Why, people have always eaten blackbird pie, haven't they? Don't you remember, 'Four and twenty blackbirds baked in a pie?'"[23]

"But that was a nursery rhyme—."

And it came to me then for the first time that I might indeed be serving something beyond the pale.

---

21   Sam Byrd (circa 1908–55) visited MKR in July 1938 to propose an adaptation of *South Moon Under*; see *Max and Marjorie*, 362, 412. He acted on Broadway as "Dude Lester" in a 1936 production of *Tobacco Road* (1932), by Erskine Caldwell (1903–87), and as "Curly" in the original production of *Of Mice and Men* (1937), by John Steinbeck (1902–68).

22   MKR was unaware that the red-winged blackbird (*Agelaius phoeniceus*) was a federally protected species at this time.

23   From the Old Mother Goose nursery rhyme "Sing a Song of Six Pence."

"But it's ridiculous. I make it often. Whenever the blackbirds are around in quantities."

He shuddered. Like a novice in the snake department at the zoo, he poked at his portion. He cut a piece of the small, succulent brown breast. He buried it between two wisps of flaky crust, brushed it with gravy—holy water, I presume, against evil—, closed his eyes, and swallowed it. He opened his eyes. He blinked them. He laid his hand on mine.

He said in low voice, "My dear friend. To think I didn't trust you—."

He wrote the other day asking for the recipe for the Sam Byrd cook-book. Here it is:

Like the recipe for rabbit, you must, of course, first shoot your blackbirds. Pluck them dry if you have the patience or the services of a little Negro boy. Split them down the back and dress them, but leave them whole. Roll them in flour. In plenty of butter in a deep kettle, brown the floured birds; and with them a tea-spoonful or so of minced onion and minced green pepper. When brown, cover with hot water. Add salt, pepper, a bay-leaf, and a dash of allspice. Simmer gently about two hours, or until the birds are tender. Add tiny whole onions, potatoes cut in balls or small squares, and carrots cut in the shape and size of shoe-string potatoes. When the onions are nearly tender, remove the bay-leaf, add a table-spoon of minced parsley, then thicken slightly, turn into a deep casserole, add a few tablespoons of sherry, cover with thick, rich pastry crust, and bake in a hot oven. Serve with a dry red wine, an endive and kumquat salad, and follow with tangerine sherbet.

This is the way I cook my small squab-sized chickens when I'm tired of waiting for them to reach broiler size:

Dress whole. Stuff with browned buttered crumbs and pecans. Roll in flour, well seasoned with salt and pepper. Brown on all sides in butter. Arrange in baking-dish. Almost cover with hot water that has been poured into skillet containing the butter in which the chickens were browned. Add sherry, one-eighth cupful to each chicken. Cover tightly and bake until very tender, when chicken will have absorbed most of the liquid. I sometimes prepare in this fashion the smaller game birds, quail, doves, snipe;[24] squirrel; small individual pot roasts of venison; or chicken too large for frying, cut into portions.

I am sorry my space does not permit a discussion of frogs' legs; or of the time my pet raccoon grew instantly to manhood by imbibing one whole Alexander cocktail; and of how, after sleeping it off on the pillows of my bed, he came

---

24   The "Sam Byrd cook-book" has not been found, but he did publish *Small Town South* (Boston: Houghton Mifflin, 1942), a book in which he describes his rural North Carolina upbringing and his concerns about development in Florida.

swaggering to the dinner-table and fell growling on a pair of frogs' legs tossed him by an alarmed guest whose leg he tried to climb; of how he ate—after all his previous life on warm milk from the nursing bottle—six pairs; of how the guest said:

"But, after all, frogs' legs are his natural diet, aren't they?"

"Yes," I answered, "but not French fried—."

Marjorie Kinnan Rawlings

"I Sing While I Cook," *Vogue* 93 (15 February 1939): 48–49.

*   *   *   *   *   *   *   *   *

Regional Literature of the South

I do not know what astute phrase-maker coined the expression "regional literature." The ill-assorted mating must be recent, for *Webster's New Unabridged Dictionary* of 1934 makes no formal acknowledgment of the union. The modern ghost writers for the shade of the great master of words define "regional" as "of or pertaining to a region or territory, especially a geographical region," which does indeed leave the word available to any man's use. "As," says Webster, "regional governments; regional symptoms." I seem to have heard lately of "regional housing," which is an appropriate and decent joining, since the shelters over men's heads must be suitable protection against whatever climatic elements are peculiar to the section. "Regional literature," to the best of my knowledge, is an expression only a few years older than New Deal phraseology. It is as glib as W.P.A., C.C.C., and N.R.A.[25] Time has not yet determined whether these terms are false or true—whether the Works Progress Administration truly progresses, or whether the Civilian Conservation Corps truly conserves. But I believe the phrase "regional literature" is not only false and unsound but dangerous

---

25   All three are New Deal programs. The WPA, or Works Progress Administration (1935; name changed to Work Projects Administration in 1939), employed thousands of workers on a wide range of major and minor projects during the Great Depression. The CCC, or Civilian Conservation Corps (1933), conducted public works projects such as the planting of trees, the building of bridges, and the maintaining of parks (the Appalachian Trail, for example, was a CCC project). The NRA, or National Recovery Administration (1933), encouraged companies to establish codes for fair competition and expanded the rights of workers. It was declared unconstitutional in 1935.

to a sharp appreciation of values, for the linking of the two words has brought in the connotation that if a piece of writing is regional, it is also literature.

Webster, again, defines literature as "literary productions as a collective body; as (a) The total of preserved writings belonging to a given language or people. (b) Specifically, that part of it which is notable for literary form or expression, as distinguished, on the one hand, from works merely technical or erudite, and, on the other, from journalistic or other ephemeral literary writing."

Accepting the specifications of dictionary preciseness, I dare to say, as a writer who often suffers under the epithet of "regional," that there is very little regional literature of the South. I dare go farther and say that the sooner we divorce the two words the sooner we shall discourage the futile outpourings of bad writing whose only excuse is that they are regional, regionalism being at the moment a popular form of literary expression.

Regional stories are obviously stories laid in a circumscribed locale, dealing with characters peculiar to that locale. Somehow or other, regionalism has come to connote ruralism, perhaps because cities are much alike, and offer no localized customs or speech or human types to the field glass and butterfly net of the literary collector. Yet the customs of travel, the mode of life and of thought of natives of New York City are so specialized that a book written about New York City with the passion for detail and for the odd patronizing condescension brought to many studies of remote rural sections would be truly a piece of regional writing. It would be tempting to write such a book, for the New Yorker's acceptance of his subways and his taxis and his cliff dwelling seems as outlandish and worthy of note as an Alabama poor white's acceptance of mules, drought, and boll weevil. The truth is that the congregating of a high percentage of the American population in urban centers and the fluid nature of that population have within a generation made any stationary rural group, maintaining its own customs, a matter for wide-eyed contemplation.

I may be mistaken, but I believe that the words "regional literature" call to the average reader's mind either Middle West farm stories or stories of the South. In a greater number of cases my guess is that the first thought is of the latter. Middle West farm stories have sprung from a common nostalgia, recognized or unrecognized, for the land. They have usually been written either by one who has left the land or by one who has returned to it. Regional stories of the South have sprung from a recent and not quite explicable resurgence of interest in the South and in southern ways.

The Mason and Dixon line is as invisible but as definite as ever. Freer travel back and forth between the two sections has accentuated, rather than minimized, differences in mode of life and thought. Yankee tourists in Florida can be spotted across a hotel dining-room for their fluttery air of knowing themselves to be in a strange land. When grits, looking like Cream of Wheat, are served them for a vegetable, like potatoes, and when their puzzled eyes light on natives buttering or gravying those grits and eating them along with the meat and bread, they are as sheepish and as delighted as any Occidental set down at a Chinese table with a set of chop-sticks, or confronted in Hawaii with the first dish of *poi*.

Fortunately, perhaps, though the South still disapproves of the North, the North has come to take—if, indeed, it ever lost it—a literary and faintly maternal interest in the South. It is not too far a step, after all, from the North's preoccupation with Fanny Kemble's *Diary* and Harriet Beecher Stowe's *Uncle Tom's Cabin*, to its horrified and rapturous embracing of *Tobacco Road*.[26] Of recent years the South has been again fresh literary meat. To subtitle a book "A Tale of the South" was to guarantee a closer attention than would be given a similarly mediocre story laid in Buffalo.[27] The South simply became popular as a divertissement. And, after several generations of mistrust of the "rebels," the southern cause has come to be looked on with a sentimental sympathy.

There is a distinct parallel between recent interest in writings about the South and interest in the Irish revival of letters of a generation or so ago. The Irish cause, lost and losing, was picturesque and remote. Almost any stereotyped tale with the brogue thick enough could be published. And within the last ten years, to make an arbitrary demarcation, almost any articulate story of the South, be it of the past or of the present, of a tenant farmer chopping cotton or a julep-drinking aristocrat under the unpainted pseudo-Greek columns of the ancestral mansion, was sure of an audience. The great wave, to the best of my memory, began with *So Red the Rose* and *Tobacco Road*, and reached its crest with *Gone With the Wind*.[28] The success of the last no longer seems phenomenal when, to

---

26 Fanny Kemble [Frances Anne Butler] (1809–93), *The Journal of a Residence on a Georgian Plantation* (1863), an antislavery document. Harriet Beecher Stowe (1811–96), author of *Uncle Tom's Cabin* (1852), an antislavery fiction so influential that according to lore, when Lincoln first met her in 1862, he said, "So this is the little lady who started this big war" (David Herbert Donald, *Lincoln* [New York: Simon, 1995], 542). Erskine Caldwell (1903–87), *Tobacco Road* (1932).

27 MKR may be alluding to George F. Robertson (born 1853), *King John: A Tale of the South* (Lowell, N.C.: Lowell, 1927).

28 Stark Young (1881–1963), *So Red the Rose* (New York: Scribners, 1934). MKR felt that Young addressed the "larger implications of the Civil War" by recognizing "the fact that the old plantation south went down, not so much under the Union armies, as under the sweep of a hypocritical industrial civilization" (*Max and Marjorie*, 256). Margaret Mitchell (1900–1949), *Gone With the Wind* (New York: Macmillan, 1936). Mitchell and MKR were good friends. Both MKR and Norton Baskin were special guests of Mitchell and her husband, John Marsh, at the première

this peak of interest in the material itself, was added the author's terrific gift for swift narrative and, above all, for characterization. When a milieu that had long fascinated sprang to physical life in the persons of characters so real that one could recognize them in the flesh—giving rise, incidentally, to the passionate furor over a choice of actors and actresses who should not betray that fleshly reality in the cinema version—an entranced reading public took the book to its bosom. The reading public includes the Old World, which has always found the American South glamorous.

The South also reads books about the South. That is because, while not too much concerned with what outsiders say about us, we are all agog to know what we say about one another.

Regional writing may be done either by outsiders or by insiders. It may be done by either outsider or insider from one of two approaches. It may be done deliberately—may I say "perpetrated?"—solely because it is regional. A business-man said to me the other day, "I should think the big market right now would be for war stories. Aren't they the easiest trash in the world to write?" I said, "I wouldn't know. I never wrote trash on purpose." Regionalism written on purpose is perhaps as spurious a form of literary expression as ever reaches print. It is not even a decent bastard, for back of illegitimacy is usually a simple, if ill-timed, honesty. Regional writing done because the author thinks it will be salable is a betrayal of the people of that region. Their speech and customs are turned inside out for the gaze of the curious. They are held up naked, not as human beings, but as literary specimens.

Regional studies are legitimate when the purpose is sociological and scientific. The form in which such studies are presented should be a scientific form. When customs are quaint and speech picturesque, and it is desirable that a record be made, I suggest a Doctor's thesis or the *National Geographic* as proper outlets. I cannot believe that regionalism, for the sake of regionalism, is valid material for creative fiction. I know that it is not literature. I know it from Webster's definition. For literature is, specifically, that part of the preserved writings of a given language or people which is notable for literary expression, as distinguished, on the one hand, from works merely technical and erudite, and, on the other, from journalistic or other ephemeral literary writing. Without Webster, I should know it by the sense of shame with which I read it, and the even greater sense of shame with which I sometimes catch myself in possible danger of writing it.

The second approach to regional writing, whether by an outsider or an in-

---

of the film in December 1939, an affair MKR described as a "riotous occasion" (*Max and Marjorie*, 435).

sider, is valid. It may or may not result in literature, but it is honest. It is the approach of the sincere creative writer who has something to say and who uses a specialized locale—a region—as a logical or fitting background for the particular thoughts or emotions that cry out for articulation. This approach results in writing that is only incidentally, sometimes accidentally, regional. It is only out of this approach that we can look for what may truly be called literature. For the producer of literature is not a reporter but a creator. His concern is not with presenting the superficial and external aspects, however engaging, of an actual people. It is with the inner revelation of mankind, thinking and moving against the backdrop of life itself with as much of dramatic or pointed effect as the artistry of the writer can command. The creative writer filters men and women, real and fancied, through his imagination as through a catalytic agent, to resolve the confusion of life into the ordered pattern, the co-ordinated, meaningful design, colored with the creator's own personality, keyed to his own philosophy, that we call art. Occupied with this magic-working, the creative writer finds a fictional character's speech, dress, and daily habits of importance only as they make that character emerge from the printed page with the aura of reality, so that the author has a convincing and effective medium for the tale he means to tell.

The degree of artistry that emerges from regional writing is proportionate to the writer's ability. If he writes badly, the most fascinating material in the world is only a fine horse to carry a crippled rider. If he writes well, he is almost independent of material, for his genius is able to transmute dross into gold and clay into sentience. Yet the best writing is implicit with a profound harmony between the writer and his material, so that many of the greatest books of all time are regional books, in which the author has used, for his own artistic purpose, a background that he loved and deeply understood. Thomas Hardy is a compelling instance.

So it is reasonable, I think, to expect to find this honest and artistic regionalism to a greater degree among native or long-resident writers than among writers-in-search-of-material who may be struck by the novelty and usableness of a particular region.

But while native regionalism is more likely to be honest than what might be called journalistic or itinerant regionalism, it is artistic only as a writer is himself an artist. It is literature only as the author is literary. Without going to the moot question of sectional percentages, and with no intent to imply that the North, or the West, or New England, has a greater quota, I think it is indisputable that the present-day South, which has emitted literally tons of regional writing, has produced very little regional literature.

The matter of personal tastes and prejudices enters, dangerously, any specific evaluation of southern regional writing. The history of literature is crammed with mistakes in contemporary judgments. I have no desire to assume a voluntary and unnecessary martyrdom. I prefer to suggest this demarcation between regional writing and regional literature as a standard of judgment of whose soundness I am certain, and to retreat. Yet martyrdom and folly are the more comfortable companions than cowardice, and I am willing to venture my personal opinions on a few southern writers as proof of the courage of my convictions.

To my mind, Ellen Glasgow stands alone in our generation as the creator of the only unmistakable regional literature of the South. Pulitzer Prizes for "distinguished" novels are amazing anomalies when they ignore work of her literary distinction. Her literature, like Hardy's,[29] is inherently regional, for while she would have written with great art of whatever people came into the ken of her interest, she is so steeped in the Virginia which she knows that it is an inextricable part of her work, like the colors of a painting or the dye of the wool of a tapestry. But she is first an artist and then a Virginian. If her books—unspectacular, but all the more sound—do not become part of "the total of preserved writings belonging to a given language or people" then I for one am willing to see the other bound volumes go unpreserved.

It is, on the other hand, the spectacular quality of *Gone With the Wind*, or, more exactly, the spectacular quality of the book's popular success, that makes me unable to insist with equal certainty that it is literature. At the moment, I am inclined to think that it is. Five years from now, when the tumult and the shouting shall surely have died, and I read it again, I believe I shall know, and others with me. A few critics, like little whirlpools isolated and individual in the sweeping flood of acclaim, have lamented the lack of "style." The charge is serious, if we are to stand firm with Webster on the specific need of literature to be "notable for literary form or expression, as distinguished . . . from . . . [MKR's ellipses] ephemeral literary writing." Yet we ask of style principally that it be an effective medium of expression for the material itself, and it seems to me that no narrative, no set of characters, could carry the excitement and the living conviction of this book unless the style were at least adequate.

There are three distinctly regional southern writers, some of whose books seem to me very close to literature. Yet, again, permanence, or relative permanence, is too difficult for me to gauge, short of the peculiar certainty that I feel for the work of Ellen Glasgow. Those are, especially, Julia Peterkin and after

---

29   Glasgow was known especially for her realistic portrayals of political and social life in her native Virginia. For MKR's notes for her biography of Glasgow, see *The Private Marjorie*, especially the letters for 1952–53. In his novels, Thomas Hardy recorded the life of his native Dorchester.

Elizabeth Madox Roberts and the negress, Zora Neale Hurston. My personal reaction to *Black April* and *Scarlet Sister Mary* is that they are of permanent value.[30] If time deals harshly with them, at least there is no question but that they stand very high indeed in the intermediate zone, between "literature" and "ephemeral literary writings," of contemporary literature.

My reservations as to Elizabeth Madox Roberts are, first, that she evinces such a scholarly preoccupation with dialect speech, as to force her work into the class of technical or erudite writings, invalidating its objective artistry; and, second, that the overpoetizing of the prose form invalidates the purity of the literary expression. Yet Mary Webb overpoetized the prose of *Precious Bane*,[31] and the result was still literature. Frankly, I do not know.

It is the newest book by Zora Neale Hurston, *Moses, Man of the Mountain*,[32] that tempts me to admit her to my own private library of literature. The book is reminiscent of Thomas Mann's great *Joseph in Egypt*.[33] A timeless legend, part of man's priceless literary and spiritual heritage, is here revivified through the luminous negro mind. The book is racial, rather than regional, and I had best avoid a positive judgment on the excuse of irrelevancy to my subject matter.

There is a body of workman-like southern writers whose regional writings are completely free from the taint I so deplore, who write out of love and understanding of their sections, but whose ultimate artistry is inadequate for a claim to the creation of literature. The ice here is too thin for me to venture from shore. The list, at best, could only reflect personal prejudice and, no doubt, erroneous judgments. And of the writers guilty of regionalism for its own sake, the less said on a shameful subject matter the better.

This is patently not the place to discuss other southern writers whose work is not regional. There is perhaps question as to whether Faulkner is or is not a

---

30   Julia Peterkin (1880–1961), *Black April* (Indianapolis: Bobbs-Merrill, 1927), and *Scarlet Sister Mary* (Indianapolis: Bobbs-Merrill, 1928), each about the life of the Gullahs on a South Carolina plantation. Elizabeth Madox Roberts (1886–1941), known for her novels, poems, and short stories about rural Kentucky life. Zora Neale Hurston (1903–60), MKR's correspondent, visitor at Cross Creek, and respected friend (see *Private Marjorie*, 114–15, 208–10).

31   Mary Webb (1887–1927), *Precious Bane* (London: Cape, 1924), set her romantic novels mainly in Shropshire.

32   Hurston, *Moses, Man of the Mountain* (Philadelphia: Lippincott, 1939), a folk interpretation of the biblical Jews.

33   Thomas Mann (1875–1955), *Joseph in Egypt*, 2 vols. 1st U.S. edition (New York: Knopf, 1939).

regional writer,[34] but I should not so classify him. The storm-swept realm of the libido knows no geography.

Marjorie Kinnan Rawlings

"Regional Literature of the South," *College English* 1, no. 5 (February 1940): 381–89; *English Journal* 29, no. 2 (February 1940): 89–97. In both published versions, there is a lengthy editor's note following the article that describes MKR's presentation of this essay as a lecture: "The foregoing paper was written for the Annual Luncheon of the National Council of Teachers of English in New York, November 25, 1939, but when the occasion arrived Mrs. Rawlings handed the manuscript to the secretary and faced her auditors with no paper between her and them. Her informal talk, which completely won the audience, made a number of revelations not in the formal essay. With Mrs. Rawlings' permission some of them are restated here from the editor's longhand jottings" (388). In the rest of his note, the editor recounts MKR's numerous literary accomplishments.

*   *   *   *   *   *   *   *   *

Marjorie K. Rawlings, Author of 'The Yearling,' Places the Laurel on an Epic of Kentucky

Any people, speech, customs or locale at all out of the ordinary, are meat for the passing journalist. "Regionalism" is as tempting to the run-of-the-mill writer as an open counter of goods to the kleptomaniac. The honest journalist presents such material as he does any other items of novelty, emphasizing frankly the strangeness, making no pretense at anything more creative than discovery. He buys and sells, shall we say, rather than steals. The dishonest journalist runs furtively with his find to the nearest bushes and emerges with what he attempts to palm off on the reading public as a creative or created novel. Back of most bad regional writing—and there is much of it—is this mental dishonesty. Back of the remainder of bad regional writing is simple literary incompetence.

There is, fortunately, beyond good journalism, and most happily bad regional writing, good and creative regional writing. James Still of the Kentucky mountains—Dead Mare Branch, Littcar, Kentucky—is one of the most delightful and satisfying exponents. James Still would write, and write beautifully, in whatever milieu he found himself. He is not quite dependent on any chance quaintness for his writing, for its source is within his own heart and humor, his love and

---

34   The novels of William Faulkner (1897–1962) are set, for the most part, in Mississippi.

knowledge of human beings. The Chaucerian archaisms of Kentucky mountain life are only incidental to his art.

It is the good fortune of his readers that this poet, for he is perhaps primarily a poet, is enchanted with the Kentucky mountain folk, for the combination is rich fare. Elizabeth Madox Roberts wrote of the same people, also as a poet.[35] But however gracefully she wrote, she wrote almost without humor, and with too great a poetizing for effectiveness in a prose form. James Still offers us the rhythm of the poet's phrasing, the excitement of the word, the expression, that strikes like a little silver hammer, along with an uproarious humor and the lustiness of living of the common man.

"On Troublesome Creek" is vital, beautiful, heart-breaking and heart-warmingly funny, and there are few books or stories of whom [which] so many divergent yet harmonious adjectives may be used. The Elizabethan vitality of speech of the characters is undoubtedly derived directly from the Kentucky mountain people and James Still deserves here credit principally for his accuracy. The beauty, the heart-break and the humor derive directly from Still.

While the book is not done in the conventional novel form, it is not a mere succession of anecdotes, but a rounded picture of a family. I should quote from the book if I could give its flavor without spoiling its points. I can only recommend it earnestly. I yield to temptation in the matter of the incident entitled "The Proud Walkers." Mother and Father and Fern and Lark and the boy through whose eyes the scene is vivified have saved their wage-money from the Kentucky coal-mines to buy a mountain farm against the inevitable day of adversity. Father has not the wisdom nor the competence of Mother, but in his own way brings about the family's welfare. Mother yields in a marvel of understatement.

"The nature of a man is a quare thing," she said.

Marjorie Kinnan Rawlings

"Marjorie K. Rawlings, Author of 'The Yearling,' Places the Laurel on an Epic of Kentucky," *Chicago Daily News*, 3 December 1941. This essay is a review of James Still (1906–2001), *On Troublesome Creek* (New York: Viking, 1941).

---

35   Elizabeth Madox Roberts, also a native Kentuckian, published her last collection of poetry, *Song in the Meadow* (New York: Viking, 1940), just a year before her untimely death from lymphoma in 1941, see also above, "Regional Literature," n. 6.

Robert Faherty's *Big Old Sun*

Long after the events of this novel have left my mind—and they are already fading—I shall have the sense of its "big old sun," of its snakelike mangrove roots, its winds and rains and waters. Its physical atmosphere is so strongly and vitally created that it seemed to me I read the book not with my mind but with my body.

The characters are one with the setting, seeming to have been created out of its primitive elements, along with its alligators and crocodiles. They have the strange reality of a nightmare. The shrewd and lusty Mis' Penny, middle-aged and strong, the pretty bitch-in-heat Sylla, her Cracker-man Horace and her Sugar-boy conch, Mis' Penny's brother Luke, and the fish-man whose meddling is the weaving of the Fates, emerge to haunt one from the swamp mud and the salt tides.

The story is as harsh as the midsummer Florida sun. It is raw with hate and lust and greed and killing. Yet it has the naturalness and inevitability of a tropical storm, and when it is over, the reader has the same feeling of the passing by of a dark violence.

When a reviewer's personal prejudices are involved, it is difficult to estimate the appeal of a book for others. The reviewer is so enamoured of the Florida Keys that it is impossible to know whether the impact of "Big Old Sun" stems from a personal delight or from the author's artistry. I believe it is a safe guess that any reader who can be charmed by color, by a restrained style, by the eddyings of stark human nature against the elements, will find a definite enchantment.

Marjorie K. Rawlings

"Robert Faherty's *Big Old Sun*," *Saturday Review* 23 (29 March 1941): 12. This is a review of Robert Faherty, *Big Old Sun* (New York: Putnam, 1941).

*   *   *   *   *   *   *   *   *

Virginia Sorensen's *A Little Lower Than the Angels*

I have read "A Little Lower than the Angels" with pleasure. It is completely mature, wise and vital.

Marjorie Kinnan Rawlings

"Virginia Sorensen's *A Little Lower Than the Angels*," *New York Herald Tribune Book Review*, 17 May 1942, 9; blurb for Virginia Sorensen (1912–91), *A Little Lower Than the Angels* (New York: Grosset and Dunlap, 1942). Sorensen wrote mainly of growing up in the Mormon community of Utah.

*   *   *   *   *   *   *   *   *

"Fanny—You Fool!"

My wonderful, impudent grandmother Who had a Beauty's ways

All my life I have watched beautiful women in the manner of a small boy peering in a pastry window. Women were surely intended to be beautiful, and it is a low trick on the part of Creation to make some of them ravishing and to give Phi Beta Kappa keys to the rest of us as a sop.[36] It is only as middle age has moved in that I have discovered the compensations of being born "plain." The greatest of those is that where the glamour girls of my generation have lost all, I and my kind have had nothing to lose. And a great understanding has dawned on me, as well, that the beautiful woman has a certain philosophy that makes her desirable. This philosophy may be had by any woman. My maternal grandmother possessed the quality in the highest degree.

Fanny was not beautiful. She was too small and too impudent. She was pretty, and I think the prettiness itself came largely from the impudence. She was five feet two at most, pleasantly plump, with naturally curly hair and eyes as blue as an April sky and with the peculiar wickedness of a kitten's. But what gave her her charm was what Grandfather called her foolishness.

Many a woman would have lost all charm under the circumstances of her life. She came of Michigan pioneer stock, as did Grandfather. They were married when she was sixteen and he was nineteen. He had his own inherited farm of some two hundred acres, and they set out, a pair of children, by our notions, to make a life. Grandfather, to the day of his death at eighty-odd, was always fatuously enamoured of her. Abe was six feet four, lean and awkward, with no sense of humour with which to defend himself against her super-abundance if it.

As a young mother, she appeared at the backdoor of the farmhouse one day completely disguised as a tramp. How she evaded her offspring to get into her rig

---

36   MKR was elected to Phi Beta Kappa in 1917; see above, "[On Poetry and Vachel Lindsay]," n. 1.

of ragged trousers and shirt, straw hat and false mustache, I would not know, but there she stood, growling a demand for food. Honest and solemn Abe having warned his young against such predatory folk, they set upon the intruder with broom and shovel. It was only when her shrieks of laughter gave her away that they recognized with horror that the vagrant was their female parent.

Fanny's Nonsense,

Grandfather Called It Charm.

She played one practical joke with never-failing success on her sober husband. He would drive to the village on business, and returning at dusk, drooped in all his length and brooding earnestness over the reins, would see a white-sheeted apparition jump out from the bushes under the heads of the horses. The horses never became accustomed to Fanny's nonsense, either, and would bolt and run with satisfying regularity. Arriving at the house, the horses at last under control and stabled, Abe would find Fanny rocking placidly and would storm in on her, shouting, "Fanny—you fool!"

She was the only human being who could upset him. She managed this in all ways known to such a female. Being a presumably settled married woman, she wore her lovely chestnut curls piled in a discreet knot on the top of her head. But until her children were full grown, Abe would beg her to come to him where he was at work. There he would take the pins from out her hair so that it fell in a whirlpool around her face and shoulders. He would run his long, bony fingers through it, and I have sometimes wondered indiscreet things about the beginnings of some of the seven children.

Typically, Fanny delighted in telling it on him that, for all his Puritan severity, he loved to have her play the hussy. On these occasions, again, he would rise, even in old age, from his chair and bellow, "Fanny—you fool!" Then he would subside and sit watching her by the hour, unaware that his grave face was luminous with his idolatry.

Her Household,

Casual, Humorous, Efficient

He was not alone in his adoration. Her kitchen, her pantry, her cellar, her dining-table, enslaved her grandchildren. She managed her household and her cuisine with casual efficiency. I have never, at any great table, amateur or professional, eaten more delicious food than she served daily as a matter of course. An enormous kitchen garden adjoined the poplar-bordered lawn. Through a wicket gate we entered a Paradise of lush rows of peas, corn, squashes, all varieties of beans, potatoes, tomatoes, cucumbers, lettuce, onions, herbs, and strawberries.

At the far end were heavy bushes of raspberries, gooseberries, blackberries, and currants.

To one side were grape arbours of Concords, Niagaras and Delawares. To the other side were all manner of fruit-trees: peach, pear, cherry, plum, apple. It was only this abundance of fresh fruits and vegetables that prevented Fanny's groaning table from killing off the whole family in early youth. There was always a divine odour in her house, and I finally traced it to the raspberry tarts always in the pantry, to the buckwheat honey in crocks, to the molasses cookies forever on tap, and to the black walnuts and hickory nuts waiting to do their bit in a salad, a layer cake, or a batch of cookies.

A Beauty's Ways,

She Played to Her Gallery

The food would account for the devotion of Fanny's grandchildren. But, above all, we loved her for her absurd tricks. Of many of them I dare not tell. But I remember that in her latter years we made excuses to invite strange children into the house, solely to show off one of her accomplishments. She would be sitting innocently and would suddenly and unconcernedly protrude her false teeth and roll her eyes at the visitors. This appalling picture invariably brought shrieks of delight. From Abe it brought, out of habit, the old "Fanny—you fool!" Then he would beam at her.

The key to Fanny is that she was sublimely herself. She was not indifferent to those who worshipped her, certainly, or she would not have played to the gallery. But she quite simply went her own way, saucy, ribald—and took admiration for granted. It came to her as a moth flies to the flame. The point of view is natural to a beautiful woman. I recommend it as well to the merely pretty and to the plain.

Marjorie Kinnan Rawlings

"'Fanny—You Fool,'" *Vogue* 100 (15 July 1942): 42. Fanny Osmun Traphagen and Abraham Traphagen, MKR's maternal grandparents; for another description of them, see *Blood of My Blood*, 4–8.

Christmas at Cross Creek

Where It's the Mode to Cook for Dinner
Whatever the Men Bring in from Hunting

It seemed to me that my first Christmas at Cross Creek would break my heart. I knew better than to expect snow on Christmas Eve. It was unreasonable to be outraged by a temperature of 75 degrees, hot blazing sunshine and red birds singing lustily instead of Christmas carolers. A half, or is it a fourth, of the world is warm at Christmas time. I had moved to the sub-tropics, and the lush life had become my life. Yet the bland air infuriated me. In pique, I built a great roaring fire in the living room of the old Florida farmhouse—and was obliged to fling wide all doors and windows. But as I set the table on the sunny veranda for Christmas dinner, the yellow flames in the open fireplace were comforting.

I was further appalled when, at one o'clock, shortly before I was ready to serve dinner. Two rural neighbors named Moe and Whitney appeared in clean blue jeans and blue shirts for a visit.[37] I hinted that the family dinner was ready and their expressions grew polite and also acquiescent. Why didn't they go home? In desperation, I invited them to dinner with us. To my horror, they accepted. The wreck of the day was complete.

Since then, I have come to love the lazy and casual Florida backwoods Christmas. The function of all such festive days is to give us a sense of cozy hominess, of belonging to something stable and lovely. And it is all a matter of the things to which one is accustomed. Now that Cross Creek is "home," I should be as infuriated as on that first Christmas day, if snow fell, and sparrows pecked at ice. The red bird's song is the accepted Christmas paean. And miracle of miracles, we have in abundance our own holly and mistletoe. The Christmas tree is not a symbol in Cracker Florida, but every family breaks mistletoe to hang above the fireplace, and cuts a large bough of holly to stand upright, bright with red berries, in a corner of the pine cabin.

The men, and some of the women, consider Christmas as one of the great days for hunting. That, too, goes back to something solid and important, when men made their living, pioneer fashion, in the woods. The relationship of man to nature continues. It is the mode to cook for Christmas dinner whatever the

---

37   Moses J. ("Moe") Sykes (1889–1938) did carpentry work for MKR, who considered him among her best Cracker friends. She devotes chapter 12 of *Cross Creek* to their friendship. The famous Christmas dinner with Moe and "Whitney" or Whitey, known only as Moe's friend, is described in *Cross Creek* (109–11).

men bring down with their guns. That, too, is stable and good. I myself consider that game, quail, dove, rabbit, turkey, or venison, is better when aged a bit in the ice box. But in the old days there were no ice boxes, and folks lived and ate from day to day and from meal to meal. And having partaken of Christmas dinner in the Big Scrub and in other remote places, I cannot say that fresh-killed meat is any less delicious. The men have brought it in and the women have cooked it, and an old, good way of life is maintained. The beverage is likely to be Florida "corn," or moonshine liquor, with, for the more delicate or puritanical woman, homemade Scuppernong[38] or blackberry or elderberry wine.

What the men hunt for Christmas dinner depends on what game frequents their locale. In the Big Scrub, in Gulf Hammock, in the Florida Everglades, it is wild turkey or deer. At Cross Creek it is quail or dove or rabbit or wild ducks. On Christmas morning, after the cows have been milked, the wood for kitchen ranges and fireplaces brought in, "Little Will," the colored grove man,[39] asks for permission to hunt. I understand why the morning chores have been done so early and so efficiently. Permission is given. This last year, Little Will was gone exactly one hour. He came in with five wild Mallard ducks for Christmas dinner at the tenant house. I questioned him. All through the fall, he had observed, bringing in the cows from the lakeside hammock, that a flock of wild Mallards was "using" in a little grove on Cross Creek. All Little Will had to do was crouch on the bank and bring down his Christmas dinner. I was, frankly, jealous, having gone to great trouble in far places to shoot wild ducks. Little Will had never mentioned to me the flock at my back door. He was assuring his own Christmas, and quite rightly.

Turkey is not necessarily the main Christmas dish in rural Florida. Unless one can have wild turkey, so many other meats are available and more than acceptable. Little Will's acquisition of wild ducks put an idea into my own head. For some years I have had my own flock of Mallard ducks. They were raised originally from a setting of eggs from the Carolina marshes, hatched under one of my game hens. The flock grew in size, until some years I have had as many as seventy ducks. They live and range freely, never leave the orange grove, and their meat is especially flavorsome because of their diet of mash, scratch feed and skimmed milk, in addition to their natural foods of greens, frogs and insects.

---

38   The "Scuppernong" (*Vitis rotundifolia*) is a muscadine grape native to the southeastern United States, although MKR writes in *Cross Creek* (222–24) that "old Carolina and Georgia vines" were imported to Florida by pioneers.

39   "Little Will" Mickens, brother of Martha Mickens, the black matriarch of Cross Creek. Little Will was not dependable, which led MKR to call him a "Poor black devil" (*Private Marjorie*, 468).

They are fatter and in flavor much sweeter than truly wild ducks, yet less fat and greasy and insipid than market domestic ducks. While I still sometimes have turkey for Christmas dinner, I am more than likely to have my Mallard ducks. The day makes a suitable occasion for cutting down their inordinate and expensive numbers. The flock costs as much to feed as two or three mules.

Here is my menu for Christmas duck dinner at Cross Creek:

Baked sherried grapefruit
Roast duck
Wild rice
Giblet gravy
Tiny cornmeal muffins
Braised white onions
Sweet potatoes in orange baskets
Crisp celery
Tart jelly,—currant, wild grape or wild plum
Green salad
Dry red wine, Burgundy or claret
Tangerine sherbet

RECIPES

Baked Sherried Grapefruit

Cut grapefruit in halves and separate sections entirely through. Turn upside down to drain off excess juice. Dot grapefruit with butter, brown sugar (or honey) butter and powdered clove. Fill centers with sherry. Brown under broiler or in very hot oven.

Roast Duck

In using wild duck, I do not make the conventional stuffing of onion or celery or apple. I dress the ducks whole, salt and pepper them, and place them breast side up in a tightly covered roasting pan with an inch of hot water in the pan. The oven is at 450 F. for the first 15 minutes. Then I reduce the heat to 350 F. Young ducks will roast a little over one hour. For older ducks, I allow 2 to 3 hours. They should be basted every 15 minutes with the liquid in the pan. I allow ½ duck per person. An occasional greedy or hungry guest will eat a whole duck but is not encouraged. I boil the giblets in hot water until tender, put through the meat grinder, and add to the gravy, which is made by adding 2 to 4 tablespoons of flour, salt and pepper, to the fat in the roasting pan.

Wild Rice

Wild rice expands in cooking more than white rice, and a half-cup serves where a whole cup of white rice is needed. Boil 20 minutes in salted water, or until tender; drain, pour hot water over it; drain and let stand in a colander over hot water 5 to 10 minutes.

Cornmeal Muffins

1¼ cups flour	¼ cup milk
¼ cup cornmeal	1 egg
½ teaspoon salt	¼ cup melted butter

4 teaspoons baking powder *or* vegetable shortening

Sift together dry ingredients. Add milk, then beaten egg, then melted shortening. Bake in tiny muffin pans in a hot oven (425° F.). Makes about 20 small muffins.

Braised Onions

Peel small to medium white onions and cook them whole in a small quantity of salted water. Allow 4 small onions or 2 or 3 medium ones per person. Cook until extremely tender, allowing all the water to boil away. Add 1 tablespoon butter and 1 tablespoon sugar for every 4 to 6 onions. Simmer until onions are well browned, turning often. Serve with the brown juice.

Tangerine Sherbet

1 cup sugar	4 cups tangerine juice
1½ cups water	Juice of 1 or 2 lemons
Grated rind of 4 tangerines	

Boil sugar and water 10 minutes. Add the grated tangerine rind to sirup while hot. Let cool slightly and add tangerine juice and lemon juice. Taste for sweetness and acidity, as the tangerines vary. Chill thoroughly, strain and freeze.

Marjorie Kinnan Rawlings

"Christmas at Cross Creek," *American Cookery* 47 (December 1942): 168, 184.

Trees for Tomorrow

A Boy in Mississippi swung off his bicycle and trundled it across a narrow-gauge railroad track that led to an abandoned lumber mill. He had sandy hair, reddish in the late afternoon sun. He was prodigally freckled. His eyes were direct and clear. His jaw was firm, outthrust in a way that made me feel good about his future.

He will need that jaw. For he is looking ahead, with something of a frown, into precisely nothing. He refused money for his posing. Look at the picture. The background is the abandoned lumber mill. It has destroyed his future in his own community. American greed and American thoughtlessness have destroyed the community itself. The tall steps behind him lead—nowhere.

It seems a peculiarly unsporting thing to have done to a typical American boy who would not accept pay for being photographed. There was, of course, nothing personal about it. No one set out deliberately to interfere with the future of this boy or any other boy. The boy in Mississippi is one of millions of potential victims, direct or indirect, of that combination of greed and thoughtlessness.

This is the story of that combination working in one field—timber—forests —trees. It is a story of people as well, for on this earth, man and the products of earth are bound up together. While the earth and its products would continue to exist, and very comfortably, without us, we could not exist without them.

When the first settlers came to these American coasts, when they penetrated inland, all were struck by the vastness of the forests. Trees had been precious in the Old World. Here in the New World, men went wild with the bounty around them. There was more than enough of everything. Men could dip into these virgin forests, and beyond them were other virgin forests and, beyond, still others. There was an infinity of trees. We learn with difficulty what is finite and what is infinite. To this moment, there are men who say, "There's plenty of timber."

I have just returned from a five-thousand-mile swing through the southeastern United States, looking at timber. It is home to me, as New England is home to the Vermonter and the man of Maine, as the great Northwest is home to the last of the pioneers. I have seen with my own eyes what is happening to the trees of my home, and I am both frightened and angry. I am equally disturbed to know that the same thing is happening in other sections of the country, sections that are home to other people.

It appears, after all, that our American forests are not infinite. The extremely simple fact is that in the South alone the cutting of our trees for saw timber has exceeded the annual growth by three billion board feet, even before the new and rigorous needs of the war.

The war demands are the final tragic note. The Army and the Navy are now using a minimum of one million board feet a month. Wood is being used to make ten thousand Army truck bodies a month to save the precious steel. Higgins of New Orleans has just been given a contract to make one hundred and eighty million dollars' worth of all-plywood troop- and tank-carrying planes. This will take a lot of plywood.

Wood Scarce as Aluminum

Recently in Jacksonville, Florida, D. Leon Willams, priority specialist of the Southeastern regional WPB office,[40] informed the Florida Lumber and Millwork Association that the United States faces in 1943 a probable shortage of nine billion board feet of lumber. It has been estimated by experts that if the war should last for several years, usable wood will be as scarce as aluminum is today.

Before I met the boy in Mississippi who is looking ahead into nothing, behind whom steps lead nowhere, I talked with a very sad man. He had been the bookkeeper for the great lumber company that a year and a half ago had closed its mills where the boy rode by. Until 1941, there had been some eleven hundred people in the community. The day I visited there only a handful remained, four or five families. The place was utter desolation.

I said to the sad man, "What has happened to your town?"

He stared at me as though I were very stupid.

"Why," he said, "the timber's gone. Just cut and gone."

We looked down the empty streets of the ghost town. It was almost impossible to imagine a day when a yearly pay roll of $960,000 had animated that town. The vacant houses had been good houses. A good American life had been lived in them. Eleven hundred people expected to go on living here, had built a good way of life around the timber, and now the timber was gone, and the mill open to wind and weather, and the people had gone too. . . . [MKR's ellipsis].

I inquired if the owners of the mill had lived here, but I knew the answer. Few owners of the 190,000 acres of commercial timber live on the land. They are absentee owners and they call the timber "investment." They move their operations from one investment to another.

Indiscriminate cuttings, which have built communities only to destroy them, along with the forests, are spectacular, but they are not isolated. I saw them

---

40   The War Production Board (WPB), established by executive order in January 1942, was given the task of converting the peacetime U.S. economy to a war footing. It was abolished in November 1945.

everywhere I went. I drove through mile after mile of pine forests in my own Florida without seeing a single pine tree sixteen inches in diameter. And it is the sixteen-inch stuff that is absolutely necessary for crossties, for bridge supports and pilings, for the mountings of large guns, for basic timbers of all buildings, for the massive construction of our modern world. I drove from Cross Creek, Florida, clear beyond Alexandria, Louisiana, before I saw a sizable stand of virgin longleaf pine, the most desirable, sometimes indispensable, wood for these purposes.

"But will not the young stuff grow fast enough to replace the heavy timber?"

There is no young stuff where forests are cut clean. Mile after mile, useless weed trees had followed the clean cutting. That or fire. That or appalling erosion in the hilly regions of north Georgia, Alabama, Tennessee and the Carolinas. That or sterile fields unsuited for the growth of anything at all but trees. When the forests are cut clean, "That's all there is—there isn't any more."

An Appalling Deficit

"Man's needs must be met," some say. "War needs, above all, must be met. This is no moment in which to count the cost."

It is precisely the moment in which to count the cost. Mathematicians may divide a 1943 deficit of nine billion board feet, first, the American supply of timber, then into the supplies of the world, and estimate neatly how many years will bring the day when usable timber is no more. Some of us today will not be here if that day comes. But experts have estimated that another war twenty-five years from now will see the United States without wood for war.

It seemed to me that I could not bear any longer the sight of such devastation as I had seen. Five million acres of virgin longleaf pine have been cut clean in Louisiana. The aftermath is hideous.

Lest I give the impression that this story of the danger to our land is an outcry against capitalists or big owners, it is a good moment to mention the fact that of the forest lands in the United States, 40% are in the hands of small owners and small farmers. It is only that the large areas of devastation are more startling. Where big owners have handled timber through greed, and thoughtlessness, small owners have handled it through need—and thoughtlessness.

I have seen the small farms from which all the timber has been cut clean because a man needed money for a sick child; because modern plumbing added to the farmhouse seemed of more value than twenty acres of pine trees on the west hill.

But after the desolation, after the ruthless destruction by both big and little men, I came on a fact that shone like a beacon in the darkness. Once known, it seems incredible that we have not known it always. It is this: Trees are not like a gold mine. They are not like a coal mine. They are not a vein of platinum to be worked out. Trees are a crop. Trees not only can be grown, starting from scratch, but with only the slightest of human help, the least human hindrance, they will grow themselves. Only the simplest ingredients make up the formula for the perpetual growth of trees. Trees may be cut selectively. That is, only certain trees of a certain size are cut, the rest left to grow; successive cuttings to be made as younger trees reach their growth.

On the other hand, where desirable or necessary, an area of trees may be clean cut, but a very few mature trees, three or four or five to an acre, are left standing, to scatter their seed and reproduce their kind. The natural method is both cheap and simple. In both types of cutting, fire must be kept out, so that the seedlings have a chance to grow. It is as easy as that. It seems unbelievable that we have gone against so plain a law of nature.

It was good to reach places where men have understood these simple facts. I found them among rich men and poor, among owners of hundreds or thousands of acres of forests and owners of little dozens of acres.

I found them in the few national forests. It was a delight to see the Osceola National Forest in my own Florida. Trees of all sizes and all ages grow side by side. Each year the largest are cut and sold at good profit. National forests pay 25% of their gross take each year to the county in which they are located. The Osceola last year returned $9,000 to its two counties.

It was a delight to see privately the W. T. Smith forests in Alabama.[41] There will be no end to the timber on this holding. The owners are raising their trees as a crop, not mining them. There is a handful of similar large owners raising forests instead of devastating them. They are unfortunately a minute percentage.

I found, unexpectedly, two small owners of timber about whom moralists might, if inclined, draw morals. I should call them, simply, good Americans, if in so doing I did not seem to call other men, big and little, who are destroying our forests, bad Americans. There are almost no bad Americans. There are selfish Americans, shortsighted Americans, careless Americans. None of them means harm to the country. So I shall only call the two small owners of timber wise and farsighted Americans. One is a white man and the other is black.

---

41   The W. T. Smith Lumber Company, Chapman, Alabama, became the largest producer of lumber east of the Mississippi River under the management of Norman Floyd McGowin (1900–1981) and his brother, the Rhodes Scholar and Alabama state legislator Earl Mason McGowin (1901–92).

Timber-bred Philosophers

The white man is Bryan Johnson, of Roxie, Mississippi. He is everything we like to think of as American. He is lean and wiry and blue-eyed, with an unmanageable forelock of hair. His Irish ancestors came into the deep South from Virginia in 1821. Johnson has a farm, a filling station and twenty-one hundred acres of wooded land. He has two children in college and a twelve-year-old son, Bryan Leston, who helps at the filling station.

Johnson touched the boy on the shoulder. "This is manpower," he said.

Twenty years ago Johnson worked for a big lumber company. He was horrified at the devastation of timber.

"Those fellows figured, 'I'll be gone tomorrow, so I'll cut today.' Seemed to me that was a poor way to figure."

In 1923, he began working his own land. He began cutting timber as a crop. Something to grow year after year. He had seen the ways of cotton on a depleted soil.

"It takes twenty-five cents to raise a pound of cotton on poor land, and the best price anyone gets is twenty-five cents a pound. Down here we have two crops, cotton and trees. It doesn't cost a cent to raise a tree. It looked like horse sense to me to raise trees."

Americans are supposed to be noted for horse sense. Sometimes it is necessary to travel over quite an area to find it. Of Johnson's twenty-one hundred selectively cut acres, one thousand and fifty are in young pines that will be ready for their first cutting in less than ten years.

"I don't need insurance," he said. "Those trees are my old-age pension. I don't need to save cash money for my children." He touched his small piece of "manpower" again. "When this boy is twenty-one years old, I'll have more trees than I have today."

I was equally proud to meet Ambrose Cole. He is as black as the ace of spades. He is erect, with grizzled hair, and looks any man square in the face. He has been on his two hundred acres nearly forty years. He began as a poor renter. This year he will make the last payment on his mortgage. He grows cotton, corn, sugar cane, sorghum, peanuts and cowpeas on eighty acres. The other one hundred and twenty are in timber. He has raised ten children. They have lived well. Ida, his wife, was spick and span in a clean blue gingham apron and a white bandanna. I asked Ambrose to what he attributed his prosperity.

"Hard work and a good wife," he said.

Scientific Tree Farming

There was more, too—the same horse sense of Bryan Johnson. Ambrose's timber brings him from four to five hundred dollars per year, and that is a lot of money in a section where cash income is among the lowest in the country. On Ambrose's type of timber the proper cutting, which he follows, is a matter of thinning. He cuts the average trees from year to year for pulpwood and he leaves the larger trees to increase in size for future saw timber. Meantime, seedlings spring up in the thinned area and are growing for future use. A man with a family is bound to look a little further ahead than one without.

I suggested that the larger timber left on his place would take care of him and Ida in their old age.

"I got what I need for me and Ida," he said. "I just studied on having something for the children."

Wilson Curtis, in the North Carolina mountains, is logging boss for a large lumber company. His is the key job in actual operations. He is young, thin and red-blond, of mountain stock, slow-moving, drawling of speech, with expert judgment on timber. His company is one of those practicing selective cutting. Seed trees are being left for every acre, and a growth of young stock.

Curtis said, "We've got to leave something for the future generations. They'll be shorter than we are."

His work is so vital that his boss has asked deferment for him from the draft. Curtis himself has not asked it.

"If they don't need me here," he said, "I sure want to go. A man can't shun any responsibility."

What is to be done? There is only one answer: A national law must be passed by our representatives, the Congress of these United States, decreeing a national system of controlled cutting (varied to suit the needs of specific regions) that shall assure the perpetual growth of trees "for the greatest good to the greatest number, in the long run."[42] There can be no reasonable opposition to a national plan of controlled cutting. It is not even as though such cutting ruined any man's profits "in the long run." Such cutting helps them. We must protect ourselves against our own carelessness.

Whose trees are they? Thirteen million people in the United States derive their livelihood directly from industries connected to wood. Check the items drawn from trees: building lumber, posts, telephone poles, almost all our paper, fuel, plastics, cellophane, high explosives, lacquer, edible sugars, alcohol, char-

---

42 MKR echoes the classic statement of Utilitarian principle, "the greatest good for the greatest number."

coal, acetic acid, tannic acid, wood tar, volatile, essential and pharmaceutical oils, dye-stuffs, drugs, nuts, herbs, fruits, turpentine and rosin.

Trees assure watersheds with consequent power and water and light. They prevent floods and erosion. They are my trees and your trees. They are our trees. No selfish minority, no careless majority, can continue to jeopardize our common interests.

Surely we are wise enough and farsighted enough to prevent catastrophe. Sooner or later, and "time is of the essence," the question, which has risen before, will again come before our Congress. We must demand that the nation's trees—our trees—be allowed to grow, to reproduce themselves for our benefit, five, ten, twenty years from now—and for the benefit of those who will come after us and whom we should wish to bless us rather than curse us.

We are fighting today for many valuable things. We must fight also at this critical moment to preserve the God-given forests without which we should be helpless atoms on a sterile earth.

Marjorie Kinnan Rawlings

"Trees for Tomorrow," *Collier's Magazine* 117 (8 May 1943), 14–15, 24–25.

*   *   *   *   *   *   *   *   *

A River That Flows through Florida History

Mr. Hanna Supplied the Facts, Mr. Cabell the Art and Irrelevancies, for a Glamorous Book

A Moses has led Jurgen out of the lovely wilderness of Poictesme into the reality of American history.[43] The new, true land is made, through the gift of a prophet, and the tongue of an angel, as enchanting as that fabulous realm in which the generation of my youth wandered with what we believed to be pagan cries.

"The St. Johns," the latest and best in the Rivers of America series, is a fortunate piece of genuine collaboration. Dr. Hanna, author himself of the fine historical study "Flight Into Oblivion,"[44] has provided with patient research

---

43   James Branch Cabell, *Jurgen: A Comedy of Justice* (New York: McBride, 1919), a provocative fantasy set in the fictional medieval province of Poictesme, was so sensational that efforts were made to ban it.

44   A. J. Hanna, *Flight into Oblivion* ([Richmond, Va.]: Johnson Publishing, 1938), about the flight of the Confederate cabinet from Richmond near the end of the Civil War.

facts on one of the most beautiful of American rivers. Mr. Cabell has provided glamour, served up with delicious wit and irony, in a style that has no equal in our time for glittering precision. One sees an engaging picture of the pair at work. Mr. Hanna skirts the mystic forest that is the Cabell imagination, dangling choice bits of data, of intriguing personalities, irresistible bait. The shy satyr is lured forth, step by step, into the world of day. At last he takes the fragments in those familiar cloven hooves, breathes on them, polishes them on his silky goat-hair, and hands them back alive and glowing.

The St. Johns is a rich river to work with. Folk who think of Florida in terms of orange groves, of Crackers, of tourists and Miami, are constantly amazed at news of its basic history. That history begins with as colorful a crew of Spaniards, at once buccaneers, hypocrites and idealists, as can be found anywhere.

The bright and blood-stained threads of French and English maritime and colonization history mingled with the Spanish thread to produce a violent tapestry. Ponce de Leon, De Soto, Menendez, founder of St. Augustine; Jean Ribaut, Napoleon's nephew, Prince Murat, Admiral Drake and General Oglethorpe, to say nothing of the European sovereigns behind their piety, their greed and their depredations, played an intricate game in the Land of Flowers and sunshine. Bartram and Audubon were here. Andrew Jackson and Thomas Jefferson had a hand in Florida matters.[45] The Seminole Indian is to this day a picturesque relic of wilder times. Through all of it runs the St. Johns River, a main artery of inescapable portent. Mr. Cabell and Mr. Hanna have brought the panorama to life.

This reviewer, when she learned of the project for the book, was disturbed lest Mr. Cabell, who is concerned with the cynical angles of human nature and never with background, with places, should neglect the physical personality of the great river itself. She expressed her anxiety, whereupon Mr. Cabell dutifully had himself borne off and "sat alone for a whole hour on the banks of the St. Johns." "And what did you feel?" "I disliked it intensely," he said. Yet for all the

---

45   Ponce de León (1460?–1521), Hernando de Soto (1500?–1542), Pedro Menéndez de Avilés (1519–74), Jean Ribaut (1520?–65), Napoleon Achille Murat (1801–47), Francis Drake (1540–96), James Oglethorpe (1696–1785) were, except for Murat, explorers who pillaged Florida, particularly the east coast near St. Augustine, where Prince Murat lived for a time. William Bartram (1739–1823), especially known for his *Travels* (1791), which in part describes his journey through Northeast Florida; he in fact passed quite close to Cross Creek, near the hamlet of Micanopy, which is about ten miles to the west. John James Audubon (1785–1851) became famous for *Birds of America* (1827–38). Andrew Jackson (1767–1845), seventh president of the United States, as a general fought the Seminoles and British at Pensacola in 1818. Thomas Jefferson (1743–1826), third president of the United States, led efforts to acquire Florida from the British, French, and Spanish, who all laid claim to parts of it.

paucity and scorn of his single hour, he caught the feeling of the magic river with its floating hyacinths, its ibises and egrets, its moss-hung edges. The artist has the privilege of re-creating the thing he has not known. For instance, take Stephen Crane's "The Red Badge of Courage," one of the most superb of war tales.[46]

Which brings us to the apparently irrelevant epilogue of "The St. Johns," in which Mr. Cabell and Mr. Hanna engage in a dialogue in an ostensibly violent quarrel over the material of the book. Mr. Hanna insists that the personal story of Stephen Crane and his wife Cora—hostess to strange characters in Jacksonville before, as Crane's wife, she becomes hostess to Conrad and the literary great—has no part in the book.[47] The fact that they lived in Jacksonville, Fla., accidentally situated on the St. Johns, is, says Mr. Hanna, no excuse for ending the book with their tale. I agree with him. But Mr. Cabell is mercury in the hand, and Mr. Hanna should feel proud that he contained an evasive element within limits as superbly as he did. He has kept Mr. Cabell to the chronological timing he employs so successfully in his own historical writings. Mr. Cabell has dallied along the banks and up a few irrelevant and bawdy byways, but the course of the book flows as steadily as the river.

The epilogue itself is necessary. It brings the history of the river up to date. If the modern characters are dull, that is not the fault of Cabell or of Hanna. The narrative of the St. Johns transcends any immediate mediocrity. Delightful illustrations by Doris Lee carry out the scholarship of Hanna and the wicked insight of Cabell.

Marjorie Kinnan Rawlings

"A River That Flows through Florida History," *New York Herald Tribune Weekly Book Review,* 5 September 1943, 3. This is a review of James Branch Cabell (1879–1958) and A. J. Hanna (1893–1978), *The St. Johns, A Parade of Diversities* (New York: Farrar and Reinhart, 1943). She mentions the review to Norton; see *Private Marjorie*, 117. The Cabells and the Baskinses were good friends. Hanna, a prominent historian and professor at Rollins College, in Winter Park, Florida, would give testimony during the Cason libel trial that MKR's depictions in *Cross Creek* of Florida and its people were of "tremendous importance to the State" (Silverthorne, 252).

---

46 Stephen Crane (1871–1900), *The Red Badge of Courage* (New York: Appleton, 1895). Although the realistic quality of his depiction of war has caused the novella to remain a staple of high school and college classrooms, Crane famously claimed that his inspiration was the newly popular sport of American football.

47 Crane married Cora Taylor (1868–1910), once the madam of a Jacksonville brothel, and they were forced to move to England, where they entertained famous writers, among them the novelist Joseph Conrad (1857–1924). Crane's journalistic tale "The Open Boat" (1897) remains his classic story involving Florida.

Parodies of Emily Post

Dear Mrs. Post:

Mother always said to me, "Bill, sooner or later you will have to follow Emily Post, if you live long enough." It's a wonder I'm alive, after what happened, but I just want you to know that I am certainly following you. Life can be beautiful—and formal dinners can be exciting. Hell, Mrs. Post, I had no idea! I get the most fun out of doing just as you say.

I read that terribly exciting chapter of yours on formal dinners before I went to Mrs. Eatenpoop's. I made up my mind nobody was going to put any bread and butter over on me.[48] People think the younger generation doesn't have any manners, Mrs. Post, but I just tell you we hang on your words. This time you had me hanging on the ropes, but oh boy, that damn butler was in worse shape than I was.

Did you know that formal dinners don't begin until about nine o'clock? I suppose you do. It sure gives a chap a chance to catch up on his drinking. I tell you, I believe in formal dinners. I got into white tie and tails and hit the Eatenpoop's about seven o'clock. The old lady was still in the bath-tub, I guess. Anyway, I didn't see anything around but a bunch of wage slaves, and boy, do those slaves make wages. One of them, that goddamn butler, lifted his eyebrows and said, "Young sir, Mrs. Eatenpoop did not expect guests until nineish." "Well," I said, "so it's sevenish. So the early bird gets the rum. So here I am stuck. Mrs. Eatenpoop certainly doesn't expect me to hang my white tie and tail over the gutter for two hours, does she?" About that time an old guy stuck his head out of the library door and said, "Oh God. Buttocks, shut him up with a bottle." "On the head, sir?" said Buttocks with bright hopeful eyes. "I wish we dared," the old guy said. "Put him in the east room with a bottle. Maybe he'll just get drunk and go home. I wish everybody would just get drunk and go home."

So I sat from sevenish to nineish with a fifth of Scotch. That doesn't happen every day, I tell you. You brought me luck, Mrs. Post. Comes nineish, and a swarm of characters out of Peter Arno and Helen Hokinson drift in,[49] and

---

48   The first parodic letter is a response to an actual column by the well-known etiquette authority Emily Post (1873–1960). In a clipping from an unknown source, found in the MKR/Baskin correspondence along with the three parodies, Post closes a response to an unsigned letter, "If there are no bread and butter plates, then bread that has the least touch of butter on it must be put on the edge of the dinner-plate and not on the tablecloth" (Kinser, "Marge and Emily," 3).

49   Peter Arno (1904–68) and Helen Hokinson (1893–1949), satirical cartoonists for the *New Yorker* known for their caricatures of wealthy socialites.

Helen and Jim Eatenpoop and a few more our age, and of course I have to drink Martinis, or be rude. Comes about half-past nineish and the bastard Buttocks in his knee breeches announces dinner, and I was so empty I could have eaten his rosettes. I'm not talking dirty, Mrs. Post. He had little round ribbons at his knees. Well, the soup was a joke. It wasn't supposed to be a joke, but it just struck me it was something from discontented horses and I let out a "Ha! Ha! Ha!" in one of those pauses in conversation. Ye ancient lackey Buttocks was helping pass, I guess on account of the help shortage. He acted as if the dishes were something the veterinarian had just finished examining. He came by me and filled my wine glass and leaned over my chair and murmured, "Mrs. Eatenpoop prefers dignity at a formal dinner." I said, "If the next course isn't better than the soup, she'll get it." Old Eatenpoop was hunched over his plate like a frustrated buzzard and he looked up and said, "Young man, now you're talking," and he winked at me.

Comes the main course, after some nasty little messes, and Sir Walter Raleigh helps out again.[50] He passes the bread, by God, and by God, Mrs. Post, it wasn't of the variety that will not soil the table linen. It was little rolled-up curls of bread with the least touch of butter on it. I hadn't read your exciting chapter on formal dinners, with Mother holding Dad's gun on me, for nothing, I tell you.[51] I gave the bread a dirty look and I put it on the edge of my dinner-plate, just as you advise. Bozo leaned over me and whispered, "Formal, if you please. On the tablecloth." "Why, you son of a bitch," I said, "can't you see it has the least touch of butter on it?" "I'm sure that's an accident, sir," he whispered, "just like you." And about then, Mrs. Post, that formal dinner really began to be an exciting chapter. I picked up my wine glass and emptied it over my shoulder on the knee-breeches, and King Henry put his knee through the fiddle back chair into my middle-back,[52] and I eased around and gave him a belly-punch and all Hell broke loose.

I stood up and shouted, "Ask Emily Post! If you were going to have the least touch of butter on the bread, you have to expect cultured people to put it on the edge of the dinner-plate instead of on the tablecloth. And if you were going to have the least touch of butter on the bread, you should have had bread and but-

50   Sir Walter Raleigh (1554–1618), writer and explorer whose legendary sacrifice of an expensive cloak, which he placed over a mud puddle for Queen Elizabeth I (1533–1603), is a representative example of good manners.

51   See Post's *Etiquette* (New York: Funk, 1937). In the enclosed clipping (see note 48 above), Post describes the chapter on formal dinners as "one of its most exciting" (Kinser, "Marge and Emily," 3).

52   An allusion to Henry VIII (1491–1547), king of Great Britain, known for his youthful exuberance and the later execution of his wives.

ter plates, and any Dead End kid knows you don't have bread and butter plates at a formal dinner. Ask Emily Post!" And I took a swing at Lord Fauntleroy and he took one at me,[53] and everybody at the table stood up, and one Helen Hokinson dame said, "The young man is quite right. I was myself astonished at the least touch of butter," and an old Peter Arno guy said, "But with such confusion in table etiquette, the proper thing to do is to refuse entirely the bread with the least touch of butter," and something out of Steig said,[54] "What! Insult one's hostess by refusing?" and he took a poke at Peter Arno's nightmare, and the nightmare poked back, and Mrs. Post, there was the goddamdest free-for-all you ever saw.

I was busy with elegant Ethelred, and I think he must have been Jack Dempsey's sparring partner[55] before he decided to handle the ham for the Eatenpoops. I was swinging wild, and he had the advantage of probably having eaten his dinner at six o'clock without a previous dose of a fifth of Scotch and Martinis not to be rude. He had me backed up against the Eatenpoop coat of arms on the wall, virgins prone and butter rampant, when old Eatenpoop got into it. He picked up the silver salver of squabs stuffed with almonds and brought it down on the Blue Boy's head, and while the squabs didn't stop him, the silver salver did. Buttocks crumpled up like Mrs. Roosevelt getting an indecent proposal.[56]

Old Eatenpoop took me by the arm. "This is our chance," he said, "let's make a break for it." We slipped out of the marble foyer and tidied each other up.

"I've been wanting to lay into that damn Buttocks," he said, "ever since he came high-hatting me around. Young man," he said, "we've made social history."

We shook hands and hailed a taxi and went down to Jack and Charlie's and ate hamburgers, and Old Eatenpoop told me all about his sad life.

------

53 The six young actors who played in the Broadway version of the play *Dead End* (1935), by Sidney Kingsley (1906–95), and who were subsequently hired en masse to appear in the film version (1937) directed by William Wyler (1902–81), were known as the "Dead End kids"; Frances Hodgsen Burnett (1849–1924), *Little Lord Fauntleroy* (1886), an immensely popular book that set fashion trends.

54 William Steig (1907–2003), cartoonist and cover illustrator for the *New Yorker*.

55 Ethelred (ca. 968–1016), known as "the unready," Anglo-Saxon king, who legend says defecated in his baptismal font. Jack Dempsey (1895–1983), Irish-American heavyweight boxing champion.

56 *The Blue Boy*, by Thomas Gainsborough (1727–88), British landscape and portrait painter, a painting that features a jauntily dressed young aristocrat. First Lady Eleanor Roosevelt (1884–1962), who was idolized for her feminist and social political views.

"Ain't elegance awful, Bill," he said.

"Why, no," I said, "it's exciting."

* * *

Memorandum to N. B.

Dear Mrs. Post:

I am soon going to have a big wedding (two bridesmaids, orchids, etc.) at the First Nazarene Church here in Broggsville. A matter of protocol is plaguing us. Where should the bride's mother be seated?

Muffie J.

Dear Muffie:

Much happiness and luck to you.

At a formal wedding such as yours, the bride's mother should be escorted down the aisle by a reasonably sober usher and directed to the second pew on the left. There she will put herself in the second spot to the left, thus leaving a retreat for your pappy after he says, "*I* do." Once pewed, the bride's old lady should plump herself roundly on both buttocks because tilting is not considered *de rigeur* in polite circles. This second-row location is traditionally popular on account of the proximity of an in-law always helps to upset the groom—along with his hangover and imminent "duties."

Write soon.

E. P.

* * *

Memorandum to N. B.

Dear Mrs. Post:

I am a young man twenty years old. Last night at a small party I went to the family bathroom and walked in on a pretty girl, who was—to put it frankly— "sitting on the can." I said, "Excuse me," and left. Then I heard hysterical screams. What *should* I have said?

Jake

Dear Jake:

There are two solutions to your problem. One is to shut up and leave. The other, and preferable, is to make a tactful speech such as this: "Mam, I deplore this unfortunate intrusion. Your functional purposes are your own affair. But I cannot help admiring you perched there with your paradisical dress histed up to reveal so many charms. May I add that Church, Tuffy, and all other makers of comfort saddles would be overwhelmed to see you gracing one of *their* seats. So adieu, my lovely sittant." Do it that way next time, Jake.

E. P.

"Parodies of Emily Post," *Journal of Florida Literature* 10 (2001): 4–8. These three "Parodies" were found among the correspondence of MKR and Norton Baskin. She sent them to him while he served in India before 20 October 1943, the date she first mentioned them to him (see *Private Marjorie*, 153). Baskin asked and received (6 November 1943) permission to have one or all of them published in his company newspaper, which is unidentified (see *Private Marjorie*, 168; see also Kinser, "'the least touch of butter'").

*   *   *   *   *   *   *   *

Florida: A Land of Contrasts

Florida has been, since its discovery by Ponce de Leon in 1513, "in the time of the Feast of the Flowers,"[57] to the present moment, an enigma, a trap for the unwary, and a combination of sustained glamour and disillusion. The rich and the poor have over-run it through a turbulent history under five flags—the Spanish, the French, the English, the American Federalist, and the American Southern, or Rebel. The sub-tropical peninsula at the extreme south-east tip of the United States has taken them all in, the exploiters and the refugees, while maintaining a strange aloofness. The idealists and the money-makers have been brought up short against the terrain and have been obliged to adapt themselves to it, or fail, as the Spaniards failed. The geography of Florida made its early history; climate and topography account for its present.

Florida is kindly. It is also repellent. It is beautiful and also ugly. Some of the coastal stretches, the Atlantic Ocean on the east, the Gulf of Mexico on the west, are tropically lovely; some consist of barren sand dunes. Inland, the traveller may find magnificent "hammocks" (from the Spanish "hamaca"—a highly arable type of soil) dense with great live oaks, sweet gum, holly, magnolia, bay, hickory and palm trees; orange groves, green-leaved and fruited the year round; vast stretches of pine forests, dusky as cathedral aisles; or he may find depressing

---

57   The explorer Juan Ponce de León (see previous essay, n. 3), landed on 2 April 1513, during the Spanish Easter season "pascua florida" [feast of the flowers], for which he may have named the new land "La Florida."

and impenetrable low marshes and expanses of the poorest open sand soil, where rains and fertilizers leech away unprofitably and the summer sun is merciless.

Florida began and has continued as a combination of man's dreams and man's greediness. The motives of the Spanish Conquistadores were frankly those of "God, glory, and gold." The Catholic faith was to be carried to the savage natives at any cost of blood. Glory should consist of the establishing of new trade routes, of military, naval and trade bases, to extend the power of the Crown and the prestige of the adventurers. Gold, as well as silver, furs, pearls and other precious gems were believed to be here in abundance. Ponce de Leon, fatuous man, searched for the fabulous Fountain of Youth. The result was that the native Indians fought long and bloodily; France, and later England, also laid claim to the trade routes and the bases, and sporadic war, actually a series of reciprocal massacres, stained the Florida soil for nearly three hundred years (the name of the Matanzas River at St. Augustine, means the river of blood); the gold, the silver, the pearls, were not here; nor the Fountain of Youth. Florida, for all its lush heat, looked on coldly and spewed out the trespassers.

Dr. Kathryn Abbey, who has written the only definitive history of the State, "Florida, Land of Change,"[58] has divided the period of Florida into the Spanish, the plantation and the modern. Of the Spanish, the only traces to-day are in the city of St. Augustine, the oldest town in the United States, founded by Don Pedro Menendez de Aviles on the Atlantic coast a little south of Ponce de Leon's place of discovery and landing. Here there still stand a fine old Catholic cathedral; the ancient shrine of La Leche; the old Spanish fort of Castillo de San Marco,[59] perfectly preserved with moat, gun mounts and black dungeon; the old Spanish Treasury; and a few quaint Spanish houses of native coquina rock with overhanging wooden balconies and flower-filled patios, down streets so narrow that modern cars must sometimes creep behind the horse-drawn carriages still used for showing the sights to the visitors. There are such streets as Hypolita, Cordova, Saragossa and Valencia.

The plantation period, from the mid-1800s to the disastrous freezes of 1894–95, belongs to the French and the English, particularly the latter. French aristo-

---

58   Kathryn T. Abbey (1896–1967), *Florida, Land of Change* (Chapel Hill: University of North Carolina Press, 1941). Abbey would become the second wife of A. J. Hanna by November 1946 (see MKR's "Princeling in Florida" in this volume, a review of Hanna's *A Prince in Their Midst: The Adventurous Life of Achille Murat on the American Frontier* [Norman: University of Oklahoma Press, 1946]); both served on the faculty of Rollins College.

59   Our Lady of La Leche Shrine was established by the Spanish in St. Augustine about 1615. "Castillo de San Marco," the fort at St. Augustine, was built between 1672 and 1695. Many historians claim that Ponce de León landed farther south, near what is now Melbourne Beach.

crats who gave glamour to the plantation era included the nephew of Napoleon, Prince Murat, who owned and developed a vast acreage near the capitol city of Tallahassee. English settlers of good blood came in numbers, the greatest movement being from about 1870 to 1894. In the same era, Florida was a favorite locale for the English remittance men, for younger sons, subsidized sometimes in hopes of making a fortune, sometimes merely to stay away from home. Cotton was planted, and profitably, citrus groves set out, cattle raised, and lumber and turpentine exports became extensive. Yet there were few large plantations and only a minority of proprietors were slave holders. The Old South, the Deep South, as portrayed in "Gone With the Wind," has never truly included Florida.

The basic white population of the rural areas drifted down over the years from the south-eastern seaboard of the United States, from Virginia, North and South Carolina, Georgia, Alabama and Tennessee. The stock is English, Scottish and Irish, sturdy and honest Anglo-Saxons who, in the more remote sections, still use in their speech a picturesque Chaucerian and Shakespearean idiom. Many of the old Scottish and English ballads are still sung here to the accompaniment of guitar or fiddle or harmonica. These backwoods residents have come to be known, as in Alabama and Georgia, as "Crackers." Most believe the name came from the habit of frontiersmen of cracking long rawhide whips over the backs of their oxen. A distinguished naturalist, Dr. Thomas Barbour of the Agassiz Museum at Harvard University,[60] believes that the name stems from William Bartram, who wrote in 1790 of the journeying into "the land of corn and crackers." One of the staple foods of the Florida countryman is corn, cracked in a form known as hominy grits, or ground into meal.

No naturalist, no historian, will ever be found to depict Florida so accurately, with such fascination, as William Bartram, son of John Bartram, an English Quaker and botanist who became the friend of Benjamin Franklin.[61] William Bartram's "Travels" (1792) [1791] had a great vogue in England and on the Continent. The book influenced many poets and writers, including Wordsworth and Coleridge. Coleridge's "Kubla Khan" was inspired by Bartram's descriptions of

---

60   Thomas Barbour (1884–1946), director of the Museum of Comparative Zoology at Harvard University from 1927 to 1946, also known as the Agassiz Museum, after its founder Jean Louis Rodolphe Agassiz (1807–73). MKR was not as charitable about Barbour to her husband, Norton: "[He] seems to have a chip on his shoulder about me (perhaps because 'Cross Creek' beat him to the gun!) and in the May issue [of *Atlantic Monthly*] disagreed with me on something that was purely a matter of personal opinion" (*Private Marjorie*, 398).

61   Benjamin Franklin (1706–90), the legendary author, printer, inventor, scientist, statesman.

the mysterious underground rivers in Florida that rise "from caverns measureless to man" to form crystal-blue springs, flowing thence with vast sudden volume to make runs and little rivers.[62]

The modern Florida may be said roughly to date from the rapid extension of railroads about 1880. Travel facilities, and the building of enormous and luxurious hotels on the east, or Atlantic, coast, at St. Augustine, Ormond, Daytona Beach and Palm Beach, and at Tampa on the west, or Gulf of Mexico, coast, brought the beginning of what to-day is probably Florida's largest industry—the tourist, in search of winter warmth and comfort. The super-tourist city of Miami, and its adjacent Miami Beach, is a development of the last twenty years. St. Petersburg, on the west coast, is little older, and here it is said that good Yankees go to die—or to put off dying, for the legend of perpetual youth persists. The development of these large cities owes its impetus to a phenomenon that occurred in the middle 1920s, "The Florida Boom." The affair was mass hysteria, like the California Gold Rush, with real estate prices sky-rocketing, worthless backlands selling for fabulous figures, land changing hands day by day at profits of tens of thousands, whole towns erected in the pine woods—until the inevitable crash, with losses, mostly on paper, running into millions. The aftermath of the boom was a more conservative development.

The tourist is a good or bad thing for Florida solely according to one's personal bias. The Chamber of Commerce, the hotels and business places, the owners of some of the exceptional beauty spots, such as the astonishing springs, cannot have too many paying visitors to please them. Those of us who prefer Florida's lush wildness to profitable commercialization regret the increasing so-called "development." But it would be selfish to deny a share in the bland sunshine, in the enjoyment of the palm trees, the exotic birds, the fishing and the hunting, to "transients," and it is only to be hoped that while more and more travellers come inevitably to the State, the natural beauties, the native flora and fauna, will be preserved. Social consciousness toward preservation of the irreplaceable is increasing, and the once almost extinct egret with its beautiful white plumage, the prehistoric alligator, are now protected by law and may be seen in their natural habitat.

The Indian figures only casually in the modern story of Florida, yet he was once a formidable enemy, the more so because he was the rightful possessor and lived in harmony with the land. Florida belonged to him many hundreds, per-

---

62   William Wordsworth (1770–1850), the English Romantic poet. In Coleridge's "Kubla Khan," the sacred river Alph, which runs "Through caverns measureless to man" (lines 4–5) momentarily erupts from its chasm as a "mighty fountain" (line 19) and thus establishes one of the great metaphors in literature for the source of human imagination.

haps thousands, of years, before the Spanish conquest. The original inhabitants bear almost no anthropological relation to the Indian of to-day, or to the Indian the Spaniards found. The Indians in modern Florida are known as the Seminoles, the word meaning literally "refugee." They are made up of members of various tribes who fled to Florida, one of the last frontier out-posts in the United States, as the hand of the white man became heavy. The Seminoles still live a primitive and happy life in the Everglades section, deep in the cypress swamps. They are technically still at war with the United States, never having signed a peace treaty, but they are a quiet and unobtrusive people, asking only not to be disturbed in their simple farming and hunting and fishing for a livelihood. The greatest influence of the Indian on Florida to-day is probably in the matter of names, for towns, counties, lakes and rivers still bear such lovely appellations as Tallahassee, Alachua, Ocala, Miami, Lahoula, Withlacoochie, Ocklawaha, Caloosahatchie and Okeechobee.

The Negro has never been in Florida in such disproportionate numbers to the white population as in such southern States as Georgia, Alabama, Louisiana and Mississippi. He does not have here so extensive a history of serfdom. For this reason, many Florida Negroes are home and land owners, and the vicious share-cropping system of the Deep South, has not yet operated here to make of them still, in practice, if not in theory, slaves. Their schools, churches, and general opportunities are somewhat better than the Southern average.

If the tourist is Florida's first industry, others crowd him. Citrus has been important since the Spanish sweet orange was first grafted, or budded, on the indigenous wild orange stock. Timber, mostly pine and cypress; naval stores; tobacco; sugar cane; vegetable crops of all sorts, beans, peas, lettuce, cabbage, tomatoes, okras, peanuts, potatoes, supply the nation. Fish, shrimp and oysters from the coasts and the tidal rivers are plentiful. At Tarpon Springs, near Tampa, on the Gulf of Mexico, Greek sponge divers carry on the trade of their Attic ancestors, with modern equipment. Florida is second only to Texas in the production of cattle in the United States. Florida provides 80 per cent. of the world's phosphate. But the gold and silver and pearls and the Fountain of Youth are not here.

The state is a sportsman's Paradise. Deer (white-tailed, or Virginia deer) abound in several sections. Game birds include quail, snipe, doves, ducks of all varieties, geese and wild turkeys. The thousands of lakes teem with fish: big-mouthed bass, very sporting and weighing up to fourteen pounds, black, or small-mouthed, bass, bream, perch. Off the coasts, large game fish offer superb sport; tarpon, tuna, marlin, sailfish, and scores of smaller varieties. There are still bears here (the black bear), and pumas, or panthers.

A. J. Cronin once told me that he considered "Transients," one of the most depressing expressions in the "American" language.[63] A sign consisting of this one word hangs over the entrance of half the once-private homes and small hotels and apartment houses in resort, or "tourist" or "tripper" Florida. Miami is the garish and gaudy queen, exciting, cheap, but touched with inescapable tropic loveliness. Palm Beach, totally artificial, almost beautiful, is softened by expensively trained bougainvillea, bignonia, hibiscus and transplanted coconut and royal palms. For my taste, the true, the valuable Florida is the little-known country off the beaten path. Two of my books, "South Moon Under" and "The Yearling," are laid in one such unique section, "The Big Scrub." This isolated area, almost as unlived-in as a hundred years ago—even Bartram passed only along its edge—is forbidding, yet has its own primitive majesty, its still occasional bear and panther, its deer and wild-cats, its prevalent but unobtrusive rattle-snakes.

The great glory of Florida is its hammocks and its rivers. Under the vast live oaks, draped with the soft, sad, gray Spanish moss that arouses and eludes the painter—I know of no artist who has caught its feeling—there is a perpetual half-shadow, shot with shafts of sunlight such as stream across the aisles of old cathedrals. Red birds and blue jays, mocking-birds and mourning doves, wood ducks and whippoorwills, cry by day or by night through the trumpet and bamboo vines, the magnolias and the yellow jessamine. Eagles scream overhead, and on the fringes, where there is almost surely water, swamp, pond or lake, egrets nest and herons and ibis turn from their feeding into the cool dusk of the forests.

The rivers are rivers of a dream. Their water is clear, but ordinarily of the colour of amber, from the dropping of magnolia and oak leaves and cypress needles. The pneuma[to]phoric cypress knees are not factual but the imaginings of Doré.[64] The rivers, doubling and curving, pressed in by the towering trees so that there are often no banks at all, run in and out of the sunlight, and rustle under over-hanging thickets of wild rose, clematis and lavender aster. Water-turkeys, or snake-birds,[65] dive for fish, and spotted limpkins walk stiffly, as on stilts, in search of snails and crawfish and river shrimp. Turtles sun themselves on logs, and a rare alligator slides his prehistoric bulk soundlessly into the water from his warm mud-wallow. Here and there a clearing appears in the denseness and the river flows past a small open field with a little unpainted pine cabin, the home of a fisherman or poor farmer or perhaps one in search only of silence. And the

---

63 A. J. Cronin (1896–1981), the Scottish novelist and MKR's friend.

64 Gustave Doré (1832–83), best known for his weird and fantastic illustrations.

65 Both are common names for the anhinga (*Anhinga anhinga*), also known as the darter.

salt tidal rivers on the west coast, flowing into the Gulf of Mexico, pass, before their absorption into the larger waters, through ancient shell-banks thick with cedars, low and twisted by the winds.

At the moment, Florida is a vast armed camp. The climate is suitable for training posts for all purposes. Camp Blanding, in the central interior of the State, maintains a steady listing of Army trainees of about 50,000. There are airfields everywhere, and the drone of training planes is steady over the coasts, the marshes, the pine woods and hammocks. At some of the Navy air bases, the amazing new Celestial Navigation Trainer is being used. Here the cadet pilot and navigator learn air navigation, under a mechanical canopy of stars. The cockpit, complete with all equipment, looks down on land and sea charts from a simulated height of 10,000 feet, and simulated bombs are dropping, the mechanics able to observe their striking. All the elements of flight, including wind and direction, are duplicated, so that lives now need not be lost by training only with actual planes in actual flight. Veteran pilots and navigators return from overseas raids to these Florida airbases for refresher courses.[66] Artillery ranges strew the flat backwoods.

The future of Florida is perhaps a trifle too rosy from the point of view of the quiet citizen and the nature lover. The climate is too inducive to many forms of industry, its charms of summer in winter too attractive. It remains to be seen whether the Florida of Bartram will survive, or whether the Chambers of Commerce will kill the goose that lays the golden egg.

Marjorie Kinnan Rawlings

"Florida: A Land of Contrasts," *Transatlantic*, no. 14 (October 1944): 12–17.

---

66   The Link Celestial Navigation Trainer—invented in 1941 by the pioneer simulator designer Edwin A. Link (1904–81) and the celestial navigation authority P. V. H. Weems (1889–1979)—was also immense; it held not only the pilot and navigator but the bombardier, and it was housed in a 45-foot-tall building.

Introduction to *Letters from Caleb Milne*

The essence of a man is never physically visible. Because of his few letters to me,[67] and these to his mother, I can say that I knew Caleb Milne, and knew the best of him. That best is something choice and beautiful.

This collection of his letters seems to me of permanent value, far beyond satisfying our avidity for news of the working of the minds of men who are fighting, for us, our battle. They reveal a rare soul, who passes on to us his own perceptions of the beauty and glory of living; and they are written in the style of true Belles-Lettres.

One feels humble and a little frightened that such a man has died for us, untimely. So much of the writing of men actively in the war has had that impact. They love life, they see so clearly what is good and what is bad, and seeing intimately the base in man, they are hopeful of the good. The responsibility on us who survive is overwhelming. We have been through this too often, always with the trust "that these our dead shall not have died in vain."[68] What does it take to teach us? How and when shall we learn? Shall we continue to kill off our Rupert Brooke's, our Joyce Kilmer's, our Caleb Milne's, and be as stupid as before?[69]

Young Milne wrote of the death of one of his comrades, "I have always felt the pain exists only for the bystanders. I don't understand life, so naturally death seems very simple to me." None can understand life. It is given to the wisest only to appreciate the gift of life. This he did, and the stirring record is here.

Marjorie Kinnan Rawlings

"Introduction to *Letters from Caleb Milne*," "*I Dream of the Day . . .*": *Letters from Caleb Milne* (Woodstock, N.Y.: Van Rees Press, 1944; New York: Longmans, Green, 1944).

---

67   Milne was among the large number of servicepeople who corresponded with MKR during World War II, although his letters were of special import to her. Milne, a stretcher bearer, was killed by a German mortar shell in North Africa on 11 May 1943, as he was giving aid to a wounded French Legionnaire.

68   MKR is quoting from Lincoln's Gettysburg Address (1863): "We here highly resolve that these dead shall not have died in vain."

69   Rupert Brooke (1887–1915), British poet, died of a septic mosquito bite off the island of Lemnos in the Aegean Sea on his way to serve in the battle at Gallipoli (February 1915–January 1916), in which 131,000 soldiers of the two sides were killed and 262,000 were wounded. Alfred Joyce Kilmer (1886–1918), widely known for his poem "Trees" (*Poetry Magazine* 2 [August 1913]: 160), was killed by a sniper at the Second Battle of the Marne (July-August 1918), in which the two sides suffered nearly 390,000 casualties.

Florida: An Affectionate Tribute

My good friend, the Honorable Joe Hendricks,[70] has, with a politician's naïve and simple approach to art, asked me, "to describe the beauties of Florida, the lakes, streams, trees, flowers, birds, etc., in just a brief story." I myself have written six full-length books in such an attempt, and the total volumes of this inexhaustible subject, in more than four centuries of Florida's chaotic history, must be of equal bulk to that of the *Congressional Record.*

Yet it can be said, and, briefly too, that Florida is unique among States in that her history is founded on that very beauty. Other States grew for reasons of agriculture, of forests and of gold; were sought out in search of political or religious freedom. But from the moment of Ponce de Leon's dream of the Fountain of Youth, to the same dream today in the heart of the graybeard who totters or is wheeled to the sun of St. Petersburg or Miami, men have sought Florida out of the purest and most aesthetic human impulse, the love of beauty. Like her sister, California, and that sister's, shall we say politely, fatherless child, Hollywood, Florida's stock in trade is glamour. And her glamour does not depend on the ephemeral flicking of the silver screen, but on the timeless, again to quote the Honorable Mr. Hendricks, "lakes, streams, trees, flowers, birds, etc."

Much of Florida is unchanged down the ages, and the ancient Spaniards came on the same wonders as delight us today. Pine forests, half shadow and half sunlight, like cathedral aisles, stretch for miles. The pines break, and there is hammock land, black of soil, lush with magnolia, sweet gum, bay, holly and live oak. The live oaks are pendulous with gray Spanish moss, stirring in the wind like the beards of long forgotten gods. The hammock breaks, and the orange groves lift their bright balls of light to the good sun. The golden apples of the Hesperides, the gold apple of Atalanta, were the orange.[71] Limes and lemons, mangoes and papayas—all the rich fruits of the Tropics and the subtropics, offer their succulence. Everywhere are the palms, shaggy-topped and noble. And scattered throughout, like necklaces of diamond, of aquamarine and amber, are the lovely lakes, and cypress-bordered magic rivers run shining to the sea. Some of these rivers have their sources in fabulous underground springs. Silver Springs, near

---

70   Joseph Edward Hendricks (1903–74), Florida congressman from 1937 to 1949.

71   In Greek mythology, the "Hesperides" were nymphs who, together with a fierce serpent, guarded an Arcadian garden where golden apples grew. Compare the title of MKR's *Golden Apples.* Atalanta, the virgin huntress and athlete who vanquished and then killed all her suitors until she raced Melanion (also called Hippomenes), who rolled into her path three golden apples, which she stooped over to pick up, thus slowing her and causing her defeat and marriage.

Ocala, are the proved inspiration for Coleridge's famous poem Kubla Khan, in which "Alph, the sacred river ran, through caverns measureless to man, down to the sunless sea."[72] Lakes and rivers and off-shore waters teem with fish of every variety.

Redbirds and mocking birds, rustling jorees[73] and sweet-calling wood ducks, snowy egrets and tall blue cranes, limpkins, and baldheaded eagles, the true American eagle, move and cry and sing through the dense green growth. White-tailed deer crop the myrtle buds, are startled and are gone; black bear lumber through the swamps, wildcats and panthers stalk their prey, and countless small woods creatures—raccoons, possums, foxes, scamper by night or day about their business.

And now, in spring, the yellow jessamine fills the air with spicy sweetness, and the orange groves are in bloom, their perfume almost unbearable through the long nights of moonlight. To the south, the bougainvillea and the hibiscus are flamboyant, and such an array of flowers and of garden vegetables is ready for man's delight as to make one wonder why the capitol of the United States was not placed in the Floridian Eden instead of in Washington, D. C. And the climate! Take the lies of California, and in Florida, they are truth.

If human wantonness and human greed have here and there destroyed Arca-dia,[74] with the careless cutting and burning of forests, the useless and destructive draining of lands that were refuges for all the wild things; with the erection of billboards and transient camps; if avid purveyors of Florida's great cash crop, the tourist, have a little spoiled the beauty and overcharged the seeker of loveliness, lay the blame fairly where it belongs, as all such things as greed and war and man's general inhumanity to man,[75] must be laid, on the frailty of human nature, and not on Florida, great and gracious tropical queen. She waits, as she has done through the centuries, to be all things to all men.

[Unsigned]

"Florida: An Affectionate Tribute," *Congressional Record* (2 March 1945): H 1692–93.

---

72   That Silver Springs is the source for the description of the river Alph in Coleridge's poem is not as definite as MKR asserts.

73   A Florida variety of the rufous-sided towhee (*Pipilo erythrophthalmus*), known commonly (and in *The Yearling*) as "jorees."

74   Arcadia, the mythological home of the Greek god Pan and the symbol of ideal natural simplicity, as opposed to Utopia, which, although similarly idyllic, is created by humans.

75   MKR is quoting Robert Burns (1759–96), "Man Was Meant to Mourn: A Dirge" (1796): "Man's inhumanity to man / Makes countless thousands mourn!" (lines 55–56).

Sacred and Profane Love

Men's lips have not lain on my mouth
With the unearthly grace
Of wind, importunate from the south,
Brushing across my face.

I have not found embrace of men
So strong, so fierce, so sweet,
As surf, drawing, again, again,
Vast hands from head to feet.

I dare not breed a mortal child
Lest, called by some far tune,
He meet half-brothers running wild,
Bastards of the moon.

"Sacred and Profane Love," *Journal of Florida Literature* 13 (2004): 32–33. This poem was found in the correspondence of MKR and her friend the Reverend Bertram C. Cooper. She probably enclosed them with a letter to him dated 8 June 1945. See Kinser, "'I'd Much Rather Write You Instead," appendix.

*   *   *   *   *   *   *   *   *

Princeling in Florida

How Napoleon's Nephew Ate Boiled Owl and Alligator and Served as a County Judge

After a flood of fictionalized biographies of various members of Napoleon Bonaparte's family, it is a rare pleasure to read a scholar's biography of one of the less publicized of Bonaparte's nephews, Prince Achille Murat. In A. J. Hanna's "A Prince in Their Midst," there are no dreamy thoughts or sentimental comments placed by an author in the minds and mouths of long-dead people, unable to warn us, "These interpolations are spurious." Yet such is the power of Mr. Hanna's straightforward prose that the facts are more exciting than fiction.

All the Bonapartes contained within their characters and their contradictions the stuff of drama. A family of Corsican peasants, precipitated from poverty to thrones, turned into figures in a fantasy. None of them is more fabulous than the Crown Prince of Naples, who "lived on wild game and slept under the stars" of the American Florida frontier more than a hundred years ago.

Achille Murat's mother was Caroline, Napoleon's youngest sister, a spectacular woman whom rumor linked in an illicit love affair with Metternich,[76] and in whom Napoleon observed, "Much stuff, much character and unbounded ambition."

Achille's father was Joachim Murat, a French divisional commander who fought with Napoleon in Egypt, and became King of Naples with the rise of the Bonaparte star.[77] Achille inherited, or was cursed by, the unbounded ambition, certainly with some of the "stuff," only to blaze and fade like an uncharted meteor across the Florida wilderness. This was not so much for his lack of character, as for his crucial weaknesses.

After a childhood as a Neapolitan crown prince, with all that implied of Bonaparte glory, the help of Napoleon saw a twenty-two-year-old lad, mature past his years, setting sail in the spring of 1823 for the new Republic, the United States of America. The fatal contradictions in his nature were established in this migration. Although of a most spurious second-generation "nobility," young Achille was on fire with the ideals of the new American land of freedom, as Lafayette had been.[78] These ideals carried him through infinite hardships in Florida in establishing, with insufficient funds, first his plantation "Parthenope," within sight of the Atlantic Ocean south of St. Augustine, and later, the larger plantation near Tallahassee, "Lipona."

Yet for all his passion for "Liberté, egalité, fraternité," Achille considered the institution of slavery a correct one, and profited by it, as far as he might, with his improvidence and delusions of grandeur, profit by anything at all. He mar-

---

76   Caroline Bonaparte (1782–1839), youngest of Napoleon's sisters, married Joachim Murat (see note 77 below) in 1800. Fürst von Metternich (1773–1859), irrepressible Austrian diplomat and arbiter of post-Napoleonic Europe.

77   Joachim Murat (1767–1815), marshall of France, king of Naples (1808–15). As he rose with what MKR calls "the Bonaparte star," so he fell: he was executed on 13 October 1815, in Corsica, where he had fled after his service in the Waterloo campaign (20 March–28 June 1815). Whether or not his wife had conducted an affair with Metternich, it is said that his last act before the firing squad was to kiss her image on a medallion he was wearing. He himself then ordered the squad to fire.

78   The Marquis de Lafayette (1757–1834), French general and statesmen, who served with renowned distinction in the American Revolutionary War (1775–83).

ried a Virginia aristocrat, a great-grandniece of George Washington,[79] and was at the same time such an *homme nature* that "a contemporary report insisted that 'nothing swims the water, flies the air, crawls or walks the earth but that he served it upon his table: alligator steaks, frogs, boiled owls, and roasted crows were found palatable."

In a brief lifetime, for he died at the age of forty-six, Prince Achille Murat managed to become a County Judge in pioneer Florida, to influence Southern agriculture for generations to come, to leave a considerable body of valuable and all but unknown writings on the subject of American life, to set Europe in a tizzy by popping up there at moments when the return of the Bonaparte dynasty seemed impending or remotely possible, and to die as a failure, as far as his ambitions were concerned.

In Florida, Prince Murat is more of a romantic legend in Tallahassee, where he is buried, than in St. Augustine. True, there is a "Prince Murat House" in St. Augustine, which, it appears, the pioneer prince merely rented for a brief period. And your reviewer did not realize, until reading this book, that when an old Minorcan fisherman said, "There's an old place near your cottage I'd like to show you, where they say a French prince lived," he was referring to "Parthenope," Murat's first plantation.

Mr. Hanna has written a fascinating book that should appeal to a wide variety of interests: to scholars, of course for Mr. Hanna and his second wife, Kathryn T. Abbey, are Florida's leading historians; to biographers and to many novelists who could profit by the direct narrative style; to all readers who might be intrigued by a factual story of a European prince pioneering in America, claiming milk and whisky as a cure-all for all-ills, traveling through Florida jungles with "slaves, cattle and a pet owl," weighing royalty against the American idea.

The illustrations by John Rae contain as much magic as the book.[80]

Marjorie Kinnan Rawlings

"Princeling in Florida," *New York Herald Tribune Weekly Book Review* (17 November 1946): 7. This is a review of A. J. Hanna, *A Prince in Their Midst: The Adventurous Life of Achille Murat on the American Frontier* (Norman: University of Oklahoma Press, 1946).

---

79   In 1826, Murat married Catherine Daingerfield Willis (1803–67), who played an important role in raising funds to preserve Washington's home at Mount Vernon.

80   John Rae (1882–1963), illustrator and artist.

Introduction to *Katherine Mansfield Stories*

A writer experiences the work of a master writer with not the purity of reaction, perhaps, of a lay reader. His spirit is as widely open to enjoyment, he is easily hypnotized by the peculiarly magic spell cast by fine writing. But while his pleasure is at its keenest, he is conscious of the technique that has created that pleasure. He is the earnest young violinist hearing Heifetz,[81] he is the little old drawing-teacher who came at last to know that he could never be an artist, rapt before a Goya and a Raphael.[82] Those apparently easy sentences, flowing surely from inspiration, he happens to know, were carved, were hewn; those airy edifices in which live such enchanting characters, were built stone by heavy stone, out of stark hard work and even out of agony.

Katherine Mansfield has been considered a writer's writer, and so she is, for the rest of us come to her with respect and awe. We still do not know her secrets. I can remember when to have read and admired "The Garden-Party" stamped one almost with the mark of the *précieuse* [precious].[83] Yet I know of no other author who may so well be unwrapped from a long veiling in ethereal gauze and presented plainly for sheer reading delight. Art and aesthetics aside, she is a raconteuse, a superb teller of tales.

Mansfield is obviously not for the addict of the popular weeklies or the women's magazines, though a few of her stories might, most deceptively, appear these days in the latter. "Feuille d'Album," for instance, has a surface sweetness that could be a trap for the unwary.[84] A college text-book that fell recently into my hands announced pontifically that although Mansfield was ranked with the great short-story writers, her work lacked depth and range. This is of course nonsense. If there are "deeper" stories than "The Man Without a Temperament" or "The Stranger," in both of which lives are seen collapsing quietly before one's

---

81   Jascha Heifetz (1901–87), Russian-American violin virtuoso.

82   Francisco de Goya (1746–1828), Spanish master, often called the Father of Modern Art. Raphael (1483–1520), High Italian Renaissance artist known especially for his frescoes in the Vatican.

83   The title story of Mansfield's *The Garden Party, and Other Stories* (New York: Knopf, 1922), 59–82, explores a young girl's confrontation with death in the context of her family's spring fête.

84   "Feuille d'Album" [Album Leaf], in *Bliss, and Other Stories* (New York: Knopf, 1920), 218–27, is a voyeuristic tale of a young Parisian artist who follows the girl with whom he is fascinated. At the end of the story, he works up the courage to confront her and gives her an egg that she has supposedly dropped.

eyes,[85] I do not know them. The very quiet is perhaps the snare. She works her wonders so subtly that the shallow-minded no doubt read no more than the actual words. As to range, call Poe "limited" if you must, but not the writer who could move from "Life of Ma Parker" to "Poison."[86]

It is an indication of Katherine Mansfield's major position in her field that even the text-book writers bracket her with Poe, Chekhov and De Maupassant.[87] She produces on occasion, too, as O. Henry a surprise ending as you could ask, as in "Bliss."[88] Yet in my opinion she owes nothing to earlier masters save the inevitable debt to all creative folk, including the iconoclasts such as Whitman, Joyce, Proust, to the artists who have preceded them.[89] The college tome that so irked me gave a full page to identifying her as a disciple of Chekhov. If the author of nearly a hundred published stories, all exquisite, some of them acknowledged classics, was a "disciple," she was more faithful than Peter or Paul.

Now if there is any recognizable influence at all, in Mansfield, why not that of Hans Christian Andersen's so-called "fairy-tales"? Andersen's tales are faery only in their occasional Thumbelinas,[90] their brothers turned into swans, but the world of all the characters is a painfully real one, sorrowful to the point of morbidness, if it were not for a redeeming tenderness. Katherine Mansfield lived and wrote in that world.

She wrote much of children, as did Andersen, and those children are hor-

---

85   "The Man without a Temperament," in *Bliss, and Other Stories* (New York: Knopf, 1920), 172–93. "The Stranger," in *The Garden Party, and Other Stories* (New York: Knopf, 1922), 211–30.

86   Edgar Allan Poe (1809–49), American writer, "limited" because of his inevitably macabre stories. MKR contrasts Mansfield's range, from the possible mercy killing in "Life of Ma Parker," in *The Garden Party, and Other Stories* (New York: Knopf, 1922), 140–50, to the more metaphoric poisoning of life by a failed relationship in "Poison," in *The Little Girl and Other Stories* (New York: Knopf, 1931), 235–43.

87   Anton Chekhov (1860–1904), Russian writer especially known for his stories of human folly and banal trivialities. Guy de Maupassant (1850–93), French writer especially known for his detail of character, called psychological realism.

88   William Sydney Porter [O. Henry] (1862–1910), prolific short story writer known for his surprise endings. At the end of "Bliss," in *Bliss, and Other Stories* (New York: Knopf, 1920), 116–36, Bertha, who has just realized how much she desires her husband, Harry, unexpectedly sees him kiss Miss Fulton good-bye.

89   Marcel Proust (1871–1922), French novelist especially known for his penetrating look into the human psyche through interior monologue.

90   Hans Christian Andersen (1805–75), Danish writer especially known for his tragic, often gruesome children's stories; although more innocent than usual, even "Little Tiny or Thumbelina" (1835) has its disturbing aspects.

ribly mature. They are lost children, knowing too much of the ways of men. Her stories have the cosmic sadness of "The Snow Queen."[91] They have, too, "the strange, beautiful excitement" of the fairy tale. There is even a relation to the Andersen style, superficially simple, almost naïve, so that textbook writers are quite misled; a style carefully calculated by an artist to sheathe her meaning. This is not influence. This is kinship.

One may ask legitimately what is expected, what is required, of the short-story form. The only honest answer is, each to his own taste; so that "a good story" may range from ten minutes of casual entertainment in a neatly executed plot, to the little incomplete sketch or vignette that merely suggests a story, or to the stream-of-consciousness study, comparable to surrealism in painting. I do think, whatever its manner, that a greater perfection is demanded of the short-story form than of the novel, just as flaws might be acceptable in a large canvas, but become intolerable in a miniature. Beyond this, one is obliged to ask what is expected *artistically* of the short story or any other piece of creative work. Joseph Conrad best answered the question in his Preface to *The Nigger of the Narcissus*. He wrote there that the function of the artist was "to make you understand, to make you feel, above all, to make you *see*."[92]

Katherine Mansfield does this to a superlative degree. She does it tangibly and intangibly. She is a great deal of a painter, of a visualist. She uses physical color, sometimes as rawly as Van Gogh, then surprises you the next time with the pale luminosity of Corot.[93] The more important light is that one never seen on land or sea, the psychic illumination which Conrad had in mind. For her great gift is a passionate awareness, and this, through her flawless technique, she is able to convey to the reader. She is "the eager, serious traveler, absorbed in understanding what was to be seen and discovering what was hidden."

There are fine writers, there are sensitive readers, who never will be attuned to the Mansfield stories. It seems to me that those who do not understand her must be those to whom the sun is only "a bright, metallic light," to whom rain represents only a difficulty in getting a taxi, to whom a child's heartbreak is only a distant wailing in a nursery. For the others of us, to many of whom this all-

---

91   In "The Snow Queen" (1845), another of Andersen's stories, the little girl Gerda suffers much before she cries for the little boy Kay and melts his frozen heart with her tears.

92   In his preface to *The Nigger of the Narcissus* (1897), Conrad writes: "My task which I am trying to achieve is, by the power of the written word, to make you hear, to make you feel—it is, before all, to make you *see*. That—and no more, and it is everything."

93   Vincent Van Gogh (1853–90), Dutch postimpressionist painter. Jean-Baptiste Corot (1796–1875), French landscape painter.

too-short collection of stories will open a door, Katherine Mansfield stands for a magnificent revelation of human emotions.

Marjorie Kinnan Rawlings

"Introduction to *Katherine Mansfield Stories*," *Katherine Mansfield Stories* (Cleveland: World, 1946), 9–12. Katherine Mansfield (1888–1923), of New Zealand, was one of the great short story writers of the Modern period of literature.

*   *   *   *   *   *   *   *   *

Josephina Niggli's *Step Down, Elder Brother*

I can only describe the book as enchanting, in the broadest sense . . . [MKR's ellipsis] The stories, in themselves have the classic quality of Isak Dinesen's *Seven Gothic Tales*,[94] yet taken as a whole, they make a complete narrative.

Marjorie Kinnan Rawlings

"Josephina Niggli's *Step Down, Elder Brother*." This is a review of Josephina Niggli (1910–13), *Step Down, Elder Brother* (New York: Rinehart, 1947).

*   *   *   *   *   *   *   *   *

Langston Moffett's *Devil by the Tail*

I am most enthusiastic about Langston Moffett's book and consider it utterly fascinating. It packs a terrific wallop . . . [MKR's ellipsis] instead of being merely one psychological episode, it is the saga of the wandering drunk.

Marjorie Kinnan Rawlings

"Langston Moffett's *Devil by the Tail*." Blurb for Langston Moffett (1903–89), *Devil by the Tail* (Philadelphia: Lippincott, 1947).

---

94   Isak Dinesen [Karen Blixen] (1885–1962), *Seven Gothic Tales* (New York: Smith and Haas, 1934).

The Use of the Sitz-Bath

A Study Based on Experiments
in the Brown's Hollow Laboratory[95]

Man's first bath was undoubtedly an accident. It seems certain that our aboriginal ancestors used water but internally, and then only until the fermented juices of wild fruits and grains brought enlightenment, and civilization as we know it, began.

Man was Homo Fragrans before he was Homo Sapiens. He had no need to disguise his scent, for he was usually the hunter and not the hunted, and soon learned to stalk up-wind. A rich aroma was no deterrent to success, and it is significant that the modern use of perfume is designed to further this aim. Madame of the advertisements is merely compensating for not having lain in a bed of wild violets, and Monsieur is attempting to simulate the woodsman fresh from pines, the agrarian come from a roll in the hay, or the hard-riding cavalier still redolent of his saddle-leather.

Ipecacus[96] has given us our clue with his deciphering of the twin stone tablets unearthed so long ago in Asia Minor. The first indicates "Water all over," followed by a symbol for horror. Its mate indicates "Water all over," followed by a symbol for pleasure. We can re-create that ancient picture: a Neolithic man stumbled headlong into a deep pool, or his rude dugout spilled him over a gentle cataract, or he was caught out of his cave in a heavy rain, perhaps far from home, with a dinosaur panting on his heels, and to gain speed, stripped himself of his dripping and leaden bear-skins.

His first feeling was one of utter distaste as the violation of his own private and enjoyably dirty skin, and it is indubitable that the violent rejection of the bath by small boys is an honest and atavistic reaction. There followed for this early Homo Fragrans a surprising sensation of freshness and delight, and it is within the realm of possibility that sheer novelty made him the Clark Gable of his day,[97] and incident became usage.

Now our establishment of "Water all over" as an accident must not delude the scientist into the conclusion that the Sitz-bath was designed to preclude ca-

95   "Brown's Hollow," the home near Van Hornesville, New York, which MKR occupied before buying her own (see *Private Marjorie*, 487–88).

96   MKR is playing on the word *ipecac*, a common purgative for children.

97   William Clark Gable (1901–60), who played Rhett Butler in the film version of *Gone With the Wind*.

tastrophe as a result of total immersion. Quite the contrary. The Teutonic origin of the word, "Sitz-bad," has been traced by François Dumont to a savage custom of the Huns.[98] It was their habit (1210–1342) to take their fattest captives before the Chieftain, give them a cake of soap and a Sitz-bad, and order them to bathe thoroughly and get all the soap off, without flooding the court or breaking a leg. Since the inevitable failure meant death, the only captive to survive was one Hans Hund, who by wiles postponed his Sitz-bad, starved himself to gauntness, and achieved the impossible with only severe bruises, which, by backing from the Court's presence, he managed to conceal.

The continuing existence of the Sitz-bath in remote areas is but one further indication of man's inhumanity to man. Before public opinion quite forced it from the land, your humble servant feels it a duty to offer, concisely and precisely, the results of experiments designed to discover the least dangerous method of achieving the nowadays-required cleanliness, using no other facilities except the Sitz-bath, for the benefit of the traveler who finds himself at its mercy.

Test Method No. 1 (Wet): Lower away slowly and carefully into the Sitz-bath, partially filled with water of the desired temperature. If possible, avoid allowing the spine to fall sharply against the back of the so-called tub. Vertebrae are easily disjointed and the human neck is a frail reed. The knees will now be on a level with the nose, the soap and wash-cloth will be found to be left behind on the distant basin, and it is necessary to throw the upper part of the body violently forward, heaving the torso from the bath, to retrieve the cleansing adjuncts. Repeat the lowering process. Human psychology is such that this time one invariably forgets caution, fair plops into the Sitz-bath, jerks the neck, cracks the nose with the knees, and displaces a volume of water that surges across the floor like the Mississippi in spate.

Soap, rub and rinse the upper portion of the body. The pitifully small amount of water left in the bath is now blue with soap and probably cold. Make haste, and attempt to bathe the remainder. This is found to be impossible, for one is sitting on it. Forget it. Lift the left leg in the air, soap, rub, rinse. Lift the right leg in the air, soap, rub, rinse. The eyes will be blinded by soap-suds and the arms will require another rinsing. Heave the torso out again, clutching at the door-frame to avoid skidding. If failure ensues, crawl on hands and knees until some object is encountered on which one can obtain a firm grip. The tail of a friendly dog has been known to save the life of one prostrate. If the dog does not immediately yelp and start moving, cry "Hie away!" or "Yoicks! Yoicks!" and hang on.

---

98   MKR is borrowing the authentic-sounding name of François Dumont (1751–1831), French painter of miniature portraits.

Method rejected.

Test Method No. 1a (Dry): The same as above, except that one begins with an empty, or dry, Sitz-bath, and turns on the faucets after making a three-point landing. Occasionally the water runs ice-cold, but ordinarily the Old Faithful Geyser is found to have been piped into the house, and a seething, scalding torrent boils under one. Think of the torture to which we subject lobsters in cooking. GET OUT OF THAT TUB.

Method rejected.

Test Method No. 2 (Yogi or Spiritual): Begin as before. Cross the legs in Yogi or Buddha fashion. Lave the upper portion, chanting "Om! Om!" the whiles. Now try to uncross your legs. TRY, YOU IDIOT, IT MAY BE DAYS BEFORE ANYONE FINDS YOU.

Method rejected.

Test Method No. 3 (Narcissus, or Nymph by the Pool): Stand before the nearly filled Sitz-bath. Lean gracefully over and wash the face and arms with dainty swabs and swipes. The rest of the anatomy will be dripping, but there is nothing for it but to step into the bath anyway and finish up. This is also known as the wall-spattering method.

Method perhaps as physically safe as any, but slow and nerve-wracking and least likely to get the soap off. Rejected.

Test Method No. 4 (Sissy, or Compromise): Sit on the two inches of tub opposite the faucets, and facing them. If you are not built to sit on two inches, whose fault is it? Remember Hans Hund. You've been threatening to reduce for five years. The front may now be washed in complete comfort. All right, all right, when you begin on the back, the water flows outside, under the Sitz-bath, and will probably rot the floor. Stand up. WATCH THAT SOAP UNDER YOUR FOOT. WHOOPS.

NOTE: We offer this incomplete study with regret, since it seems unlikely that it will ever be finished. Dr. Rawlings became totally paralyzed in the course of these experiments, and at last report, was sinking rapidly. The last intelligible words of this unselfish scientist were, "Hold on to your hats, boys, here we go again."

Dr. M. K. Rawlings Baskin

"The Use of the Sitz-Bath," *Dumpling Magazine*, 11, no. 2 (6 July 1947): 3–7. Only one copy of the *Dumpling Magazine* was published annually by Richard Young, the son of Owen D. Young, and contained contributions from the family and close friends. MKR proudly contributed five pieces to the magazine (see Tarr, *Bibliography*, 233–34).

About Fabulous Florida

Study of One of the Strangest, Most Fascinating and Blood-Stained Regions of Our Continent

"There are no other Everglades in the world." So Marjory Stoneman Douglas begins a fabulous book about fabulous Florida, certainly one of the best in the series "Rivers of America." Hervey Allen, the editor of the series,[99] was inspired when he persuaded Mrs. Douglas to apply her rich and sensitive style, her gift for scholarly research, her knowledge, to the first comprehensive study of one of the strangest, most blood-stained, regions of our continent.

"They have been called the mysterious Everglades so long," she writes, "that the phrase is a meaningless platitude. For four hundred years after the discovery they seem more like a fantasy than a simple geographic and historical fact . . . [MKR's ellipsis]. The shores that surround the Everglades were the first on this continent known to white men. Their interior was almost the last. They have not yet been entirely mapped."

Sparing neither the cruelty of the terrain nor of the men who have inhabited or impinged upon it, passing on to us its beauty in lyric prose, Mrs. Douglas has traced the history of the Everglades from the first rising from the sea of "the great pointed paw of the state of Florida" to the present perilous moment.

The beginning was "late in the earth's history, a mere geologic yesterday." Yet fossils have been found there of the saber-toothed tiger, of the mammoth and the mastodon. The ancient crocodile still suns himself and catches his prey in the Miami River, one of the many outlets of the Everglades, "river of grass." The grass is saw-grass, inimical, and the river is that grass with the swift current of water running through it—or it was until the white man of recent years rushed bodily in to attempt to combat a balance of nature that he has not, until today, halfway understood, and has all but ended the water.

It is difficult to say which is the more fascinating in this chronicle, the study of nature or the uncompromising study of man. The book leaves ones breathless with its descriptions of the Glades and of the wildlife, birds, beasts, and reptiles, and then goes on to astonish the reader in its revelations of the truly cultured aboriginal Indians and of their sickening betrayal by the "white men" of past and present generations. The early Spaniards who took easy slaves in the West Indies, who conquered Mexico in the false guise of gods, found themselves up against

---

99   William Hervey Allen Jr. (1889–1949), more often remembered for his best-selling novel *Anthony Adverse* (1933).

a new sort of Indian in the Glades. These Indians, with a democratic pattern of life in which women had a vote long before our American democracy, were forewarned and fore-armed against the voracious and "Christian" intruders. The chapter in Florida history that deals with the early relations of the Conquistadores to the "aborigines" will always be exciting and heart-breaking, and none has told it with greater impact on the mind and the emotions than Marjory Douglas.

She explodes a dozen myths, and the new, true stories are better than the old. Her facts, derived from fresh source material, show Ponce de Leon as reaching the Florida coast far more to the south than is claimed by the commercially minded of St. Augustine, and the new facts are most engaging. Captain John Smith's rescue by Pocahontas is traced to a similar incident in earlier Florida, where Juan Ortiz was rescued by a chief's daughter.[100] It was only in his second version of his experiences with the Indians that Captain Smith told his romantic story, nearly sixty years after the authentic Ortiz experience. His first account made no mention of an enamored Indian maiden.

The tale of the Everglades from Spanish times until today is a consistent one of white man's avarice and insensitivity. The "Seminole" Mikasukis, the "Muskogee-speakers," the Yemassee, a tribe of Talasis, and so on, played consistently fair with the invading white man, and received only treachery in return. The Seminoles and their Everglades were betrayed, and betrayal continues to this moment. The Seminole is now harmless. But through the long historic years, the white American has taken without giving.

The latter-day development of this part of Florida is a story of greed. The railroads,[101] the hotels, the pandering to tourists, the cattle and truck-farming industries, the illicit hunters and fishermen, the misbegotten drainage of the Glades, the cruel fires in the rich muck land, are all here indicted. Mrs. Douglas will not be popular with many of her neighbors when her book appears. Yet she offers hope, for it is not too late to save the Everglades, where the saber-toothed tiger has been replaced by predatory humans. She ends her story of the mastodon, the Indian, the Spaniard, the Englishman, the American, "Perhaps even in

---

100   The claim that John Smith (1580–1631) got the idea for his famous adventure story with Pocahontas (circa 1595–1617) from the actual experience of Juan Ortiz, who was rescued by the eldest daughter of Chief Hirrahigua in Florida one hundred years before, remains impossible to verify, although the experiences are strikingly similar.

101   The building of the railroad from Jacksonville to Miami by the industrial magnate Henry Flagler (1830–1913) was considered an engineering triumph, but the resulting damage to Florida's ecosystems has proved incalculable.

this last hour, in a new relation of usefulness and beauty, the vast, magnificent, subtle and unique region of the Everglades may not be utterly lost."

This beautiful and bitter, sweet and savage, book may be recommended not only to residents and tourists of Florida, but to all readers concerned with American life and the general relation of man to nature.[102]

Marjorie Kinnan Rawlings

"About Fabulous Florida," *New York Herald Tribune Weekly Book Review*, 30 November 1947, sec. 7, 4. This is a review of Marjory Stoneman Douglas (1890–1998), *The Everglades: River of Grass* (New York: Rinehart, 1947). Not quite a week after this review appeared, Harry S. Truman (1884–1972), thirty-fourth president of the United States, formally dedicated the 1.3 million-acre Everglades National Park (6 December 1947).

*   *   *   *   *   *   *   *   *

Apology to an Old House

"What would the Root boys think," my neighbor said,
"Of all this fixing up. They kept things mended
"Like doors and panes and shutters, garden tended,
"Stoop swept each day, but My," he shook his head,
"Two bath-rooms now, one up, another down.
"They had a wash-bench by the wood-shed door.
"Lem was the widower, Rufe the bachelor.
"Lived quiet. Never took a toot in town.
"They'd be real troubled by that cocktail bar.
"Ate in the kitchen, where they saw the hills.
"A pity you've not left things as they were."

I know—. I too have mourned the new and strange,
And I have seen the dear familiar pass
Like stricken ghost before a looking-glass.
I too have known the treachery of change.

Forgive me, House—and Neighbor. Let me prove
Houses were meant for life, for living in.

---

102   Rinehart later used the last paragraph of this review as a blurb for Douglas's *Road to the Sun* (New York: Rinehart, 1952).

Take it, I beg, atonement for my sin,
This rape was done most humbly, and with love.

Marjorie Kinnan Rawlings

"Apology to an Old House," *Dumpling Magazine* 11, no. 4 (5 September 1948): 10. MKR purchased her Van Hornesville house in July 1947. At the time, she acknowledged to Norton that it needed a "partial new roof, plumbing, electricity, new plastering, etc." (*Private Marjorie*, 492).

*   *   *   *   *   *   *   *   *

If You Want to Be a Writer

There are two kinds of writers. One writes as a way of making a living. This sort of commercial writing is a trade or business, like bricklaying or stenography. Sometimes it is extremely profitable and sometimes it brings very small returns.

The other kind of writer writes out of the inner depths of his heart. He writes because life seems tremendously exciting, because it seems beautiful or sad, because he understands people better than the average person, because he burns to express in words the things that he sees and feels. He writes when he is cold and hungry, although he could keep warm and well fed in some other kind of work. He writes even when everyone tells him that his work is of no account, when magazines and publishers refuse his stories.

He writes because he must. It is his life. If finally his work appears in print, he is pleased, because it means that someone is interested in what he has said and how he has said it. If he makes what we call a "success," he is pleased, because it means that a great many people have been touched by him.

Let us take one by one the questions usually asked by young writers. Some of them apply to commercial writing, some to creative writing, and some apply to both.

Q. How do I know whether I can be a writer?

A. If you feel that nothing else will satisfy you, and if you have a natural talent, it is possible to become a writer. Unfortunately, there are many who feel this burning desire without realizing that they lack genuine ability. Merely wanting to be a writer is not enough.

Q. How can I tell whether or not I have a natural talent?

A. If you delight in the use of words; if you have writings accepted by your school newspaper or magazine; if your teachers say that you have a gift, you may take it as encouragement. However, many geniuses have been discouraged by everyone. Also, there have been some with little natural talent who have compensated for their lack and become writers by sheer hard work. The final answer depends on you alone.

Q. How hard does a writer work?

A. The creative writer works very hard indeed, and for long hours. One writer has said, "Genius is the application of the seat of the pants to the seat of the chair." Another has called genius "an infinite capacity for taking pains."[103] This means the writer can not depend on "inspiration" but must stick at his work and build it as a carpenter builds, one board after another. Sometimes creative writing flows like a river, as it did with Thomas Wolfe.[104] Again, it is like digging a deep well with a teaspoon. The commercial writer may also work very hard.

Q. How do I know whether I will prove to be a commercial writer or a creative one?

A. This is difficult to tell when you are just beginning. Sometimes a creative writer becomes discouraged and turns to commercial writing and makes a success of that. Sometimes he tries commercial writing and is a dismal failure. Sometimes one who begins as a commercial writer puts all thought of making money behind him, does finer work, and becomes a creative writer.

Q. How do I learn to be a commercial writer?

A. You can read magazines that give advice to commercial writers. You can take courses, either in school or in college, or by mail. You can try to get a job, even a lowly one with small pay, in an office where you can pick up what are called "the tricks of the trade." This applies particularly to advertising and to writing for the radio or the movies. A special technique is required in these lines.

To learn to write for the stage, it seems best to get a job in the theater in any capacity—stage-hand, scene-shifter, extra, office boy, stenographer—anything that gives you a chance to see plays actually being worked out.

To learn commercial short-story writing, you can try to get a job on the staff of a magazine, although the field is crowded. Short-story courses are helpful. You can study the successful stories in popular magazines and learn the for-

---

103   MKR is quoting Mary Heaton Vorse (1874–1966), feminist, writer, and original member of the Provincetown Players: "The art of writing is the art of applying the seat of the pants to the seat of the chair." The other definition is from Thomas Carlyle (1795–1881), Scottish historian, philosopher, and essayist: "Genius is an infinite capacity for taking pains."

104   Thomas Wolfe (1900–1938), MKR's friend and fellow star at Scribners, known for his nearly uncontainable use of language.

mulas, just as you learn a formula in chemistry. You add your own imagination or experience to the formula or to one of the standard plots, so that you have something new to offer an editor.

A course in journalism is almost necessary to prepare for newspaper work.

Q. How do I learn to be a creative writer?

A. You can not learn this except by and for yourself. You are creative or you are not. You can develop style, you can develop your own technique, you can discover the faults in your writing and correct them, you can learn to co-ordinate your material. It is necessarily a lonely job. Occasionally a great editor, such as the late Maxwell Perkins of Scribner's,[105] gives invaluable help to a writer in learning and working out these things, but such assistance is rare.

The creative writer must be his own sternest critic. He must always be dissatisfied with his own work. He must struggle perpetually to turn his original dream or inspiration into a completed work that says a fraction of the things he wants to say.

Q. What education is advisable in preparation for writing?

A. The amount of formal education is not too important. A college education is like life itself: we get out of it what we put into it. Treasures for the mind are ready in college courses, but the same treasures are waiting in the great books of all time, and in the mere fact of living, experiencing and feeling.

Q. Is newspaper work good training for a creative writer?

A. It is splendid training. In newspaper work one has to write so that one is understood clearly. One learns human nature in the raw. One learns to see human beings objectively.

However, it is difficult to get a job on a newspaper. The requirements are high. Newspaper work should never be thought of as an easy road to a writing career. It is best done when one makes it a career in itself. It is often literary in quality and creative in spirit.

Q. How long does it take to write a book?

A. Some writers dash off a book in a few months or even weeks, but such books are usually mediocre at best. Other writers work many years on one book. From one to two years is a reasonable time for the actual writing.

Q. Should books and short stories be planned out completely before beginning the writing?

A. Short stories should be planned from the beginning to end, except for details. There is no room in their limited space for feeling one's way.

---

105   Maxwell E. Perkins (1884–1947), famed editor of MKR and many others at Scribners, including Wolfe, Fitzgerald, and Hemingway; also MKR's treasured friend, the memory of whom no doubt influences her remarks in this essay.

For a book, a writer should know in advance his general theme; the final result for which he is heading; a rough outline of the story, as to plot or development; and his principal characters. The rest must be worked out as he goes along. Sometimes a character comes to life and takes over and becomes more important than the author planned, or even runs away with the story. Plot changes usually occur as the characters themselves develop.

Q. Does a writer use real or imaginary characters?

A. They are usually a combination of the true and the imaginary. John Galsworthy said that he never invented a character in his life.[106] He undoubtedly meant that even his most fictitious characters had traits of, of physical resemblances to, real people he had known, or heard speak, or merely passed on the street. *The Story of the Novel*, by Thomas Wolfe,[107] includes a wonderful study of this aspect of writing.

An author often draws a literary portrait straight from life. Real people turned into characters in fiction are called "prototypes." Even so, the author invariably changes them in some way, to his plan.

Q. How does a writer become established? How does he first get into print?

A. He usually begins by selling little essays or sketches or verse or stories to small magazines or papers or house organizations. He learns a great deal from seeing his own stuff in print. Competition is keen in the large and popular, or the purely literary magazines, and it is seldom advisable to submit manuscripts to them until after a start in a less crowded field. Almost every library has magazines that give lists of possible outlets for your writings, according to type. It is a waste of time to submit a nature study to a magazine of love stories, for example.

There is no easy road. "Pull" will not help. Knowing an editor, or a publisher, or a successful writer, or having a friend who knows one, will not make up for a poor manuscript. Do not write to editors, or established writers asking them to criticize your work, or for help or advice in getting your book or story published. They are unable to help you, even if they were willing to spend half their working hours trying to assist the beginner. Your work must speak for itself.

The young or beginning writer must realize that every manuscript mailed into a publishing office of any sort is carefully read by trained and competent readers. This does not mean that such readers necessarily read every word or every page

---

106   John Galsworthy (1867–1933), British novelist and playwright, winner of the Nobel Prize for Literature (1932), known for his social commentary and his depiction of unhappy marriages.

107   Wolfe, *The Story of a Novel* (New York: Scribners, 1936).

of a submitted manuscript. A few paragraphs often tell the sad tale that the piece of writing is worthless. Amateur writers have been known to place a small object between pages, and finding it undisturbed, to announce triumphantly that the manuscript had not been read. But one does not need to eat a whole apple to know that it is no good.

Manuscripts showing any promise at all are passed on to a higher editor. These are read thoroughly and sometimes discussed by the entire staff before acceptance or rejection. Sometimes an editor will ask for changes, or make suggestions for the improvement of a story or book. A personal note from an editor instead of a printed rejection slip may be taken as genuine encouragement. Editors make mistakes, of course. Fine books and stories have been turned down. This does not happen often.

Q. Should I have an agent?

A. Reputable agents usually handle only the work of writers who have already broken into print. They are extremely helpful to the established writer in the making of contacts and in placing material properly. They are, however, engaged in a specialized business, and have no time for anyone without an already marketable product. Beware of "agents" or "advisers" who charge fees for reading manuscripts.

Q. Is it true that established writers have a strangle hold on the literary market; and that the new writer finds it almost impossible to get a hearing?

A. This is not true. The most successful writers frequently have books and stories refused by editors. Editors are constantly on the lookout for fresh, new talent.

Q. In what form should I submit my manuscript?

A. Manuscripts must be typed, double-spaced, on one side of the page only, with your name and address in the upper left-hand corner of the first page. They should be mailed flat unless very short. A stamped, self-addressed envelope should be enclosed for the return of the manuscript if it is rejected by the publisher.

Marjorie Kinnan Rawlings

"If You Want to Be a Writer," in *The Book of Knowledge Annual*, ed. E. V. McLoughlin (New York: Grolier Society, 1948), 247–49.

The Key

"Though I speak with the tongues of men and of angels, and have not love,
I am become as sounding brass, or a tinkling cymbal."
"And though I have the gift of prophecy, and understand all mysteries, and all knowledge; and
though I have all faith, so that I could remove mountains, and have not love, I am nothing."
—I Corinthians 13:1–2

The ancient words of Paul have always seemed to me to hold the complete answer to all of human living. Man, in his struggle out of the prehistoric mire, becomes proud and arrogant with each new step of progress. He becomes wise and clever. Surely, we must match each pace forward with a corresponding love, or compassion, or understanding, else we perish. We stand at a moment in human history when, to survive, we must choose between love or hate. "And now abideth faith, hope and love, but the greatest of these is love."[108]

Marjorie Kinnan Rawlings

Author of "The Yearling"

"The Key," in *Words to Live By: A Little Treasury of Inspiration and Wisdom Selected and Interpreted by Eighty-Four Eminent and Women*, ed. William Nichols (New York: Simon and Schuster, 1948), 129.

* * * * * * * * *

Lament of a Siamese Cat

THERE is no sorrow half so deep as mine,
No fate so personal as falls on me,
Unloved, unwanted, trapped by treachery,
No life worth living, not a one in nine.

Doors cruelly closed against me; doors
Only ajar to catch my trusting end,
No one waiting with a light, no friend
To bear me down the lonely corridors.

---

108   1 Corinthians 13:13.

Starvation stalks me. Did I not demand,
Profanely, too, in no uncertain words,
My plate, I'd be dependent on stray birds,
A hungry orphan in an empty land.

I cannot reach the far, unfeeling sky
To voice my anguish full.
      But boy, I try.

Marjorie Kinnan Rawlings

"Lament of a Siamese Cat," *Dumpling Magazine* 9, no. 5 (4 September 1949): 8. MKR no doubt has in mind her beloved Siamese cat Uki, who became seriously ill at the end of the month but miraculously recovered (see *Private Marjorie*, 530–31, 549–50).

*   *   *   *   *   *   *   *   *

[An Address Given at the University of Florida Library Dedication]

I'm both grateful and comforted that the University of Florida Library is going to accept as part of this new collection my manuscript materials. I feel that I have found a useful home for my illegitimate children, to use a euphemism. And, of course, it is very important that all serious Florida writers contribute manuscript materials of all sorts to this collection, because there must be a mass of it to be of use.

And letters, particularly those of more than casual interest, I think, should be a very important part of the collection. Because anyone who has done research of any sort knows the treasure trove in coming across letters that picture the period and the personalities in a period far beyond the publications of the day, I think.

And the special interest of the so-called "original manuscripts" is, of course, that there the student of writing can come pretty close to seeing how it's done. I was at the Huntington Library in California,[109] all excited because I'd heard of the wonderful material they had. And I asked if they had an original manuscript of Keats or Shelley.

I thought if one could see a corrected manuscript of one of those poets one

---

109   The Huntington Library, San Marino, California.

would see where the felicitous phrase had either been a matter of inspiration or had been worked or slaved over. Unfortunately, the Huntington didn't have it. But in any corrected manuscript you see where the writer's mind reaches out toward the better word, the better idea.

There is no other special value as I see it to so-called original manuscripts. If there were at one book sale a copy of the original manuscript without its author's final editing and corrections, and one fifty-nine-cent reprint of the author's finished book, the fifty-nine-cent reprint would be infinitely more valuable than the so-called original manuscript.

And I think I had my most serious lesson in, shall we say, literary values— whereby the only purpose of a book is to be read—from my friend Leonard in the Big Scrub. This is a favorite of Mr. Young's, and if it's a little rough, I'm going to blame Mr. Young.[110]

Leonard was the prototype of the principal character in my first book, *South Moon Under*. I lived in the Big Scrub for weeks at a time with Leonard and his mother Miss Piety. They knew what I was doing, and Leonard would take me for perhaps miles down the Oklawaha River and introduce me to a friend or neighbor. And he would day, "Now here's Miss Marge here, and she's writin' a book about the old days and the old ways, and you tell her about that bear hunt."[111]

Then when the book was in proof, I took it to Leonard so he could go over part of it and catch any errors in the nature lore, because I was not too familiar with the Florida nature, the flora and fauna, at that time.

When the book was published, I drove for about fifty miles into the Scrub with the first copy that came from my publisher and inscribed it with gratitude to Leonard and his mother. The next time I went over to see them, the book wasn't in sight, and of course I was interested to know how the people of whom I had written, about whose lives I had written, thought about it when they read it in its final form.

So I said, "Leonard, I don't see the book. Have you loaned it to anyone?"

He said, "Yes, it's loaned out right now, but I'm mighty careful where I loaned it." He said, "Now my Aunt Eulie, she wanted to borrow it, but I was afraid she'd burned it."

I said, "But why would she do that?"

---

110   Stark Young (1881–1963), Mississippi novelist.

111   Perhaps a reference to Barney Dillard, who lived on the St. Johns River and who took MKR on bear hunts (see *Max and Marjorie*, 250).

He said, "Well, you know you got a right smart cussin' in the book" (which I had gotten straight with Leonard), and, he said, "Aunt Eulie, she's one of them Christian-hearted sons-a-bitches, and peculiar as hell to boot."

"And," he said, "now, you know her boy Lester, she'd be feared Lester would learn to cuss from that book. Now Lester can out-cuss the book right now, but his momma don't know it."

Well, just a few years ago Leonard came to visit me at Cross Creek and I had guests from New York. So I told the story on him in his presence. And I said, "Do you still have that book, Leonard?"

He said, "Yes. But," he said, "I'll have to tell you. I loaned it to Uncle Enoch and he hid it out in the bushes. And there came a little sprinkle of rain on it, and that book now looks like pure hell."

And I said, "Well, would you like a fresh copy?"

And he said, "I sure would, if it don't disfurnish you none."[112]

I assured him that it wouldn't, and I handed him a fresh copy. And in the years that have passed, I have written several more books, and, what with having come to the University of Florida at one time or another, have been asked for autographs very often. So I thought I'd be very gracious, and I said to Leonard, "Would you like me to autograph it? to write in it for you?"

Leonard said, "Hell, no, Miss Marge. That don't benefit nobody."

[Unsigned]

"[An Address Given at the University of Florida Library Dedication]." This address was delivered on 30 March 1950 at the dedication of a new addition to the University of Florida library. MKR left most of her papers to the library in 1950 and later added to the bequest with other invaluable materials. The address was published posthumously: *An Address Delivered by Marjorie Kinnan Rawlings at the Dedication of a New Addition to the University of Florida Library March 30, 1950. Published in Honor of Senator George A. Smathers*, ed. Carmen Russell Hurff (Gainesville: University of Florida Libraries, 1991), 5–7.

---

112   MKR recounts the episode of the loaning of *South Moon Under* to Leonard Fiddia in a letter to Maxwell Perkins, adding Fiddia's exclamation, "You done a damn good job, for a Yankee" (*Max and Marjorie*, 103). MKR's inscription in the "fresh copy" of *South Moon Under* reads: "For my friends the Fiddias—with deep thanks for their assistance in gathering and preparing the material for this book. Affectionately, Marjorie Kinnan Rawlings."

Portrait of a Magnificent Editor
As Seen in His Letters

Toward the end of his life, Maxwell Evarts Perkins, head editor for twenty of his thirty-seven years with the house of Scribner, wrote a carping correspondent, "Editors aren't much, and can't be." In these nearly two hundred letters, 1914–1947, he totally disproves this statement.

He continued, "They (editors) can only help a writer realize himself, and they can ruin him if he is pliable, as Tom (Thomas Wolfe) was not. And that is why editors I know shrink from tampering with a manuscript and do it only when it is required of them by the author, as it was by Tom. When an editor gets to think differently from that, to think he knows more about a writer's book than the writer—and some do—he is dead, done for, and dangerous. When he thinks he is a discoverer because he doesn't fail to recognize talent—was a jeweler ever praised because he knew a diamond from a lump of glass?—he is a stuffed shirt, and through. But I've known it to happen."

In the case of Maxwell Perkins himself, it seems undeniable that no editor has ever so influenced and "helped to realize themselves" so impressive a number of writers. The long list includes such names as John Galsworthy, F. Scott Fitzgerald, Ring Lardner, James Boyd, Marcia Davenport, Taylor Caldwell, Thomas Wolfe and Ernest Hemingway.[113] Of his association, intimate and personal, with Hemingway, however, he wrote, "Nobody ever edited Hemingway, beyond excising a line or two for fear of libel or other legal dangers."

Perhaps the most intriguing, even the most valuable, of the "letters" are those to Thomas Wolfe. A unique and magnificent editor is here dealing with a distraught genius. Although most of Perkins' work with Wolfe was done in person, there are enough letters in this volume to give the complete story of the self-realization to which the great editor helped the great writer. There is here, too, the nearly full picture of the one-sided quarrel that shook the publishing world, and of its tender resolution.

Several of us who had the privilege of his counsel have asked one another, "What was it that he gave us?" We agreed that his special gift was his ability, as creative as that of the author himself, to enter into the mind of the individual writer, to understand what that writer was attempting to do and to say, to direct

---

113   Ring Lardner (1885–1933), sports and short story writer; James Boyd (1888–1944), historical novelist; Marcia Davenport (1903–96), novelist, biographer, and MKR's good friend; Taylor Caldwell (1900–1985), novelist.

all criticism and all help toward the writer's own best expression, whether Max himself agreed or not. And again and again in the "letters" we find:

To Ernest Hemingway: "I do not want to put anything so emphatically that it will embarrass you to over-rule me if you must."

To Scott Fitzgerald: "Do not ever defer to my judgment."

To this reviewer: "When I write in that do-as-it-seems-right-to-you way, it is because it has always been my conviction—and I do not see how anyone could dispute the rightness of it—that a book must be done according to the writer's conception of it, as nearly perfectly as possible, and that the publishing problems begin then."

Maxwell Perkins was a Yankee, of aristocratic descent, shy, modest, conservative except when such challenges came to him as the writing of Hemingway, Wolfe and Fitzgerald. He understood nevertheless the violent, and to him, with his balanced approach, unreasonable exuberance of the writer and of the "progressive" worker. To the same fanatical critic he wrote, "I stand with Erasmus, and you with Luther.[114] It seems to me that the issue joined by them typifies the tragedy of man . . . [MKR's ellipsis]. Erasmus loved the good as much, or more, than Luther did, but he believed the good could not be accomplished by violence—by charging like a mad bull . . . [MKR's ellipsis]. Any man admires Luther, and sympathizes with him, because emotions are stronger in all of us than reason." And later writes of his argument, to Dexter Wecter, "A weakness in it is, of course, that, as I have come to believe, no progress would be made, perhaps, without the impetuous ones."[115]

For all his strain of Puritanism, his personal reserve, he could write with fire in defense of the right of John Stanley Pennell and of Hemingway to use obscene words. "But if they belong, if they are the words that would actually be used in the circumstances of the book, then artistically they should be used, and an author feels as if he were playing false in evading them."[116]

---

114 Desiderius Erasmus (1466?–1536), Dutch humanist who disagreed with Martin Luther (1483–1546), German leader of the Protestant Reformation, on church reform; Erasmus later denounced Luther's position on predestination. Perkins's now famous statement, "I stand with Erasmus, and you with Luther," made to an unnamed correspondent, occurs in a letter of 25 May 1944 (*Editor to Author*, 242).

115 Dixon Wecter (1906–50), American social historian, was the literary executor of the Mark Twain Estate. In the letter to Wecter, 4 December 1940, Perkins also wrote, "Erasmus did represent the man of cool intelligence, and Luther the impetuous and intense one" (*Editor to Author*, 182).

116 Joseph Stanley Pennell (1908–63), whose *The History of Rome Hanks* (New York: Scribners, 1944) caused a unnamed correspondent to complain to Perkins about its "dirty" language.

Perkins' humor was unexpected and dry. "D— had the time of his life. We started for home about 11:30, when Chapin proposed that we visit a certain night-club where he said he knew the girls.[117] I felt I must go along in line of duty, but I never would have if I had supposed we would stay in an underground, airless place until four in the morning... [MKR's ellipsis]. Chapin did know the girls, but there was not much to boast of in that they were very easy to know."

The last letter in the volume, written shortly before his death, sums up his integrity, as well as his passion for free, creative expression.

"While we are, therefore, wholly in favor of the intentions of your league, (The Anti-Defamation League) it does not seem to us as publishers that it would be proper for us to edit a classic ("The Arabian Nights") of some centuries' standing.[118] Only the author would have the right to do that, it seems to us, and if we did it, we should in some degree betray an obligation of our profession." "Nowadays, publishers are under pressure from all sorts of groups. What if they should trim their books to suit every point of view and every element of religious and racial pride? What, then would remain of that one relatively free realm left, the republic of letters?"

Entirely aside from the value of Perkins as an editor, as friend and comforter of authors, there emerges the portrait of a man and a thinker. Only time can determine whether the "Letters" will take their place in Belles Lettres for their literary quality and their revelation of an individual. It is likely that the name of Maxwell E. Perkins will outlive many of the authors to whom he addressed himself so generously. It is certain that the Perkins' "Letters" will become required reading for other editors and troubled creative writers anywhere, and for, as he put it, "Those useless courses in composition which they give—which were better abolished." He cannot but help them all, as he helped three generations of Scribner authors, infinitely more than he would ever have admitted.

In a letter of 13 November 1944, Perkins responded that it was not the duty or right of a publisher to alter an author's language (*Editor to Author*, 155–57). Hemingway's use of obscenities and Perkins's attempts either to stem them or to apologize for them are now part of Scribners lore.

117   Joseph H. Chapin (1869–1939), once the head of the Scribner art department. This bar-hopping episode is reported to Roger Burlingame (1889–1967), historian and biographer, in a letter of 20 June 1928 (*Editor to Author*, 56–57).

118   The Anti-Defamation League, founded in 1913 to combat anti-Semitism. The objection to the tale of Aladdin in *The Arabian Nights [The Thousand and One Nights]* and Perkins's rejection of such censorship appear in a letter to an unnamed correspondent, 4 June 1947 (*Editor to Author*, 303).

John Hall Wheelock,[119] his long associate, has written a most sensitive and revealing introduction. From the thousands of Perkins letters in the Scribner files he has selected those which best present a unity of editorial and personal philosophy. Wheelock has edited them with restraint, never impinging his own ideas and personality; the rare but proper way, Max Perkins would have said, for an editor to follow.

Marjorie Kinnan Rawlings

"Portrait of a Magnificent Editor As Seen in His Letters," *Publishers' Weekly* 157, no. 13 (April 1950): 1573–74. This is a review of *Editor to Author: The Letters of Maxwell E. Perkins*, ed. John Hall Wheelock (New York: Scribners, 1950).

*　　*　　*　　*　　*　　*　　*　　*　　*

Dubious Praise in Dubious Battle

or

"Who Said That—And Why?"

"A garden is a lovesome thing, God wot"
Which, if not wot-ched, goes woefully to pot.
So, lest the spotted, panting plants should die,
I water wildly while the weather's dry.

A garden is a beauteous bwitch [*sic*], God knows.
Each pampered pansy, ruddy-cheeky rose,
Opens her hoarish heart, predaceous prey
To every insect, which I then must spray.

The blasted blossoms bloom 'neath pouring flood,
So I must clip my crop in clinging mud,

119　John Hall Wheelock (1886–1978), poet and editor at Scribners (see Matthew Bruccoli's edition of Wheelock's oral autobiography, *The Last Romantic: A Poet among Publishers* [Columbia: University of South Carolina Press, 2002]).

All summer, cash, and potty patience spent.
My garden came. At last, thank God, it went.

Marjorie Kinnan Rawlings

"Dubious Praise in Dubious Battle," *Dumpling Magazine* 11, no. 8 (1 September 1950): 7.

*   *   *   *   *   *   *   *   *

I Remember Christmas

I knew it was to be a miracle Christmas, for I heard the reindeer. I roused drowsily and out of my window I saw a shadow pass across the snow in the bright moonlight. The next instant I heard the sleigh and reindeer rest lightly on our roof. The sharp hooves, the runners, scraped unmistakably. It could not possibly be only the squirrels who sometimes found a way from the bare oak tree tops into our attic—not when you were a little girl of seven and believed with all your heart in Santa Claus.

Somehow it was morning in a moment, and the long, black, ribbed cotton stocking hung bulging at the foot of the bed. It held the always exciting barley candy animals, red and yellow, a box of colored crayons, the usual orange in the heel, Brazil nuts in the toe, all most acceptable. The special gift that would stand alone, like the star at the top of the Christmas tree, was not here.

There was the race to see who of the family could first cry out, "Merry Christmas," and Father said grace over the breakfast that must be eaten before going to the tree, else it would never be eaten at all. The sliding doors into the parlor were opened. And the tree shone with its glory of tinsel and sparkling balls, the birds with spun-glass tail, and all the candles mysteriously lighted. The important gifts were piled around the base, most of them recognizable through their wrappings—the doll, the books, the toddling brother's drum. And to one side an old gray hat box tied with ribbon, the cover a trifle ajar, and I knew.

They had come and gone for five of my seven years, the neighbors' dogs enticed home and having to be taken back again with sobs and lamentations; above all the stray cats, an army of them, vagrants who stayed a day or two to regain strength on my hoarded meat and milk, then went away into the void from which they had come, and even the going of the fierce yellow tomcat with ragged ears who had all but scratched out my eye when I hugged him too tightly, had left me desolate. There had been five years of heartbreak, of that strange, passionate yearning of many children to possess an animal.

I untied the ribbon and lifted the lid of the hatbox. A small gray kitten lifted blue eyes to me trustingly. I took it in my arms and laid my cheek against its soft fur. It gave a little cry of recognition, for we belonged at once, and began to purr. It was my own. This was the miracle gift that fed a child's heart-hunger—a gift of life, of love.

Marjorie Kinnan Rawlings

"I Remember Christmas," *Better Living* 2, no. 2 (December 1952): 23, 40.

*   *   *   *   *   *   *   *   *

The Man and the Place

Last summer I sat alone with Robert Frost in his cabin work-room in Vermont.[120] He talked of writing.

"It has to have roundness," he said. "There's a big roundness and a little roundness, but if it comes out round, it's all right."

Cryptic or no, I thought I knew what he meant. And it occurred to me that this may apply as well to human character.

St. Augustine said, "Men should serve the understanding of things."[121]

And Alcuin, the scholar and theologian of the eighth century wrote, "There is in men a royal mind."[122]

Once in a great while—only a handful of each generation—we find a man who combines these qualities. He has roundness. He serves the understanding of things. He has a royal mind. Such a man is complete and great. Of those I have been privileged to know, Owen D. Young is indubitably the greatest.

---

120   Frost and MKR became close friends during her Van Hornesville years. She visited him and he her. It is interesting that MKR in this tribute would associate Frost and Young, since Frost for many years resented Young because he once dated Frost's future wife, Elinor White (1872–1938), while both were at St. Lawrence University (see *Private Marjorie*, 575–77).

121   Augustine of Hippo (354–430), sainted and named Doctor of the Roman Catholic Church in 1303, author of the enormously influential *Confessions* (c. 400) and *City of God* (after 412), which have exerted enormous influence on Western theology and epistemology. In addition, his exploration of the "understanding of things" has had an immense impact on the Western approach to semiotics.

122   Alcuin of York (735?–804), monk who became the main ecclesiastical and educational advisor to Charlemagne (742–814); as such, he was largely responsible for creating medieval curricula, and he wrote often of the importance and method of educating the "royal mind."

That same Alcuin also wrote, "If place could help, never had angels fallen from Heaven, nor man sinned in Paradise."

I dare to disagree with the renowned abbot. I wrote in *Cross Creek*, "There is an affinity between men and places." I believe that place can help.

When Owen D. Young went from his father's farm some sixty years ago, young and brilliant, to St. Lawrence University, he must have met that affinity. No University could have harmed him, not even Yale or Harvard or Princeton. But this small liberal arts college must surely have helped his mind and spirit. It has maintained its tradition of roundness; of serving the understanding of things; of feeding and nourishing the royal mind in men.

Marjorie Kinnan Rawlings[123]

"The Man and the Place," *Dumpling Magazine* 12, no. 2 (5 July 1953): 10–11.

*   *   *   *   *   *   *   *   *

A Word about Her Life and Her Work as a Novelist

I have lived in Florida since 1928. From my first moment here, I have felt more at home than since my childhood days on my father's farm in Maryland.[124]

For thirteen years, I lived alone in a rambling farmhouse on my orange grove at Cross Creek. I have done most of my writing on the screened veranda, from which I could watch the comings and goings of the birds to the feed basket in the crepe myrtle bush, and to the bird bath.

There are always assorted animals on the place; my bird-dog, or pointer, and old Martha's "varmint dog" to drive away or catch the skunks and 'possums that slip in at night after the chickens and eggs;[125] my pet house-cat and Martha's sturdier rat-catchers; chickens; a flock of Mallard ducks raised long ago from

---

123   After MKR's signature is the following: "Notes from a brief talk at Canton, June 7, 1953"; Canton, New York, is the home of St. Lawrence University, from which MKR earned an Honorary Litt.D.

124   Arthur Kinnan Sr.'s dairy farm; see the headnote to "Sad Story of Little Pip" in this volume.

125   At this point, Moe was in residence as MKR's beloved pointer. Martha Mickens, the matriarch of Cross Creek.

wild eggs from the Carolina marshes, but now so tame that they eat from the hand and could not be induced to fly away; and one or two milch cows.

GOLDEN APPLES, while entirely fictional, is laid on the site of my own grove, in the fertile north-central "hammock" country. CROSS CREEK is the story of my own life there, in its relation to Nature and to the other residents of the tiny community.

SOUTH MOON UNDER and THE YEARLING are laid in the Big Scrub, a strange section bounded by the Ocklawaha and the St. John's rivers. I have lived off and on in the scrub, where the few remaining inhabitants have been glad to pass on their memories of the old days and fast-vanishing way of life that characterizes the Florida Cracker, or backwoodsman.

I consider THE YEARLING the most unified of my books, as to theme and technique. It was in mind for many years, and could just as well have been laid in any other remote section of the Big Scrub. I began making notes for it at the same time I wrote SOUTH MOON UNDER. I gathered material for five years. The actual writing took about two years.

The boy "Jody" is entirely imaginary, except that I might say that he was born of the memories of old men. As two old hunter friends told me their tales,[126] I visualized a boy who might have lived that simple, yet difficult, life in the scrub country.

Penny Baxter is my favorite character. He comes closer to expressing my own philosophy of life than any other character I have worked with. I meant to be much harsher with Ma Baxter, because I disliked her; or, more exactly, I disliked her type of nagging woman. But it swept over me, when she was being disagreeable about the death of Fodder-wing, how much such a woman has to endure. In spite of myself, I softened, and could never again, in the course of the story, be too severe with her. As I said in GOLDEN APPLES, it is impossible to hate what one understands.

In 1943 I began work on THE SOJOURNER. The basic idea of a sensitive man, such as Ase Linden, mute and puzzled, had been in the back of my mind for many years. I made half a dozen beginnings, one almost a third of book-length, and destroyed them as totally unsatisfactory. The war was too disturbing for work, for one thing. For another, the book had a Northern setting, somehow necessary for this peculiar man's relation to Nature, and I had been away from the North a long time. I felt the need of following again its seasons, the richness

---

126   Cal Long, who suggested the story of Flag, the pet deer, and Barney Dillard, who took MKR on bear hunts.

of a Northern autumn, the bird migrations in reverse, of living with deciduous trees, of seeing once more the ice and snow.

In 1947 my friends Mr. and Mrs. Owen D. Young loaned me a cottage near Van Hornesville, N. Y.,[127] to make a fresh start on the book. I fall easily in love with a new countryside, and this time I was fatally stricken. Whether or not there be such a thing as racial memory, I had returned to the land of my fathers, and my very bones responded. My earliest ancestors in America, on both sides of my family, were Hollanders who settled not far from here in the middle 1600's. Again, I had come home.

I bought an irresistible small house, long untenanted, "the Root house," on Pumpkin Hook Road halfway up Mt. Tom. Many of the hand-blown glass window panes had been shot through by vandal hunters, so that the house looked sightless, and the shutters sagged, and the yard and ancient garden were a mass of rank weeds, thistles and burdocks, with only a great clump of old-fashioned rose peonies to show the place had once been cared for. But the style was Greek revival, with charming pillars, the house was sound and solid, the butternut paneling and the wide-boarded chestnut floors made from trees cut on the place. Local artisans restored it lovingly, and beside the date of building found scratched in the stone of the deep cellar, 1848, they cut a 1948, knowing the Root house was now good for another hundred years. I worked on THE SOJOURNER there of long summers, sometimes into mid-December, and at Cross Creek of winters.

For answers to many technical questions let me refer you to an article of mine, "Writing as a Career," in the 1948 Annual of the Book of Knowledge available at most libraries.[128]

Marjorie Kinnan Rawlings

"A Word about Her Life and Her Work as a Novelist." This is a typescript on the "News of Scribner Books and Authors" stationery. It seems from the context to have been written after the publication of *The Sojourner* in January 1953. Following this autobiographical sketch, there is a brief biographical sketch, more than likely written by another individual.

---

127   "Brown's Hollow," which MKR describes to Bernice Gilkyson, 9 July 1947, as "deep in the woods above a rushing trout stream, old, furnished with antiques, but with modern conveniences" (*Selected Letters*, 300).

128   See "If You Want to Be a Writer," in this volume.

Marjorie Rawlings Tells Story of Her Long Struggle to Write

Lean Early Years Led to Novels

I was born in Washington, D.C. My father was principal examiner in the Patent Office but he lived the true life of his mind and heart on his Maryland farm, 10 miles away on Rock Creek. From him I learned my love of nature. Summers on the farm and visits to the Michigan farm of my mother's father planted deep in me a love of the soil, the crops, the seasons and a sense of kinship with men and women everywhere who live close to the soil.

New York Alone

It was 15 years after my father's death in 1913 before circumstances took me back to the land, 15 years of urban life not to my taste. From college at the University of Wisconsin I assailed New York City alone, certain of my future as a writer, armed with a briefcase of manuscripts and a new purse containing $60, which must last until I got a job. Some depressingly discerning thief stole my purse and ignored the briefcase.

I had three letters of introduction from one of my college professors. One had been to the old magazine, The New Republic. I walked from Upper New York down to their offices. Here Signe Toksvig, then the bride of Francis Hackett,[129] dried my tears and lent me $20.

I said, "But I'm a stranger to you. Suppose I don't pay it back?"

She said, "If you can't it won't matter. Someday you'll have a chance to give a lift to some other young writer."

Takes Wartime Job

I have not seen her since the day I was able to repay the money but I often think of her if I am inclined to feel impatient with young writers who ask for various kinds of help, usually the answer to some unanswerable questions as to "how to write" and "how to sell," and I try to give them my best. I now have an article, "Writing as a Career," in the 1948 Annual of the Book of Knowledge[130] and

---

129   Signe Toksvig (1891–1983), novelist and biographer; Francis Hackett (1883–1962), historian, biographer, and historical novelist.

130   See "If You Want to Be a Writer," in this volume.

I refer the young questioners to this, unless they present some personal problems as well.

The $20 was gone when a college friend got me a job as a writer and editor on the War Work Council of the YWCA national headquarters. The first World War ended and with it the job. Free-lancing tided me over for another year, including three Boy Scout manuals. I was married to my college fiancé, Charles Rawlings, and there were moves to Louisville, where I did some feature writing for the Courier Journal, and to Rochester, N.Y., where I had a job as a feature writer on the Journal-American.

I learned more on the newspaper job than in all my "composition" classes. There was no place here for the purple prose to which all young writers are addicted. The story must be told with no waste of words, and the superfluous adjectives and adverbs fell like dead leaves by the wayside. My features were based on local happenings, often tragic, and to have the sometimes stricken subjects tell me their stories, I found that I must forget myself and enter with sympathy into their own lives. This necessary objectivity was priceless training for a self-absorbed young writer. The sympathy and understanding of others that began as part of my job, turned into genuine concern with and for other human beings.

All the while I was writing short stories, all of them promptly rejected.[131] I was 32 years old and I began to despair. Perhaps I couldn't write, after all.

Buys Orange Grove

In 1928 my husband and I moved to Florida, where my purchase of a small orange grove and shabby farmhouse at Cross Creek represented my inherited share of my father's Maryland farm. This was not the Gold coast of Florida, with its wealthy Northerners and idling tourists. It was a primitive section off the beaten path, where men hunted and fished and worked small groves and farms for a meager living, where the lean, sun-browned women did their washing outdoors in iron kettles over smoky pine fires; men and women who spoke with a refreshing and vivid dialect that was Chaucerian, Shakespearean, and that went back to their English and Scottish ancestry, to the more immediate Appalachian highlands and the hills of Georgia and Alabama from which they had drifted south. And the country was beautiful, with its mysterious swamps, its palms, its great live oaks, dripping gray Spanish moss, its deer and bear and raccoons and panthers and reptiles.

I was on the land again. I was poor and a little frightened, but I was once more at home. I decided never again to try to write stories with one eye on possible

---

131   MKR apparently has forgotten "His Little Cabbagehead," a story published in *Young's Magazine* and appearing in this volume.

sale and publication. I must write of this land and these people as I saw them, stirred by my new love. I should write in what would surely be an unpopular style, but that could not be helped. With any encouragement, I should go on. Without it, I should forget writing altogether, except for secret poetry, which I have always written to ease my own need for expression.

Boiling With Stories

I submitted my first piece, little sketches called "Cracker Chidlings," to the old Scribner's magazine, which had given me my only encouragement in once "almost taking" a story based on newspaper life. I enclosed a timid note, asking if the material and my way of handling it had any value at all. The sketches were accepted, and Maxwell Perkins began his 20 years as editor and friend by asking: "Have you any thought of doing any actual short stories laid in that locale and about those wonderful people?" Needless to say, I was not only boiling with such stories, but was already at work.

With the first story, "Jacob's Ladder," accepted by Scribner's, Mr. Perkins wrote: "Have you ever thought of writing a novel laid in that locale and about those wonderful people?" My first novel, "South Moon Under," was already begun.

The years passed at Cross Creek. My husband, a newspaper man, and I were amicably divorced in 1933. I was alone at the Creek. There were bad years for the grove, years of freezes and low prices. The money from the few short stories did not quite cover expenses. I was down one day to a box of crackers and a can of tomato soup.

I hung my washing on the clothesline and stamped my foot and said aloud: "Things will have to get tougher than this to run me away from the Creek!" The rural mail carrier stopped at my box and in the mail was a check for $500, the O. Henry first prize for a long story, "Gal Young Un." The $500 saw me through the winter, until royalties began coming in from "South Moon Under." It never occurred to me that publishers were not in the habit of letting their authors starve and that I could have had an advance.

In the fall of 1941 I was married to an old friend, Norton Baskin, a hotel man, now a restaurateur at Marineland.[132] He lived in puzzled patience while I abandoned him for six summers to write "The Sojourner."

Because the book is necessarily laid in a northern setting, and because I must feel close to the background of any book I write, I bought in 1947 a little abandoned farmhouse in the Classic Greek Revival style. It is near Van Hornesville,

---

132   Marineland, south of St. Augustine, opened in June 1938 as the world's first oceanarium. Baskin took over the management of the Marineland restaurants in March 1946.

N.Y., to which I was introduced by my friends Owen D. Young and his wife, who knew of my need to renew my northern knowledge. I have lived again through the seasons, sometimes late into December, through snow and ice storms and howling northern winds. Cross Creek is still "home," but it has become a race between me and the robins in our mutual yearning to return. To quote Edwin Way Teale, "North With the Spring."[133]

'Sojourner' Developed Slowly

I wrote "The Sojourner" because I was haunted by a grandfather I had not known. I was never to know him, and I was obliged to create another man and another life, that may or may not have resembled his own, but which I came to know as well as I know myself.

The book developed slowly. It is Ase Linden's book, but his wife Nellie kept threatening to take it over. I began as I did with Ma Baxter in "The Yearling," with an almost total lack of sympathy for her. Nellie did not appreciate Ase, nor truly love him. Her standards were materialistic. She kept saying extremely vulgar things that I was obliged to delete. I had to give up and let her be herself, a much nicer and kinder little soul than I had intended, "a good wife," after all, as Ase himself said of her in the end.

Answer Comes at Last

Something of the same sort happened to Benjamin, the lost brother. He seemed cruel in his abandonment of Ase; he was apparently heartless toward their mother Amelia. I meant Ase's lifelong devotion to him to be unwarranted, a sign only of his capacity for love, but I found, almost with surprise, as Ben lay dying, that he had valid reasons, and that he was worthy. I remember exclaiming aloud, "Ase was right about him all the time."

Although I knew from the first approximately how the book must end, I could not see how Ase Linden might possibly triumph over the trespasses against him, how he might manage to speak at last. As he met with one betrayal after another, as he failed in his inarticulacy to speak for the good and against the evil, knowing himself that he was failing, I had a sense of hopeless plodding, for myself and for him. Through the latter-middle part of the book I could scarcely put one word after another, as though my feet sank in the terrible bog on the Linden farm. The answer came only toward the end of the final rewriting of the

---

133   Edwin Way Teale (1899–1980), *North with the Spring* (New York: Dodd, Mead, 1951), a travel narrative in which Teale drives north from the Everglades literally to follow spring up the east coast.

book. By this time I was so identified with Ase that I felt the same soaring release that came to him. I realize now that subconsciously this was what I had always intended.

*   *   *   *   *   *   *   *   *

Author Tells of Life in 'Yearling' Land, Birth of 'The Sojourner'

Exact Topography Needed; Book Completed

Abed after Heart Attack

An almost exact topography is necessary for me for background. I begin with a true location, then build or move houses, change hills and streams and fields, to suit my purposes. For "The Yearling" and "The Sojourner" I drew maps for my guidance, indicating the compass points as most important, for the north and the south, the east and the west, having an ineffable effect on men; then the layout of the farm buildings, the dwelling, the fields, the woods. The casual reader might never notice that a man walked north to his barn, where at another point he walked south, but I could not accept such a discrepancy.

Once the background is specific for me, I can write in almost any isolated setting. For instance, I began "The Yearling" in a remote cabin in the North Carolina mountains. I had been away from the North for so long that I needed to live there again for most of the writing of "The Sojourner." I revisited my grandfather's farm in Southern Michigan (no longer in the family) and used its general topography.[134]

Began Writing 'Sojourner'

I visited a beloved aunt, who re-created much of the Michigan farm life for me, who answered my questions as to which crops were planted first in that latitude, who turned over to me the old farm records and letters that spoke of crops and seasons. I lived from six to eight months a year for the last six years in Central New York State, co-ordinating this section's crops and seasons and farm

---

134   Blowing Rock, in the North Carolina mountains, about seventy-five miles northeast of Asheville. The Michigan farm of MKR's maternal grandparents was just west of Holly, which is about seventeen miles south of Flint.

timing with the Michigan one. Yet during the winters I was able to continue the writing in the Florida subtropics at Cross Creek, for I was still living imaginatively in the North.

I began the actual writing of "The Sojourner" in 1943, soon after my husband, Norton Baskin, went overseas to serve in the American Field Service as an ambulance driver in India and Burma. I stayed through most of the war at our beach cottage on a high dune above the Atlantic Ocean near St. Augustine. I was alone, and housekeeping there was simpler than in the sprawling farmhouse at Cross Creek. The "perfect maid" of whom I bragged in my book, "Cross Creek," had chosen that moment to leave me without notice.[135] My faithful bird dog Moe was stolen that same week, just as my husband announced that he had been accepted by the Field Service.

Half-Dozen Beginnings

I mourned: "In one fell swoop I've lost a good dog, a good maid, and a good husband."

Baskin said sadly, "Named no doubt in the order of their importance."

I stayed.

I made half a dozen beginnings on "The Sojourner." None was right. I had not yet discovered that I must renew my northern contacts. The horror of the war made creative writing difficult. I walked on the lonely beach by day, skirting the ominous oil from the ships torpedoed off the coast, the burned debris, the empty sailors' trousers. After sunset the beach was forbidden, the blackout was vital, the Coast Guard patrolled all night long. The world of Ase Linden was very far away.

Daily letters to my husband and correspondence with men in the service absorbed me. The dog Moe made his way home on foot, emaciated and bleeding. My husband returned in 18 months, skin and bones from tropical illnesses. The "perfect maid" reappeared some three years later, vowing undying fidelity "this time," only to disappear, again without notice when I had reached the crucial point on "The Sojourner" and when I was exhausted and needed her quiet care.

In February, 1953, with only two more weeks of work to be done on the book, a heart attack caught me alone at Cross Creek. Three months of convalescence were ordered after three weeks in the hospital but the ending of the book was so clear in my mind and so insistent that rest was impossible and I finished the book in bed.

---

135   MKR's cottage, now privately owned, is in Crescent Beach, Florida. MKR's "perfect maid" is, of course, Idella Parker.

Intimate Anguish Gone

I was reluctant to turn over even my rewritten manuscript to my publishers. I was not satisfied with it. I felt that I should put it away for still another year, for perspective, then try to make a better job of it. But when Scribner's read and approved it seemed too late, as though a child had been born. Whatever its imperfections, it must now begin its life in the world.

Once a book is actually published, it seems as though I had had almost nothing to do with its writing. The intimate anguish of composition is forgotten. I look at it objectively, pleased with a good sentence, annoyed by a bad one. Many of the characters, I find then, have taken on a life of their own. They are completely real to me. They are no longer "characters" whom I created, but people whom I know. I should recognize Ma and Penny Baxter and Jody, of "The Yearling," if I saw them in the Florida scrub. I should recognize Ase Linden of "The Sojourner" if I saw him in a wheat field. I should know his wife Nellie, his mother Amelia, his strange Indian and gypsy friends, his children, anywhere. Sometimes a character remains "a character," and shadowy, and then I realize with embarrassment that here I have failed.

A book-club selection is rather frightening. How many tens of thousands of people will now decide whether one's book is good or bad!

Writes Voluminous Notes

MGM did a fine job of filming "The Yearling." However, only the superb and sensitive acting of Gregory Peck and Jane Wyman made them acceptable to me as Penny and Ma Baxter,[136] for Penny was a little runty man and Ma was as big as a barn. Now, the physique of Gregory Peck is that of Ase Linden in "The Sojourner," his face would reveal Ase's lonely brooding, his mute love for his pretty little wife Nellie and his daughter Doll[,] and it seems to me that if filmed the movies really owe me a Gregory Peck for "The Sojourner" in a role that would fit him like a glove.

I make voluminous notes always. Some are random, in the nature of unrelated ideas and phrases. I keep no actual notebooks for these, but jot them down on the backs of envelopes, sometimes along with a grocery list, so that after "butter - dogfood - lettuce - soap, etc." I find weeks later, in cleaning out my purse, at the bottom of the list such notes as "When a man is sleeping, is he asleep or dead?

---

136   Gregory Peck (1916–2003) and Jane Wyman (1914–) received Academy Award nominations for best actor and actress for their work in *The Yearling*. The winners that year, however, were MKR's old college friend Frederic March, for *The Best Years of Our Lives*, and Olivia de Havilland (1916–), for *To Each His Own*.

Only another, watching his breathing, can say, 'The man is not dead, but only sleeping.'"

Sometimes wakeful in the night, ideas, phrases, sentences, come to me, and I scramble for paper and pencil to put them down for otherwise they are usually gone.

Lived in Scrub Land

When working on a long book, I make some purposeful notes. Some are derived from research, if that research is only talk with people who have help to give me, about nature aspects, old tales relevant to my story, or actual specific information of one sort or another.

After the conception of "The Yearling" was clear in my mind, I lived for weeks at a time in the Florida scrub country, with two old-timers who took me hunting, fishing and prowling, as they and their ancestors had done. The sons and daughters of one of these old hunters were frankly mistrustful of me.[137] For all they knew, I was about to tell a scandalous tale of their father's life, while reaping millions of dollars in profit. The elder son overheard my question to his mother. I was asking about the old herb remedies that were used almost 90 years ago in that lonely scrub.

He said: "Miss Marge, I had no idea that was the kind of thing you want to know about. Excuse me a minute."

Fiction Predominates

He returned with a hunting horn he had carved himself, and said: "This'll do you good the next time you go deer hunting with pa."

My research on "The Sojourner" was simpler. My aunt had preserved old family documents, so I knew that it was of the period for Ase Linden to have his father's "gold hunter's watch," and so forth. My aunt turned over to me records of crops and their prices so that I knew the dates when farmers in the general belt across Central New York and Southern Michigan were prosperous or impoverished.

There were records in the books in my grandfather's small library, and I was able to get a few of these.

Yet I used almost nothing of this material in "The Sojourner" for in the relation of fact to fiction, fiction must predominate, if the finished job is to be remotely artistic.

---

137   Cal Long and Barney Dillard; it was Dillard who had fifteen children, some of whom were suspicious of MKR's intentions (see Silverthorne, 118).

Mrs. Rawlings Adapts Characters to Meet Novel's Creative Need

Delineations Are Based on People She Knows

I think that no writer has ever completely copied a true "character." He may begin with an actual living person, but his imagination takes him further to adapt the character to his own creative needs, so that the final characters, even though dozens of people claim to recognize him or her, is fiction.

Many of my own characters are "based" on people I know, but not a single one is a life copy. The closest I ever came to a true depiction is Uncle Benny in my story, "Uncle Benny and the Bird Dogs." Even here, the real man departs in many ways from the fictional one.[138]

None of my novels has satisfied me. "The Yearling" is perhaps the most co-ordinated of my books. Its theme is direct and simple. I am reasonably satisfied with three of my short stories: "The Parson," "The Shell," and "The Pelican's Shadow."[139] The short story form permits of a maintained subtlety and a certain roundness. Robert Frost said to me not long ago that a piece of creative work has to have roundness. He said, "There's big roundness and little roundness, but if it comes out round it's all right." I think that complete roundness, complete perfection in writing is possible only in a poem, and not too long a poem at that.

Dog Aroused Readers

I got myself into very hot water with a chapter, "The Catch Dog" in my book "Cross Creek."[140] My husband sulked for days after reading it, and finally blurted out, "You threw rocks at that poor dog." Ellen Glasgow wrote me in anguish about to take back her friendship. Readers swamped me with distressed or angry letters. To begin with, it wasn't rocks, it was gravel, and I had not actually thrown gravel nor anything else. What I had done was to let myself be carried away by making a good story from a minor incident, with the intent of having the heart break for the dog (whom in real life I had met only casually) and totally oblivious to the fact that in fictionalizing the truth, I was making a monster of myself.

---

138   The model for "Uncle Benny Mathers" was MKR's close Cracker friend Fred Tompkins.

139   "The Pardon" (*Short Stories*, 216–25), "The Shell" (*Short Stories*, 338–43), and "The Pelican's Shadow" (*Short Stories*, 290–97).

140   Actually a story from chapter 19 of *Cross Creek*, entitled "Summer," 294–97.

Penny Baxter of "The Yearling" is one of my own favorite characters. He was wise and tender, and he was a little man who was big against odds. I enjoy Quincey Dover in three of my stories: "Benny and the Bird Dogs," "Varmints," and "Cocks Must Crow."[141] She is a big, fat countrywoman who can take a joke on herself, and who has a tolerance and understanding of the male that I like to think of as my own. I am too close to Ase Linden of "The Sojourner" at the moment to know whether or not I shall continue to care for him. I rather think so, for there is perhaps more of every man's struggle in him than in any other of my characters.

Devoted to Forresters

I am devoted to the Forresters in "The Yearling." They are a shocking family, vulgar, brawling, fiddling, dancing, drinking before dawn, unclothed, uninhibited, "naked jay-birds," as Ma Forrester called them herself with a toddy in hand. Their uncomplicated zest for life is a relief from the more serious and worthy characters.

I hate only one character of whom I have written—Amelia Linden, Ase's Mother, in "The Sojourner." Because of her madness she cannot be held entirely responsible for her evil, but her very madness comes largely from mental self-indulgence. She is selfish, self-centered, without concern for others that alone redeems all egotistic humanity.

I hope to write more short stories in the near future and to rewrite half a dozen that have been tucked away for several years. A long novel calls for so much carpentry and brick laying, while a short story is conceived almost whole and is more amenable to being molded into Robert Frost's "roundness."

Avoids Petticoat Trails

Robert Frost's liking for my short story "Benny and the Bird Dogs" has pleased me as much as any reaction to my work. He corners people and reads it aloud to them. He insists "it's a man's kind of humor." This pleases me because I feel that no writer's accident of sex should obtrude on his work. I long not to be of the "lady-author" ilk who, as Dorothy Parker said of one of them, "trails her petticoats through literature."[142]

Perhaps the most astonishing applause that has come to me was when James

---

141   "Benny and the Bird Dogs" (*Short Stories*, 198–215), "Varmints" (*Short Stories*, 226–42), and "Cocks Must Crow" (*Short Stories*, 252–72).

142   Dorothy ("Dot") Parker (1893–1967), writer and poet known for her brilliantly sardonic wit.

Branch Cabell, master of the subtle delicacy of style and theme, scholar and sophisticate, wrote me about that great lusty Cracker woman, "For I am, to speak frankly, heels of head in love with Quincy Dover."

At the time "The Yearling" was being filmed, a woman approached me at a cocktail party. She had the appalling coyness of a former belle, southern, middle-aged. She lifted her Martini and said: "If I was just 10 years younger, honey, I'd be right out there in Hollywood this minute, playing 'Scarlett' in your book."

Such Is Writing Fame

I had just been awarded the Pulitzer Prize for "The Yearling," and, alas, am afraid that for a moment I was sure the world knew of it. I was introduced to a woman as "Marjorie Rawlings, the writer." "Indeed," she said with interest, "and have you published anything?"

At the time of my marriage to Norton Baskin, he owned a hotel in St. Augustine.[143] Most of the time I escaped to Cross Creek from the too-public life. A little mousy woman scuttled into the lobby of the hotel, approached my husband furtively and asked if she might have tea. Assured that she might, she went into the dining room and gave her order to a waitress. She scurried back into the lobby and asked, "Will I see Mrs. Rawlings?" Told that Mrs. Rawlings was away, she sighed and said, "Oh dear, then I won't have tea." Baskin said courteously and bravely, "I'm sorry madam, but Mrs. Rawlings comes only with the blue plate dinner."

True Story Touching

Many readers of "Cross Creek" were touched by the story of the old colored Martha. She received fan letters and gifts, among them an arm band from a naval unit, entitling her to the rank of "Navy cook first class. I was at the Creek after an absence, and as Martha and I stood "visiting" in the front yard a plane swooped low over the farm house then did a double barrel roll. Martha waved and smiled.

"That's a friend of mine, she say, 'Proud to know you. I flies over here 'bout twice a week. You watch for me, I'll do for stunts for you.'"

Her fine brown face shone.

"Here I is, Sugar," she said, "'way out of the world, but the world comes to us."

---

143 Norton, with financial backing from MKR, purchased the Castle Warden Hotel, near the Castillo de San Marcos in St. Augustine, in December 1941; he sold it in March 1946; the hotel is at present a "Ripley's Believe It or Not" museum.

MGM Films 'Yearling'

"The Yearling" was filmed by MGM. Most of the background and the animal and nature sequences were made in the Florida scrub, on the site that I had used for the book. The director, cast and crew offered me every courtesy, and I spent a day on the set, but it had been agreed beforehand, at my request, that I was to have nothing to do with the production.

A friend visited MGM in Culver City about two years after the filming of "The Yearling" and was surprised to come across hundreds of tin cans containing carefully tended stalks of corn. His question produced an investigation, and the fact that in producing part of the Florida sets in Hollywood it had been necessary to keep corn growing in the various stages, for shots of Jody and Penny Baxter in the cornfield. The order had been to raise corn and for two years no one had thought to countermand the order.

A story of mine, "Mountain Prelude," was serialized in the Saturday Evening Post.[144] MGM bought it for a movie with the understanding that I was to rewrite it, but still in fiction form, for making a script closer to Hollywood needs, especially for enlarging the dog's part for Lassie. I had no objections, for I could even see ways in which the story could be made more dramatic.

Wrote in Swank Misery

MGM ensconced me in a large and elegant suite in the Waldorf Towers, while Robert Sisk,[145] the producer, occupied modest quarters at the Astor, to be available at the end of every day for consultation. The lap of luxury is never to my taste and I wrote my husband in misery: I am trapped like a dog in the Waldorf Towers." I had no sooner made enough of an adaptation to the unsuitable elegance to settle down to work, than MGM headquarters in New York announced that I must move for the week end to a smaller suite on a lower floor as Deborah Kerr was due in on the Queen Elizabeth and must have the swank suite.[146] I protested the move violently, insisting that Lassie was just as valuable

---

144   In "Top Dog in Hollywood," Helen Colton wrote of Lassie's stature in the movie business: "Lassie is remarkable not only to MGM but to the whole film industry. Her photograph appears on the screen ahead of the titles of her films. A Pulitzer Prize novelist, Marjorie Kinnan Rawlings, has tailored a screen story, 'The Sun Comes Up,' to her talents. By beauty standards, Lassie's too fat (80 pounds), to [*sic*] tall (26 inches), her face is too wide and her upper jaw sticks out too far over her lower one, and yet she is loved for her looks" (*New York Times*, 27 February 1949). MKR never forgave MGM for their treatment of "Mountain Prelude."

145   Robert F. Sisk, MGM producer of *The Sun Comes Up* and other "Lassie" movies.

146   Deborah Kerr (1921–), Scottish film actress, received an academy award nomination as best actress for her work in *Edward, My Son* (1946). The luxurious ocean liner RMS *Queen Eliza-*

a property as Miss Kerr. The protest, which was made only because of the difficulty for most writers in switching a base of operations, was in vain, and I was bundled away to a lower floor. The smaller suite was infinitely more cozy and I had a consoling view from it of real trees, and I was able to work harder than ever. Two bellboys and a maid appeared to move me back to the gilded cage, and when again I raised a howl it was totally incomprehensible to my hosts, who attributed both protests to temperament—or temper.

Jeanette Sang Well

I finished the rewriting to my satisfaction and that of Robert Sisk. The story of a famous woman concert pianist, retreating from her career and her world in self-pity because of the accidental death of her only son, of her regeneration through her friendship with a Carolina mountain lad (played by Claude Jarman, Jody of "The Yearling,"[147] and his collie dog played by Lassie), of a boy's harmonica playing of a mountain ballad's leading to her composition of a "Mountain Prelude" (which a good composer was already commissioned to do) pleased us immensely.

I was paid my large fee, I escaped, and months later I received Hollywood's own script. The concert pianist was now a singer, there was no "mountain prelude" at all, and the finished film appeared, Heaven knows why, as "The Sun Comes Up." Jeanette MacDonald was very pretty and sang very well.[148]

* * * * * * * * *

Character May Take on Life of His Own

Mrs. Rawlings Cites Linden of 'Sojourner' as Example

I have always waited to begin a book until the principal characters at least were clear to me. Since I am lost away from the background of nature, I know precisely where the action of a book will take place. The characters, as for all

---

beth, of the Cunard Steamship Company (1938–68), served as a troop transport during World War II.

147   Claude Jarman (1934–), child actor who played Jody in *The Yearling* (1946).

148   Jeanette Macdonald (1903–65), singer and actress known for her film duets with Nelson Eddy (1901–67); her last operatic performance was in a 1951 production of *Faust*, by Charles-François Gounod (1818–93).

writers, are a combination of fact and fiction, as the background may be. It is vital that the writer know and understand his main characters at the start, even if in actual life he would not be in sympathy with them, else he can never bring them to life for a reader.

Let dilettantes prate as they will of "the ivory tower," of writing "for himself," a book is not a book until it is read, just as there is no sound without the ear to hear it. The honest author writes to meet his own preferably severe standards, true, but he must have an audience if he is to communicate.

Soars to Ending

Often even a major character changes in the course of the writing of a book. If he is truly living and real for the author, he takes on a life of his own, and his creator is obliged to yield to the circumstances that arise. An instance of this is Ase Linden in "The Sojourner." I knew the man; I thought I saw the outcome of his life, which I had planned to end in a noble and unselfish suicide. Yet suicide, however warranted, is always an admission of defeat, and Ase Linden, after a life of frustration, would not accept it, and he soared to an ending that was more triumphant than I had believed possible for him.

The minor characters often create even greater difficulties for the writer. Again and again they "take over," and the writer must fight or give in to them, according to the major needs of the book and the author's own ability to control them for artistic purposes.

Lived With Characters

When writing of more or less true people, as in "South Moon Under" and "The Yearling" ("Cross Creek" was entirely true), I lived with the people and on the terrain. After the prototype of the hero in "South Moon Under" read the book, he said, "Marge, while you were living out here in the scrub with Ma and me, you must have done a hell of a lot of writing."[149] And so I had, under my mosquito net on my cot in their cabin, I had made endless notes. For "The Yearling" I made a circular outline of the months of the year, with arrows leading outward to indicate the incidents that took the boy Jody from adolescence to manhood.

I rewrite a book, sometimes several times. Infinite, apparently small, details require rewriting to give harmony of character and situation, even to accent the style. Again, there may be major changes, as in the case of Ase Linden of "The Sojourner," who could not commit suicide as I had planned.

---

149   Leonard Fiddia was the prototype of Lant, the hero of *South Moon Under*.

Household Chores Wait

When I was young, I was able to write anywhere, at any time, under any circumstances. I write most easily and rapidly, if not best, when there are household chores waiting to be done. This stems back to the hypocrisy of my youth, when I was supposed to dust the furniture and clean the silver and wipe the dishes. I soon learned that if I sighed and murmured something about "inspiration," my mother would say, "If you have an inspiration, you may go and write." Most writers live half their lives in shame. I have been ashamed of this, but the habit was fixed, and I still am fired to frenzy when I have no maid and there are two days of unwashed dishes in the sink.

During most of my writing life, at least on novels, I worked from 8 or 9 in the morning to 5 or 6 o'clock in the evening, and toward the end of the book, often late into the night. There is more than a 10-year gap between my last book and "The Sojourner," and I find now that a half day's work exhausts me, and I can do no more. I spend that half day in bed, my portable typewriter on a bed tray, even when I have no household help. The bed is a refuge, the counterpart of the ivory tower, no distractions can approach. The work goes joyously forward when I have someone bring me breakfast and luncheon; but through the period when the perfidy of the "perfect maid" has left me entirely alone, I still take comfort and rest an unreliable back, propped up in bed, typing away like mad.

In writing a long book, my goal is and always has been a minimum of a thousand words a day. This often proves impossible and there may be only a page, a paragraph, a sentence to show for a day's work. Then again, it is possible to make it up, when the ideas come and the words fly, and the chapters flow one into the other.

I have used the typewriter since I was in college and use it always for my work. I compose much more easily on it than I could in longhand. Yet when I write my very private verse, I use a pencil, for the slow thoughts, the attempt at perfection, which I know I shall never attain, require such plodding.

I have written ever since I can remember. I made off with the brown grocery paper and hid myself, to put down on it the ideas and emotions which stir a child. I showed my father one of my "poems," in which I had rhymed something like "rain" and "again," and my father said, "But that's poetic license." For a long time I dared write no more "poems" thinking it was necessary to go to the post office to buy a license.

It Was too Late

My life of writing may possibly be due to a misunderstanding at the age of 6. My composition, "The Bluebird," was complimented by my first grade teacher.

I was called on to read it aloud at home whenever there were guests. There was invariably terrific applause. I knew I had found my vocation. Years later I found "The Bluebird" among my mother's souvenirs. The printed letters on the old-time ruled sheets ended: "Miss Bluebird and Mr. Bluebird were married. The next day to their great surprise there were four little bluebirds in the nest." So, the applause had come because adults have low minds, but by this time I was a newspaper writer and it was too late.

My publishing and financial success was at the age of 11, when I won a prize of $2 for a story on the Sunday children's page of the Washington (D.C.) Post. No book club royalty or Pulitzer Prize check has ever looked so large. I won other prizes on the same page. One was for a long "poem" on the anniversary of the death (or birth) of James Whitcomb Riley, in which I imagined myself a lonely orphan with no friend in the world but Mr. Riley.[150] The unspeakable gloomy business was reprinted in an orphanage magazine and I shudder today at its possible effect on really lonely orphans. I doubt if it endeared them to the Hoosier bard.

Roundly Denounced

My first adult work in fiction was a group of sketches, part fiction, part fact, "Cracker Chidlings," in the old Scribner's magazine in 1929. I was roundly denounced in a nearby newspaper for writing libelously of "no such people," while at the same time the mother of one of the true subjects was sending me notes threatening to horsewhip me. I made friends later with both editor and mother.[151]

I received, as I mentioned before, the O. Henry prize for a long short story, "Gal Young Un," and the Pulitzer prize for "The Yearling." Incidentally, "The Yearling" has been translated into French, German, Italian, Polish, Czech, Rumanian, Hungarian, Spanish, Portuguese, Hebrew, Japanese, Norwegian, Swedish, Danish, Finnish and Burmese, which may be something of a record.

Something called, I think, the Southern Book Award, was offered me, but with the stipulation that I must receive it in person at the annual luncheon in New York City and must make a speech. The trip was impossible and I refused.

I have received honorary degrees from Rollins College, the University of Tampa and the University of Florida. The last one touched me deeply for at the

---

150   The story is "The Best Spell," which appears in this volume; MKR was in fact thirteen years old when she published it. The poem, "To James Whitcomb Riley," also appears in this volume.

151   For MKR's response to the editor's complaint, see "Author of Cracker 'Chidlings' Protests," in this volume.

time at least an honorary degree had been given only to one other woman by
this university.

*   *   *   *   *   *   *   *   *

Marjorie Rawlings Writes of Other Writers

She Praises Today's Writing

And Stands in Awe of Proust

A great amount of good writing is being done today and I could scarcely
begin to list the contemporary writers I admire. I stand in awe before Marcel
Proust, as a stylist first, for even the most involved of his sentences climb rhyth-
mically to a superb climax, like Bach organ music. His ability for evocation of
visual and sensual and, what shall I say, heartbreaking nostalgia has seldom been
surpassed. Sigrid Undset, who became my friend through my admiration, was
magnificent in the sweeping range of her historical novels, her re-creation of
characters and background, her bitter understanding. And oddly, the book she
chose to inscribe for me as a gift after her visit to me at Cross Creek was one of
her lesser books, too much based on her own life, so that her usual artistry was
lost.[152] So seldom can a writer judge his own work. Isak Dinesen (Karen Blixen)
is stirring.

Chekhov Is Moving

Guy de Maupassant seems to me to have attained a near perfection in the
short story. Tolstoi, Dostoevski, Chekhov move me, as do some of the French
novelists, Stendhal, Balzac.[153] Among the dead Englishmen there are, of course,
the poets, Shelley, Keats and some of Wordsworth. If I must be pinned down
to my "favorite" writers of olden times I should have to insist on whatever true
writers translated the King James version of the Bible. There has been no such
style before or since.

I had the great fortune to see the three Barrymores, Ethel, Lionel, and John,

---

152   Sigrid Undset (1882–1949), Norwegian novelist, winner of Nobel Prize for Literature
(1928), and especially beloved by MKR; the "lesser book" is either *Stages on the Road* (New York:
Knopf, 1934) or *The Longest Years* (New York: Knopf, 1935), both of which are autobiographical.

153   Leo Tolstoy (1828–1910), Russian epic novelist; Fyodor Dostoyevski (1821–81), existential
novelist; Marie-Henri Beyle [Stendhal] (1783–1842), psychological novelist; Honoré de Balzac
(1799–1850), one of the fathers of Realism.

in their greatest character roles on the living stage. Time has killed one of them, the exigencies of radio and movies have lowered a bit the acting standards of the others, yet the Barrymores still stand in the great tradition of acting. On stage today Marlon Brando and Judith Anderson are unique. They maintain a complete integrity of acting. Fredric March also maintains this integrity. I should include Helen Hayes, except that she has allowed herself to act in so many inferior plays and movies.[154]

Hepburn Preferred

Among screen stars I prefer Katharine Hepburn, Greta Garbo, Gregory Peck, Henry Fonda, Gene Kelly and Spencer Tracy.[155]

I do not "collect" first editions as such, nor autographed ones. It is pleasant to have a signed "first" when one knows the author, and I have some that mean a great deal to me including Sigrid Undset, Ellen Glasgow, Wendell Willkie, James Branch Cabell, Robert Frost, A. J. Cronin, Marcia Davenport, Edith Pope, Bernice Kenyon. I have an American "first" of "Bartram's Travels."[156]

---

154   Ethel Barrymore (1879–1959) won an Academy Award for best supporting actress in *None but the Lonely Heart* (1944); Lionel Barrymore (1878–1954) won an Academy Award for best actor in *Free Soul* (1931); he is perhaps best remembered as Mr. Potter in *It's a Wonderful Life* (1946); John Barrymore (1888–1942), known for his Shakespearean acting and uproarious lifestyle. Marlon Brando (1924–2004) achieved stardom for his role as Stanley Kowalski in the play *A Streetcar Named Desire* (1947), by Tennessee Williams (1911–83); Brando reprised the role for the film version (1951). Judith Anderson (1897–1992) received an Academy Award nomination as best supporting actress for her work in *Rebecca* (1940), directed by Alfred Hitchcock (1899–1980), and starred in several films of the 1940s. The prolific Helen Hayes (1900–1993) was later to be widely acknowledged as the "First Lady of the American Theater."

155   Although keenly disappointed because she did not receive the role of Scarlett O'Hara for the film version of *Gone with the Wind*, Katharine Hepburn (1907–2003) in 1951 received her fifth Academy Award nomination as best actress for her work in *The African Queen*; she was defeated by Vivien Leigh (1913–67), the actress who played Scarlett (MKR, incidentally, thought Leigh was "perfect"; see Silverthorne, 176). Greta Garbo (1905–90), one of the most glamorous actresses of the 1920s and 1930s; by 1940, she had received four Academy Award nominations for best actress. Henry Fonda (1905–82), actor who played Tom Joad in the Academy Award–winning *The Grapes of Wrath* (1940). MKR's Aunt Ida had said of Steinbeck's book, "This is a wonderful book for anyone to read that's moving" (*Private Marjorie*, 418). Gene Kelly (1912–96), whose first film role had been with Judy Garland (1922–69) in *For Me and My Gal* (1942), had recently appeared in what became his signature role, *Singin' in the Rain* (1952). Spencer Tracy (1900–1967), originally chosen for the role of Penny Baxter and very complimentary of MKR's work on *The Yearling* (see Silverthorne, 176–77), had been in his now legendary relationship with "Kate" Hepburn since 1941 and had recently appeared with her in *Adam's Rib* (1949), and also with Deborah Kerr in *Edward, My Son* (1949).

156   Wendell Willkie (1892–1944), Republican politician, author of *One World* (1943). Edith

I find myself accidentally with a collection of china and porcelain cats. For years my husband had given me one whenever he couldn't think of anything else.

In a modest way, I collect Audubons in the elephant folio Havell edition. My one dream is stumbling on a complete folio in some obscure bookshop and buying it for a song.[157]

I cannot live happily without a flower garden, so that I may always have flowers in the house. I have many times bought a bunch of posies when I needed stockings.

Blissful When Cooking

I am blissful when cooking. I was once a wonderful cook, but ten years of the "perfect maid" spoiled me, and now that she is gone, I find that I have lost a great deal of my knack. Like music, cooking must be practiced constantly to maintain one's art. Perhaps nothing in life still gives me more satisfaction than making jams and jellies. Here, perfection is attainable, results are tangible. I make a wild raspberry syrup the flavor of which has a more devastating effect on strong men than strong perfume.

My favorites among war books are Tolstoi's "War and Peace," Stephen Crane's "The Red Badge of Courage," Hemingway's "For Whom the Bell Tolls," James Jones' "From Here to Eternity," Herman Wouk's "The Cain Mutiny," Montserratt's "The Cruel Sea," and "A Convoy through the Dream" by Scott Graham Williamson.[158]

Write or Fight

The question of whether a writer should write or fight during a war has tormented the best of them. It is almost impossible for anyone but a philosopher or a scholar to maintain the necessary objectivity during a war. Theoretically, he

Pope (1905–61), a dear friend whom MKR introduced to Scribners, who published her best-selling novel *Colcorton* (1944). Bernice Gilkyson [Kenyon] (1897–1982), author of *Night Sky, and Other Poems* (New York: Scribners, 1951), which was dedicated to MKR. In 1944, MKR reported to Norton, "Monday morning discovered the termites had completely destroyed my precious Bartram's Travels" (*Private Marjorie*, 438). She replaced it in 1949 (see *Private Marjorie*, 529).

157   Audubon's *The Birds of America* (London: Audubon, 1827–38), known as the "Havell edition" because the 435 plates were engraved by Robert Havell Jr. (1793–1878).

158   Tolstoy, *War and Peace* (1865–69); Hemingway, *For Whom the Bell Tolls* (New York: Scribners, 1940); James Jones (1921–77), *From Here to Eternity* (New York: Scribners, 1951); Herman Wouk (1915–), *The Cain Mutiny* (Garden City, N.Y.: Doubleday, 1951); Nicholas Monsarrat (1910–79), *The Cruel Sea* (New York: Knopf, 1951); Scott Graham Williamson (1899–1948), *A Convoy through the Dream* (New York: Macmillan, 1948).

should write, yet his skin is seldom more valuable than that of the doctor, the teacher or anyone who contributes to the welfare and spirit of mankind, and he usually ends by taking a more or less active part in the conflict to satisfy his conscience.

During the last war, I did airplane spotting. I wrote propaganda for the Writer's War Board and the Red Cross, did a "minute movie" for the bond drive. My only contribution of any value was a voluminous correspondence with men in the service. Three of my books, "South Moon Under," "The Yearling" and "Cross Creek," were in the armed services edition, and lonely soldiers and sailors wrote me from all over the world, literally from Greenland's icy mountains to Africa's tropic shore. They were of many races. I felt I had something to give here, and most of my time went to answering these men at length and with great thought and care.

Too Old for Adoption

A Filipino wrote me, "I am lonesome orphan boy 25 years old in American Navy. I read your books and you seem like a kind mother lady. Will you adopt me please for son?" I answered that I was fortunate enough to be free of any race prejudice, but that, alas, 25 did seem too advanced an age for an adopted son.

There have been some sad aftermaths to some of this correspondence; letters from mothers or sisters saying that Bob or Harry had been killed in action.

I believe in every man to his trade, and it is presumptuous for the novelist to offer solutions to the problems of the world where the leaders, the sociologists, the economists have failed. Yet since humanity itself is the writer's business, I can say that the main world and domestic problem is more basic than the social and economic factors involved which are slowly, too slowly, being solved. I see the basic problem as a spiritual one, at home and abroad.

Plain People Ahead

Man's prehistoric savagery and personal selfishness and greed, his materialism which seems to increase in direct ratio to the technical advance of the so-called civilization, are the stumbling block, the impasse. Plain people seem to me to be ahead of the "leaders" in some respects. It was the insistence of such, most of them farmers who know the meaning of crop failures, that finally put enough pressure on the American Congress to vote for wheat for starving India.[159]

---

159   In February 1951, President Truman asked Congress for two million tons of grain for India. Congress resisted but approved a $190 million loan for Indian famine relief later that June.

The ordinary man will not see his neighbor go hungry nor cold nor un-clothed, while somehow the manipulations of "governments" allow whole na-tions to starve and shiver. A world-wide free vote would be overwhelmingly against war, and for justice and tolerance and equity.

In the Face of God

The immediate problem, none can doubt, is the enslavement of too many hundreds of millions of plain, decent people by a Soviet minority, the ideals of whose original revolution have been dissipated in the cruel inhumanity and blind lust for power, and who must be halted lest the whole universe be enslaved. Yet the military defeat or the ideological containment of the ruling Soviet will not solve the continuing problem which might be reduced to that of man's ar-rogance, his lack of love and humility, tiny bit of dust that he is, in the face of God and the Cosmos.

As to my present and future work, I am now spending several months in Richmond, Va., doing research on the life of Ellen Glasgow. I have been asked to do the biography of this beloved Virginia authoress. I knew Ellen Glasgow and admired her very much. She was important as a social historian[,]`and I am deeply interested in doing this biography.

I am still undecided as to where the emphasis should go—on Ellen Glasgow the woman, or Ellen Glasgow the writer. Up to now my research has mostly been gathering personal anecdotes about her from her few remaining close friends. Everyone is being most co-operative. However, I shall not actually write the bi-ography for several years, and I hope to do another novel as soon as the Glasgow book is completed.

In the meantime I have short stories on my mind that I am anxious to do, and that is about all I can say about my life and work thus far.[160]

Marjorie Kinnan Rawlings

"Marjorie Rawlings Tells Story of Her Long Struggle to Write," *Los Angeles Times*, 26 April 1953; 3 May 1953; 10 May 1953; 17 May 1953; 24 May 1953. See [Autobiographical Sketches], Tarr, *Bibliography*, C645.

---

160   MKR died the following December (1953), and none of these literary ambitions would be realized.

Doris Betts's *The Gentle Insurrection*
and Other Stories

The Doris Betts stories are completely mature and effective. They are as fine as any stories I have read in a long time. I decidedly vote that the prize should go to them. I feel these stories will receive a splendid critical reception.

"Doris Betts's *The Gentle Insurrection*," blurb for Doris Betts (1932–), *The Gentle Insurrection and Other Stories* (New York: Putnam, 1954). Published posthumously, the blurb was taken from MKR's response as a judge for the G. T. Putnam–University of North Carolina Prize Contest for 1953. Now Alumni Distinguished Professor of English (Emerita) at the University of North Carolina, Chapel Hill, Betts to date has published nine novels and short story collections.

Bibliography

Kinser, Brent E. "'I'd Much Rather Write You Instead': The Letters of Marjorie Kinnan Rawlings to Bertram C. Cooper." *Marjorie Kinnan Rawlings Journal of Florida Literature* 13 (2004): 1–33.

———. "'The least touch of butter': Marge and Emily on Manners." *Marjorie Kinnan Rawlings Journal of Florida Literature* 10 (2001): 1–9.

Rawlings, Marjorie Kinnan. *Blood of My Blood.* Edited by Anne Blythe Meriwether. Gainesville: University Press of Florida, 2002.

———. *Cross Creek.* New York: Scribners, 1942.

———. *Cross Creek Cookery.* New York: Scribners, 1942.

———. *Golden Apples.* New York: Scribners, 1935.

———. *Max and Marjorie: The Correspondence between Maxwell E. Perkins and Marjorie Kinnan Rawlings.* Edited by Rodger L. Tarr. Gainesville: University Press of Florida, 1999.

———. *Poems by Marjorie Kinnan Rawlings: Songs of a Housewife.* Edited by Rodger L. Tarr. Gainesville: University Press of Florida, 1997.

———. *The Private Marjorie: The Love Letters of Marjorie Kinnan Rawlings to Norton S. Baskin.* Edited by Rodger L. Tarr. Gainesville: University Press of Florida, 2004.

———. *Selected Letters.* Edited by Gordon E. Bigelow and Laura V. Monti. Gainesville: University Presses of Florida, 1983.

———. *Short Stories by Marjorie Kinnan Rawlings.* Edited by Rodger L. Tarr. Gainesville: University Press of Florida, 1994.

———. *The Sojourner.* New York: Scribners, 1953.

———. *South Moon Under.* New York: Scribners, 1933.

———. *When the Whippoorwill—.* New York: Scribners, 1940.

———. *The Yearling.* New York: Scribners, 1938.

Silverthorne, Elizabeth. *Marjorie Kinnan Rawlings: Sojourner at Cross Creek.* Woodstock, N.Y.: Overlook Press, 1988.

Stevens, Wallace. *Letters.* Edited by Holly Stevens. New York: Knopf, 1966.

Tarr, Rodger L. *Marjorie Kinnan Rawlings: A Descriptive Bibliography.* Pittsburgh: University of Pittsburgh Press, 1988.

———. "Marjorie Kinnan Rawlings and the Rochester (N.Y.) Magazine *Five O'Clock.*" *American Periodicals* 1, no. 1 (Fall 1991): 83–85.

———. "Marjorie Kinnan Rawlings and the *Washington Post.*" *Analytical and Enumerative Bibliography,* n.s., 4, no. 4 (1990): 163–68.

Index of Titles

Lady Alicia Thwaite

"Live Women in Live Louisville"

Poems

Reviews/Introductions/Blurbs

Stories

Index

Rodger L. Tarr is University Distinguished professor, Emeritus, at Illinois State University. His books on Rawlings include *Short Stories of Marjorie Kinnan Rawlings* (University Press of Florida, 1994), *Marjorie Kinnan Rawlings: A Descriptive Bibliography* (University of Pittsburgh Press, 1996), *Collected Poems of Marjorie Kinnan Rawlings: A Descriptive Bibliography* (University Press of Florida, 1997), *Max and Marjorie: The Correspondence between Maxwell E. Perkins and Marjorie Kinnan Rawlings* (University Press of Florida, 1999), and *The Personal Marjorie: The Love Letters of Marjorie Kinnan Rawlings to Norton S. Baskin* (University Press of Florida, 2005). Tarr is an Honorary Trustee of the Rawlings Society and a Consulting Scholar on the Hemingway Letters Project.

Brent E. Kinser is an assistant professor of English at Western Carolina University. He serves as an editor of *The Collected Letters of Thomas and Jane Welsh Carlyle* (Duke University Press) and as co-editor of *Carlyle Studies Annual*. Kinser is also coeditor of the *Marjorie Kinnan Rawlings Journal of Florida Literature* and vice-president elect of the Rawlings Society.